Palgrave Studies in Economic History

Series Editor
Kent Deng, London School of Economics, London, UK

Palgrave Studies in Economic History is designed to illuminate and enrich our understanding of economies and economic phenomena of the past. The series covers a vast range of topics including financial history, labour history, development economics, commercialisation, urbanisation, industrialisation, modernisation, globalisation, and changes in world economic orders.

Denggao Long · Xiang Chi

The Institutions of Land Property Rights in China

Transformation and Development, 1560–1950

palgrave
macmillan

Denggao Long
School of Social Sciences
Tsinghua University
Beijing, China

Xiang Chi
Institute of Modern History
Chinese Academy of Social Sciences
Beijing, China

ISSN 2662-6497 ISSN 2662-6500 (electronic)
Palgrave Studies in Economic History
ISBN 978-981-97-5114-3 ISBN 978-981-97-5112-9 (eBook)
https://doi.org/10.1007/978-981-97-5112-9

Jointly published with China Social Sciences Press.
The print edition is not for sale in China (Mainland). Customers from China (Mainland) please order the print book from: China Social Sciences Press.

Cover image: courtesy of Denggao Long

This Palgrave Macmillan imprint is published by the registered company Springer Nature Singapore Pte Ltd.
The registered company address is: 152 Beach Road, #21-01/04 Gateway East, Singapore 189721, Singapore

Contents

List of Figures

List of Tables

CHAPTER 1

Outline of the Institutions for Farmland Transactions in Traditional China

As the primary production source in an agricultural society, farmland and its related institutions underlie the processes of resource allocation and business operations. To analyze them is the first and most fundamental task if one wants to understand the transformation of China from a traditional society to a modern one. Such understanding is also key to the current agricultural reforms and is of exceptional theoretical value for world economic history. While previous understanding and assessments of this fundamental issue were anything but uniform, breakthroughs have been made over the recent two decades.[1]

[1] In the past decade, Taisu Zhang, Madeleine Zelin, Zhao Gang, and other Chinese middle-aged scholars, such as Qin Hui, Gao Wangling, Luan Chengxian, Cao Shuji, and others, have made new explorations. See Taisu Zhang, *The Laws and Economics of Confucianism: kinship and Property in Preindustrial China and England* (Cambridge University Press: 2017); Madeleine Zelin, Jonathan K. Ocko, and Robert Gardella eds., *Contract and Property in Early Modern China* (Stanford: Stanford University Press, 2004); Zhao Gang, "Cong ling yige jiaodu kan mingqing shiqi de tudi zudian" (Viewing the Land Tenancy System of Ming and Qing Dynasties From Another Perspective), *Zhongguo Nongshi* (Agricultural History of China), no. 2 (2000); Zhao Gang, "Lishi shang nongdi jingying fangshi de xuanze" (The Choice of Agricultural Land Management Mode in History), *Zhongguo Jingjishi Yanjiu* (Researches in Chinese Economic History), no. 2 (2000); Fang Xing, "Zhongguo fengjian shehui de tudi shichang" (The Land Market of China's Feudal Society), *Zhongguo Jingjishi Yanjiu* (Researches in Chinese Economic History), no. 2 (2001); Gao Wangling, "Zudian guanxi xinlun" (A New Perspective on the Tenancy

D. Long and X. Chi, *The Institutions of Land Property Rights in China*, Palgrave Studies in Economic History,
https://doi.org/10.1007/978-981-97-5112-9_1

This chapter reconstructs China's traditional farmland property rights and transaction system by examining primary sources, especially farmland transaction deeds and farmland disputes, in *Xingke tiben*. It offers an in-depth analysis of the institutional legacies of China's farmland system and its transformation. On this basis, we try to provide a comprehensive analysis and explanation of the resource allocation processes and business operations in the farmland tenure system based on economic principles and tools. We also offer a systematic framework for understanding and explaining the historical transformation of the traditional economy, which revolves around farmland rights (or farmland tenure) and impacts the economic reforms of modern China.

1.1 Theoretical Construction of Types of Farmland Rights

Private (family and private) property rights, corporate property rights, and state property rights in farmland coexisted in traditional China. Among them, private property types were much more mature and demonstrated an innovation of Chinese origin based on the theoretical reconstructions of China's traditional farmland property rights system.

First, farmland rights can exist independently and be traded in the market at different levels and at different times, thus making up types of property rights such as ownership, possession, and user rights, as well

Relationship), *Zhongguo Jingjishi Yanjiu* (Researches in Chinese Economic History), no. 3 (2005); Gao Wangling, *Zudian guanxi xinlun—dizhu, nongmin he dizu* (New Theory of the Tenancy Relationship—Landlords, Peasants and Land Rents) (Shanghai: Shanghai shudian Press, 2005); Cao Shuji, "Su'nan diqu 'tianmian quan'de xingzhi" (The Nature of Top-soil Land Rights in Southern Jiangsu Province), *The Journal of Tsinghua University*, no. 4 (2007); Cao Shuji, "Liangzhong 'tianmian quan'yu Zhejiang de 'er'wu jianzu'" (Two Kinds of Permanent Tenancy and Rent Reduction in Zhejiang Province), *Lishi Yanjiu* (Journal of Historical Research), no. 2 (2007); Cao Shuji and Li Feiqi, "Qing zhonghou qi zhenan shanqu de tudi diandang—jiyu songyang xian shicang cunde 'dangtian qi'de kaocha" (Land Mortgage in Mountainous Regions of Southern Zhejiang during the Mid- and Late Qing: A Study Based on 'Land Mortgage Contracts' from Shicang Village, Songyang County), *Lishi Yanjiu* (Journal of Historical Research), no. 3 (2008); Cao Shuji and Liu Shigu, *Chuantong zhongguo diquan jiegou jiqi yanbian* (Traditional Land Property Rights Structure and Its Transformation) (Shanghai: Shanghai jiaotong University Press, 2014); Li Deying, *Guojia faling yu minjian xiguan: minguo shiqi chengdu pingyuan zudian zhidu xintan* (National Decree and Civil Customs: A New Probe into the Tenancy System of Chengdu Plain during the Republic of China) (Beijing: China's Social Science Press, 2006).

as their corresponding types of transaction, which constitute the farmland rights transaction system. Second, all these different levels of realization of various types of property rights can be acquired through investment and trade. This results in rules universally accepted by society, licensed by the government, and regulated by the legal system, thus giving them the force of law. Third, documents of property rights and transactions expressed through contracts have a long history in civil practices and have been recognized and regulated by successive governments through laws. Fourth, the property rights of legal persons (corporate property rights) were derived and developed from private property rights.

There was a long-term belief—which still remains influential today—that China lacked property rights and failed to develop contracts. In fact, a simple idea of property rights and a related legal system existed in traditional society, and both were deeply rooted. Both private farmland and corporate farmland were titled and traded by deed, and different levels of farmland rights could be acquired through investment capital (in addition to inheritance, etc.). Non-landowners could also obtain a corresponding disposition of farmland rights by investing and controlling land yields and the appreciation of land, and they could thus share land rights with the landowners. One instance is the so-called top-soil rights of farmland (*tianmianquan*). It coexisted with the subsoil rights (*tiandiquan*) as a property rights and differed from the regular tenancy rights (*dianquan*). Similarly, the *dian* (conditional sales) rights resembled the top-soil rights, and both were distinctive types of farmland tenure and the sale of property rights.

Corporate property rights are derived by extension from private property rights, reflecting the degree of development of the private property rights system. For example, clans, religious temples, academies of classical learning and private schools, nonprofit organizations, charitable organizations, and various associations (*hui*) and societies (*she*) in the industrial, commercial, financial, cultural, sports, and entertainment industries could all form a property unit, a transaction unit, and a taxing unit, with features such as integrity, indivisibility, and exclusivity, and developed an efficient management model based on the independence of property.[2] They

[2] Long Denggao, Wang Zhenghua, and Yin Wei, "Chuantong minjian zuzhi zhili jiegou yu faren chanquan zhidu: jiyu qingdai gonggong jianshe yu guanli de yanjiu" (The Governance Structure of Traditional Civil Organizations and Legal Person Property Rights

were recorded as "public properties" (*gongchan*), as opposed to "governmental properties" (*guanchan*) owned by the government and "private properties" (*sichan*) owned by private individuals.

State-owned farmland existed for generations and was usually not tradable. It could be traded only when privatized. At that time, its character had been changed to private or corporate property, which did not happen in every dynasty. There was, however, a general tendency for the share of state land to diminish gradually.

1.2 Debate on Farmland Transactions

The Dian Rights and Transaction

There has been an intense concentration on studying *dian* (conditional sale) since it was a form of farmland property rights and transaction with the most traditional "Chinese characteristics," but many controversies have continued to surround it. Some regarded *dian* as the transaction of user rights. In contrast, others argued that there was no difference between *dian* and the practice of *huomai* (revocable sales).[3] Based on our analysis of original deeds and employing economic theory, *dian* referred to a transaction regarding the management of farmland with all of its profit and interest in an agreed period and not to the "balancing of rent

System: A Study Based on Public Construction and Management in the Qing Dynasty), *Jingji yanjiu* (Economic Research), no. 10 (2018): 175–191.

[3] Dai Jianguo and others argued that *dian* was a transaction of user rights. See Dai Jianguo, "Songdai de mintian dianmai yu 'yitian liangzhu zhi'" (The Dian Transactions of Civil Lands and the System of "One Piece of Land with Two Owners" in the Song Dynasty), *Lishi yanjiu* (Historical Research), no. 6 (2011): 99–117. Quite a few scholars, on the other hand, argued that *dian* was a revocable sale (*huomai*), which means that *dian* was a transaction of ownership. For example, Ye Xiaoxin argues that *dian* "can also be called *huomai*." See Ye Xiaoxin, *Zhongguo fazhi shi* (History of the Chinese Legal System) (Beijing: Peking University Press, 1999), 249. Chen Zhiying clarified the meaning of *dian* and the difference between *dian* and sale, especially irrevocable sale (*juemai*), but still customarily thought of *dian* as "a revocable sale (*huomai*)." See Chen Zhiying, *Songdai wuquan guanxi yanjiu* (A Study of Property Rights Relations in the Song Dynasty) (Beijing: China's Social Science Press, 2006, 140–147). Li Li argued that Qing people saw *dian* as a sale. However, the deeds that his article used were all deeds of sale. See Li Li, "Qingdai minjian tudi qiyue duiyu dian de biaoda jiqi yiyi" (The Expression and Significance of Qing Dynasty Civil Land Deeds to the Dian), *Jinling falü pinglun* (Jinling Law Review), no. 1 (2006): 111–118.

and interest" (*zuxi xiangdi*), as claimed by some scholars.[4] A "conditional sale" (*dian*) was a property right in the form of a possessory right and can form the function of a security interest; farmland becomes collateral. In other words, *dian* practice was a transaction between the right to occupy farmland and the interest in the capital. It is different from the sale and purchase of ownership and tenancy was a right, thus clarifying previous misunderstandings. The *dian* seller (*chudianren*) actually realized the future interest on the value of land to obtain a loan, while the *dian* buyer (*chengdianren*) received possession for the agreed term and could choose between either operating income (self-farming), investment income (leasing), or realizing future income (*dian* transfer), depending on their own preferences and needs. Moreover, the *dian* buyer could rent out the *dian* farmland, even to the landowner and *dian* seller. It reflects a pattern of shared farmland rights constructed by landlords, *dian* owners, and tenant farmers relying on market transactions and sheds light on the characteristics and orientation of the traditional farmland rights market.[5]

Analysis of Various Farmland Transaction Types

In different periods, different levels of farmland rights could be transacted, forming a diversified regime of farmland transactions such as sales, conditional sales (*dian*), rent deposits (*yazu*), tenancies, mortgages (*di*), and loans using farmland as collateral (*taijie*). The system became mature during the Ming and Qing dynasties. Depending on the order of user right, possession, and ownership, the greater the rights of farmland, the higher the returns, and the higher the transaction price.

The multi-layered farmland rights and diversified types of farmland rights transactions were quite complicated in reality. Ambiguities, disputes, and misunderstandings related to them in the past were due mainly to the lack of a theoretical explanatory framework. Therefore,

[4] Some scholars, such as Wu Xianghong, misunderstood the core rule of *dian* practices. We characterize their misunderstandings as "balancing rent and interest" (*zuxi xiangdi*), because they have ignored the differences between different categories of *dian*. See Wu Xianghong, "Chapter 7," in *Dianzhi fengsu yu dianzhi falü* (Customs and Laws of Dian) (Beijing: falü Press, 2009).

[5] Long Denggao, Lin Zhan, and Peng Bo, "Dian yu qingdai diquan jiaoyi tixi" (Dian and Qing's Land Rights Transaction System), *China's Social Science* (Social Sciences in China), no. 5 (2013): 125–141. The article was awarded the 18th Sun Yefang Prize in Economic Sciences (2018).

we offer an analytical framework regarding the different levels of farmland rights and the development of regulations across time, distinguishing between the roles of the different farmland rights transactions and paying attention to differences and interconnections.

Dian (conditional sales) originated from sales. In the Tang and Song dynasties (618–1279), the term *dianmai* was used, and both transaction rules and tax payment procedures were not clearly separated. The main distinction between a "conditional sale" (*dian*) and a "sale" (*mai*) was made by the contractual form and by the fact that, although even for a "conditional sale," the tax duty was transferred to the new owner, the administration continued to consider the original owner as possessing the "field bone" (*tiangu*). In the Qing Dynasty, the two were further clearly separated. On the one hand, the "sale" (*mai*) of ownership was broken down into "revocable sale" (*huomai*) and "irrevocable sale" (*juemai*). The nature of an "irrevocable sale" was an ownership transaction. In a "revocable sale," the title to the farmland could be redeemed, but only as a right of first refusal. In a *dian* transaction, on the other hand, the redemption of land ownership signified the conclusion of the transaction.

Tenancy was a transaction of the user right. A regular tenancy was a post-rental payment, while a rent deposit (*yazu*) was a partial prepayment. There was a progressive relationship between farmland rights as tenancy and *dian*. When a rent deposit was maximized (C in Fig. 9.1), it gets close to *dian* from the landowner's point of view, but a partial rent deposit cannot create a security interest (full collateral). If the rent deposit was considered an investment and a purchase of farmland user rights, then, in the case of a rent deposit, the tenant can acquire the top-soil rights similarly to the *dian* rights. At this point, the top-soil rights of farmland were also rights of possession with property attributes.

Both *dian* and mortgages can constitute security interests (represent collateral). However, farmland mortgages were usually short-term loans with a high risk of title transfer, whereas *dian* transactions effectively buffer the eventual transfer of landownership. Therefore, the *dian* practice was popular and recognized by the government. This was one of the reasons for the long prevalence of *dian* in the market of farmland rights. As institutions of *dian* and *huomai* effectively reduced the transfer of farmland ownerships and acted as hedge factors against the concentration of landownership rights, they helped peasants weather the storm and restore and re-establish independent farming. Practices such as "supplementary payments" (*zhaojia*) and "joyous-gift silver" (*xiliyin*)[6] could also be seen, to some extent, as relief for landless peasants. Thus, the customary practices and legal provisions of *dian* protected the vulnerable while preserving peasants' ownership rights and contributed to traditional Chinese society's socioeconomic stability.

The above differentiation and analyses have revealed the interconnection and logical relations among various farmland rights transaction types.[7] The farmland rights transaction system thus meets the diversified preferences and demands of factor market actors and reduces the systemic risks of farmland rights transactions, especially ownership transfers.[8] The development of a market for farmland rights on this basis was conducive to the strengthening of the ability of individual farmers to operate independently and contributes to the stability and development of the traditional economy and society.

Transmutation of a Farmland Right System

Since the Warring States Period and the Qin and Han dynasties (471 BCE–220 CE), the types of farmland rights transactions have gradually multiplied, and the types of farmland property rights have become more varied, including *dian* rights in the Tang and Song dynasties, the permanent tenancy system in the Song and Yuan dynasties, and the emergence

[6] When a landowner sold his land, the original landowner asked for and usually received "joyous-gift silver" from the buyer. This custom was widespread, and there were more than 20 cases recorded in *Xingke tiben* 2.

[7] Long Denggao, and Wen Fangfang, "Chuantong diquan jiaoyi xingshi bianxi—yi dian wei zhongxin" (Identifying Traditional Forms of Land Rights Transactions. A Case Study of *Dian*), *Zhejiang xuekan* (Zhejiang Academic Journal), no. 3 (2018): 172–182.

[8] Some scholars today question the efficiency or rationality of redemption transactions, which is actually a misinterpretation (for details, see Long Denggao and Wen Fangfang, "Lun zhongguo chuantong dianquan jiaoyi de huishu jizhis—jiyu qinghua guancang shanxi qiyue de yanjiu" (On the Redemption Mechanism of Traditional Chinese *Dian* Transactions: A Study Based on the Shanxi Deeds in the Tsinghua Collection), *Jingji kexue* (Economic Science), no. 5 (2014): 172–182. In the traditional period, the opposite was true: the "conditional sale" (*dian*) was regarded as the "correct *dian*," and the mortgage was subject to moral attack. In fact, each transaction method has its own preferences and should not be viewed in isolation but should be embedded in the trading system so that it is understood that the coexistence of trading methods with different preferences can reduce systemic risk.

of top-soil rights, rent deposits, and revocable sales in the Ming and Qing dynasties. The transmutation and differences of the farmland rights from the Song to the Qing Dynasty and their differentiation reflect how the farmland rights transaction rules developed from spontaneous generation to gradual improvement and standardization. Social perceptions and government management also changed along the way.

The Song Dynasty was at the beginning of the development of the *dian* right. It was relatively simple to apply, so it was easy to grasp the original nature of *dian*. In the Qing Dynasty, the development of the *dian* rights led to complex and diverse types and manifestations, and the rights derived from it gradually became explicit and were no longer forbidden, as during the Song Dynasty. Nevertheless, they also contributed to obscuring and distorting the original nature of *dian*.

First, regarding the origin of *dian*, in the Song Dynasty, the fundamental norm was "*dian* selling the land off the property" (*diantian liye*). The control of the farmland and the transfer of all business income during the agreed period were the origin and core of the *dian* right. Second, the derived rights and the manifestation of diversity of *dian* were highlighted by the different ways to transact farmland in *dian* sales. Misconceptions of *dian* in the Song and Qing dynasties were also related to these different transaction procedures. For example, the practice of the *dian* buyer renting out farmland to the original landowner was not recognized in the Song Dynasty, while in the Qing Dynasty, this form was widely popular.

Third, the different policies and regulations of the Song and Qing dynasties regarding *dian* transactions were also compatible with the rules mentioned above. In the Song Dynasty, the transaction of *dian* fields required the transfer of the tax obligations of farmland tax and corvee and payment of a transaction tax. The form of the deed was correspondingly contractual meaning that the deed consisted of two parts, which would be put together at the date of redemption, a practice referred to as *heqi tongyue*. In the Qing Dynasty, the management of *dian* fields was simplified, and the tax was exempted for a long time, so there was no need to go through the transfer of farm tax. The contractual deeds of *dian* farmland also changed into a single-deed form, adapted to the increase of subsequent transactions or related transaction types in the Qing Dynasty. People could record and practice *dian* transfer, *dian* supplementary payment, and other additions to the original deeds and agreements.

These phenomena and differences cannot be understood in isolation but were interrelated and corroborate each other according to an internal logic; thus, they constitute an explanatory framework. The different stages and traits of the development of dian rights show how the rules for farmland rights transactions changed over time. This helps us learn more about how farmland property rights and transactions worked in traditional China.[9]

1.3 Farmland Rights Market, Family Farms, and Characteristics of the Traditional Economy

Connection and Influence of Farmland Tenure Market on Individual Farms

The markets for farmland rights and individual family farms were interrelated and constituted two of the most fundamental features of China's traditional economy and its unique development path. The two promoted and reinforced each other, improved economic efficiency and farmland output, contributed to the stable development of the traditional economy, and inhibited its transformation and change into modern economic types. It helps to explain the difference in the evolution of the Chinese and Western economic types and was one of the most important reasons why China's traditional economy could not spontaneously move toward an Industrial Revolution.

Self-employed, semi-employed, and tenant farmers established individual family farms under their ownership, possession, and user rights and produced and reproduced with the help of a combination of market factors and resources. A multi-layered farmland rights transaction system enabled peasant households to make choices according to market prices and risk appetites and to cater to their own needs; it also helped to achieve regulation between current and future profits, thereby facilitating the combination of farmland circulation and productive factors and improving economic efficiency.[10] The redemption mechanism, which

[9] Long Denggao, Wen Fangfang, and Qiu Yongzhi, "Diantian de xingzhi yu quanyi—songdai yu qingdai de bijiao yanjiu" (The Nature and Rights of Dian Land—A Comparative Study of the Song and Qing Dynasties), *Lishi yanjiu* (Historical Research), no. 5 (2016): 54–70.

[10] Long Denggao, "Diquan jioayi yu shengchan yaosu zuhe, 1650–1950" (Land Rights Transactions and Production Factor Mix, 1650–1950), *Jingji yanjiu* (Economic Research),

included the use of *dian*, *huomai*, and *yazu*, effectively preserved the willingness of peasant households to secure and resume their landownership. It also made less complicated but potentially unfair property transfers, like irrevocable sales or mortgages, less likely to happen.

The land rights market that supported individual family farms was characterized by a low threshold, separability, and easy replication. Farmers could support their families even when encountering natural and human-made disasters, and members of an increasing population coming from existing families and villages were able to establish their own independent farms. Since the Chinese used to have a system of equal inheritance among sons (*zhuzi junfenzhi*), rather than a system of primogeniture, families, farmland, and individual farms were constantly divided and regenerated.

However, the self-regeneration and dynamism of individual family farms also inhibited the growth of large-scale and capitalist operations. As a result, it was difficult for new factors to emerge while the original essence of the Chinese agricultural economy was continuously reinforced.

Reconstructing Share Tenancy: A Reflection on the "Optimal Owner-Peasant"

Tenancy and farmland rights transactions enabled the owners of factors with different endowments to cooperate effectively, increased the mobility and efficiency of the factors of production, brought about changes in different classes and changes in management, and thus reflected the social mobility of the time. Previous studies have generally considered tenant peasants to be the landowners' labor, similar in nature to hired labor, and remunerated on a par with hired labor, a stereotype which has led to misconceptions in economic interpretation and historical understanding. In fact, during the Ming and Qing dynasties, tenant farmers already managed businesses independently. They combined different factors of production from the family, the landlord, and the market to create wealth and use diversified farming methods. Moreover, they dominated the residual claims, reaping under risk and uncertainty the rewards only for an entrepreneur; and the future benefits of investment in the land and farm could be realized through trade. In all these cases, the hired farmers had no connection to them, just like today's entrepreneurs, who do not own

no. 2 (2009): 146–156; Long Denggao, *Diquan shichang yu ziyuan Peizhi* (Land Rights Markets and Resource Allocation) (Fuzhou: Fujian People's Press, 2012).

capital, farmland, labor, or technology but rather integrate these factors of production and resources through the market to build enterprises which create wealth. Economic efficiency and farmland output were driven by the transfer, selection, and allocation of factors of production under the system of farmland rights transactions, and tenancy was an important source of dynamism for tenant farming and the smallholder economy.[11]

History and theory have refuted the prevalent traditional myth that tenant farmers were less productive and exploited by landlords while peasant farming was fair and efficient. In a free market situation, the structure of farmland rights depends on the transaction costs and the level of the total surplus of the system. We use the theory of optimal ownership structures to look at the total institutional surplus of owner-farmers, tenant farmers, and hired laborers. We argue that the choice of tenure structure will depend on the best level of technology, land endowment, and market conditions, and that owner-farmers were not always the best choice. By examining the impacts of the degree of marketization of agricultural products, transportation costs, the scale of farmland management, and the degree of dispersion of farmland rights on tenancy rates using statistical methods and by comparing the scale of production and profits of modern owner-farmers with those of tenant farmers, it is clear that the tenant economy exhibited advantages in many respects. The explanation lies in the fact that tenancy separates the asset function of farmland from the factor production function, makes the area of farmland management independent of the area of farmland ownership, and leads to a meritocracy among the cultivators.[12]

Corporate Property Rights, Civil Organization, and Grassroots Social Order

If the rights of private ownership of farmland were the cornerstone of the independent operations of peasants, then the rights to corporate ownership were the basis for the independent development of civil society

[11] Long Denggao and Peng Bo, "Jinshi diannong de jingying xingzhi yu shouyi bijiao" (A Comparative Study of the Nature and Profitability of Tenants in Modern Times), *Jingji yanjiu* (Economic Research Journal), no. 1 (2010): 138–147.

[12] Zhao Liang and Long Denggao, "tudi zudian yu jingji xiaolü" (Land Tenancy and Economic Efficiency), *Zhongguo jingji wenti* (China Economic Studies), no. 2 (2012): 3–15.

organizations, which together constitute the organic system of the private and public spheres of traditional society.

Non-governmental and nonprofit micro-objects, represented by various civil society organizations, were prevalent in grassroots society and the public sphere. They have independent property, especially estates and funds (*huijin*), with future value-added income for long-term operation. Such separate property was a corporate property right, exclusive, integral, and indivisible and was guaranteed by the government and the law. Corporate property rights existed not only in "bridge societies" (*qiaohui*) and "free Ferry" (*yidu*) but also in water conservancy societies (*zhahui*), industrial and commercial societies, guilds, and secret societies, and more generally in families, temples, schools, and charitable and relief institutions. They became the basis for the independence and sustainability of any such social organization, which developed and existed over time, independent of the power of government and administration.

The micro-subjects of corporate property rights have formed an effective organizational system and governance structure. They operated openly and transparently, were accountable to society and stakeholders, had clear regulations and institutional safeguards, and were able to embark on the path of sustainable development. Their effective incentive and discipline mechanisms were not only directly related to their economic interests but were also compatible with the prevailing religious, ethical, and moral values. The directors of social organizations were willing and committed, and their employees worked hard. Meanwhile, strict regulations and public supervision prevented them from taking advantage of the situation and being passive. Thus, rent-seeking and corruption were overcome effectively.

In short, independent property rights of corporate entities, clear statutes and rules, effective governance structures, open and transparent operations, incentives for social and economic interests, and supervision and restraint by the public all constitute the institutional arrangements of traditional Chinese civil organizations. The government manages grassroots society indirectly through social organizations and social elites, which become the dominant force in the public sphere and provide public goods and services to the grassroots.[13] The grassroots private and public

[13] Chen Yueyuan, Long Denggao, "Qingdai shuyuan de caichan shuxing jiqi shichanghua jingying" (The Property Attributes of Qing Academies and Their Market-Oriented Operation), *Zhejiang xuekan* (Zhejiang Academic Journal), no. 3 (2020):

spheres, provided by independent and autonomous micro-entities, allow the governmental authorities to achieve and maintain unity at a low cost.

1.4 Modern Farmland Rights and Their Misconceptions

Power and violence have undermined the system and order governing China's farmland rights in modern times, and this deterioration has contributed to the socioeconomic upheaval and decline in the late Qing Dynasty and the early Republican Era. People often blame it on the private property system itself, and, in particular, they meant that free trade in farmland rights leads to farmland appropriation and concentration. However, the new scholarly findings over the last two decades have shown that the traditional view has been significantly exaggerated.

Examination of Farmland Holdings

The amount of farmland held by wealthy landowners and peasants was an important indicator of the distribution of farmland rights since 1949 and fundamental for judging the farmland tenure system and modern economy, yet there has been a lack of convincing data. A detailed nationwide survey was conducted on land reforms, and although accurate national data were not published, it laid the foundation for statistical work. Based on the land reform survey data from 1949 to 1952, we were able to establish that the proportion of farmland held by the top 10% of the wealthy rural landowners on the eve of the land reforms was around 30% (±5%) in the southern provinces, while it was much lower than that in the north. This figure would be lower if the occupancy status of land rights such as top-soil rights, permanent tenancy rights, and public land were taken into account.[14] In other words, the rural rich held about 30%

205–216. Long Denggao, Wang Zhenghua, and Yin Wei, "Chuantong minjian zuzhi zhili jiegou yu faren chanquan zhidu: jiyu qingdai gonggong jianshe yu guanli de yanjiu" (The Governance Structure of Traditional Civil Organizations and Legal Person Property Rights System: A Study Based on Public Construction and Management in the Qing Dynasty), *Jingji yanjiu* (Economic Research), no. 10 (2018): 175–191.

[14] Long Denggao and He Guoqing, "Tugai qianxi diquan fenpei de jianyan yu jieshi" (An Examination and Interpretation of the Distribution of Land Rights on the Eve of Land Reforms), *Dongnan xueshu* (Southeast Academic Research), no. 4 (2018): 150–161.

of land, but their land rights and benefits were shared with the rest of the population.

Farmland concentration phenomena and trends were exaggerated. Another important reason was that this was an inevitable consequence of free trade. The lack of convincing academic analysis has caused neglect of the negative feedback mechanisms that inhibit and hedge against the concentration of landownership.

Apart from the well-known equal inheritance rule among various sons, other important factors were hedging against the concentration of farmland rights and the causes of the fragmentation of farmland rights. First, the more diverse the types of transactions, the more likely they were to reduce systemic risk, such as redemption mechanisms to protect the rights of vulnerable groups and also to delay the transfer of farmland rights, providing the possibility for farmers to weather the storm, recover and rebuild their farms, and operate independently. Second, regarding farmland tenure, it is not just about ownership but also possession. It was a fact that many middle- and lower-class farmers had the rights of the topsoil of land and the rights to sell the land in a conditional sale, which was also a property right. Third, the farmland under corporate property rights, such as family-owned lands (*zutian*), temple fields, school fields, various association's fields, and community fields, had to some extent reduced the unevenness of privately occupied land. For example, the proportion of public land in Guangdong and Fujian could have reached about 30%. These institutional arrangements enabled individual farmers to gain ongoing competitiveness and vitality and, to some extent, inhibited land concentration and mergers.

Equalization of Farmland Rights: History and Reality

Sun Yat-sen's political slogan, "equalization of farmland rights" (*pingjun diquan*), has been the dominant ideological trend in China and was put into practice nationwide in the mid-to-late twentieth century. The Land Reform Movement of 1949–1952 was a compulsory change to equalize farmland ownership, whereas the Collectivization Movement since the late 1950s and the 1981 Family Contract Responsibility System were about the equal distribution of farmland user rights.

The initial equalization of ownership or use rights was disrupted by factors such as female marriage, changes in household composition, population mobility, and farming capacity. The dynamic combination of land

and labor was difficult to maintain when combined with other variables. In the twenty-first century, the shift in national policy toward encouraging farmland transfers meant a shift from government allocation of agricultural land to an enhanced role for the market.[15]

From an academic perspective, it was rare to find economic "experiments" and research materials on how tenure status changed after the initial measures of tenure equalization, so what does exist was of great value. Although there were many results on equal land rights and land system reforms, there were limited coherent, systematic studies. In reality, each change has had a profound impact on the economy and politics of China and provides inspiration and lessons for the current land system reforms to grasp their orientation and basic ideas. The transformation helps in understanding the fundamental characteristics of Chinese society and the economy.

In fact, the one-sidedness of mainstream thinking of the twentieth century, such as the theory of optimal self-farming, the theory of the unfairness and inefficiency of tenancy, and the theory of equal farmland rights, was due to the lack of a market mentality. It was all static thinking, based on the premise of farmland immobility and other production factors. It became mainstream thinking under the strong influence of China's economic backwardness and the quest for a strong state able to resist foreign imperialism in the modern era.

Transition from a Traditional to a Modern Economy

Owning farmland and trading it to create wealth can be deeply rooted in the nature of traditional Chinese people. However, in modern times, it lost importance due to the chaos created by backwardness and economic and military aggression by foreign powers. People sentimentally attribute poverty and backwardness to the concentration of farmland rights due to private ownership of land, which led to the bankruptcy, migration, and poverty of peasants, and the disorder of the economy due to factors and commodity markets. They believed that China could break out of the chaos and attain the goal of becoming a prosperous and strong country only through governmental control of the allocation of resources.

[15] Long Denggao, "Cong pingjun diquan dao guli liuzhuan" (From the Equalization of Land Rights to Encouragement of Circulation), *Hebei Xuekan* (Hebei Academic Journal), no. 3 (2018): 142–147.

It became the dominant ideological strain during most of the twentieth century. However, the leading external cause of the economic decline of modern China was, in fact, the incessant wars. In contrast, the fundamental internal cause was the failure of the transition from a traditional to a modern economy (or the industrialization of the agricultural economy).

Many scholars have hypothesized that if China had been able to generate an Industrial Revolution of its own, as Britain did, it would have been able to avoid being left behind. Similarly, many scholars have discussed why France, Spain, India, and the Muslim world did not have a spontaneous Industrial Revolution. In fact, all other regions industrialized by learning and imitating the "British model." The absence of a spontaneous Industrial Revolution does not indicate stagnation and a lack of dynamism in the traditional Chinese economy, nor does it entirely negate the traditional Chinese system and culture.

On the one hand, comparing the form of property rights and business operations between China and Western Europe in the premodern period, we find that the characteristics of traditional China—individual farming based on private property rights of farmland and market transactions with low thresholds, divisibility, replicability, and easy recovery—created a substantial middle class of peasants in the agricultural era and achieved relative economic and social stability. On the other hand, this stability and the self-reinforcement of essential attributes inhibited the emergence of factors such as the alienation of farmland from poor peasants—as, for example, in Britain—which would constitute the workforce in newly emerging factories. Here, we can observe some of the essential characteristics of the traditional Chinese economy, which were at least partially responsible for a path of economic development different from that of Western Europe.

1.5 Conclusions

Through systematic investigation of the traditional farmland property rights system over the past millennium, this chapter has re-examined the farmland rights system and the traditional economy and reflected on some profoundly influential existing theories to form a new understanding. Meanwhile, the all-round excavation of this irreplaceable institutional heritage, as well as the in-depth investigation of farmland property rights and the diversified types of transactions, has resulted in new academic discoveries and theoretical innovations and contributed to forming a systematic understanding and an explanatory framework.

In this chapter, we have reflected on the established theories; however, we do not intend to create new ones but rather to base our own perspectives on the explanatory framework of a self-contained logical system. The interpretation of the relevant issues is not based on deduction from certain theories or models but rather on new insights based on reassessing historical facts. The unique heritage of the traditional farmland tenure system has reference value for the current market-oriented reforms of the agricultural land system. The recent construction and development of a market economy rest on specific traditional institutional and cultural foundations. However, these institutional legacies have not been properly explored; on the contrary, they have been neglected and even presented in a distorted way by historical research.[16] This chapter has aimed to present these valuable legacies to enable a better understanding of the market economy system with Chinese characteristics and highlight its theoretical value for further research.

[16] Li Bozhong, "Preface," in Long Denggao, *Zhongguo chuantong diquan zhidu jiqi bianqian* (China's Traditional Land Tenure System and Its Changes) (Beijing: China's Social Science Press, 2018).

CHAPTER 2

The Types of Farmland Property Rights

2.1 Farmland Rights Stratification and Conceptual Analysis

Concerning farmland property rights, there were several groups of concepts. This book will focus on explaining farmland rights in as simple terms as possible without entangling the identification of legal terms. It pays attention to farmland rights, including rights at different levels and at different periods; they were not only civil customs practiced by ordinary people but were also recognized and protected by government and law. First were private property rights, legal property rights, and state property rights, and we will discuss these later.

Second were ownership rights, possession rights, and user rights. This series of concepts is widely used in economics. Ownership is an exclusive and independent farmland right, and what needs to be explained is the rights to possession. In this book, possession typically refers to de facto control, which includes rights of use, proceeds, and disposition that were distinct from the owner's will and interests and enjoyed by non-owners; disposal rights include transactional rights, particularly real rights for security (*danbao wuquan*), such as mortgages. Possession contains all rights other than ownership or certificate and is a property right with an agreed-upon time limit. Rights to the conditional sale (*dianquan*) and rights to the top-soil (*tianmianquan*) were typical rights of possession

D. Long and X. Chi, *The Institutions of Land Property Rights in China*, Palgrave Studies in Economic History,
https://doi.org/10.1007/978-981-97-5112-9_2

that were epitomized in conditional sales in the Song Dynasty, where the landowner retains the deed root (*qigen* that represents ownership), and the *dian* buyer (*chengdianren*) had the right to possess the land.

Third were real rights, which include ownership, usufruct, and security rights. Jurisprudence, particularly civil law, extensively uses this range of concepts. Usufructuary right, as the name implies, is the right to use and gain. Real rights for security include mainly mortgages and pledges. In particular, if a piece of farmland cannot form a security interest, its property attributes were incomplete. In other words, the presence or absence of a security right is an important marker in determining the attributes of farmland property.

Real rights can be divided into the right of full ownership (*jus in re propria*) and the right over the property of another (*jus in re aliena*). The right of full ownership is ownership, and other rights in this book refer to the breakdown of usufruct and security rights by the owner, which may be simplified and equate to possession.[1] Possession or rights over the property of another involving the sharing of farmland rights with the landowner were not well known in contemporary China and may not be well understood at the outset of contact. However, in the earlier periods of China's history, when farmland rights were highly developed, the phenomenon of possession rights was prevalent. They were the product of the development of the farmland rights market and were beginning to appear more and more in China today.

The stratification and trade of farmland rights in the market have undergone a long history of evolution and gradual diversification. In the Warring States, the Qin and Han dynasties, and the Sui and Tang dynasties, farmland transactions usually took the form of tenancy of user rights, the purchase and sale of ownership, and, later, mortgages or loans secured by farmland rights. During the Tang and Song dynasties, there emerged *dian*, commonly known as conditional sale, between tenancy and finalized sale, which became popular thereafter.[2] Among the 415 deeds of conditional and finalized sales in the *Selected Economic Contract Documents of Fujian in the Ming and Qing Dynasties* (Mingqing Fujian jingji qiyue

[1] Right over the property of another was also called "limited real rights" (*xianzhi xing wuquan*) or "real rights at certain limits" (*dingxian wuquan*), which seems not to fit with what it really infers.

[2] Kong Qingming, Hu Liuyuan, and Sun Jiping, *Zhongguo minfa shi* (The History of Chinese Civil Law) (Changchun: Jilin People's Press, 1996), 360–362; Chai Rong,

wenshu xuanji), 171 deeds were conditional sale contracts, about 41.2% of the total.[3] In the Ming and Qing dynasties, there was also the emergence of *yazu* (loan through the farmland as a guarantee) between *dian* (conditional sales) and tenancy and *huomai* (irrevocable sales) between conditional sales and irrevocable sales. In the abovementioned database, the number of contracts for irrevocable sales was 115, which accounted for 22.7% of the total. In addition, there were also land rent transactions in Fujian and Taiwan called *taijie* (loans through the land as security).[4] In this way, various channels of farmland circulation and transaction have been formed, such as "*taijie* (loans through the farmland as collateral), *zudian* (tenancy), *yazu* (rent deposits), *dian* (conditional sales), *huomai* (unfinalized sales or revocable sales), and *juemai* (irrevocable sales)." Revealing the historical evolution of farmland property rights and their transaction system will help us understand the differences among various types of farmland rights transactions (Fig. 2.1).

2.2 Certificates of Ownership: Expression and Validity of Deeds

In early modern China, the transaction contract was a kind of free and voluntary exchange of interests and mutual benefits and a true reflection of equality and credit; a deed or contract was also proof of property rights and protection of rights and interests. The development of contracts and credit had given rise to innovative private credit currencies that have promoted the spontaneous growth of the market economy. In particular, farmland deeds present a variety of transaction types and multi-level types of farmland rights, based on which farmland circulation and resource allocation have improved economic efficiency and farmland output.

Zhongguo gudai wuquanfa yanjiu—yi tudi guanxi wei yanjiu shijiao (Research into Property Rights Law in Ancient China: Land Relations as a Research Perspective) (Beijing: Zhongguo jiancha Press, 2007), Chapter 4.

[3] Thanks to Prof. Peng Kaixiang for showing me the database. Fujian Shifan University Lishixi (Department of History, Fujian Normal University), ed., *Mingqing Fujian jingji qiyue wenshu xuanji* (Selected Economic Contract Documents of Ming and Qing Dynasties in Fujian) (Beijing: People's Press, 1997).

[4] Long Denggao, "Qingdai diquan jiaoyi de duoyanghua fazhan" (The Diversification of Land Transactions in the Qing Dynasty), *Qingshi yanjiu* (Research into Qing History), no. 3 (2008): 44–58.

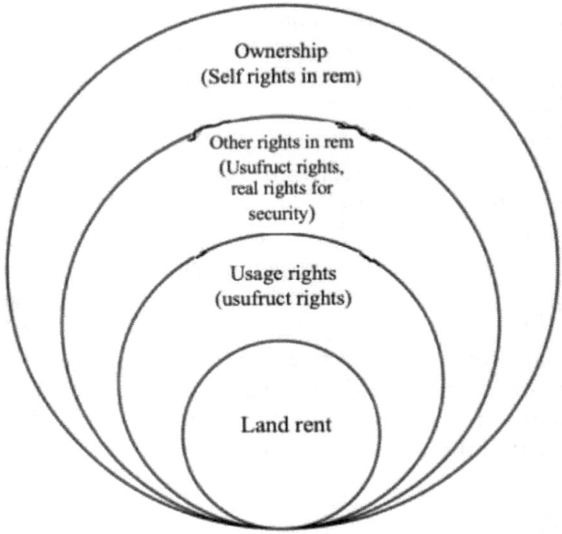

Fig. 2.1 Hierarchical farmland rights

The Regulatory Effect of Deeds in Property Transactions

The existence of contracts is ubiquitous and long-standing. From Dunhuang to Taiwan, Hainan to Northeast China, and Huizhou to Shanxi, contracts exist in almost all regions. They even go from the human world to the underworld. For example, there were the so-called deeds of the underworld (*mingqi*) and ghost deeds (*youqi*) in the form of "farmland purchase vouchers" (*maidiquan*). Deeds were prevalent not only in transactions of farmland rights but also in other civil transactions. In the contracts of Dunhuang and Turpan in the Sui, Tang, and Five dynasties, there were contracts for crop fields, melon fields, vineyards, orchards, homesteads (*shedi*), slaves, maidservants, young girls (*nizi*), sons, camels, oxen, horses, carts, metal products (*dang*), etc. Other contracts include borrowing coins, silver, wheat, barley, bean seeds, millets, grains, raw silk, miscellaneous silk, brocades, clothes, blankets, ropes (*xie*), and clothes made of coarse cloths (*he*). There were also contracts for long-term and short-term employment, documents of family separation, servants dismissed by masters and turned into civilians (*fangliang*), and goods collection.[5] In addition to sales and purchases, the transaction types also include *dian* (conditional sales), *lin* (leases), *zu* (rentals), and *jie* (loans), such as those for children and themselves.

Does the early modern Chinese contract have the meaning of a modern contract? Western civil law, or modern civil law itself, had developed out of custom. Its existence was not based on present-day or Western-specific civil practice but on the internal logic of market transactions and a natural sense of property rights. We randomly selected an unnumbered contract from the Contract Collection of Tsinghua University Library and tried to analyze the normative validity of deeds in property transactions from the perspective of modern contract law.[6]

> A land sale contract in perpetuity signed by Gong Yujin (finalized sale contract, *juemai qi*)
>
> I, Gong Yujin, the maker of the land sale contract in perpetuity, due to the shortage of grain, am willing to sell my proportions of land located in Xinzhuang Village (*xinzhuang cun*) of two and a half *mu*, between two field boundaries of north and south, east to the Feng's, west to the Zhang's, south to the slope at the edge of the field, and north to the road. Also, another piece of hollow land (*wodi*) of ten *mu*, one-third in the west of the field, is sitting in a north-south position. It is located east of the Du's, west of the Sun's, south of the slope, and north of the road. Another piece of land is in the east of eighty *mu* and twelve *mu*. It was a north-south position, extending east to the Du's surname, west to the Feng's, south to the road, and north to the Mud River canal (*nihequ*). The boundaries of the four directions were clear, and large and small trees on the ground were included. I am willing to sell them to Zhu Jinfa for farming and management and to receive 4300 coins (*daqian*) for the transaction, which he did not owe. I also attached 3.1 *sheng* of local grains under the Beijing measuring standard, stored in the warehouse. Under my name, Gong Yujin, I transfer ownership to Zhu Jinfa. The payment is in full, and the amount of grains is clear, so I have no other opinions. If there is a dispute within the household in the future, the seller side will take all

[5] Zhang Chuanxi, *Qiyue shi maidi quan yanjiu* (A Study of the History of Deeds and Land Purchase Certificates) (Beijing: Zhonghua Books, 2008): 9–38.

[6] I thank Liu Yuejing for her work.

the burden. I am afraid the verbal deal is difficult to rely on; I have made this finalized sale contract for reference.
December 11, The Fourth Year of the Xianfeng Period (1854)

Signed for sale in perpetuity
Gong Yujin
Witness (*yantongren*) Wang You
Written by Sun Xiaoda

According to the general principles of contemporary contract law, the basis for the establishment and effectiveness of a contract was the agreement of the buyer and the seller; the core terms of the sales contract were those related to the subject matter and its price and the transfer of rights to trees and other attachments on real property (large and small trees were included). Evidentiary effect provisions of contracts in dispute resolution were that "it is difficult to rely on the verbal evidence, and it shall be written down and preserved for reference in perpetuity." Therefore, there was no substantial difference between early modern and modern contracts. The rights of both parties (mainly the seller's claim for price and the buyer's claim for delivery of property rights) were carefully considered from the conclusion of the contract to its enforcement and even in the dispute resolution procedures that may occur after the enforcement of the contract. From the perspective of modern civil law, the contractual form of real estate transactions in early modern China developed to a more mature stage, with a well-established mechanism of normative effect. As for registration by the government, it belongs to another administrative relationship between the government and the people, which was not directly related to the transfer of ownership.

Deeds with red official seals, commonly known as the official deed (*guanqi*) or the red deed (*chiqi*), have full legal effect. In contrast, deeds without red official seals, the so-called white deeds (*baiqi*) or draft deeds (*caoqi*), were also recognized by the public and used by the local government as a basis for deciding cases in lawsuits. Many deeds did not have an official counterpart; namely, they did not need to be confirmed by the authorities (in the form of copies of deeds with official seals). These deeds also had the force of civil practice. In general, for transactions without tax payments to the government, the deeds may be processed without going to the government and do not necessarily have a corresponding official deed (with a red seal). In fact, most of the transactions were not taxed. Regarding the farmland rights transactions of the Qing Dynasty, there was no transaction tax on the tenancy of the user rights of farmland or on *yazu*. Mortgages (*diya*) and pawns (*diandang*) were considered debt transactions without transaction tax. Generally, only the ownership transaction was subject to transaction tax, and an official deed must be filed because, in addition to the transfer of ownership, there was also the payment of future tax on the land.

The defect guarantee system was highly critical in contract law and was divided into the defect guarantee of goods and rights. It refers to a kind of security obligation the seller has to the buyer. Liability for defects in goods means that the subject matter of the warranty should be of the usual or specially agreed quality; liability for defects in rights means that the seller warrants that third parties shall not claim any rights against the buyer in respect of the delivered subject matter. For example, the deed states that "In the event of future disputes between the parties, the seller will be liable," which means that in the event of a dispute over the ownership of the land, the seller should settle all the disputes, and the buyer's ownership should not be affected by the previous dispute, which was clearly defective security of rights. The consideration of the defect guarantee of rights indicates that, at least up to the time of this transaction, the requirement of defect-free ownership had already arisen in the farmland transaction. It must be mentioned that the emergence of such defect guarantee clauses dramatically improved the credibility of farmland transactions and was a major guarantee of the security of the transaction.

The creation and possession of property, like the creation and possession of knowledge, were as much a part of life as knowledge, and the simple system of the contract was deeply rooted in the hearts of Chinese people. As evidence of property transactions, the early modern Chinese contracts have formed a set of relatively mature mechanisms of normative effect in property transactions. Early modern Chinese contracts, as a definition and evidence of property rights, were based on which property owners can claim property rights according to the land boundaries (*sizhi*). Although the legal protection of private property rights may not be as well developed or expressed in different ways in the West, it is still generally effective in ensuring the realization of private property rights.

First, the making of a contract represents a free and voluntary transaction between two parties, which reflects equality and credit. In general, the contract should make clear that "both parties were willing to have this transaction and have no complaints" and that there is no coercive transaction or economic compulsion.

Second, contractual transactions were usually mutually beneficial and a kind of interest exchange, which means that all parties to the transaction were meticulous about their own interests and will fight for every coin. The provisions of the contract should be specified to the extent that even the smallest amount of money, such as one *fen*, one *li*, one *si*, and one *hao*, was to be carefully specified.

Third, both parties should abide by the contract. Otherwise, they should receive penalties for non-performance or breach of the contract. For example, failure to enforce or breach the contract will be punished, and the penalty for breach of contract is also explicitly stated in the contract. The deed's terms and language were precise, and a seal is required to confirm the addition of even one word.

Fourth, when settling a dispute or lawsuit, the local governor would recognize the deed as evidence instead of the person. It is stated that "fearing to make a verbal agreement without proof, I thereby establish a contract for future reference." Therefore, the contract has malleability that goes some way beyond the limitations of an anthropomorphized transaction.

Once a contract is signed, it is respected by all parties, especially in anthropomorphic villages, where the rural people usually consciously abide by the agreement. As the scope of the transaction expands, intermediaries and witnesses can play a coordinating role. The Crown arbitrates disputes that were not mediated at the civil level, but this is the usual case when lives were at stake or interests were not reconciled. Civilians respect contracts, and so do local governments, because contractual rules were compatible with the law, or the legal provisions were formulated based on contract rules that were recognized by the public. In disputes, provincial and county officials usually arbitrate and decide them strictly according to the contract.

It was a long tradition that "government officials follow the state code and civilians follow private deeds" and a government rule in dealing with civil affairs. The government should intervene in civil affairs as little as possible, leaving it to operate with its own spontaneous customs and rules, of which the contract is the core. There was even a "pardon-off clause" (*dishe tiaokuan*): if the contractual provisions conflicted with the emperor's amnesty, then the effect of the amnesty gave way to the contractual provisions. This is the connotation of the so-called private deeds rule (*renyi siqi*), which guarantees the validity and continuity of the contract to a great extent.

The change of dynasty does not affect the continuity of deeds and property rights. There were some illustrative cases in *Xingke tiben*:

> In Huichang County, Jiangxi Province, during the Ming Dynasty, Qiu, the tenant of Jin, farmed Jin's ritual land (*sitian*, land used for rituals with rental income), with an area of three *shi*, three *dou*, and three *sheng* (about one *mu*, and nine *fen*, and four *li*). During the Qianlong Period of the Qing Dynasty, Qiu Shichuan, the tenancy owner, moved to Wan'an County, where he transferred the tenancy to Qiu Tingfeng, who paid the "top-soil rent" (*dingzu*) to Qiu Shichuan every year and paid the Jin family's rent for grain. In the twelfth year of Qianlong's reign (1747), Qiu Shichuan returned from Wan'an to Huichang to collect the *dingzu*, but because of the inconvenience of the long distance, he wanted to return the land to someone to undertake the farming. The landowner, Jin, invited the tenant, Qiu Shichuan, to wine and agreed to return the deposit of the top-soil price of 12,000 coins, and the owner, Jin, would cultivate the land himself. However, Qiu Shichuan sold the top-soil rights of land to Wang Shihuai through the middleman and received 24,600 coins. The tenant owner, Qiu Shichuan, chose the high bidder for the transaction. However, the landowner, Jin, although dissatisfied, could only ask for a refund of the money for the banquet.[7]

Qiu's top-soil rights of farmland were not affected by the transfer from Ming to Qing, or by the landlord, but only by the market.

Middlemen and Guarantors

In making a traditional contract, one of the most distinctive participants was the intermediary, with titles such as "eye to person" (*yantongren*), "relying on the middle" (*pingzhong*), "middle seeing" (*zhongjian*), "standing in the middle" (*juzhong*), "witness to conclusion" (*jianli*), "middle person" (*zhongren*), "just-centered" (*zhengzhong*),

[7] Diyi lishi danganguan (No. 1 Historical Archives of China), and Zhongguo shehui kexueyuan lishi yanjiusuo (Institute of History, Chinese Academy of Social Sciences), eds., *Qianlong xingke tiben zudian guanxi shiliao Qingdai dizu boxue xingtai* (The Documents of Tenancy Relationships in Grand Secretariat Memorials on Criminal Matters in Qianlong's Reign, and Types of Exploitation of Land Rents in the Qing Dynasty) (hereinafter referred to as the "Memorials on Criminal Matters"), item 344.

"off-centered" (*pianzhong*), "witness person" (*zhengren*), and "quoting the middle" (*yinzhong*). There were also known as "relying on lineage" (*pingzu*) and "relying on kin" (*pingqin*). In an anthropomorphized society, the relationships of family and lineage may involve land origins or related interests. In fact, *pingzu* and *pingqin* actually contain a description of interests. In addition to the signatures or marks of both parties to the transaction, the middleman and the scribe (*shuren*) also signed the contract. Generally, the scribe was a specialist and calligrapher drafting the contracts whose contractual text usually reaches a certain level. The scribe receives a modest amount of remuneration for doing so.[8] In all, the middleman was a crucial element in making the contract.

First, the middleman was a witness to the transaction. In some cases, the deed contains words such as "seeing person" (*jianren*) and "witness person" (*jianzhengren*) to put the deed in effect. In case of a breach of contract dispute, the middleman will be a witness in the arbitration.

Second, some intermediaries were also guarantors, with joint and several liabilities. Once one party breaches the contract and fails to fulfill the compensation liability stipulated in the contract, the middleman will be responsible for compensation. This situation was clearly stated in the deed. In a farmland transaction with the legal person, commonly a tenancy deed, they usually had wealthy households as guarantors in case the tenant defaulted on the rent.

Finally, the officially authorized middlemen were called "official middle" (*guanzhong*) and "impartial" (*gongzheng*).[9] They often appear in official deeds and grant formal legal effect to the deed. Some deeds were signed by both official middlemen and civil middlemen. In the case of "Pawn Contract Made in the First Year of Tongzhi" (*Tongzhi Yuannian li dianyue*) of the Tsinghua University Library Collection, there were two official middlemen and one civil middleman.

[8] In the Southern Song Dynasty, there were people in Raozhou (Rao Prefecture) called *yongshuren*, who wrote land deals on behalf of buyers and sellers and who were paid hundreds of coins at a time (Hongmai, *Yijian sanzhi* (Three Records of Yijian), *Xinji* (Xin Collections), vol.7.

[9] Wang Zhenghua, "Wanqing minguo huabei xiangcun tianzhai jiaoyi zhongde guanzhong xianxiang" (Phenomenon of *Guanzhong* in the Dealings of Land and House in Rural North China in the Late Qing and Republican Period), *Zhongguo jingjishi yanjiu* (Researches in Chinese Economic History), no. 6 (2017): 104–119.

In the customs of Nanchang, there were two kinds of middlemen: "just-centered" (*zhengzhong*) and "off-centered" (*pianzhong*). In farmland transactions, both the seller and buyer invite *zhengzhong*, one from the buyer and one from the seller, and the number of *pianzhong* varies. There were also two kinds of fees for middlemen: one for the banquet and the other for the thanks (*xiezhongfei*). The buyer pays three-fifths of the banquet fee, while the seller pays two-fifths of the fee, which depends on the price of the land. If the farmland price was 100 *yuan*, the banquet fee was 5 *yuan*, and the two sides share it proportionally. If the farmland price was 100 *yuan*, then 103 *yuan* will be the total price, of which 98 *yuan* will be paid to the seller. As for the payment of thanks, whose proportion was the same as the banquet fee, *zhengzhong* receives the most, and *pianzhong*'s remuneration varies. Therefore, it can be seen that the role of the middleman in farmland transactions remains essential. It was necessary to invite middlemen to the site following village rules and regulations and to be highly cautious when signing contracts.[10]

The manner and amount of fees charged to intermediaries also vary from place to place. In some areas, the contracting parties share the cost of the middleman, while in others, only one party was required to bear the cost. In some areas, payment was in the form of money, while some middlemen accept goods and drinks, or both goods and money were collected. According to the Civil and Commercial Custom Survey (*Minshang xiguan diaocha*), the typical rate was about 5% of the total transaction price, in which the buyer pays 3% and 2% was paid by the seller.[11]

Still, in Nanchang, for example, the buyer was independently responsible for the cost of the middleman and was also charged for alcoholic beverages. It was called "three percent for the middleman, one percent for the scribe, and two percent for the banquet" (*Zhongsan biyi jiu'er fen*).

[10] Nongye tuiguangbu (Ministry of Agricultural Extension), "Nanchang quanxian nongcun diaocha baogao" (Report on the Rural Survey of Nanchang County), *Jiangxi sheng Nongyeyuan zhuankan* (Special Issue of Jiangxi Province Agricultural Institute), 1935.

[11] Xingzheng sifabu (Ministry of Justice and Administration), *Min shangshi xiguan diaocha baogaolu* (Report of the Survey of Civil and Commercial Customs) (hereinafter "Customs"), 1930, 435, 478, 551, 555, 575, 642.

In addition to the property price, the buyer must pay three *fen* (percent) for the middleman, one for the deed writer and two for the banquet. Among the three *fen* for the middlemen, one for the *zhengzhong* (the main middleman), and the rest of the *sanzhong* (those who assisted the main middleman) divide equally one point five *fen*. One *fen* of the pen money goes to the deed writer alone; two *fen* of the banquet fee was required, and if the buyer was willing to host the banquet, he was not required to pay for the wine. It has been the custom of buying and selling for a long time.[12]

In Nanchang customs, the middlemen at the site of the purchase and sale of lands and houses obtain the middleman money (*zhongrenqian*), all paid by the buyer. For example, if the price of the farmland was traded for one hundred *yuan*, the buyer should give the middleman three *yuan* of silver; if the house price was one hundred *yuan*, the buyer should give the middleman four *yuan* of silver, so the middleman's thank-you money, known as "three *yuan* charged for the transaction of an estate and four *yuan* for that of a house (*tiansan wusi*)."[13]

In the cases of Hubei, Fujian, and Nanping, middlemen in tenancy and borrowing contracts do not charge intermediary fees.[14] Middlemen, commonly known as "middle seeing" (*zhongjian*), show up on occasions such as transactions, borrowing, and mortgages. In addition to loans and borrowing, the middlemen might not have charged fees; otherwise, they must be paid. The remuneration standard was "five percent of the price," in which "three percent is paid by the buyer and two percent by the seller," according to the deed.[15]

Many middlemen and guarantors in contracts bear joint liability for guarantees. The guarantor must be responsible if a party defaults and fails to fulfill the obligation. For example, in a credit purchase case in Luonan

[12] *Xiguan* (Customs), the second part, 574.

[13] Ibid., 572.

[14] For example, in Hubei, as for tenancy farming, Shang County, Kai County, and others do not have the custom of giving thank-you money to middlemen (*xiezhongqian*). If you buy and sell pigs, cattle, and sheep or grain and all other goods, Zhushan and Badong counties do not have the custom of giving thank-you money to middlemen; Jingshan County has the custom of giving money in thanks for buying and selling pigs, cattle, and sheep; the transactions of grain and rice are extracted according to measures of hu. *Xiguan* (Customs), the second part, 663.

[15] *Xiguan* (Customs), the second part, 642.

County, Shaanxi Province, Zhou Dezhang, the guarantor was asked to fulfill his responsibility. According to the sources, "On the tenth day of December in the first year of Daoguang (1821), Yuan Linfu begged me to serve his guarantor and bought one *shi* of corns from Wei Youcai on credit for 1300 coins, which was due at the end of the month. However, it was not paid after the expiration of the period."[16]

In farmland rent transactions, there were also specialized agencies called "rent firms" (*zuzhan*) in the Yangtze River Delta and other places where landowners usually live far away in the city or outside the region, especially the owners of subsoil rights to the land. As the amount of land rent may be rather small and the cost of trips to collect rent was too high, they entrust an intermediary to collect the land rent on their behalf.[17] The land in Jiangnan was mostly divided into top-soil rights and subsoil rights, and most people favored intermediaries to collect the rent, resulting in the gradual formation of a specialized intermediary agency, the "rent firm." Both the tenants and the rent collectors dealt directly with the rental agency so that the tenants and rent collectors did not have to know each other as long as the agency guaranteed the payment of rent, and the tenants were able to trade the top-soil rights of farmland as freely as possible. As a result, both sides of the subsoil and top-soil rights were increasingly isolated. Thus, it was possible that the landowners and their descendants did not ask for the natural locations of the farmland for a long time or several generations and would gradually become unfamiliar with the exact locations of their farmland property in some sense.

In modern China, a particular agency in charge of farmland rent collection emerged, and it was a product of the development of delegated agency relationships in the tenancy system. As the tenants could not afford to pay the deposit in advance, a group of ten people in Sichuan formed a rural association called *tianyuanhui* (Rural Association). They obtained funds as a deposit for renting large areas of land, which were then transferred to peasants. The annual fund collection of the Guangdong Rural

[16] *Xingke tiben tudi zhaiwu lei* (Board of Punishments Routine Memorials, Land Debts) 6120, September 12, 1823 (Dai Junyuan Memorial).

[17] The reason for this is, on the one hand, the development of absentee landlords and, on the other, the regularization of the rural anti-rent movement. Muramatsu, Yuji, *Kindai Kōnan no jozan—Chūgoku jinushi seido no kenkyū* (Renting Firm in Modern Jiangnan—A study of the landlord system in China) (Tokyo: Tokyo University Press, 1970): 697–740.

Association often amounted to thousands of *taels*, which was also used in the traditional "joint association" (*hehui*) in tenancy relations.[18]

In the contract "A Conditional Sale Contract Made by Ji Fengcheng" [立典地约人冯继成] in the first year of Tongzhi (1862), collected by the Tsinghua University Library, it states:

> "Mediated by the middleman, I agree to make the land a *dian* under Ning Xiutang, and he will plow the land."

The notaries (*gongzheng*) were Cao Jinzhi and Cao Peizhi, and the middleman was Peng Zhenrong. At the end of the contract, it states:

> "In the first year of Xuantong (1909), Sir Tong's (*Tonggong*) land, which is valued at nineteen *taels*, according to the original contract, and is estimated to be fifteen hundred coins,[19] according to the market price, is to be under the name of Cao Yunliang for farming. In the future, if the landowner wanted to redeem the land, it would have nothing to do with Xiu Ningtang."

In the third year of the Republican Period (1914),

> "The *dian* contract maker, Ning Xiutang, is willing to sell this land to Cao Yunliang as a conditional sale."

In 1935 (the 24th year of the Republican Period), "Cao Renji and his mother sold this land to Cao Dengying in perpetuity, and this page, therefore, became invalid." (The original contract stated that "the redemption of *dian* was limited to eight years." By then, 73 years had passed. According to the laws of the Republican Era, the owners of *dian* were allowed to obtain full landownership and dispose of the land at will.)

[18] Qu Mingzhao, "Zhongguo nongtian yazu di jinzhan" (Progress of the Leasehold of Agricultural Land in China), *Zhongguo nongcun* 1 (Rural China), no. 4, 1935.

[19] It was probably a writing error in this deed. It might be (壹千五百文).

2.3 Types of Realization of Farmland Property Rights

Property Acquisitions

A property right was a bundle of rights consisting of a bundle of sub-rights. The economic subject can have all or part of a property right or have the property right for a certain period or within an agreed-upon time. Gaining control over land through investment in labor refers to the incremental land gains that peasants receive as a result of investment and labor, including investment in the construction of water conservancy facilities that increase the fertility and output of land. It was not only a natural law but also a civil custom to obtain land property rights through investment and transactions, which were also recognized and protected by state law.

In the case of Nanping, Fujian Province, it records that "for example, in the land of A, he could collect 100 *shi* of grains per year and recruited B to take over the tenancy; and B, because of his hard work, did not hesitate to spend efforts and fertilizers, so that this piece of land was able to produce 150 *shi* of grains one year."[20] We show it as a formula, as below:

$$100 + 50 = 150\,shi$$

The extra 50 *dan* collected by B was called "tax land" (*shuitian*); the original land of A was called "seedling land" (*miaotian*). Both types of land "can be sold, transferred, and inherited separately." If the cost increases further, the output will continue to increase to 250 *shi*; then we have:

$$100 + 150 = 250\,shi$$

Increases of up to 150 *dan* surpassed the original harvest. It was logical and understandable that obtaining the corresponding land yields created by the tenants gives them more than the original landowners. This was the so-called dirt soil silver (*fentuyin*) and gray fertile land (*huifeitian*), a way to form the top-soil rights of land.[21]

[20] *Xiguan* (Customs), 599. The customs of the Republican Era were inherited from those of the Qing Dynasty.

[21] If people don't trade, there will be no added value. This was the increased benefit of resource allocation.

In the farmland transaction of Zhuxi County, Hubei Province, there exists the so-called top rights of loan (*dingdangquan*), also known as "rent on the top-soil but conditional sale de facto" (*mingzu andian*). For example, "A wants to buy B's land at 400 *taels* of silver after negotiation. However, A does not have enough money, so he has to rent out the land to C at 300 *taels* of silver, known as the "top head silver" (*dingshouyin*), and pays off B. C will pay land rent to A annually. Within the time limit of the duration of top-soil (*dingtian*), C may transfer the land to D at will, and A should have no right to intervene."[22]

$$100 + 300 = 400\ taels$$

It can also be regarded as a joint investment by Party A and Party B to purchase land and share land rights. Party A obtains ownership for a quarter of the land price and obtains the land rent. Party B dominates the independent rights over the property of another with three-quarters of the land price. Because B has invested three-quarters of the land price, his rights will not be interfered with by A. The top-soil had the "top rights of loan" (*dingdangquan*) reflecting the combination of elements and the allocation of resources.

Partial landownership by land investment was particularly evident in the tidal land (*shatian*) case of Baoshan, Jiangsu Province. Tidal land, like the uncultivated (*huangdi*), became fertile only after the tenant peasants enclosed the riverbank and cultivated it. Landlords and tenant peasants drafted a piece of paper known as a "sub-degree voucher" (*fuduju*), and "this receipt was tradable."[23] The *fuduju* could be traded and had nothing to do with the landowner; the current income and future income were thus guaranteed. As future income can be realized through transactions, it incentivizes the tenants to invest in the land. This *fuduju* was a certificate of property right, specifically the certificate of top-soil rights of land, which contains the future land income. To sell this property right certificate was to realize the future income tenants will get from the land investment. The Pearl River Delta's tidal land and the other reclamation areas have similar characteristics.

The upward mobility of Han tenants in Taiwan was also related to this. In the Qing Dynasty, Fujian people crossed the sea to rent the

[22] *Xiguan* (Customs), 337.

[23] Ibid., 344.

farmland owned by Taiwan natives (*fanren*). Afterward, Han tenants became the creditors of Taiwan's indigenous landowners. This situation was common in nineteenth-century Taiwan.[24] Fujian's skilled peasants brought advanced technology and spared no effort to invest in water conservancy construction that increased land fertility and made the land increasingly productive. The increment of land yields and interests was obtained and controlled by the skilled Fujian cultivators, and the land rights and prices of top-soil rights rose higher and higher, gradually surpassing the subsoil rights of Taiwan natives.

Meanwhile, with the land output and social surplus continuing to increase and the living standards in Taiwan improving, the living expenses of natives were also rising, but their access to social resources was relatively declining. Therefore, Taiwan natives contracted the land to Fujian peasants or collected more rent by "heavy deposit and light rent" (*zhongya qingzu*), a loan and cash flow in the form of future earnings. They constantly looked for supplementary payments (*zhaojia*) and borrowed loans from Han tenants. As time went by, the interests and prices of the subsoil rights became lighter and lighter, but the living expenses of the natives increased unabated, and the debts rose daily. The natives had to sell the subsoil rights to the tenants to offset the deficits. In this way, land rights and property rights were quietly transferred from natives to Han tenants.

How can a tenant exploit the landlord in turn? Scholars in Taiwan have revealed the history of Fujian tenants' "exploitation" of the Taiwan natives, leading to their land loss. However, according to the Marxist point of view, the landlord (landowner) usually exploits the tenant. In fact, in modern China, there have been many "hardcore tenants" (*wandian*) and "unruly tenants" (*diaodian*) that reneged and resisted rent payment. As a result, landlords constantly faced the loss of their rights and interests.

Before the First Industrial Revolution, the development of British tenant farmers was somewhat similar. The grain imports from the North American colonies freed up scarce land in the British Isles for more efficient production. The large-scale enclosures of tenant manors for sheep grazing and the high income of wool export made these tenants into

[24] Chen Qiukun, *Qingdai Taiwan tuzhu diquan* (Indigenous Land Rights in Taiwan during the Qing Dynasty) (Taipei: Institute of Modern History, Academic Sinica, 2009), Chapter 7.

an emerging wealthy class whose fortunes surpassed those of the original feudal lords and aristocrats. Therefore, their power influenced the parliament and further propelled the establishment of the British property rights system. The Agricultural Revolution and the Property Rights Revolution laid the foundation for the First Industrial Revolution.

Farmland Appreciation Rights and Investment

The farmland can confirm the property's security and realize the property's appreciation in circulation and transactions. The transferability of farmland rights facilitates the transfer of resources from lower-value uses to higher-value uses. In addition, the transfer of property rights facilitates the dynamic security of the property and, on this basis, achieves the preservation and appreciation of the property's value, analyzing from the perspective of the security of the property. From the social point of view, goods do not serve their purpose, and social wealth may be wasted in idleness; from the private point of view, the claims of rights holders were limited, full realization of benefits was difficult, and the incentive from the rights was thus weakened.[25]

Farmland Appreciation Rights

Clear and stable property rights in the farmland attract owners to invest in it, and multiple levels of property rights enable various classes of capital to invest in the farmland through numerous transactions. Landowners, businessmen, and urban dwellers invest in farmland and were enthusiastic about the stable benefits of landownership. This section focuses on the fact that stable operational farmland rights, such as top-soil rights of farmland and permanent tenancy rights, create new and constant yield increments on limited land that make tenant farmers and land cultivators willing to make long-term investments in land.

With the security and expectation of property rights, tenants could acquire tenancy or land rights according to customary law, inherit, transfer, and sell freely without interference from the landlord. The landlords could not withdraw the tenancy at will. Therefore, the tenants were willing to increase inputs to improve the land yield or devote themselves

[25] Zhou Linbin and Li Shenglan, "Wuquan xinlun: yizhong fa yu jingjixue fenxi de silu" (A New Theory of Property Rights: A Method of Law and Economic Analysis), *Xiangtan University xuebao* (Journal of Xiangtan University), no. 6 (2000): 26–33.

to water conservancy and infrastructure to increase future land income. If there were no guarantee of land titles such as top-soil rights of land (*tianpi*) or permanent tenancy rights, the current tenant would not invest in the land; if there were no guarantee of the validity of the deed and no guarantee of future returns, the tenant would not invest his capital and labor in the land. Because the investment in arable land and its supporting facilities cannot be fully paid for in the current period, the remuneration was shared over the annual crop harvest in the future. So, tenancy rights were not just the rights to farm; they themselves have future expected benefits. A tenant peasant not only earns income from farming but also earns income from the top-soil rights of farmland and the tenancy rights even if he does not farm the land, as shown in a case from *Xingke tiben*.[26]

In the 36th year of Qianlong (1771), Ladian, from Pinghe County, Fujian, bought eight *dou* of Huang Zhongliang's land and collected fifteen *shi* and three *dou* of grain annually, which had been done twice. Laidian wanted to grow crops on his own and ended his tenancy. However, Huang Xi, the tenant on Laidian's land, refused to cancel his tenancy as he claimed that there should be tenant silver for manure. It was only after Laidian paid 50 *yuan* of silver that the tenant peasant agreed to write a letter to cancel.[27]

The 50 *yuan* was the tenancy price that condensed the future earnings. The top-soil rights could be traded, and the price was specified in the deed at the time of trading. They were known as *quetian*, *fentuyin*, among others. The term "dirt silver" *fentuyin* means that the tenant peasant's investment in the fertility of the land was discounted as silver, and the small farmer had a clear view of his own interests and was careful with every coin. Initially, the price of the top-soil rights and the subsoil rights of land was agreed upon by both parties, and the price of the rights of the land would increase continuously or even exceed the current price as the tenant farmers invested their labor costs to increase the productivity of the land. The "Jiangyin Gazeteer-Custom" (*Jiangyin Xianzhi-fengsu*) records that the tenant farmers freely controlled the local tenancy rights; "the old shared the land, the poor sold the land, and it was called *que*." The amount of money obtained was called landed money (*shang'anqian*),

[26] Fang Xing, Wei Jinyu, and Jing Junjian, eds., *Zhongguo jingji tongshi—Qingdai jingjishi* (General Economic History of China: Economic History of the Qing Dynasty) (Beijing: Jingji ribao Press, 2000), 1783–1785.

[27] *Xingke tiben*, 288.

which was more than the initial price of the land. For example, "two *taels* of silver for one *mu*, and three or four *taels* for the landing money." The "landing money" here was the price of the top-soil rights of land.

Property rights were unparalleled in motivating tenant farmers to invest in the land. A deed in the fifteenth year of the Guangxu Period in Taiwan's land resettlement, entitled "Willingly to return the land for the silver of the cost of labor" (*Ganyuan tuigeng shouhui gongbenyin*), records the following: Huang Wujiu was responsible for a section of the Dengying College's paddy field, which was prone to flooding and could not be harvested whenever the water rose, and therefore his debts in grains were piling up. Huang Wujiu "prepared the capital and labor, carried the mud to fill the lowland, and built the new field, which cost quite a lot." Huang hoped to make a profit in the future. Therefore, when the new tenant, peasant Zhang Shuiwen, wanted to acquire the tenancy rights, in addition to paying off the 50 *shi* rentals of grains owed by the original tenant, he had to make provision for a sum of 190 *taels* of "Buddhist face silver" (*fomianyin*)[28] to be paid to the original tenant, Huang Wujiu, for Huang's capital investment and the related future interest and income.[29]

A clear property rights system and well-developed land rights transactions allow land to gain value like capital, bringing land rights owners more equity. Property rights have an incentivizing function and a reasonable expectation of economic benefits, giving people a motivation to create wealth. The exclusivity of yield rights gives tenant farmers and landowners an incentive to invest in the land. As long as a certain amount of labor and cost was invested in the land, the increase in the value of the land resulting from that input goes to the inputter, including both the tenants and the landowners.

Future Gains from Farmland to be Transferred and Discounted

Tenant farmers do not fully benefit from the various capital and labor inputs into farmland management in the current year but usually expect to receive future returns that were spread over a period of time: either as a deposit under the security of tenure system or as a "cost of labor," often referred to in deeds of title, including the construction of water

[28] The Mexican silver dollar.

[29] Taiwan yinhang jingji yanjiushi (Bank of Taiwan Economic Research Office), *Taiwan sifa wuquan bian* (Private Law Property Rights in Taiwan), the second part (Taipei: Taiwansheng wenxian weiyuanhui, 1999), 697.

facilities on agricultural land. With the upfront capital investment, future investment returns were enjoyed, i.e., annual "profit rent" (*lizu*) or "top-soil rent" (*dingzu*) or access to "work capital grains" (*gongbengu*). In the case of the *Xingke tiben*, Lin Yajian, a tenant peasant in Yong'an County, Guangdong, had "spent nine *taels* of silver for labor" on 26 *mu* of tenant land. As he moved back to his hometown in Heyuan, he "transferred the land to Zhang Weihao and Zhang Yaxin for farming," who agreed to pay back nine *shi* of grains a year for "grain for labor cost" (*gongbengu*). It was about getting nine *shi* of grains a year in future profits.[30]

This means that when a tenant farmer withdrew from farming the land, he could receive a transfer commitment of future earnings from the tiller and therefore did not have to worry about the loss of future earnings from past and present investments in the land. The future return on the tenant's investment in the land could also be cashed in on the spot by the tiller at the time of the transaction. Again, let's look at a case from *Xingke tiben*:

> "Because of the barren land, the tenants donated their own capital, built stanks, and farmed the land according to their quota."

It implies an increase in the tenant's share, which was derived from the tenant's labor cost, and the tenant consequently obtains the rights to freely dispose of and transfer the top-soil rights of the land. Between the sixth and eighteenth years of the Qianlong reign (1741–53), many transfer transactions took place concerning these tenancy rights. For example, Chen Shiqing successively purchased the top-soil rights (*dinggeng*) from the original tenants, Ye Zisheng and Ye Boling, and Pan Yuren purchased the top-soil rights of land from Chen Shebo. The tenant owners said,

> "Because there was no stank in the past, we had many poor harvests. Later, we, the small ones (*xiaode*), paid for hired labor to build the stank so that the harvest could be made, and the rent was paid as usual. If any tenants can't grow crops on their own, they will be given a price for the cost of construction work and find substitutes to plow the land (*dejia dinggeng*). They will still pay the landowners' rents and will never be in arrears."

30 *Xingke tiben*, 317.

"To transfer the top-soil rights of land for a price" (*dejia dinggeng*) was where the future return on the investment was realized on the spot.[31] If future returns to farmland inputs could not be transferred or discounted, this would limit tenants' free choice and reinforce the land's binding effect so that those tenants could not leave the land or receive their own investment returns when they did. It was also an exit mechanism, a right, and a benefit of free choice. It is a very important point that has been overlooked.

Institutional Framework for Top-Soil Rights

Two property rights—"top-soil right" and "subsoil right"—are created on the same piece of land. The landowner (subsoil rights owner) owns the land and harvests the land rent, while the top-soil right owner owns the rights to manage the land and the rights to dispose of the proceeds and transactions of the "top-soil" (*tianmian*). They were able to not only lease, transfer, and exchange the top-soil but also exercise mortgage, pawn, and security. A lease of the top-soil may bring another kind of land rent, known as a "top lease" (*dingzu*) or "tenancy" (*dianzu*), and loans can be granted by a mortgage of the top-soil. The transfer of the top-soil rights of land did not affect subsoil rights of land or the proceeds of its land rent.

The top-soil rights of farmland contain the rights in the bundle of the property rights of use, proceeds, mortgage, transfer, etc., and were owned exclusively and without interference from the owner of the subsoil rights of the land. Regarding the series of ownership-possession-use rights, top-soil rights of farmland should be incorporated by possession, similar to that of *dian* rights. From the point of view of civil law systems, top-soil rights not only had usufruct right but also formed a security right by which it can be pledged, pawned, and so on, and can take the form of a real right—"a right over the property of another" or "possession." When top-soil was leased out, it means that the owner of the top-soil transfers the rights to use the field, and the three parties share property rights of the land, each acquiring different levels of land rights.

The subsoil and top-soil rights of the land were interrelated and mutually binding, and the two parties enter into a contract by negotiation,

[31] Ibid., 284.

specifying their respective interests. The subsoil and top-soil rights of the farmland were traded and circulated relatively independently, forming the corresponding market prices (Tables 2.1, 2.2, 2.3).

The price of the subsoil and top-soil for each plot of farmland was agreed upon by both parties and depends mainly on the degree of investment contribution of the top-soil owner. It was also agreed who will pay the tax, usually the owner of top-soil, if the subsoil owner was out of town or lives in a city, or by a third party. The top-soil-to-subsoil ratio was on an upward trend. According to surveys in Wu County, Wuxi, and Changshu, before the Second Sino-Japanese War, it was generally 1:1, and after the war, the price of the subsoil fell, the price of the top-soil remained largely unchanged, and the ratio of the top-soil to the subsoil of the farmland rose.

The prices of top-soil rights in Pinghu and Qidong were higher than those of subsoil rights. The price of Pinghu farmland top-soil was as high as 100 *yuan*, medium up to 60 *yuan*, which was higher than the highest 60 *yuan* and medium 40 *yuan* of the farmland subsoil base price. At the lowest price only, the subsoil rights were slightly higher than the top-soil right. The situation in Qidong was somewhat unique. Qidong was a sedimentary plain at the mouth of the Yangtze River, most of which was only two or three hundred years old. Soil fertility was derived mainly from the investment of labor by the tenant peasants so that they acquired top-soil rights and controlled the main land rights, the price of which was much higher than that of the subsoil rights, which accounted for 85–90% of the total price. Farmland rights of subsoil were only 10–15%, almost symbolically.

Original tenant farmers who have acquired top-soil rights to leased land should be granted land with a value equivalent to the prevailing market value of local top-soil rights.[32] The provisions of the East China Land Reforms Implementation Measures (*Huadong tudi gaige shishibanfa de guiding*) state: "When allocating land based on original cultivation, for original tenant farmers who have acquired top-soil rights to leased land, the price of these top-soil rights is generally calculated based on pre-war

[32] *Tudi gaige shouce* (Handbook of Land Reforms) (Beijing: Xinhua shudian huadong zong fendian, 1950), 12.

Table 2.1 1929 Pinghu agricultural survey form no. 2 (*Diaocha pinghu nongye shi diaocha zongbiao di'er hao*). *Source* "Condition of the Agricultural Economy in Pinghu, Zhejiang" (*Zhejiang pinghu nongye jingji zhuangkuang*), Office of Statistics, Legislative Assembly, *Monthly Statistics* (Tongji Yuebao), no.3, 1929

General table of agricultural survey No. 2	*A bumper harvest of important agricultural products of Pinghu County*			
Products	*Rice*	*Broad Bean*	*Wheat*	*Mulberry tree*
Where to plant, water, sand, or other	*Paddies and lowlands with water*	*Paddies and lowlands with water*	*Paddies and lowlands with water*	*Paddies*
Estimated number of *mu* countywide or rural	324,858 *mu*	13,105 *mu*	24,501 *mu*	1365 *mu*
Value per *mu*				
Subsoil				
Highest	60 *yuan*	60 *yuan*	60 *yuan*	60 *yuan*
Medium	40 *yuan*	40 *yuan*	40 *yuan*	40 *yuan*
Lowest	30 *yuan*	20 *yuan*	20 *yuan*	30 *yuan*
Top-soil				
Highest	100 *yuan*	100 *yuan*	100 *yuan*	65 *yuan*
Medium	60 *yuan*	60 *yuan*	60 *yuan*	45 *yuan*
Lowest	15 *yuan*	15 *yuan*	15 *yuan*	15 *yuan*

Table 2.2 Average farmland price, Qidong districts, in per *mu* (*yuan*), 1925–28. *Source* Xiuqing, "Agricultural Economy and the Tenancy System in Qidong" (*Qidong nongcun jingji yu zudian zhidu*), *Jiangsu Agricultural Bank Monthly* (Jiangsu nonghang yuekan) 3, no. 6, 1936

Districts	*Land rights Categories*	*Drylands*			*Paddies*		
		Highest	*Medium*	*Lowest*	*Highest*	*Medium*	*Lowest*
First District	Subsoil rights	10	8	5	–	–	–
	Top-soil Rights	60 (85.7%)	48	30	–	–	–
	Total	70	56	35	–	–	–
Second District	Subsoil rights	10	8	6	7	6	5
	Top-soil Rights	85 (89.5%)	70 (89.7%)	44 (88%)	40	25	20
	Total	95	78	50	47	31	25
Third District	Subsoil rights	8.5	7.5	6	–	–	–
	Top-soil Rights	65 (88.4%)	50 (86.9%)	37 (86%)	–	–	–
	Total	73.5	57.5	43	–	–	–
Fourth District	Subsoil rights	8.5	7.5	6	–	–	–
	Top-soil Rights	75 (89. 8%)	50	30	–	–	–
	Total	83.5	57.5	36	–	–	–
Fifth District	Subsoil rights	10	8	5	–	–	–
	Top-soil Rights	85 (89.5%)	60	40 (88.9%)	–	–	–
	Total	95	68	45	–	–	–

Table 2.3 Changes in the price ratio between top-soil and subsoil in Jiangnan (*jiangnan bufen tudi tianmian yu tiandi de bijia bianhua*). *Sources* See Zhonggong sunanqu dangwei nongwei hui [the Agricultural Committee of the Party Committee of the Communist Party of China, Sunan District], "Preliminary Survey of the Rural Land System in Sunan" [*Sunan nongcun tudi zhidu chubu diaocha*], 1 May 1950. JF328.8-2431

	Change in land top-soil to subsoil Ratio in Parts of Gangnam		*Unit:* shi
Districts	*Time*	*Subsoil price*	*Top-soil price*
Three towns in Changshu	Before the war	5–10	5–10
	After the war	3–5	5–8
Districts	*Time*	*Subsoil price*	*Top-soil price*
Songjiang Xinxiang	Before the war	8–9	2–4
	After the war	7–8	2–4
	The eve of the founding of the PRC	1–4	3–5

prices. However, specific cases should be determined according to local conditions."[33]

Under long-term property rights incentives, top-soil owners have spared no effort to acquire value-added interests in water facilities, soil improvement, and enhancement of farmland production. On the other hand, out-of-town and urban dwellers can invest their capital in land and agriculture by trading subsoil rights. In Tao Xu's *Zuhe* (core elements of land tenancy), it was said:

The separation of top-soil rights and subsoil rights lowered the threshold for land transaction and circulation and therefore enriched peasants' choice, as in the case of the *Xingke tiben*. Huizhou Zhu Tianyou had two *shi* and one *dou* of land. In the second year of Yongzheng's reign (1724), he sold his "pledge property" (*zhiye*, known as top-soil rights of land) at the price of twelve silver *taels* of silver and four thousand coins to the Zheng Ruifa brothers for farming, with an annual land rent (*liangye*

33 "Huadong tudi gaige shishi banfa de guiding" (Provisions of the East China Land Reforms Implementation Measures), 1950-aa-26. Jiangsu Provincial Archives: 3006-Chang-22.

zuyin) of one *tael* of silver, four *qian*, and seven *fen*. In 1734, he sold his "grain property" (*liangye*, which is the subsoil rights of land) to the father of Zhu Secai for eleven *taels* of silver. The land was still being farmed by the Zheng brothers.[34]

When Zhu Tianyou needed funds, he dismantled his clear land (*qingyetian*) and retained the subsoil rights of the land himself. While selling the rights of the top-soil of the land (*zhiye*), he obtained more than twelve *taels* of cash, leaving only a little more than one *tael* per year of future land rental income. Ten years later, when he needed cash again, he had to sell his subsoil rights of land only to get eleven *taels* of silver.

To a certain extent, the nature of the top-soil rights of land considerably reduced the uneven distribution of land rights in modern times, expanded the "peasant middle class," and laid the foundation for long-term social stability.[35]

2.4 Legal Property Rights

Legal property rights were the derivative and developmental form of private property rights, reflecting the degree of development of private property rights; legal property rights in Chinese history have not been revealed. Legal Entity, which corresponds to the property rights of natural persons, refers to the property rights owned by specific groups, institutions, units, associations, and enterprises; in addition, it corresponds to Public Entity, which refers to property rights owned by the state, the government, or the public, including state ownership, public ownership, and common ownership. A Public Entity was defined as the exercise of public rights and the exercise of an option over a public resource by any person that does not exclude others from exercising the same rights over that resource.

Legal property rights, often referred to as "public property," have existed extensively throughout Chinese history, including on fixed assets such as farmland and houses owned by families, temples, churches, schools, charities, guilds, and various "associations" (*hui*) and "societies" (*she*). According to Chapter 5, in a land reform survey in the early 1950s,

[34] *Xingke tiben*, item 255.

[35] Long Denggao, Yi Wei, Wang Zhenghua, Civil Society in Traditional China: Governance and Ownership System, China Economist, 2019.5.

the share of public land in total land was highest in Guangdong and Fujian, at 33% and 29.1%, respectively. Zhejiang's public land ratio was 16.3%, and Jiangxi, Hunan, Guangxi, and other places also reached about 15% and Hubei 10%. Among them, family-owned lands (*zutian*) and shrines were probably the most common. In the Land Reform, in order to highlight the inequality of tenure, the phrase "landowners occupying land and controlling communal land" was often used collectively to reflect their high share of the total land. In fact, most public lands were not controlled, much less owned by landowners. The management of various types of public land was usually institutionalized. Public land was usually leased, with the proceeds of the land rent used for specific groups, institutions, and organizations to which it belonged. In some cases, family members rotated their lineage lands, and the family allocated the proceeds equivalent to land rent for various intra-family expenses.

Legal property rights were recognized and legally secured by the government. Hunan Anhua Yongxi Bridge was built and maintained under the auspices of the Council (*shoushi*); its organization was called "Bridge Association" (*qiaohui*), a legal person, both a property unit and a trading unit, but also a taxing unit, recorded by the government as "Yongxi bridge pillar." Various contracts were signed in the name of this corporation, including contracts for the purchase and sale of land (pawn deeds can also be found), tenancy deeds, and employment deeds, and taxes were also paid in the name of this corporation. For example, in the collection of Tsinghua University, "The Transfer of the Deed of Li Xiaotang in the Thirteenth Year of Tongzhi's Reign" (*Tongzhi Shisannian Li Xiaotang zhuan dianqi*), see Fig. 2.7.[36]

> Due to the shortage of grains, Li Xiaotang, the *dian* contract maker, is willing to transfer eight *mu* and five *fen* of the *dian* land owned by Liang Haiyou. In the previous year, three *mu* of land had been transferred to Wei Nanjie. The rest, five *mu* and five *fen* on the western side, as well as two *mu* of the land of Xue jia'a, will be transferred to the Shrine of the God of Wealth at the West Gate. I state clearly with the *dian* receiver that the price is 26 *taels* and 0.6 *fen* of silver. The same price for redemption. If there is not enough silver for the redemption of the two pieces of land, regardless of the years and months, one may redeem the larger piece on one day or the smaller piece on another day. The price varied according to

[36] Tsinghua University Library Collections of Deeds and Contracts, no. T2011.

the pieces of land. In case a verbal agreement is not reliable; I made this contract and kept a copy of it as proof. Two items of land totaling five *mu* and five *fen*.

With the residents in the community [同社内人]
The *dian* transferrer, Li Haotang
April 21 of the 13th year of Tongzhi's reign (1875)

The "Shrine of the God of Wealth at the West Gate" (*Ximen Caishenshe*), the party that received the transfer, was not a natural person but an independent legal person. In "the land deed of Liang Risheng in the 16th year of the Daoguang Period" (*Daoguang shiliunian Liangrisheng diandi qi*), the transfer receiver was the "Heaven Society of Shijun" (*Shijun tianhui*): Sheng and others were willing to sell the land of their ancestral village at the west to the *Shijun tianhui* as a conditional sale for management and stated explicitly to the middleman. The *dian* price was 160 *taels* of silver for five years.

Legal property rights have at least the following attributes: first, legal entity property rights were juridically private property rights. From the late Qing Dynasty to Republican China, the "Private Free Ferry Bureau of Gua Town, Zhenjiang" (*Zhenjiang sili Guazhen yiduju*) and the "Private Society of Free Ferry of Dongsei" (*Sili dongsei yiduhui*) in Taichung were legally defined as "private." In 1925, the Dongsei Free Ferry Society was registered in the "Taiwan Governor's Office" and renamed the "Legal Body of Financial Group of Dongsei Free Ferry Society" (*Tōsei Yoshiyoshi-kai*), which corresponded to the Japanese system. In 1953, after the free ferry function disappeared, the society applied to the Taichung County Government to change its name to "Taichung Private Higashi Yidu Charity Association," and in 1986, the name was changed to "Taichung Private Dongsei Free Ferry Social Welfare Foundation" (*Taichung xian sili dongsei yidu cishanhui*). The statutes, the property catalogs, the tenant registers, the budget and accounts, the income and expenditure statistics, and the welfare assistance were meticulous and transparent.[37]

Although defined as "private property" by legal doctrine, these legal persons were referred to as *gong* (public), *gongyi* (publicly discussed), and *gongcheng* (publicly asserted) in their internal documents. They were

[37] "Dongsei yiduhui: Taiwan lishi zuiyoujiu de cishan zuzhi" (Dongsei Yidu Society: Taiwan's Oldest Charity Group), *Gongyi shibao* (Public Interest Times), June 3, 2015, sixteenth page.

different from what *si* (private) refers to in Chinese idioms or traditional user; on the contrary, these legal persons were more consistent with "collective" (*jiti*) or "public" (*gong*). From this point of view, the property rights of legal persons were related to collective property rights. From the historical evolution of the property rights of legal persons such as *yidu* (free ferry) and *chating* (charitable tea pavilion), after the establishment of new China, especially during the period of the People's Commune, they were usually inherited collectively by villages and production teams. In the case of the Tea Pavilion for relaxing in Mei Town, Anhua County, the village still arranged for people to guard it every year, and there were 1000 annual work points. After implementing the accountability system, each of the three villages associated with the pavilion subsidized the watch-keepers by 120 *yuan* per year; until 1997, when the road was opened, the pavilion was left unattended and basically abandoned. The voluntary ferry at the Large Sand River (*dashahe*) connecting Jianshi County with Enshi County in Hubei Province made accessible 5.7 *mu* of mountainous *yitian* (charitable estate) by ferry. Its income was used for the livelihood of the boatmen. After the Collectivization Movement, the land to support the boatmen was handed over to the production team for farming, and boatmen were required by the production team to register workpoints.[38]

In the Chinese property rights system, the definitions of "public" and "private" differ from those in the West. Although directly translated as "independent private institutes," Harvard University and Yale University were not individuals or families but independent institutions distinct from state universities. The word "private" in the English-speaking world corresponds to "state, government, public, and common." However, the so-called private universities, such as Harvard and Yale, have broader sources of funding and students than state universities. Funding for the former comes not only from all over the United States but from all over

[38] After the land was contracted to the household, *yidu* was transferred to the boatmen, who were compensated by the non-payment of retention money and agricultural tax. Now they are subsidized by the local government. Wangcheng, Jiwu, "Yichuan yi shijie: zusun sandai jiannuo bainian xinyi" (One boat, One world: Three Generations of Grandparents and Grandchildren Keep Their Promise of 100 Years of Faith and Righteousness), *Jiangcha fengyun* (Procuratorial Situation), no. 2 (2011): 69–70. Yuanqi and Chenhong, "Yichuan yigao: xinshou bainian yidu" (One boat, One Pushing Pole: *yidu* of One Hundred Years of Faith and Righteousness), *Wenhui bao* (the Shanghai Mercury), May 8, 2011, fifth page.

the world; public universities were funded primarily by the state's financial appropriations, and therefore the student body must be tilted toward the state's taxpayers, with lower tuition and lower admission thresholds. Tuition and admission thresholds were the same at private universities, both within and outside the state, regardless of US nationality or the world. Thus, there was no lowliness or nobleness between public and private universities. The "private" sector was more open and inclusive regarding funding and student sources.

Second, the property rights of the legal entity were independent and exclusive, and individuals, groups, and institutions other than that particular group or institution cannot claim their rights, including the government. For example, the government was not allowed to occupy the property of the *yidu* for public reasons.[39] The *yidu* was set up specifically for the benefit of civilian pedestrians, and it was stipulated that it would never be borrowed by the government or businessmen traveling around. Nor would they respond to the government or the army's demands. They specially reported to the Zhenjiang and Yangzhou governments and got approval for their requests in the form of government-issued orders.[40] Other institutions also should not take possession of their property in the name of the public.

Third, the property rights of the legal entity were integral and indivisible. Most of its property comes from donations, but after the transfer of assets, the original owner no longer had rights, nor can directors, managers, or even founders claim or divide their interests by their contributions. In a for-profit legal entity, even the owner of an equity interest cannot divide a portion of the property. The late Qing Dynasty, as mentioned in Chapter 7, was the late Qing Dynasty when the Wu Xun bought property to promote education and signed the deed of land rights transaction in the name of the legal person "Righteous Learning Zheng," which was also filed with the government. The reason for not purchasing

[39] Xiao Ben, *Cong Qingchao minguo duzhi kan hunan yidu* (Free Ferry of Hunan from the Perspective of *Duzhi* (Records of Ferries) in the Qing and Republican Era), Master thesis, Hunan Normal University, 2014.

[40] Gong Jun and Wei Zhiwen, "Guazhen yiduju shimo" (The Beginning and End of GuaZhen's Free Ferry Bureau), *Dang'an yu jianshe* (Archives and Construction), no. 5 (2016): 58–59.

a property in the name of Wu Xun was to prevent his relatives and descendants from dividing up and encroaching on the property of the righteous school in the name of Wu Xun.

In traditional Chinese grassroots society, diverse civic groups and institutions organized civil society's affairs with their own stable assets and ongoing funding sources and were thus able to maintain their independence and sustainability. For example, there were lineages by blood, temples by religion, guilds (*hanghui*) by manufactures and commerce, societies (*hehui*) by finance, guilds and societies (*hui*) by entertainment and sports, academies and schools of righteousness by education, *shantang* and life-saving societies by charity and relief, societies of the bridge, ferry, pavilion, road, and water conservancy by infrastructure and public construction, etc. Property with legal property rights and stable sources of income, as a universal and all-encompassing existence, has a long history and was the cornerstone of the independence and sustainable development of civil self-organization.

Just as the independence of peasants lies in their land property rights or the ownership of their farms, the property rights of legal persons were the basis for the functioning and development of civil organizations.

2.5 Disturbance and Reconstruction of Property Rights

Chinese civilians, through deeds, spontaneously form rules of transaction, property rights systems, and market order and were recognized and respected by the government. It was also known as "the government follows political codes, and the civilians follow private deeds" (*guancong zhengdian, mincong siqi*), which forms a system of local autonomy and self-organization based on the property rights and independent operation of peasants, as well as the property rights of legal persons of various civic groups.

Political Interference with Property Rights

It has been questioned that, although the contract was made, it may not have been well enforced in China, unlike in the West, and the emperor could scrap it at will. How could the emperor, who lived in the palace city, break the civil contract? In Bai Juyi's "The Old Man who Sold Charcoal" (*Maitanweng*), it offers a picture of the palace officer (*gongshi*): "Who arrived trippingly with two rides here? The yellow-clad officers were in white. The hand that held the document and the mouth called it an order; they yelled at the cows, pulling the cart towards the palace. A handcart of charcoal, more than 1000 *jin*, the old man was too upset to let go of his goods. Half a red veil and a piece of silk, the officers hung it on a cow's head as money to buy charcoal." The palace officers stayed in the capital (Luoyang in the Tang Dynasty), and the rest of the region was governed by officials. Namely, the emperor could only plunder civilians through his agents. Did the emperor encourage his agents to do so?

What was the emperor's greatest pursuit? was it plunder or tax maximization, or was it the inheritance of stable rulership from generation to generation? The primary pursuit of any emperor and regime is, of course, the stability and continuity of the regime, and for this long-term goal, even short-term interests may be sacrificed.[41] Under the premise of long-term continuity of the regime, it seeks to maximize current gains, mainly through taxation. The emperor does whatever he wants, and today's imagination affects how people think. A mediocre emperor may appear occasionally, and if he was bent on his actions, regardless of the consequences, his power may be unchecked, intruded upon, and deprived of civilians. However, under normal circumstances, the emperor also had restraining forces, such as ideology, patriarchal rule, bureaucratic groups, aristocratic groups, and his country. It was said that the emperors of the Qing Dynasty, each one of them, were very industrious, which was probably one of the reasons why the Qing regime lasted for more than two hundred years.

Apparently, all under heaven (*tianxia*) belongs to the emperor, and, in theory, he wants peace more than anyone else, rather than the people's grievances boiling over and the world in chaos. The emperor's raiding of the people's wealth required adopting an established tax system. In essence, the emperor wanted the people to live and work in peace and contentment on the land. What he was trying to limit was the officials' plundering of the people by power, and, in this respect, the supervision mechanisms of the Chinese bureaucracy have been relatively effective in traditional times.

[41] Fang Shaowei, *Chixu zhizheng de luoji: cong zhidu wenhua faxian zhongguo lishi* (The Logic of Sustainable Governance: Discovering Chinese History through Institutional Culture) (Beijing: Zhongguo fazhan Press, 2016), 1–7.

The emperor's greatest concern was that his agents, i.e., officials, exploited the people and enriched themselves. Faced with the incompatibility of incentives, how to motivate bureaucrats to govern affairs and manage the people for the emperor while at the same time restrain officials from seeking private profit became the emperor's first problem to solve. Successive emperors and courtiers have gone to great lengths to achieve the goal. The institutionalization of the civil service system of successive dynasties was relatively mature and efficient compared with other regimes in the world at the same time, and this was an important reason why most dynasties lasted for a couple of hundred years. However, the impression of fatuous emperors and treacherous courtiers that people observe from historical sources, historical novels, and even historical romances was so impressive that in historical thinking, they often start from a sentimental point of view that the autocratic emperors were so messed up or brutal and that they should be blamed for all historical problems.

There was even a saying that laments the vicissitudes of China's dynasties, which have changed every one or two hundred years, leading to instability. Was stability what the first emperor of Qin expected, as "lasting for ten thousand generations" (*wanshi buyi*)? In fact, the dynastic cycle of one or two hundred years was already stable enough when looking at world history. In human history, the incentive-incompatibility dilemma of bureaucracy had probably been mitigated only by democratic and decentralized regimes. The truth lies in local autonomy, which allows people to select and monitor officials. At this point, the local society of the Qing Dynasty was not directly managed by the central government.

Authoritarian centralization was a flawed system from the point of view of modernity. However, centralization and autocracy primarily directed at bureaucracy and ideology, not essentially aimed at the grassroots; instead, economic liberalism was forced upon the people and the grassroots, as discussed in Chapter 7. In fact, the stability and continuity of civil property orders must be guaranteed for their tax stability. To this end, the emperor and the central government would restrain bureaucrats from intruding on civil and property order.

In the case of land, restrictive decrees were enacted to prevent bureaucrats from relying on power to usurp people's wealth by purchasing and selling land by force. The Song Dynasty stipulated that officials were not allowed to purchase land in their jurisdictions during their term of office. Later, the Song court forbade them from purchasing land for several years after leaving office. The same rules were in place during the Qing Dynasty.

As a result of off-site tenure, the drive to buy land off-site was inherently weak in an era of inaccessibility. Thus, the disruption of the land market by the powerful was effectively curbed.

The aristocracy, in addition to the hierarchy, had the potential to interfere with the order of the civil market. In order to prevent the Manchus from interfering with the market order, the Qing court had two rules: one was that Manchus could not participate in business, and the other was that Manchus could not buy or sell land. The Qing Dynasty allocated state land to the Manchu people, who cultivated their own land and could inherit it, but could not buy, sell, or pawn the land. Subsequently, the phenomenon of *yazu* (loans through land as a guarantee) gradually increased, and there was a practice of conditional sales (*dian*) under the disguise of *ya* (mortgages).

In the twentieth century, with the rise of warlords and the decline of centralization, it was even less likely that the people could supervise land transactions, so unfettered power interfered with the market, and some land annexations took place. This anomaly was compared to the dynastic cycle and was thereby seen as the norm. It was only when the land rights market was disrupted that unfettered coercion would lead to unjustified land annexation and disorder in the farmland market. However, this was not an inevitable consequence of the private property rights of land and the land rights market itself.

Distraction and Reconstruction of Property Rights

The spirit of the contract was repeatedly destroyed during the modern revolutionary period, especially after the burning of the contract during the land reforms. However, one cannot infer that there was either no contractual spirit in Chinese history or no contractual tradition among the Chinese people. In fact, even in times of war, the Red Army and the PLA inherited the tradition of contract, as reflected in a receipt for a loan of silver in the 1930s, during the Chinese Soviet era.

The Chuan-Shaan provincial government temporarily borrowed silver from the masses for emergency wartime military supplies. The certificate shown in Fig. 2.8 was issued to borrow silver (RMB 80,000) at the discretion of the Industrial and Agricultural Bank of Kawasaki Province.

Although the Chinese Soviet Republic soon ceased to exist due to the revolutionary situation, the Red Army maintained the traditional spirit of the contract during the revolutionary period. Since the war required much grain, the Soviet Republic of China had a particular "grain loan" (*jiegupiao*), in addition to wealth acquisition by overthrowing the local deposits. For example, the "fifty *jin* of soft grain" ticket (*ruangu wushi jin*) wrote that "this ticket is designed for borrowing sufficient grain from the masses for the support of the Red Army in 1934" and was inscribed "Chen Tanqiu, People's Committee of Grains," demonstrating the Communist Party's inheritance of tradition. Chen Tanqiu was a Communist Party of China representative and one of its founders. In August 1947, the Dongjiang guerrillas borrowed grain and guns from Huang Guanrong, a landowner in Gongzhuang Town, Boluo County.

> Receipt: In August 1947, Huang Guanrong at Xia Dong, two rifles with 200 bullets, one pistol with 50 bullets, 1000 *jin* of rice, and two live pigs. Yours sincerely (Pay the debts after a new regime is established by force) Recipient: Squadron Leader Li Hanhui. August 1947.

Printed and handwritten debit notes of the Red Army, the guerrillas, and the PLA, such as these, have been found in many places. The slogan "Pay the debts after a new regime was established by force" (*Dachu Jiangshan lai suanzhang*) shows that the Red Army and the PLA hoped to seize political power by force in a few years or even decades and let the new revolutionary regime repay its debts. However, it was not known whether the rich peasants who lent the rice and grain did so out of revolutionary belief or out of helplessness, as documented in the deeds and records.

The twentieth-century revolution attempted to break with tradition by burning the deeds and uprooting the concept of property rights and the institutions on which they were based. In the period of the planned economy, government power to control resources replaced private property rights, unit "letters of introduction" (*jieshaoxin*) replaced individual contracts, and unit credit replaced personal credit. Without a letter of introduction from the unit, it was impossible to engage in various transactions (see Fig. 2.11).

> Letter of Introduction
>
> Dajiangkou Supply and Marketing Cooperative Second Railway Office 8 (71) No. 091
>
> I hereby introduce Comrade Du Renwang, one person in total, to you to contact you about the purchase of citruses for holiday condolences for the sick and disabled workers.
>
> Please accept and assist him.

Long live Chairman Mao!

Second Railway Engineering Bureau
December 21st, 1971

The top of the letter of introduction was printed in red with the supreme directive: "The most fundamental aspect of the reforms of state organs is to reach the masses."

In the period of the planned economy, individuals no longer had their own property rights; they no longer operated independently; there were few market transactions and therefore no need for contracts; they were personally dependent on the unit and the government; and there was no personal credit. The new century re-established private property rights and a market economy, but with the inevitable upheavals and misunderstandings caused by economic transformation, there was a long way to go to rebuild the spirit of the contract and the system; however, the simple tradition of Chinese contractual spirit and property rights awareness will be its source.

The Contracts Act (*Hetong fa*) was enacted in 1999. The constitutional amendment of 2004 explicitly provided that "the lawful private property of citizens shall be inviolable" and that "the state shall protect the private property and inheritance rights of citizens as provided by law." In 2007, the Property Rights Act (*Wuquan fa*) was promulgated. This series of laws marked a new stage in constructing the contract and property right system under market economy conditions.

CHAPTER 3

The Farmland Property Transaction System: A Study on *Dian*

3.1 Types and Substances of the *Dian* Rights

In China's history, land rights transactions have taken various types, each with its own characteristics and connectedness, structuring a hierarchical and inherently logical system of land rights transactions, which includes: *taijie* (loan through the land as collateral), *zudian* (tenancy), *yazu* (rent deposit), *dian* (conditional sales), *diya* (mortgages), *huomai* (revocable sales), and *juemai* (irrevocable sales). If we examine the classification of *dian* in the Qing Dynasty from the perspective of land rights stratification and transaction, we find that *dian* refers to a transaction between the land management with all of its proceeds and interest in an agreed period, rather than the so-called offset of rent and interest (*zuxi xiangdi*). The redemption mechanism, which includes the use of *dian*, *huomai*, and *yazu*, had effectively preserved the willingness of peasant households to secure and resume their land ownerships and reduced the space for easy property transfers caused by *juemai,* or *diya* of a usurious nature. A multi-layered land rights transaction system enables peasant households to make

---

The main contents of this chapter were published in the *China's Social Science* (Social Sciences in China), no. 5 (2013): 125–141. Co-authors are Lin Zhan and Peng Bo.

D. Long and X. Chi, *The Institutions of Land Property Rights in China*, Palgrave Studies in Economic History,
https://doi.org/10.1007/978-981-97-5112-9_3

choices according to market prices and risk appetites, cater to their own needs, and help to achieve cross-time regulation between current and future yields, thereby facilitating the combination of land circulation and productive factors and improving economic efficiency.

Dian is a unique and common form of land transaction in traditional China.[1] Studies on *dian* practices have been fruitful but diverse, and some of the results even contradict each other.[2] The existing studies of economic history have not systematically constructed a land rights transaction system of interrelation and intercommunity, and there is a lack of adequate discussions on its economic function. The role that land rights transactions have played in peasant household operations and resource allocations needs to be further excavated. This chapter will proceed with the primary sources of the Qing Dynasty, such as civil deeds, transaction customs, legal provisions, land transaction disputes, and legal cases, and attempts to establish a framework of interpretation. Based on the stratification and historical trajectory of land rights development, this chapter aims to provide an economic analysis of *dian* and other land transaction types and their interrelationships, delve into the inherent causes and economic functions of the formation and development of the land rights market, and reveal its profound impact on peasant household management as well as the fundamental characteristic of China's traditional economy.

Categories of Dian

Dian is a transaction between the proceeds of land and interest on capital, where the landowner transfers the rights in rem (*wuquan*) for an agreed period to obtain a loan and pays interest on capital with the rights to manage the land and all proceeds; the landowner, who was also the *dian* seller, retains final title, or rights to own property, and does not transfer

[1] This view is more general. See Huang Zongzhi (Philip Huang), "Zhongguo lishi shang de dianquan" (Dian rights in Chinese History), *Qinghua falü pinglun* (Tsinghua China Law Review), no. 1 (Beijing: Tsinghua University Press, 2016). Some European scholars argue that similar transaction types existed in modern Spain and other regions. At present, there is no specific discussion or comparison in domestic and foreign academic circles.

[2] For example, was *dian* a transaction of user right or that of ownership? Does *dian* have the function of security interest? What are the differences between *dian*, revocable sales (*huomai*), mortgages, and securities (*didang*)?

ownership in the official property registry. After the period expired, the land was available for redemption at the original price. The *dian* seller gains the loan and becomes the debtor. In contrast, the *dian* buyer, the creditor (*yinzhu*, silver lender), gets possession rights (other property rights) of the land for an agreed time. In modern Zhejiang, *dian* right was commonly known as "provisional property right" (*zanyequan*),[3] which is quite appropriate. Scholars have agreed on *dian* transactions, and we do not have to repeat its basic transaction rules. However, scholars have different arguments in their specific discussions. Some regarded *dian* as the transaction of user rights, while others argued that *dian* is no different from *huomai*.[4] Any such ambiguity is related to the diversified manifestations of *dian*, especially those triggered by the diversification of the interest payments on borrowing and lending. If we explore *dian* in terms of its classification, we may further recognize the characteristics of *dian* transactions and the difference from other types of land rights transactions and thus avoid confusion caused by generalizations or examples.

In the first category of *dian*, interest was paid on the entire proceeds of the land operation for the year. Within the agreed period, the *dian* seller transferred the land management rights to obtain a loan, and the *dian* buyer managed the land independently and earned income as interest on the loan. It was known in the Song Dynasty as "transferring the property in a conditional sale" or "*dian* selling the land off the property"

[3] Han Dezhang, "Zhexi nongcun zhi jiedai zhidu" (The System of Loan in the Villages of the Western Zhejiang Province), *Shehui kexue zazhi* 3 (Journal of Social Sciences 3), no. 2 (1932).

[4] Dai Jianguo and others argued that *dian* was a transaction of user rights. See Dai Jianguo, "Songdai de mintian dianmai yu 'yitian liangzhu zhi'" (The Dian Transactions of Civil Lands and the System of "One Piece of Land with Two Owners" in the Song Dynasty), *Lishi yanjiu* (Historical Research), no. 6 (2011): 99–117. Quite a few scholars, on the other hand, argued that *dian* was a revocable sale (*huomai*), which means that *dian* was a transaction of ownership. For example, Ye Xiaoxin argues that *dian* "can also be called *huomai*." See Ye Xiaoxin, *Zhongguo fazhi shi* (History of Chinese Legal System) (Beijing: Peking University Press, 1999), 249. Chen Zhiying clarified the meaning of *dian* and the difference between *dian* and sales, especially irrevocable sales (*juemai*), but still customarily thought of *dian* as "a revocable sale (*huomai*)." See Chen Zhiying, *Songdai wuquan guanxi yanjiu* (A Study of Property Rights Relations in the Song Dynasty) (Beijing: China's Social Science Press, 2006, 140–147. Li Li argued that Qing people saw *dian* as a sale. However, the deeds that his article used were all deeds of sale. See Li Li, "Qingdai minjian tudi qiyue duiyu dian de biaoda jiqi yiyi" (The Expression and Significance of Qing Dynasty Civil Land Deeds to the Dian), *Jinling falü pinglun* (Jinling Law Review), no. 1 (2006): 111–118.

(*liye diantian*), which was the norm of *dian*, and the primary form of *dian* rights transaction. In the first year of the Daoguang reign (1875), Zhang Shengqing borrowed silver by land pawning. The sources read: "He borrowed capital of 128 *taels* of silver this day and claimed to transfer his property equal to the same amount of silver within a few days. Busheng would take over the land, and the interest would be paid [by the proceeds from the land]. Regardless of the far or near future, the land would be returned once the silver was fully paid back."[5] It was clearly stated here that interest was the entire income from management of the property.

In the second category, interest was paid in rent in cases where the silver lender rented out the *dian* land. Tenancy relations were further developed in the Ming and Qing dynasties, where interest was paid on rent alone without the necessity for the entire land output. The *dian* buyer exchanged the lending capital for the land rights in Rem by leasing the plots and collecting rent as interest on the loan instead of farming them himself. This form became more and more common in the Qing Dynasty, so much so that "collecting rent to offset interest" (*shouzu dixi*) and "offset of rent and interest" (*zuxi xiangdi*) became the rule of *dian* on the top-soil,[6] whose essence was no different from the first category, except that the *dian* buyer leased the user rights to tenants, with whom he shared the total income of the land, and obtained rent. In contrast, the tenant peasants received their income from labor and management.

When the landowner directly *dian* sold the land to his original tenants, the roles of the two sides changed in interesting ways. For example, Wang Xianqing of Putian County, Fujian Province, had one *mu* of land. He *dian* sold it for 40 *taels* of silver to his tenants, Wang Qiguang and his son, and agreed that he would redeem his land at the original price in the twelfth year of the Qianlong Period (1747).[7] At this moment, the

[5] Liu Zhiwei ed., *Zhang Shenghe jiazu wenshu* (Zhang Shenghe Family Papers) (Hongkong: Huanan Press, 1999), 121.

[6] Some scholars saw "offset of rent and interest" (*zuxi xiangdi*) as the core rule of *dian* practices because they ignored the first category of *dian* and their common essence with the second and third categories. See _chrome burning_vocabulary _id_ 1664629871806">Wu Xianghong, "Chapter 7," in *Dianzhi fengsu yu dianzhi falü* (Customs and Laws of Dian) (Beijing: falü Press, 2009).

[7] *Qianlong xingke tiben zudian guanxi shiliao zhier: qingdai tudi zhanyou guanxi yu diannong kangzu douzheng* (The Second Volume of the Historical Sources of Tenancy Relations in the Qianlong Memorials on Criminal Matters) (Beijing: Zhonghua Books,

tenant turned into the silver lender and became the landowner's creditor. From the perspective of exploitation, it became tenant exploitation by the landowner at this point. This situation was ubiquitous in nineteenth-century Taiwan, where Han tenants turned into the creditors of the Taiwan aboriginal landowners.[8] Under such circumstances, the land rights of tenants were expanded from user rights to other property rights.

In a similar vein, plots were *dian* traded while tenants remained unchanged. In the tenth year of the Yongzheng reign (1732), Lin Xuzhang's ancestors "*dian* sold the land to an Imperial College student (*jiansheng*) Huang Zhonghan for 130 *taels* of silver. The procedure materials related to deed root and deed top-soil (*qimian*, deposit) were incomplete, while the tenants were farming and paying rent to the new *dian* owner according to the old landowner-tenant rules [典与监生黄仲汉, 得价银130两, 契载根面不全, 主佃循旧耕收无异]."[9] Such transactions often took place when the tenant peasant held the top-soil rights of the land. It was called "*diandazu*" (the great lease of *dian*) in Qing's Taiwan, where many such contract deeds were saved.[10] When the land rent was paid directly from the tenant to the creditor (*dian* buyer), it was similar to the "*taijie*" practice (loaning through the land as collateral), a popular form of borrowing in the Fujian and Taiwan provinces. The "*taijie*" practice was a form of credit that did not require any change in

1988), item 72. Below, we abbreviated it as "Memorials on Criminal Matters 2." In this case, Wang Qiguang requested that "as I inherited the tenancy from my ancestors, we should follow the village rules and have Wang Xianqing make a deed of tenancy first" (祖遗佃耕, 要照乡例, 叫王宪清先立佃批). A tenancy deed was used to maintain the right to use the land for farming purposes before returning the *dian* deed. In other words, the real rights to the land were redeemed, but the right of use remained with the tenant.

[8] Chen Qiukun, "Chapter 7," in *Qingdai Taiwan tuzhu diquan* (Taiwan aboriginal land rights in the Qing dynasty) (Taipei: Academia Sinia, 2009).

[9] In this case, those tenants, because they had worked hard to improve the fertility of the land, were given the top-soil rights of land, so the *dian* transaction could not change the tenant relationship. The Lin Family *dian* sold his subsoil rights, while Huang Zhonghan received the rent as interest. See *Qianlong xingke tiben zudian guanxi shiliao zhier: qingdai tudi zhanyou guanxi yu diannong kangzu douzheng* (The First Volume of the Historical Sources of Tenancy Relations in the Qianlong Memorials on Criminal Matters) (Beijing: Zhonghua Books, 1988), item 284. Below, we abbreviated it as "Memorials on Criminal Matters 1."

[10] Bank of Taiwan Economic Research Office, "Dishi jiedian maizi" (The Tenth Section: A Deed of *Dian*), in *Qingdai Taiwan dazu diaochashu* (Survey on the Great Lease of Taiwan in the Qing Dynasty), vol.1 (Taipei: Taiwansheng wenxian wekyuanhui, 1999).

the original tenancy relationship. The rent was used as a guarantee to pay off the interest. For example, when a landowner borrowed a debt, the debt would be repaid directly by the tenant paying rent to the debtor or, if the tenant changed, by the new tenant paying rent directly to the creditor.[11] If the land was not redeemed when due, the rent continued to be collected by the creditor.

In the third category, the landowner *dian* sold his land to the silver lender and leased it back. The landowner then cultivated the plots as a tenant and paid an annual rent to the *dian* buyer as interest payments. This is so-called paying rent to offset interest (*nazu dixi*). Such an operation was regarded as irregular in the Song Dynasty[12] and was mistakenly understood as a transaction of mortgage and pawning. However, this form was quite common in the Qing Dynasty. On the top-soil, it was only a form of land rent transaction and exchange of rent and interest, but in essence, it was a release or transfer of possession rights (other property rights) by the landowner, which was an exchange of all the proceeds of the land for interest. The two sides signed not only a *dian* contract but also a tenancy contract (or *zupiao*, a lease note), including the tenancy lease in the *dian* deed. For example:

> Father Zhao Xi and his son Zhao Wenge *dian* sold 24 *mu* of land to Gao Shan. In the 30th year of the Daoguang Period (1850), the Zhaos asked for a price add-on of a total of 4000 *diao*. "In the second year of the

[11] In 1894, a deed of taijie read: Jiang Gang, who borrowed a loan through tenancy as collateral, made this deed of taijie. I borrowed from Li Jingyi 100 yuan of fofanyin (Spanish silver coins) and would pay an interest rate of 0.16 yuan per silver yuan per year, adding up to 16 yuan of interest per year. The interest in silver would be paid to the now-tenant Xu Laoyong clear and should not owe a coin less. In the 22nd year of the Guangxu reign (1896), the tenant Xu Laoyong dropped tenancy. Jiang Gang and Li Jingyi had discussions and agreed to replace Xu Laoyong with new tenants, Liu Qi and others. Jiang Gang would then pay the silver interest to the new tenant, Liu Qi, as stipulated in the deed, daring not to break the contract, and made this statement. If, at the end of the term, I had no sufficient silver to redeem the land, I would follow the stipulations of the deed. See Wang Shiqing ed., *Taiwan gongsi cang guwenshu huibian* (Collection of Antique Documents from the Public and Private Collections of Taiwan), FSN01-10-479, Fu Ssu-nien (Fu Sinian) Library, Academia Sinica, Taipei.

[12] Long Denggao, WEN Fangfang, and QIU Yongzhi, "Diantian de xingzhi yu quanyi—songdai yu qingdai de bijiao yanjiu" (The Nature and Rights of Dian Land—A Comparative Study of the Song and Qing Dynasties), *Lishi yanjiu* (Historical Research), no. 5 (2016): 54–70.

> Xuantong's reign (1910), Zhao Wenge leased back his plots from Gao and cultivated it."[13]

In this case, the *dian* seller, while retaining ultimate ownership and transferring other property rights revolving around the land, acquired the user rights through tenancy. In contrast, the *dian* buyer owned the other property rights of the land and may exercise the rights to lease to transfer the user rights to the *dian* seller and landowner. Therefore, this form was following the rules of the *dian* transaction. In modern Hubei Province, there was a transaction custom:

> "There were cases where plots were transferred to the pledgees (the *dian* buyers), and new tenants were recruited to cultivate and collect rents; there were other cases where lands were transferred to the pledgees without recruiting new tenants, but the landowners were recruited to cultivate on their own and were required to pay annual rents." The local investigator analyzed that "although, in fact, it did not appear that the lands were transferred to the possession of the pledgees, legally it was a pledge relationship rather than that of a mortgage."[14]

This transaction of land rights at all levels may seem complicated, but it was simple and clear to both parties to the contract and was rational. The *dian* seller was already poor; without land to cultivate, he may not even have been able to survive, let alone repay the capital. As far as lenders (*dian* buyers) were concerned, they did not manage the plots themselves but leased the property directly to the debtors, i.e., the *dian* sellers. Since both parties already had some credit base, the costs of information search,

[13] A civil case in the Chengde District Court, as published in the *Shengjing shibao* (Shengjing Times) on March 14 of the third year of Xuantong (1912). South Manchurian Railway Co., "Kisaki-hen dai ni-kan furoku" (The Latter Part, Volume I, Appendix), quoted from *Manshū Kyukan Chōsa Hōkoku-sho* (Report on the survey of old customs in Manchuria), 1915, 49.

[14] Qian Nanjing guomin zhengfu sifa xingzheng bu (The Former Ministry of Justice and Administration of the GMD Government of Nanjing), ed., *Minshi xiguan diaocha baogao lu* (Record of Survey Reports on Civil Customs) (Beijing: Zhongguo zhengfa University Press, 2000), 328. (Hereinafter, we refer to it as "Civil Customs.") Several surveys of civil transaction practices were conducted during the late Qing dynasty. See Sui Hongming, *Qingmo minchu shangshi xiguan diaocha zhi yanjiu* (A Study of Civil and Commercial Customs in the Late Qing Dynasty and Early Republican Period) (Beijing: falü Press, 2005). The book reflects long-established civil customs from all through the Qing Dynasty.

negotiation, and default could all be reduced, and so reduced risk. As can be seen, "*dian* selling the land through self-tenancy" (*chudian zidian*) was a rational choice to reduce transaction costs and risks for both sides. In this transaction, the *dian* seller owned the ownership and user rights, the *dian* buyer acquired other property rights and land rent, and both parties shared the land rights and interests.

In the second and third categories, the lender's loan could not be paid back if the rent was not paid in time. At that point, the silver lender, as the *dian* buyer, had the rights to repossess the user rights and cultivate the land for his own profit, thus reverting to the first type of "transferring the property in a conditional sale" or "*dian* selling the land off the property" (*liye diantian*).

In the fifth year of the Qianlong's reign (1750), Luo Guoshi of Hengshan County, Hunan Province, "*dian* purchased Zhu Dianxuan's land at the Zhu's Valley (Zhujialing) and agreed to an annual land rent of 20 *dan*. The deed stated clearly that redemption was not restricted to either the near or far future. Zhu Dianxuan and his son would still cultivate the land and pay rents after the *dian* transaction. In the 22nd year of the Qianlong's reign (1757), the Zhu's were unable to pay enough crops and dropped tenancy voluntarily."[15]

Zhu Dianxuan *dian* sold his land and leased it back from the creditor, Luo Guoshi, to cultivate and pay back interest on the land rent. Due to the rent arrears, the silver lender terminated the tenancy relationship and resumed the user rights. Although the third form of *dian* satisfied the needs of both parties, the *dian* rights transaction compounded by tenancy triggered disputes easily. In *Xingke tiben* 2, there were as many as 20 manslaughter cases caused by such transactions.

Between the eleventh and thirteenth year of the Qianlong reign (1746–1748), in Wuning County, Jiangxi Province, Shu Yunhui owed a total of eight *taels* of silver and seven coins for taking goods on credit from a shopkeeper, Shu Jiande, and was unable to pay back. Because of that, in 1749, Shu Jiande, through a middleman (*pingzhong*), Shu Xuanshi, *dian* purchased Yunhui's land of 2.9 *mu* for 20 *taels* (Yunhui's debt plus a price add-on of 11 *taels* and two coins). However, Yunhui still cultivated his land and paid six *dan* of grain annually to the *dian* buyer, Shu Jiande. In the fifth year of the Qianlong reign (1750), Yunhui paid ten *taels* of

[15] *Xingke tiben* 2, item 82.

silver, eight *taels* in the next year, and nothing in 1752. Consequently, both parties terminated the tenancy relationship, and the silver lender, Shu Jiande, obtained the land to cultivate himself.

> Nonetheless, as a shopkeeper, it was not convenient for Shu Jiande to cultivate the plots himself. As a result, in the spring of 1753, Shu Jiande demanded Yunhui redeem his property "at full land price and return the deed." However, Yunhui had no silver to redeem the land, nor did he have the land rent to repay the interest on the loan. Since the *dian* seller could "neither pay back the rent nor pay the full price of the land," this piece of land had to be sold from a conditional sale to an irrevocable sale to close the deal. Finally, Shu Jiande purchased the property, "collected grains, and received the landownership" (*shouliang guohu*).[16]

The transfer of land title in the official registry (*jiaoge guohu*) is usually a sign of the transfer of ownership. Shu Yunhui moved from the landowner, who owned all the proceeds of the land, to leasing back the user rights by giving away his other property rights, to returning the user rights, and finally, to selling the ownership.

In the fourth category, the *dian* seller pays interest to the *dian* buyer in currency. This does not appear to have been a transfer of land property rights and looks similar to *di* (mortgages), so it was a violation in the Song Dynasty but not uncommon in the Qing Dynasty. Although the interest payment was usually made through annual rent in kind, it was also done in the form of money rent, which was consistent with the rules of the *dian* transaction.

In Le'an County, Jiangxi Province, the 76-year-old Chen Ruijiu "had accumulated tens of thousands of coins as old age pension money and lent them for loans to generate interest." In the 30th year of the Qianlong's reign (1765), Chen Ruijiu offered a loan of 25 *qianwen* (about 25 *taels* of silver) to Chen Zhiyi and accepted his eight *mu* of early crop field (*zaohetian*) as collateral. Chen Zhiyi still farmed the land and agreed to pay at least three *fen* of interest annually. If not paid on time, the property would be transferred back to Chen Ruijiu. In the first 2 years, Chen Zhiyi paid back 4500 coins in interest each year, but then he did not pay back anymore. In the 36th year of the Qianlong reign (1771), the 82-year-old Chen Ruijiu was faced with the difficult problem of interest arrears on the

[16] Ibid., item 47.

land, and he was no longer able to cultivate the land himself. Therefore, he was willing to reduce the interest rate, persuading Chen Zhiyi to come back to redeem the land.[17]

In this case, a transfer of the *dian*'s rights in rem existed in essence. Since the *dian* buyer was still in possession of the real rights of land, redemption was still required.

The above four types of transactions were all in line with the rules of the *dian*, which reflected the diversity of the types in which the *dian* rights could be realized. They thus also cleared up the controversy over the causes and reasons of *dian* rights disputes. Although the manifestations of the four types were different, the interest payment for the *dian* rights stayed the same: the payment of the land management rights and all the proceeds within an agreed period. The second, third, and fourth categories were represented by land rent in that the *dian* buyers did not cultivate the land by themselves but transferred the user rights and shared with the tenant peasants the total proceeds of the property. In other words, out of the entire proceeds of the land, the *dian* buyer paid for the cultivators' labor and kept the rest of the income for himself, which was expressed as land rent. Thus, it can be seen that the "offset of rent and interest" was not the rule of *dian* but a manifestation of the intersection of two types of transaction, *dian* and lease. Therefore, *dian* was neither a transfer of the user rights nor a transaction of ownership but an exchange of possession (other property rights).

Guarantee Function of Dian

The lender's future collection of interest and capital was uncertain and risky and thus requires credit and security. In *dian* transactions, such credit and security were derived from land management or other property rights. However, because of *dian*'s uniqueness in its various manifestations, whether it had the function of a real rights for security or not was controversial. Some scholars argued that the *dian* was a usufructuary rights transaction and does not have the capacity of a real right for security. The opposite view contended that the *dian* was similar to a mortgage (*diya*) and that it was a real right for security that a mortgage can replace. It has even been argued that the *dian* rights can be canceled and that

[17] Ibid., item 89.

instead of *dian* selling the real estate for a *dian* price, it would be better to create a mortgage on it to obtain a larger loan.[18]

Unlike the commonly known practice of mortgage as a debtor–creditor relationship without a transfer of rights in rem, the practice of *dian* obtains a loan by transferring real rights of land. However, *dian* had something in common with pledges and lien in security interests. Without the security provided by property rights, there was insufficient credit guarantee for the future acquisition of land proceeds to pay interest on loans. Therefore, the function of security interests of *dian* should not be denied based on formal differences. Concerning the discrepancy between "*dian* selling the land through self-tenancy" (*chudian zidian*) and the practice of mortgage in Hubei Province, the experts in the Republican Era held the view that "the subject matter of the security was like a mortgage if it was owned by the debtor, and was like a pawn and pledge if the creditor owned it."[19] However, if the mortgage was not repaid on time, the property title would be forcibly transferred, whereas in a *dian* transaction, if not redeemed at due time, the plots may continue to be traded.

The plots of *dian* land can also be re-pledged as security for a loan. During the term of the agreement, the *dian* buyer can either obtain the loan by assigning it to a third party or use it as collateral. "In the 34th year of the Daoguang reign (1909), Lang Yulin *dian* sold his residential house for 600 *yuan* of silver to Wang Junzhi, accompanied by a "red deed" (*hongqi*). During the *dian* period, Wang Junzhi used the red deed as collateral to borrow a mortgage from the Gaos. Neither trial court mentioned this mortgage taken out by Wang Junzhi, which did not violate the law."[20]

Dian transfers (*zhuandian*) were ubiquitous, and multiple *dian* transfers occurred from time to time.

[18] Zhang Xinbao, "Dianquan feichu lun" (abrogation of *dian* rights), *Faxue zazhi* (Law Science Magazine), no. 5 (2005): 6–10.

[19] *Minshi xiguan* (Civil Customs), 328.

[20] The civil case in the Chengde First Primary Court, as published in the Shengjing Times on the fifth day of the eleventh month of the first year of the Xuantong reign (1910); and the civil case in the Chengde Local Trial Hall, as published in the Shengjing Times on November 27 of the first year of Xuantong (1910), quoted from South Manchurian Railway Co., "Kisaki-hen dai ni-kan furoku" (The Latter Part, Volume I, Appendix), in *Manshū Kyukan Chōsa Hōkoku-sho* (Report on the survey of old customs in Manchuria), 1915, 66–68.

> Before 1875, in Taiwan, Zhang Jichun and others had *dian* purchased a "tile shop house" (*wadiancuo*) and then transferred it to Jiang Wanfu. In 1875, "Jiang Wanfu, due to lack of silver currency, was willing to re-transfer the house ... for 70 *yuan* of silver as deed transfer compensation (*qimianyin*). Money should be received on that very day with the middleman ... The silver gained for transferring the house was due in five years, and Jiang Wanfu should redeem the transfer deed at the full price of 70 *yuan* of silver. If he could not pay the price on time, the *dian* buyer (the silver lender) would be in charge of the house. Jiang Wanfu and others would not dare to cause trouble ... One copy of the deed of *dian* transfer was jointly established, and four copies of the old ownership deeds (*shangshou laoqi*) were handed over, which counted as five copies in total. All were submitted as evidence."[21]

Since the *dian* transfer was accompanied by the ownership deed, it made it easy to transfer repeatedly without interrupting the chain of transactions because of redemption. In some *dian* transfer transactions, the new *dian* buyer only needed to be noted on the original deed, which could be done repeatedly. This way, when the original owner redeemed the land, he could directly redeem it at the original price from the last *dian* buyer.

In the case of *dian* land, since the owner still owned the property (although he had *dian* sold it to others), he could always mortgage it again, as long as he could pay the debt.

In the twelfth year of the Yongzheng reign (1734), Hou yingzu from Zhijiang County, Hunan Province, *dian* sold one piece of paddy field to Yuansheng for farming at the price of 5.6 *taels* of silver. As Yingzu became impoverished again, he used the same piece of land as collateral and borrowed seven *taels* of silver from Tian Guanyin twice, with an interest rate starting at three *fen*. Thus, Hou Yingzu obtained two loans using the same piece of land, one was through *dian* and the other was through a mortgage (*di*). It led to conflicts and a fatal case, but the local court ruled that his transactions were not unlawful: "Hou Yingzu used the land as collateral, with an interest rate starting at three *fen*, and it was not a duplicate *dian*. All of the appeals were exempted."[22]

[21] Bank of Taiwan Economic Research Office, "Zhuandian cuoqi zi" (A Deed of *Dian* Transfer of Residential House) in *Taiwan sifa wuquan bian* (The Taiwan Compilation of Private Law of Property), vol.2 (Taipei: Taiwansheng wenxian weiyuanhui, 1999), 644.

[22] *Xingke tiben* 2, item 41.

It was indicated that the owner could still mortgage a piece of land that had been sold in a conditional sale. The conflict here broke out only due to the inability of the owner to pay his debts. In the fourth year of the Qianlong reign (1739), Hou Yingzu could not repay the capital and interest of eight *taels* and six coins. According to the provisions of the mortgage, the lender could enforce the acquisition of land rights, so Tian Guanyin went to transplant rice seedlings in the field. However, as the *dian* buyer still had possession of the land for the term of the contract (other property rights), Yuansheng was still entitled to cultivate the land. Thus, the interests of the two creditors of Hou Yingzu conflicted.

Suppose a mortgage was secured by a final, enforceable transfer of ownership or a right in rem. In that case, the practice of *dian* was secured by a transaction of other property rights and its continuation. Thus, the security interest function of a *dian* was established, except the form of the security was different. Some mortgages use the forced transfer of ownership represented by the irrevocable sale deed as a credit guarantee to reduce the risk of lending; correspondingly, the continuation of other property rights (rather than the final transfer of ownership) acts as a better credit guarantee and a risk barrier in *dian* transaction.

3.2 Economic Function of Types of Farmland Transactions

Because of the variety of manifestations, *dian* was easily confused with other types of farmland rights transactions, thus creating ambiguity. In the first category, "*dian* selling the land off the property" (*diantian liye*) was simple and clear; from the point of view of the *dian* seller, the form of alienation of the land's property rights was related to that of *huomai* (revocable sales); from the point of view of the *dian* buyer, acquiring the right to operate the land by paying a sum of money was similar to that of *yazu* (rent deposit). In the second type of *dian*, the *dian* buyer leased the land, and when the rent was paid directly by the tenant to the debtor (who was the *dian* buyer), it was similar to the transaction of *taijie* (loan through the land as collateral). The third type was a mixture of *dian* and tenancy. The original landowner (namely, the *dian* owner) leased back the user rights to the land after divesting himself of other property rights, turning him into a tenant peasant who paid the rent and interest to the *dian* buyer. In the fourth category, the creditor received interest, which again looked like that of a *diya* (mortgage). In the following, we will discuss the economic functions of various types of land rights transactions from a comparative point of view in order to construct a multidimensional system of land rights transactions in the Qing Dynasty and explore its impact on both sides of the transaction, especially on the production and livelihood of peasants, and the role of the land rights market on the Qing economy at the level of resource allocation.

Redemption and Transfer of Farmland Ownership

Dian (conditional sales), *huomai* (revocable sales), and *yazu* (rent deposits) all have the function of redemption, that is, to avoid the ultimate transfer of landownership rights, but the object of redemption was obviously different. In line with their respective transaction objects, *dian* redeems other property rights, *huomai* redeems the rights of ownership, and *yazu* redeems the user right. From the above, it can be seen that compliance with the norms of land transactions and preventing or postponing the eventual transfer of landownership as far as possible was internalized as a kind of institutional adhesion, which ran through the entire evolution of China's traditional land rights transaction system.

The difference between *huomai* and *dian* was whether or not a title delivery occurs.[23] Therefore, the nature of the redemption differs, and the land rights of the parties involved in the transaction were also divergent. The case of a land dispute in Lin'an Prefecture, Zhejiang Province, in the Song Dynasty was caused by the difference in recognition of the rights of redemption between a conditional sale (*dian*) and a revocable sale (*huomai*).

First transaction: in Changhua County, Lin'an Prefecture, the widow A Zhang *dian* sold his residential house and foundations to Xu Lin 11 years ago. Second transaction: following the "parent-neighbor priority," A Zhang's late husband's parental male cousin (*congxiongdi*) Xu Shi'er "redeemed" the house and the foundation from Xulin 9 years ago.

First judgment: the widow A Zhang requested to redeem the house and the foundation from Xu Shi'er. According to her, 11 years before, she had *dian* sold them to Xu Lin instead of transferring ownership to

[23] The top-soil rights of land can also be *dian* sold, which was a kind of *dian* practice of other rights in Rem. Other rights in Rem can also be further divided and traded, which involves the expansion of *dian* rights and deserves special discussion.

him. Based on this, the Changhua County magistrate ruled that Xu Shi'er accept the ransom and hand over the property to A Zhang.

Second judgment: Xu Shi'er appealed to Lin'an prefecture and demonstrated the deed of sale that he had bought from Xu Lin 9 years before, including the deed of ownership of A Zhang's property, on which the ownership of the property had been "transferred and recognized" (*ouge*) by the local government, stamped with the official seal as the "red deed."[24] Therefore, the Lin'an prefecture officials ruled that A Zhang had sold the property in a sale (*mai*), rather than a conditional sale. Thus, the widow A zhang's claim in the name of *dian* and its accompanying redemption rights were not established, while Xu Shi'er's priority of redemption was obtained and exercised after the land sale according to the principle of parent-neighbor priority. Xu Lin's property ownership was thus recognized.

From this case, it can be seen that ownership of the land in a *dian* transaction remained with the original owner, while in a sale (*mai*) transaction it did not. This was strong evidence that the redemption of *dian* presupposed that ownership had not been transferred, whereas the redemption of *huomai* took place after the transfer of ownership.

Yazu (rent deposits) refers to deposits made by the tenants to the landowner when he leased the land. From the landlord's point of view, *yazu* and *dian* were similar in that the landlord receives a sum of money in exchange for granting certain land rights. According to "Chen's Documents in a Golden Box" (*Jingui chenshi wenshu*) in the collection of the Institute for Advanced Studies on Asia, there was a kind of top-soil rights in Jiangnan in the Qing Dynasty in which tenants were required to pay a deposit to the landlord; if the tenants defaulted on rent, the landlord would redeem the farmland, and the rent would be deducted from the deposit.[25]

[24] Research Office of Song, Liao, Jin, and Yuan History, Institute of History, Chinese Academy of Social Sciences (CASS), "Yimai erbu liye" (Land sold without leaving the property), in *Minggong shupan Qingming ji* (Collections of Well-Crafted and Just Verdicts of Scholar-Bureaucrats in the Song Dynasty), vol.6 (Beijing: Zhonghua Books, 1987), 145–146. In the Song dynasty, the term "*huomai*" (revocable sales) did not yet exist, and the term "*dianmai*" (*dian* sold) here expresses this meaning.

[25] *Jingui chenshi wenshu* (Chen's Documents in a Golden Box) (Institute for Advanced Studies on Asia), quoted from KAWAKATSU Mamoru, *Meisei Kōnan nōgyō keizai-shi kenkyū* (Studies on the Agricultural Economy of Lawer Yangtze) (Tokyo: Tokyo University Press, 1992), 318–319.

An interest-bearing rent deposit was equivalent to a landowner getting loan money from tenant peasants and paying interest to them annually. It would be the equivalent of the fourth category of *dian*, as demonstrated in a case of "recruitment of cultivators" (*zhaogengzi*) in Taiwan in the thirteenth year of the Guangxu reign (1887):

> Leased an allotment with a deposit of precisely one *yuan* of silver without interest; and leased another allotment with a deposit of precisely six *yuan* of silver and an interest rate of 0.252 *yuan* per *yuan* of silver, adding up to precisely 1.60 *yuan* in total. The lease term is limited to 25 years, and the land would be returned when the original price of silver was paid back. The annual rent is 1.60 *yuan* of silver per year.[26]

It was a complicated case where, on the one hand, the tenant paid a rent deposit for the land to be cultivated and an annual rent (*buzuyin*), and, on the other hand, the deposit was equivalent to a loan that earned interest each year. The land was redeemed at the end of the term at the original price.

In contrast to the systems of *huomai*, *dian*, and *yazu*, which all created an institutional barrier to the transfer of property rights through redemption, there was no corresponding buffer mechanism for *di* (*diya*, *didang*, mortgage, and pawning).

Di (mortgages) refer to loans obtained using landownership or property rights as security. If the debt and interest cannot be repaid on time, it was settled by the delivery of the title. The orientation of mortgages differs between the past and the present. Current mortgages were often not aimed at the delivery of title, and the lender does not want the subject property. Historically, however, in the case of mortgages on agricultural land, the moneylender tended to end up with the an eventual direct acquisition of the land. The mortgage was enforced by the delivery of the title; otherwise, the lender was not compensated for his losses. The land rights ultimately transferred were all subject to the object of the transaction, either ownership, possession, user rights, or even rent.

In the 25th year of the Qianlong reign (1760), in Kaitai County, Guizhou Province, Mao Laiting "borrowed 48 *taels* of silver from the

[26] Bank of Taiwan Economic Research Office, "Zhaogeng zi" (A Recruitment of Cultivators) in *Taiwan sifa wuquan bian* (The Taiwan Compilation of Private Law of Property), vol.2 (Taipei: Taiwansheng wenxian weiyuanhui, 1999), 677.

Mu Family's Jiao festival (*Mujia jiaohui*) to trade in Sichuan." He mailed back the interest in silver annually. However, in 1765, Mao Laiting failed to do so. In the next year, the headman of *Mujia jiaohui* forcibly cultivated Mao's farmland to offset the unreturned interest and did not allow Mao's family to farm. After the conflict, the two sides went to court. The magistrate ruled that "the land should belong to *Mujia jiaohui* to cultivate" because this was a creditor's right in a mortgage transaction.[27]

The results of mortgages were often dire for peasants, who, in addition to having their land titles transferred, were likely to be trapped in an abyss of loan sharks. In the 32nd year of the Qianlong reign, in Zhijiang County, Hunan Province, Huang Yongde borrowed 19 *taels* of silver from the Yongguang brothers, using his land as collateral, and signed a deed. It was agreed that the interest rate would go up 30 percent a month [按月加三起息]. Interest was paid every 10 months, after which it would be treated as principal. The total capital and interest reached 48 *taels* and 11 coins. In the 35th year of the Qianlong reign (1770), as Huang Yongde was unable to pay up, with the help of a middleman, he bargained for 65 *taels* and five coins and sold the land to Yongguang.[28]

Generally speaking, as the peasant debtors' ability to repay was diminishing, their struggles were mostly in vain. Peasants were often forced to sell their land and even go bankrupt in order to repay their debts. As principal and interest rapidly rolled over, the burden on the borrower became more burdensome, and the lender was subject to moral attacks, with judgments in *Xingke tiben* (Memorials on Criminal Matters) often accusing the lender of being wealthy and uncaring. However, by contrast, *dian* could reduce or mitigate the harm caused by the delivery of ownership or property rights. Thus, in the Song Dynasty, *dian* was deemed a "righteous transaction," or "correct *dian*," whereas mortgage and pawn were called "unscrupulous mortgage" (*yidang*).[29] Social ethics from the Song to the Ming and Qing dynasties generally restricted and discouraged the use of such illegal mortgage transactions.

27 *Xingke tiben* 2, item 54.

28 Ibid., item 57.

29 Wu Shuzhai "used the sale as a mortgage and requested redemption" (以卖为抵当而取赎), and "unscrupulous mortgage" (*yidang*, 倚当) in *Minggong shupan Qingming ji* (Collections of Well-Crafted and Just Verdicts of Scholar-Bureaucrats in the Song Dynasty, vol.6, 168–170).

Transaction Choices Based on Prices and Risks

The price at which land rights were transacted was usually voluntarily negotiated between the two sides and was determined by market conditions of supply and demand. In traditional societies, interest rates were high due to a severe shortage of financial instruments and funds, and borrowers were often desperate for money. However, the diversification of tools for land rights transactions enabled market actors to choose between different market prices and risk preferences to meet their needs.

The price of a conditional sale (*dian*) was the amount of the loan borrowed, and the interest was the land yield for the agreed term, whereas the price of a revocable sale (*huomai*) was the underlying market price of the land without any interest paid. The *dian* price was, of course, lower than the selling price because the *dian* price was directly proportional to the length of the term; the longer the term, the greater the land yield and the higher the *dian* price. Had the end of the term not been reached, the *dian* buyer would reject any request for land redemption, as the interest yield on the loan would only be fully recovered at the end of the term.

In the fifth year of the Yongzheng reign (1727), in Qi County, Henan Province, She Kechen *dian* purchased Han Yiyuan's plots of 1060 *mu* for farming at the price of *42 taels* of silver and agreed upon 10 years before redemption. In 1734, Han Yiyuan "sold the plots to Han Yunji. However, She Kechen refused to release the redemption due to the unexpired term." Not until the second year of the Qianlong reign (1737) was Han Yiyuan able to redeem the land from She Kechen and he then sold it to Han Yunji. The selling price was 100 *taels* of silver higher than the *dian* price.[30]

For an agreed period of 10 years, the *dian* buyer had exclusive possession rights over the land; therefore, the landowner could not interfere. When the term ended after the agreed-upon period, the *dian* buyer would have no further connection with the property.

[30] *Xingke tiben* 2, item 65. Diyi lishi danganguan (No. 1 Historical Archives of China), and Zhongguo shehui kexueyuan lishi yanjiusuo (Institute of History, Chinese Academy of Social Sciences), eds., *Qianlong xingke tiben zudian guanxi shiliao Qingdai dizu boxue xingtai* 乾隆刑科题本租佃关系史料清代地租剥削形态(The Documents of Tenancy Relationships in Grand Secretariat Memorials on Criminal Matters in Qianlong's Reign, and Types of Exploitation of Land Rents in the Qing Dynasty) (Beijing: Zhonghua Books, 1988), item 344.

The price of a revocable sale was the basic market price of the land, and if an extra payment (*zhaojia*, price add-on) was added, it would equal the price of an irrevocable sale (*juemai*). Usually, if the landowner in a revocable sale could not redeem the land and necessary funds, he could ask for an additional payment to make it an irrevocable sale. In the 36th year of the Qianlong reign, in Houguan County, Yang Yongzuo sold three *mu* of his land in front of his residential house via contract (*qimai*). *Qimai* was also known as *huomai* (revocable sale). In the 38th and 39th years, Yang Yongzuo and his son Yang Chuanjun successively asked for additional payments of five *taels* and seven coins and 11 *taels* of silver, adding up to 16 *taels* and seven coins of silver, and "stated their rights for redemption in the contract explicitly." In the 45th year, their grandson Yang Lifu was going to ask for another additional payment of ten *taels* of silver but was only allowed five to six *taels*,[31] above which their redemption rights could no longer be reserved, and the revocable sale would turn into an irrevocable sale.

In a *dian* transaction, if the landowner could not redeem the land, he could ask for an additional payment from the *dian* buyer to sustain the transaction. For example, in Jintang County, Sichuan Province, in the 39th year of the Qianlong reign (1774), one person pledged his land for 1230 *taels* of silver and agreed to redeem it in 6 years. In the 45th year of the Qianlong reign, when the term expired, the person was unable to redeem the land. Instead, he requested an add-on to sustain the transaction.[32] The reason was that, at the end of the term, the interest and yield on the land also reached an end, so an additional payment was required to compensate. In the 15th and 16th years of the Daoguang reign, he successively asked for a separate price add-on of 150 *diao* and 100 *diao*, and in the 17th year of the Daoguang reign, he requested 400 *diao*. The original *dian* price, plus several additional payments, made the land's irrevocable selling price 3800 *diao*.[33] In Shunchang County, Fujian Province, similar customs of requesting additional payments were also practiced. It was recorded that "for the first request, an add-on of 10% or 20% to the original price was allowed; if the request takes place for the third, fourth,

[31] Ibid., item 202.

[32] Ibid., item 98.

[33] South Manchurian Railway Co., "Kisaki-hen dai ni-kan furoku" (The Latter Part, Volume I, Appendix), in *Manshū Kyukan Chōsa Hōkoku-sho* (Report on the survey of old customs in Manchuria), 1915, 63.

and even fifth time, the add-on price will be reduced by 50% of the original price each time requested." When the add-on request was no longer accepted, the land would be sold in an irrevocable sale.[34]

Both *di* (mortgages) and *dian* (conditional sales) required the payment of interest, but at different intervals. Mortgages could be paid monthly, while the interest on *dian* transactions was paid on the land harvest, usually after at least 1 year or 6 months. In Yulin County, Guangxi Province, in the 42nd year of the Qianlong reign (1777), Zhang Jiufu, who migrated from Pingyuan County, Guangdong Province, *dian* bought Chen Kongxiang's plots three times and paid 27,000 coins (*wen*) in total. "It was originally written in the deed that the landowner would leave the property" [原写明离耕]. If the landowner did not farm the land, it was agreed that he should pay five *dou* by grains and five *sheng* per thousand coins annually. In the end, both sides agreed that Chen Kongxiang would still cultivate the plots, and the annual payment of profit grains would be made to Zhang Jiufu. Since it was less than a year old, the *dian* buyer, Zhang Jiufu, had not received the interest due to him and therefore refused to release the redemption. It was because "private *dian* buyers purchased plots in conditional sales to collect rents and interest in autumn, which was not comparable to those who lent money and collected interest monthly."[35]

Any transaction instrument involves risk, and it was up to the parties to the transaction to determine how that risk was allocated. The risk level in turn affects the price; high risk usually means a high reward and therefore a high price. High interest rates on *di* (mortgages) stem from high risks. For lenders, the future collection of interest was uncertain, as was the recovery of the principal and interest through the compulsory transfer of title to the property. As a result, enforcement was costly and sometimes even life-threatening. Borrowers who were desperate under high interest rates may be hopeless at the first sign of conflict. All of the approximately 300 homicides recorded in the *Xingke tiben* were generally manslaughter. There were only three cases of willful killings, two of which were caused

[34] *Minshi xiguan* (Civil Customs), 301.

[35] The Zhejiang case, see *Xingke tiben* 2, item 52; The Guangxi case, see *Xingke tiben* 2, item 93.

by land mortgages,[36] showing the high risk level for mortgage lenders. Since lenders' rights may be difficult to secure, to reinforce the enforcement of deeds in the future, in some places parties to a mortgage resorted to the deed of irrevocable sale (*juemaiqi*) as a guarantee of credit. For mortgages in Yiwu, Pucheng, and Changxing, Zhejiang Province, a deed of irrevocable sale must be made first, followed by a loan note. The property may not be transferred, at which time the borrower paid interest on the loan to the lender; on the other hand, the property may also be transferred and farmed by the lender, and land yield was collected against interest. There were similarities between this process and the *dian* transaction. However, the difference was that once the debt could not be repaid, a property transfer occurred. It was recorded that "if not paid by the due date, the land shall be handed over to the lender, no matter if the deeds contained words such as a note of loan (*jiepiao*), *toushui* (tax payment), and *guanye* (possession)."[37] Idioms such as "deed first and note second" (*qianqi houpiao*), "deadhead, live tail" (*sitou huowei*), and "irrevocable sale deed, but revocable sale" (*jueqi huomai*) were descriptions of such customs. As many lenders were mostly non-local

[36] The first case was about a borrower poisoning the lender with arsenic (*Xingke tiben* 2, item 50); the second case was about three debtors murdering a loan shark in Ning Prefecture, Jiangxi Province (*Xingke tiben* 2, item 38).

[37] In Chongming County, the person who had a loan through land as collateral "made a deed of irrevocable sale and exchanged rent for interest" (有书立绝契, 以租抵息), but would not transfer the ownership. "The mortgagor did not entirely lose his land ownership. The attached deed of irrevocable sale, without a seal, was to prove the debtor's credit. The adoption of the word '*jue*' (irrevocable) on the deed was to express the creditor's hope for the early settlement of the debtor and to prepare for future negotiations, hoping that the deed will have a purely business effect." See *Minshi xiguan* (Civil Customs), 190. Similar practices of "dead deed and live contract" (*siyue huoqian*, meaning irrevocable sale on paper but revocable sale in practice) were also found in Shandong Province. "When borrowing against real estate, a deed of irrevocable sale was first made. However, a special removable paper label (*fuqian*) was attached, stating that the period was limited to a certain year, month, and day, that the mortgage would not be redeemed until that date, and that the creditor was allowed to take possession of the property after the term expired. Comments: This type of deed was to consolidate the mortgage. However, if the real estate was not redeemed by the due date, it still could not be considered an irrevocable sale. To make an irrevocable sale, it still needed both parties to negotiate and agree on an add-on price. Until then, the property could be sold off. The morals of the protection of property rights were also very detailed." See *Minshi xiguan* (Civil Customs), 135.

merchants from Huizhou and Shanxi provinces, secured mortgages must be protected by a mandatory enforcement system.

In comparison, the relationship between the two sides of the *dian* transaction could be relatively less tense and antagonistic because the *dian* buyer already had control of the land operation with little or no risk, and interest rates were likely to be lower. Meanwhile, the *dian* owner still retained ownership of the land and therefore had no worries. A *dian* transaction did not create a deed of sale as in a mortgage transaction, and its credit security was provided by a temporary assignment of the rights in rem. For example, in the customs of Minqing County, Fujian Province, "Even if the period expired and was delayed for a few years, the *dian* buyer could not resist the redemption. In some cases, redemption was still possible after several decades or more than a hundred years." If the term on the deed expired, "while the original principal and interest were not returned, the *dian* buyer should still manage the property according to the deed."[38]

Different transaction instruments have various apportionments of risk arising from market price movements. The risk appetite of both parties to the transaction usually had its trade-offs, and they choose the appropriate instruments for themselves. In the case of a mortgage (*diya*), the creditor may seek liquidation from the debtor if the amount of the claim that resulted in the realization of the security was insufficient. In a *dian* transaction, the risk of price changes was borne by the creditor, not the debtor, who was also the *dian* seller, while the debtor captured the proceeds of price changes. For example, if the *dian* price was low, debtors (the *dian* sellers) may waive redemption. Creditors were often left to bear their losses from price changes and would suffer if land prices fell below the *dian* price—of course, land prices rarely fell (e.g., after the Taiping Rebellion). The redemption price was usually the same as the original price, even if the redemption period was as long as 20 or 30 years. If the price of the land rises, the landowner (i.e., the *dian* seller) may redeem the property and sell it at a higher price to gain appreciation.

In the Kangxi reign, in Suzhou, Anhui Province, Liu Wenyuan *dian* purchased 18 *mu* of plots from Du Shijia for 1200 coins (*wen*). The land price rose after that. Liu Wenyuan *dian* transferred eight *mu* for 1500 coins and another ten *mu* for 4500 coins to Liu Mincheng, adding up

[38] *Minshi xiguan* (Civil Customs), 304–305.

to 6000 coins, which was 4800 coins higher than the original price. Liu Mincheng again transferred his share of the land at the price of 4500 coins to the father of Liu Minruan. In the 33rd year of the Kangxi reign (1694), the landowner Du Shijia redeemed the land at the original price of 1200 coins.[39]

The increase in the value of the land was solely attributable to the original landowner, the *dian* seller. However, some magistrates in the late Qing Dynasty also had the discretion to deal with disputes caused by rising land prices. For example, in 1909, the Fengtian High Court (*Fengtian gaodeng shenpanting*) ruled that "the ancestors of Guan Fusheng *dian* sold his land to Wang Youguo's ancestors ... The original *dian* price was only 1000 *diao*, but now it was 6200 *diao* after Wang Youguo transferred it to the Yi Family and the Shi family. As the land was expensive now, [I] therefore request that Fusheng Guan pay 6200 *diao* to the Yi family and the Shi family for redemption after the autumn harvest."[40]

The fact that the *dian* transaction protected the rights and interests of the *dian* sellers, including the proceeds of land appreciation, while leaving the risk to the creditor, became a reason for contemporary scholars to criticize *dian* rights.[41] Historically, however, it was to protect landowners by restricting and opposing mortgages, a usurious means of exchange that constituted the social basis for the prevalence of *dian*.

Interim Regulations and Land Transactions

To receive current income from the future sale of land interests, peasants used land rights and capital markets to transfer resources across periods. For the seller of land rights, a revocable sale (*huomai*) was a one-time realization of future land proceeds. In contrast, a conditional sale (*dian*) realized the land proceeds within the agreed period, so the current profits differed. Han Yiyuan's land in the above case cost 42 *taels* of silver in a *dian* transaction, while its selling price was 100 *taels* of silver.

[39] *Xingke tiben* 2, item 97.

[40] South Manchurian Railway Co., "Kisaki-hen dai ni-kan furoku" (The Latter Part, Volume I, Appendix), in *Manshū Kyukan Chōsa Hōkoku-sho* (Report on the survey of old customs in Manchuria), 1915, 43.

[41] Zhang Xinbao, "Dianquan feichu lun" (Abrogation of *Dian* Rights), *Faxue zazhi* (Law Science Magazine), no. 5 (2005): 6–10.

The inter-period regulation function of the rent deposit system was more prominent. For the landowner, the rent deposit was the current income, and the ground rent was the forward income. The landowner could choose to increase the current revenue by reducing the rent deposit or increasing the future ground rent according to his own needs. Let's take a look at a tenancy deed in Taiwan called "recruitment of tenants" (*Li zhaodian gengzi*):

> The native (*fanren*) landowner "had difficulty supporting his daily life and had debts owed to others. So that I had tenants to cultivate my land and deduct the interest. However, it was still difficult to pay off the debts. As unable to pay off the loan, I, therefore, would like to hire another tenant to take over the land and borrow more money". With the middleman and the new tenant, "the three sides agreed upon a high deposit of submerged land silver (*qidiyin*) and a will to lower the ground rent. It was explicitly stated that sufficient submerged land silver of seven *taels* should be prepared to be delivered and received in full". In the future, only when the landowner was able to pay the full price of seven *taels*, could he redeem the plots.[42]

In the above case, the landowner realized the future income by increasing the current rent deposit (submerged land silver) and reducing future rent. This deed explicitly proposed "a high deposit of submerged land silver (*qidiyin*) and a will to lower the ground rent." The higher the deposit, the lower the annual ground rent paid. This way, the deposit was maximized when the yearly ground rent paid was zero. This practice was similar to a *dian* transaction, where the forward proceeds of an agreed-upon term were realized in a lump sum.

This deed clearly showed the landowner's inclination to repay the debt by renting out the user rights of the land, which was "having tenants to cultivate my land and deducting the interest." In fact, since the rights of possession (other property rights) could be transferred to borrow or repay a debt, it was also natural to transfer user rights to borrow or repay a debt. A tenancy could also be a debt transaction. In this case, the landowner, unable to repay the debt, recharged the tenancy to obtain more cash. It can be seen that the rent deposit system (leasehold) was similar to the *dian* system. To a certain extent, it can also be seen as a kind

[42] Bank of Taiwan Economic Research Office, "Di erliu zhadian gengzi" (A Recruitment of Tenants, No. 26), in *Taiwan sifa wuquan bian* (The Taiwan Compilation of Private Law of Property), vol.2, 680.

of loan to the landowner, and the debt relationship of the rent deposit system was prominent here. There was a kind of rent deposit, the same as *dian*, where the landowner paid interest to the financer, as shown in the case of Minqing County. The deposit of Minqing was called "howing silver" (*chutouyin*), and the tenants deposited "root silver" (*genyin*) to the landowner. "The interest of the root silver of the year should be deducted in the ground rent." If the tenant paid 20 *yuan* for the root silver and the rent was ten loads per year, then one load of rent should be deducted. However, of course, generally, the *dian* buyer did not need to pay rent to the landowner.

Therefore, it was logical to move from a rent deposit to a *dian* transaction. For the transferor of land rights, cash flow would increase. For the assignee, it would be an expansion of land rights, from usufructuary rights to other leasehold property rights. In the 31st year of the Qianlong reign (1766), in Beiliu County, Guangxi Province, Li Zeng authorized Lü Guangshen to farm his land for an "authorization head silver" (*pitouyin*) of 9600 coins for 3 years. This process was the practice of rent deposit. In just 1 year, Li Zeng made a pawn deed, and *dian* sold his plots, including large and small, of 170 *qiu* 丘in total to Wei Tongmo for 160 *taels* of silver. The *dian* buyer Wei Tongmo "self-farmed and paid rent by grains" [自耕纳粮管业] in a 5-year term.[43]

The relationship between *dian*, rent deposit (*yazu*), and general tenancy in terms of transfers across current and forward earnings is shown in Fig. 3.1. Assuming that the term limit of the three transactions was set, for the landlord, general tenancy offers more forward yield, as B in Fig. 3.1, whereas *dian* provides more current yield, as A in the figure. Under the system of the rent deposit, the deposit as a security deposit was also a kind of current income; increasing its amount will inevitably reduce the future rent, and vice versa; the rent deposit is, in fact, the realization of the future income of the land. The rent deposit may be moved between A and B, increased or decreased to C, or decreased or increased to D. When moving from D to C, the forward yield decreases and the current yield increases. If practicing "rent-free" (*yiya mianzu*) or "pure mortgage (*ganya*), then the rent was zero and the mortgage rent was maximized, which means that all the forward yield was realized as the current yield within the agreed period, which can be equated to

[43] *Xingke tiben* 2, item 87.

dian, commonly known as "tenancy on the top-soil and *dian* in reality (*mingdian andang*)."[44] Under the circumstances, a deed of rent deposit was still used and did not need to be changed to a deed of *dian*. Such a practice was similar to *dian*, except that it did not function as a security interest. "When the amount of deposit was close to the selling price, and the tenants did not have to pay rent, it was called 'increased deposit tenancy' (*jiada yadian*)" [至有与买价相埒, 概不取租者, 曰加大押佃].[45] Therefore, *dian*, rent deposit (*yazu*), and general tenancy became interchangeable. The parties to the transaction could then negotiate the most convenient and least costly form of transaction for their own needs.

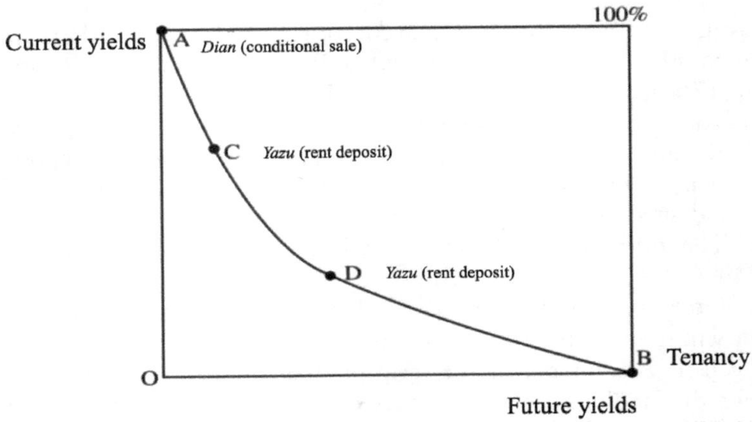

Fig. 3.1 Connections between Dian, Yazu, and Tenancy

[44] That was the perception of people then. For example, "the more the rent deposit increased repeatedly, the less the rent was paid … Therefore, there was a common saying that it was 'tenancy on the top-soil but mortgage in reality' (*mingdian andang*)" (押租屡加, 租课愈少 … 故俗有明佃暗当之语). See Yu Xiufeng et al. eds., "Dilizhi·fengshu" (Chronicles of Geography·Customs) in *Dingyuan tingzhi* (Chronicle of Dingyuan Prefecture), 1879 version (Taipei: Chengwen Press youxiangongsi, 1969), 258. Even if the rent was zero, there were differences in land rights between such a deed of rent deposit and those under a deed of *dian*. For example, the land under a rent deposit deed may not have the security interest function, meaning it could not be mortgaged and *dian* transferred.

[45] Liu Langsheng et al., Wei Linshu ed., "Juansi shihuozhi" (Volume 4, Records of Food and Commodities) *Nanchuan Xianzhi* (Chronicles of Nanchuan County) (Taipei: Chengwen Press youxian gongsi, 1976), 316.

In fact, the categories of land rights transactions were not of the utmost concern to ordinary people and could sometimes be mistaken or confused, but both parties to the transaction were very concerned about their own land rights and interests, and there was no ambiguity whatsoever. They made rational decisions about the mix and arrangement of current and future returns and the choice of which transaction method or combination of techniques they would use to optimize their cross-period transfers. The emergence of several new types of land transactions in the Qing Dynasty resulted from continuous exploration and friction between the parties to the private trade, during which the transaction rules gradually matured.

3.3 Impact of the Farmland Rights on the Traditional Economy

At this point, the practice of *dian* can be examined in the context of the farmland rights transaction system. Ground rents, land use rights, security rights, other rights (possessory rights), and proprietary rights (ownership rights) can all enter the market independently and be traded separately. Land-rent transactions were called *taijie* (borrowing through the land as collateral), land use rights transactions were called *zudian* (tenancy), other property rights transactions were called *dian* (conditional sales), rent deposits were between tenancy and *dian*, security rights transactions were called *diya* (mortgages), and ownership transactions were called *maimai* (sales). The larger the land rights, the higher the returns and the higher the transaction price, as shown in Fig. 3.2. This kind of land rights transaction system created a certain degree of flexibility and scalability, as both parties could use individual contracts or a combination of different transaction instruments to meet their own needs.

The functions of a particular form of transaction were specific and limited, but the more types of transactions there are, the greater the options for market actors. For example, a farmer who owned land and wished to obtain a loan could rent out his field for a certain amount of deposit. If he was unwilling to sell the land in anticipation of a higher loan, he might choose to temporarily dispose of the land in a *dian* transaction. If he wished to also cultivate the land for his subsistence, he could negotiate with the silver lender to lease back the property and cultivate it himself, paying the rent to the silver lender to repay the interest. If the loan still fell short of what was needed, he could choose to extend the

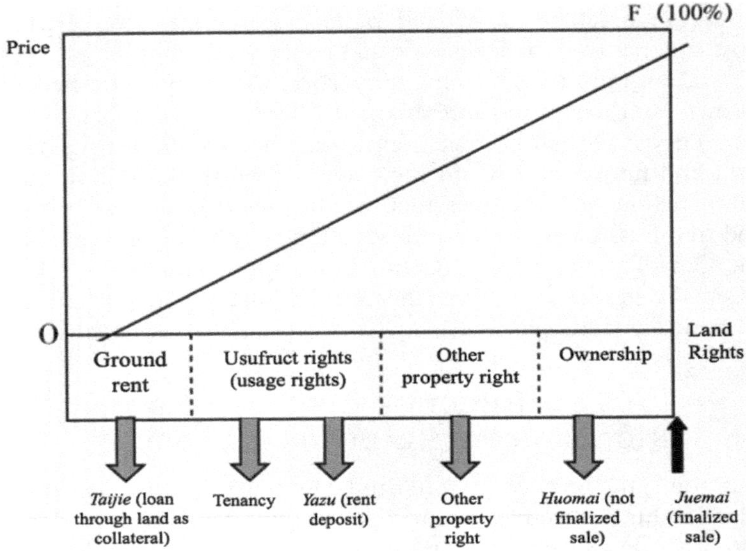

Fig. 3.2 Farmland rights and transaction prices

term of the *dian*, sell the land in a revocable sale, opt for a riskier mortgage deal, and finally, as a last resort, sell the land in an irrevocable sale. Here, peasants' options would be significantly constrained in the absence of *dian* as a transaction, and they could be forced to give up their land prematurely.

Similarly, if mortgages were prohibited because of their high risk, the availability of finance would be reduced as lenders would have no incentive and withdraw. It can be argued that no single instrument was perfect. Still, a diversified system of land rights transactions could meet the needs and risk preferences of different parties at different levels. It would be biased to judge the inadequacy of one particular transaction instrument in isolation from the entire system of land rights transactions. This isolation seems to be the source of much of the social criticism toward the mortgage in premodern China and criticism of *dian* nowadays.

The land rights transaction system had a profound impact on the economy of the Qing Dynasty. It adapted to and strengthened the fundamental characteristics of the traditional economy and became the institutional support and facilitating factor for its stability and development. Its influence on the flow of factors, the allocation of resources, and how individual peasants managed their businesses was mainly manifested in the following aspects:

First, stratification and marketization of land rights brought about various types of land rights transactions, lowered the entry threshold, provided an exit mechanism, and made it easier for all walks of society to enter and exit the land rights market. Market factors could flexibly participate in land rights transactions and distributions through different links such as investment, management, and profits. Meanwhile, land circulation was expanding and deepening, making it easier to combine production elements and allocating land and labor more efficiently in the flow.

Second, peasants' financing needs were met through transactions in the land rights market. Individual farming operations were most vulnerable. However, even in an agricultural era when financial instruments were in short supply, farmers were able to use land rights as an intermediary to meet their financial needs for production and livelihood, realize future land income through the market, and regulate needs across periods between the household economy and different stages of life, thereby increasing the peasant household economy's resilience to risk.

Third, multi-level land rights such as possession and user rights and their transactions enabled farmers with no or little land to establish individual farms and operate independently through diverse types of land circulation. A farmer could work independently by renting land—in other words, by acquiring the user rights of the property on the security of future rent. When he was able, he could obtain greater control over the land by prepaying a deposit. Then, he could get limited real rights through various channels, such as the rights of *dian*, the top-soil rights, and the rights of permanent tenancy. Here, the rights to dispose of the land, earn income, and trade can then be freely disposed of without conflict with ownership rights. Although peasants do not necessarily own the land, they can establish their farms through transactions such as tenancy, rent deposits, conditional sales, and top-soil-right transactions. Just as by leasing a plant to establish a business, a peasant would be able to acquire surplus control and surplus claim to his farm and earn operating income, investment income, and venture income instead of labor income alone, which were certainly not comparable to wages received for labor as a hired hand.[46]

Fourth, all levels of land rights, such as land ownership, possession rights, user rights, and soil rent, could enter the market in their independent types. Institutions of *dian* and revocable sale made it possible for farmers to weather the storm and re-establish independent farming, thus effectively reducing the transfer of landownership and acting as a hedge against the concentration of landownership rights. Practices such as "supplementary payment" (*zhaojia*) and "joyous-gift silver" (*xiliyin*)[47] could also be seen, to some extent, as a relief for landless peasants. Thus, the customary practices and legal provisions of land rights transactions protected the vulnerable while preserving peasants' ownership rights. The mainstay of traditional Chinese society was the independent peasant and tenant peasant, who constituted the "middle class" of the agricultural era and contributed to socioeconomic stability.

Moreover, land property development and its transaction system have reinforced two fundamental features of China's traditional economy.

First, it was reinforced the independent operation of individual peasant households. Through various types of land rights markets and supporting institutional and cultural systems, individual peasant households could not only meet their financing needs, but more importantly, they could establish and restore independent family farms through a particular level of land rights strengthening their resilience to risks. In the past, what was seen as a cultural factor, the equal inheritance rule among various sons (*zhuzi junfenzhi*), was essentially an informal institutional arrangement adapted to individual farming. This system of equal inheritance could not be sustained in the long term if individual household farming was not viable.[48] In contrast, the Western European primogeniture system

[46] Long Denggao and Peng Bo, "Jinshi diannong de jingying xingzhi yu shouyi bijiao" (A Comparative Study of the Nature and Profitability of Tenants in Modern Times), *Jingji yanjiu* (Economic Research Journal), no. 1 (2010): 138–147.

[47] When a current landowner sold his land, the original landowner asked for and usually received "joyous-gift silver" from the buyer. This custom was widespread, and there were more than 20 cases recorded in *Xingke tiben* 2.

[48] Fang Xing, Li Bozhong, and other scholars argued that during the Ming and Qing dynasties, the economy of the individual peasant household was still viable, which was the basic characteristic of the traditional Chinese economic system. See Fang Xing, "Zhongguo fengjian shehui nongmin de jingying dulixing" (Operation Independence of Peasants in Chinese Feudal Society), *Zhongguo jingjishi yanjiu* (Economic Researches

responds to the estate's holistic needs.[49] Diversified land property rights and their flexible transaction system proved to be important institutional guarantees for the viability of the independent operation of individual peasant households in China, as well as a disincentive to the growth of modern large farms or wage-labor farms. It also explains the essential characteristics of the traditional Chinese economy and its divergence from the path of economic development in Western Europe.

Second, it strengthened the resource allocation system based on land. To a certain extent, this system was inhibited the operation of the capital-centered economy, thus making it difficult for China to transform its traditional economy into a modern one.[50]

3.4 Contract and Transaction of Farmland Rights

Summary of Farmland Rights

The development of *dian* transactions highlighted the characteristics and orientation of the farmland rights market in the Qing Dynasty. The *dian* was a transaction between land proceeds and interest on capital, realized through the transfer and security of land management rights for an agreed period. There were four primary types, and they were easily confounded with other transaction types such as *huomai* (revocable sale), *di* (mortgage), and *yazu* (rent deposit), which became the cause of the debate and controversy over *dian* rights. *Dian* rights contained the functions

in Chinese History), no. 1 (1995): 10–23; Li Bozhong, *Jiangnan nongye de fazhan, 1620–1850* (Development of Agriculture in Jiangnan, 1620–1850) (Shanghai: Shanghai guji Press, 2006); Li Bozhong, *Zhongguo de zaoqi jindai jingji—1820 niandai huating-louxian diqu GDP yanjiu* (China's Early Modern Economy—A Study of the GDP of the Area of Huating County and Lou County in the 1820s) (Beijing: Zhonghua Books, 2010). Muramatsu Yūji firmly believed and argued that the Chinese tenancy system was still quite viable, at least in the early 1920s. Muramatsu Yūji, *Kindai Kōnan no sozan: Chūgoku jinushi seido no kenkyū* (Tenancy Firms in Modern Jiangnan: Study of the Chinese Landlord System) (Tokyo: Tokyo University Press, 1970).

[49] The need for the circulation of land in England did not become stronger until the Enclosure Movement, as land rights became entrenched. Private ownership of land, on the other hand, was not finally established until after the Enclosure Movement.

[50] See Long Denggao, "Chapter 9" and "Appendix," in *Diquan shichang yu ziyuan Peizhi* (Land Rights Markets and Resource Allocation) (Fuzhou: Fujian People's Press, 2012).

of usufruct (user rights and rights to yields) and security interest and could be mortgaged or pawned and, of course, leased. Therefore, *dian* rights were different from the transfer of user rights (such as tenancy) and transfer of ownership, such as *huomai* (revocable sale) and *juemai* (irrevocable sale).

From the perspectives of the stratification and transaction of land rights, it was found that land rent, land user rights, security interest, other property rights, and ownership could all enter the market independently and be transacted separately, thereby forming the corresponding transaction types: *taijie* (loan through land as collateral), general tenancy and rent deposit, *di* (mortgages), *dian* (conditional sales), *huomai* (revocable sale), and *juemai* (irrevocable sale). With the expansion of land rights, their transaction values gradually increase, forming a hierarchical land rights transaction system with an internal logic. Various transaction types were clearly distinct but also interconnected and even interchangeable. Viewed from the perspective of historical evolution, new means of transaction have gradually developed and matured under the push of the demand for private transactions. Following the Han and Tang dynasties, where ownership sales and user rights transactions were accessible, the Song Dynasty saw the takeoff of other property rights. Until the Ming and Qing dynasties, when there emerged transactions of *yazu* (rent deposits) and *huomai* (revocable sales), China's land rights transaction system came into existence.

The system, buttressed by multi-level land rights transactions, had multiple functions and influences. For example, it satisfied the diversified needs of numerous parties to the transactions and their different risk appetites, and it helped to realize the demand for the transfer of current and forward returns. The redemption mechanism of *dian*, *huomai*, and *yazu* postponed the final transfers of land ownership, compressed the space for land ownership transfer or land concentration caused by *juemai* and usurious mortgages, and effectively maintained peasants' willingness to secure land property rights.

The gradually maturing land rights transaction system not only facilitated the circulation and combination of production factors, improved economic efficiency and land output, but also profoundly impacted the essential characteristics of China's traditional economy, especially reinforcing the economic operation mechanism centered on land and the individual peasant household's capacity to operate independently.

Flexibility, Individuality, and Combinability of Contract

The various levels of land rights for the parties to the transaction or their associates were flexible and resilient and could be negotiated through individualized contracts. Legal provisions, however, strove for universal adaptability and could only be strict and even inflexible. This led to some conflicts between general legal definitions and individualized contractual agreements. Legal terminology does not necessarily cover various transactions resulting from contractual agreements. The parties to a transaction do not always use the exact language of the transaction, especially when the law was summarized, distilled, or even abstracted from Western practice, which may make it difficult to adequately explain economic phenomena and behaviors in different economies and cultures. Those unique phenomena and institutions developed over a long period of China's history may pose an interpretative dilemma within the framework of the existing or Western legal system.

Interchangeability of Transactions Types

The various types of land rights and transactions that were strictly defined by legal terminology are, in the view of the contracting parties, interlinked and flexible, with the freedom to choose between them. This was highlighted by the association of general tenancy, rent deposit, and *dian*. Under normal circumstances, *dian* and general tenancy were transactions of a different nature, and *dian* and rent deposits were also unrelated. *Dian* was a transaction of possession (other property rights), whereas a tenancy was a transaction of user rights; *dian* was a debt transaction, whereas a rent deposit was an act of leasehold. However, in Fig. 3.1, they were associated.

Similarly, a security right in rem was usually a lending relationship in which there was no transfer of rights in Rem. Thus, it has been argued that a *dian* right does not function as a security right in rem. In the absence of some underlying credit mechanism or effective risk-averse means, traditional Chinese market actors used the land as an intermediary to seek to make up for the lack of a credit facility—the creation of security by the transfer of real property rights in land to enable the parties to the transaction to achieve their individual needs smoothly. Why not? Therefore, in our opinion, it is not impossible to treat the *dian* rights of land as a special kind of security interest.

Combination of Transactions Against Risks and for Profits

Different transaction types can be combined to achieve a balance between power selection and risk aversion so that the benefits and risks of each can be avoided to meet the needs of the other.

The "property in charge" (*guanye*), after receiving the *dian* right, enjoys usufructuary and security rights over the land, which can be cultivated by the owner for management proceeds and labor income, leased, including to the original owner, or can be *dian* sold again, known as a *dian* transfer (*zhuandian*), or borrowed through other means. All these diversified options for land indicate precisely that the *dian* buyer had a real right of land, that is, the rights of control and the rights to dispose of the proceeds. Mortgages, on the other hand, do not carry these rights.

Such cross-transaction was widespread in the modern era. In Hubei Province, there was a transaction custom where "the owner's plots have been transferred to the pledgee [the *dian* buyer,] who recruited new tenants to farm and collect rents; there were also cases where plots were not transferred to the *dian* buyer to recruit new tenants separately but were transferred to the landowner to farm. An annual rent of grains was requested." The investigator stated: "Although in fact, the land does not appear to have been transferred to the possession of the pledgee, legally it is a pledge rather than a mortgage".[51]

Although the increase in the interest rate of the *dian* was normally achieved through annual ground rents, it may not have been impossible to do so in the form of money rents. The stakeholders, with their own interests at stake, were more flexible in their understanding and use of *dian*, *zu* (tenancy), and *di* (mortgage) than Song officials and modern jurists. The needs of traders were very different, and there were many ways and tools to help them achieve their needs. Here, the landowner needed to obtain a loan on the land but also wanted to obtain a return on his operation and labor on the property and, at the same time, sought to retain his ownership. The moneylender wished to obtain interest on the capital through lending, security, and control of the land but did not need to cultivate the land himself. The *dian* rights of the land property (*dianzhi liye*), the rights to control the land, also included the rights to lease it out. Regarding the object of the lease, it could also include the owner who transferred the real rights.

[51] *Minshi xiguan* (Civil Customs), 328–339.

The cross-application of tenancy and *dian* could achieve the effect of a mortgage or satisfy the desired mortgage orientation of the counterparty while avoiding the risk of a mortgage through such a cross-application. In this sense, *dian* was a way of preventing the delivery of ownership rights by transacting other property rights. The freedom of choice to avoid risk and seek to maximize the interests of all parties was an intrinsic motivation for the creation of the *dian* and for the continuous diversification of types of land rights transactions.

Economic Interpretation of Historical Heritage

Conceptual definitions, legal systems, and academic research should respond to the development and richness of reality with consequent adjustments and new interpretations rather than mediating evolving phenomena and behaviors with an established intellectual framework. If a legal concept was imported from the West—the regulation of behavior under very different historical and economic systems—it certainly cannot be defined in such a way as to cover the rich and varied historical phenomena unique to China. Therefore, it was inevitably anachronistic to explain unique Chinese characteristics in this way. To use such culturally and institutionally different norms of behavior to constrain the free choices of Chinese people, to set up a legal system, or even to eliminate the traditional Chinese legacy of effective trading choices and institutions would be tantamount to trimming the toes to fit the shoes, and nothing could be more wrong.

Law is an artificial regulation, which is essentially a restriction on people's behavior, while market transactions are the free choice of the actors. To a certain extent, the two are fundamentally contradictory. The law is designed to reduce conflict between parties to a transaction and resolve transaction disputes by regulating the behavior of people. However, if such laws restrict or even prohibit people's economic freedom of choice—contracts negotiated without prejudice to the rights of others and the public interest, to the detriment of the interests of the parties to the transaction and the welfare of society as a whole—then such laws must be amended and adjusted to accommodate the diversity of market transactions and not become an obstacle to the realization of legitimate free choices and needs. For example, mortgages were traditionally regarded as immoral usury, and Chinese society and the government have spared no effort to attack them. However, the government did not prohibit it by law but used "scrupulous *dian*" (*zhengdian*) transactions to reduce the scope for mortgages and protect the vulnerable.

Law studies what not to do and how to minimize losses, while economics studies what to do to maximize benefits—this is the different orientation of economics and law. Here, the author attempts to provide an economic explanation of historical phenomena and legal systems. Also, as contemporary academic systems were shaped by Western history and institutions and cannot explain well the unique history, culture, and institutions of China, China's original intellectual innovation should come to the fore to offer an answer.

Innovative research is needed to understand other property rights from the institutional heritage of the *dian* rights and top-soil right. At present, other property rights were still a new thing in China, and it is not easy to fully understand their functions. *Dian* rights help us realize that the rights of other property lie between the user and the ownership rights. Although the relationship was complicated, it is not difficult to grasp its essence in two key points—at the heart of this issue was the sharing and distribution of land rights within the mutual constraints of possession (other property rights) and ownership, and the key to our understanding was the evolution from user rights to possession.

Mutual and Restrictive Relationship Between Possession and Ownership

The *dian* right, as a representative right of possession (other property rights), or rather, the institutional legacy of the *dian* right, provides a rare object of study for understanding the rights of possession (other property rights). Because of their complex relationship with ownership, other property rights were not easily captured and managed when various parties were involved, especially in the allocation of rights and benefits. Regarding historical evolution, the independence of other property rights had a long development, mainly through two paths. The first was the gradual realization of the strengthening and expansion of the user rights, and the second was the separation from ownership rights and the release of rights and interests, or the mutual interaction between the two.

Separation and independence of land user rights and possession rights from ownership have undergone several stages in the development of tenancy rights. Since the land user rights holders (i.e., the tenant of the land) must divide up the owner's future income from the property, uncertainty and risk make it necessary for the owner to ensure that the tenant not only pays the ground rent after acquiring the rights to cultivate land, so that the owner receives the income from his land, but also does not damage the land's fertility. Therefore, how to bind the tenant becomes crucial.

Generally speaking, during the Wei, Jin, and Northern and Southern dynasties, this restraint was established based on the premise of physical dependence and even affiliation.[52] The landowners owned the bodies of the tenant peasants, compulsorily organized and managed production, and had complete control over the distribution of land yield. In the Sui and Tang dynasties, landowners bound tenants through labor dependency, providing the primary means of production and labor tools and dominating the distribution of earnings. The land relationship of Western Europe in the Middle Ages was similar to this in that peasants depended on the manor for pasture, livestock, and other means of production, in terms of production processes and even living conditions. It could not reproduce independently of the manor. During the Song and Yuan dynasties, China's land relationship developed into one of land rights deeds, in which owners and tenants contracted to share the land rights and distribute the proceeds—the land use rights were purchased or leased through market transactions, and the enforceability of the contract was protected by custom and law. During the Ming and Qing dynasties, tenancy rights became independent; that is, tenancy rights evolved from the user rights to the rights of possession or other property rights, commonly known as the top-soil right.

In this process, the development of market relations and the growth of independent farming ability were two indispensable conditions that led to the generalization of the *dian* rights in the Song Dynasty. Well-developed contractual and market relationships, supported by customary practices and government laws, allowed for smooth transactions between capital interest and land revenue. The increased ability of individual peasants to operate independently and the increased land output were sufficient to guarantee income distribution between owners and tenants.

During the Ming and Qing dynasties, land rights in rem were further expanded. Tenancy rights under the rent deposit system were a form of land rights that transitioned from user rights to rights in rem. Under

[52] He Ziyuan, "Hanwei zhiji renshen yifu guanxi xiang lishu guanxi de zhuanhua" (The Transformation of Personal Dependency to Affiliation in the Han and Wei Dynasties), *Hebei xuekan* (Hebei Academic Journal) no. 6 (2003), 146–150.

the rent deposit system, an advance deposit meant that the tenant paid for the rights to use the land, so the owner was not free to evict the tenant. For both landlords and tenants, it was a form of a security deposit and risk premium. If the tenant defaulted on the rent, the owner could deduct this from the deposit. In fact, maintaining a stable tenant-tenant relationship was the best way to minimize the transaction costs for both sides in a repeated game. Secure tenancy like this stimulated the tenant's incentive to produce, especially to maintain and invest in the land, and not to exhaust it through intensive farming. Tenants invested in "labor" by fertilizing and improving the soil and even constructing irrigation systems, thus obtaining an incremental yield. The expansion of their land rights started with incremental control, and the control over land management was strengthened, beginning with the investment in the land. In this way, the user rights gradually extended to include the elements of possession (other property rights). If the stock of land output was created and shared between the owner and the tenant, then the incremental land output due to the tenant's investment was controlled by the tenant alone. For example, since the proceeds of the land investment would be spread primarily in the future, the tenant peasant would then demand that the future proceeds be realizable to recoup his investment and thus obtain the rights to transact. Tenant-only investments, nicknamed "dirt silver" (*fenzhiyin*) or "dirt-tail silver" (*fenweiyin*), were the source and security of the transaction and control rights and the primary means by which user rights were extended to rights of possession (other property rights).

The landowner's rent was secured due to increased farmland output, and increased land fertility and unit output were also what the owner sought. Thus, the interests of the owner and the tenant were aligned to achieve a game equilibrium with compatible incentives. Both sides shared the land rights and their proceeds, and the tenant's rights extended from user rights to other property rights. With the development of China's awareness of land property rights, customary practices and government laws have recognized and protected this new form of land rights, resulting in the formation of restrictive rights in Rem, such as permanent tenancy rights and top-soil rights of the land.

Property Rights and Modern Reforms of Farmland

The development of other property rights from their emergence to the point where they became separate and mature types of land rights, like top-soil right, was a long-term evolution in which the rights in Rem took many different types. In the mutual restraint of ownership and rights in rem, land rights also varied in size and degree. They were shared by negotiation between landowners and tenants, as demonstrated in Fig. 3.1, moving between ownership and rights in rem. Some scholars named them "two kinds of top-soil right."[53] Historians have studied the top-soil rights in depth, but it was mostly regarded as a form of user rights in the past. Recent research has progressed, but top-soil rights were still regarded as a form of ownership and, together with subsoil right, were called "double land rights." From our perspective, neither of these two views has ever grasped its essence, and it is, therefore, even more difficult to expand the discussion. Conventional top-soil rights or other land rights exist independently of subsoil rights. Under the release and restriction of ownership, top-soil rights include the rights to control the management of the land, the rights to dispose of the incremental income, and the rights to transact. Owners of top-soil rights could lease, mortgage, or pledge them and realize their interest through circulation. People with land user rights or usufruct rights, on the other hand, only had the rights to farm and earn income and cannot had a right to trade in the real sense, not to mention to mortgage or pledge them. This was the institutional premise behind the disappearance of land *dian* rights in mainland China for more than 40 years.

Ownership was unique, and only other property rights may be released. Real rights, on the other hand, were shareable and can be differentiated again and again, and other property rights can be differentiated to another level of other property rights. For example, top-soil right, which were rights in Rem, can be mortgaged or sold in a conditional sale (*dian*), and the *dian* rights were another level of other property rights. As the standard *dian* right, it was a right to control the land management for an agreed period.

After the independence of other property rights, what was the point of the remaining land property with only a certificate of ownership? First, while the landowner's interest was subject to other property rights, the value of ownership cannot be underestimated. Fundamentally, a legally backed certificate of ownership means the ultimate ownership of the land. Second, any rents paid after the surrender of other property rights belong

[53] Cao Shuji, "Liangzhong 'tianmiantian' yu Zhejiang de 'erwu jianzu'" (Two Types of "Top-soil Land" and the Policy of "25% reduction in Tenant Rents" in Zhejiang Province), *Lishiyanjiu* (Historical Research), no. 2 (2007): 108–121.

to the owner, such as ground rents for subsoil rights. Third, title deeds can be used as mortgages, letters of credit, etc. Finally, as with the *dian* right, the rights of income, appreciation, and accommodation of the land will be returned intact beyond the term of the agreement.

The emergence of other property rights, represented by *dian* and top-soil right, as an independent hierarchy of land rights enriched the types of land rights and their transactions, promoted land circulation, expanded people's free choice, and facilitated the allocation of resources. From the Song Dynasty to the Ming and Qing dynasties, China's limited amount of arable land was able to support a quarter or even a third of the human population, rooted in the economic efficiency brought about by the optimal combination of factors of production in the flow of land property rights and its transaction system.

With the expansion of China's market economy, the separation of ownership and possession (other property rights) will become more common, and the resulting transaction disputes and conflicts will gradually increase. It is increasingly important to fully understand and enable the asset and economic efficiency of various property rights and to deal with the interrelationship between ownership and real rights. The historical legacy of other property rights, such as *dian* and top-soil right, also provides valuable lessons.

In the context of the current agrarian land reforms, other property rights and the legacy of the land rights system provide invaluable insights. If rural households' contracted management rights remain in the form of user rights, the agrarian reforms will not be able to get out of the dilemma. Moreover, if private ownership of land is practiced, there is a fear that the cost of implementation will be too high. Therefore, we propose the transformation of rural family contract management rights into rights in rem.[54] The current encouragement of land circulation was practical, and the problem was twofold. The first was that farmers lack real land rights, and the second was that types of land rights transactions

[54] Cui Yangyang, *Tianmianquan jiqi lishi qishi* (Top-soil Rights of Land and Their Historical Inspirations) (Master thesis, Tsinghua University, 2010); Ren Zhiqiang, *Nongdi chanquan jiqi zibenhua* (Property Rights in Agricultural Land and Their Capitalization) (Postdoctoral Report, Tsinghua University, 2011); Long Denggao, results from the Project "Tudi chengbao jingyingquan de wuquanhua yanjiu: tianmianquan zhidu yichan de jiejian" (Research into the Transition of Land Contract Management Rights to Other Property Rights: Lessons From the Heritage of the Top-soil Right System), Ministry of Education, Social Science Planning Project (10YJA790124).

were quite limited. The inevitable trend was to expand the user rights into other property rights, similar to the *dian* rights or the top-soil rights of land, and to establish diversified types of land rights transactions by drawing on traditional heritage. In this way, the circulation of agricultural land will be facilitated. In fact, reform efforts across the country point to the return of land rights to the peasant for self-empowerment (*huanquan funeng*), that is, the expansion of peasants' user rights into real rights while retaining collective ownership rights. Just as top-soil and subsoil rights were independent, peasants with real land rights will become property owners, and agricultural land will be transformed into colossal capital when it becomes a liquid asset. Granting peasants real rights of land on the premise of maintaining existing land ownership was not only a compromise solution that should be acceptable to all sides but also an indispensable institutional basis for safeguarding the rights of vulnerable peasants and the only way to promote land circulation out of the agricultural predicament. It will be a great institutional innovation with Chinese characteristics, and its historical basis will significantly reduce the cost of its implementation. Due to the minimal academic understanding of the meaning of other property rights and the little that was known about the relationship between ownership and other property rights, there was a lack of persuasive empirical evidence and theoretical explanations for the transition of rural family contract management rights into real rights. This article's arguments for the right of possession (other property rights) and the excavation of Chinese institutional heritage thus provide theoretical support and historical reference for this conception.

CHAPTER 4

The Transformation of Farmland Rights Transactions from the Song Dynasty to the Qing Dynasty: A Study Centering on the Nature and Rights of *Dian* Farmland

As farmland rights transactions developed, transaction rules or practices recognized by the counterparties spontaneously emerged within the market, regulated by state laws. Both the development and maturation of these rules of land rights transactions and people's understanding of them have undergone a long process. Take the example of *dian* transactions (conditional sales). In the Song Dynasty, the rule that "the *dian* transaction requires [the landowner] leaving the property" (*dianxu liye*) in fact clarified the origin of "*dian*," but its derived rights and interests and their diverse manifestations have given rise to ambiguities in the later dynasties. For instance, in the Song, it was not recognized by the government for the *dian* buyers to lease the land to the *dian* sellers; however, in the Qing, this form was widely accepted and thus created the illusion of an apparent "balancing of rent and interest" (*zuxi xiangdi*). In fact, the *dian* buyers deciding to operate or invest the income of the *dian* land, or to realize the future income, according to their own preferences and needs, was a manifestation of a shared land rights pattern constructed by the three parties: the landowner, the *dian* buyer, and the tenant farmer through market transactions.

D. Long and X. Chi, *The Institutions of Land Property Rights in China*, Palgrave Studies in Economic History,
https://doi.org/10.1007/978-981-97-5112-9_4

The right of *dian* were neither rights to use nor rights to own, but a form of other property rights, which was clearly distinguished from a mortgage. The difference in the temporality of *dian* rights was reflected in the government regulations. During the Song Dynasty, it was necessary to go to the local government to make a contract deed, transfer the agricultural land tax, and pay the transaction tax. In contrast, in the mid-to-late Qing Dynasty, *dian* transactions were exempted from transaction taxes and did not require land tax transfers. The deeds were also mainly in the form of single deeds (*danqi*), which facilitated subsequent transactions such as transfers. These stage differences and characteristics demonstrate that the rules of and social understanding regarding the *dian* were also undergoing a convoluted evolution during the development of the *dian*.

Why was the same type of *dian* transaction not permitted in the Song but allowed by the state in the Qing? Similarly, many of the perceptions and explanations of the Qing people regarding the *dian* would not make sense if they were placed under the regulations of the Song Dynasty. Further, why did the Qing differ significantly from the Song in terms of *dian* deed types, transaction taxes, and agricultural land tax transfers? Were the different regulations on *dian* transactions in the Song and Qing dynasties based on differences in understanding, or had the nature of *dian* rights changed? Finally, were such phenomena relevant to the debate on *dian* in today's academia?

As a transaction form reflecting the characteristics of traditional Chinese land property rights,[1] *dian* rights have sparked an intense scholarly interest. There were many relevant research results and debates.[2] However, these debates rarely address the above issues, or they ignore these perspectives. Previous studies have not sufficiently distinguished the differences in the rules of *dian* transactions in different periods and lacked comparative studies on the evolution of the regulations of *dian* transactions, so the grasp of the nature and characteristics of *dian* rights offered

[1] Cao Shuji sees *dian* and the rights of land top-soil as two of the fundamental concepts of traditional Chinese land rights. See Cao Shuji, "Chuantong Zhongguo xiangcun diquan biandong de yiban lilun" (The General Theory of Land Rights Changes in Traditional Chinese Villages), *Xueshu yuekan* (Academic Monthly) 44, no. 12 (2012): 117–125.

[2] Economic historians have mainly explored the economic logic and function of the *dian*. Legal historians have explored the customs and practices of the *dian* and their jurisprudential connotations in more depth, and the results are too numerous to list.

by the existing studies has been confusing or even controversial. It essentially involves an understanding of the nature of *dian* rights. The above questions may be answered if we compare the different situations of *dian* rights in the Song and Qing dynasties.

Although the current research has not been able to fully demonstrate the complete historical lineage and the differences between the various stages of the evolution of the *dian* through the Song, Yuan, Ming, and Qing dynasties for nearly a thousand years, the *dian*, as a new form of land rights transaction that began to take shape in the late Tang and Five Dynasties,[3] had in fact undergone an evolutionary process in terms of its development, social understanding, and maturation of rules. Drawing on the original deeds (especially the "Deeds in the Tsinghua University collection," *Qinghua daxue guancang qiyue*[4]) and judicial archives, this book compares the *dian* transactions of the Song and Qing dynasties from an economic-historical perspective (the Yuan and Ming dynasties were also covered). This chapter finds that the rules and expressions of *dian* transactions were dynamic, reflecting the changes in the traditional dynastic understanding of the characteristics of *dian* rights; we can, therefore, further grasp the essence of *dian* rights from these changes and clarify some misunderstandings. The specific research idea of this chapter is as follows:

In the Song Dynasty, *dian* rights were in the early stages of development. Their manifestations were relatively simple, thus making it easy for people to grasp the origin of the *dian*, but they might not have a clear understanding of the rights and interests derived from it. However, by the Qing Dynasty, the derivative interests of the *dian* gradually became visible, but the origin of the *dian* may also be obscured or misinterpreted by its complex and diverse types and manifestations, leading to misunderstandings. Therefore, this chapter attempts to show the development trajectory of traditional Chinese *dian* rights through a comparative study over a long period. In this way, we can escape the limitations of previous intergenerational studies, grasp the original characteristics, and

[3] Han Xiao, "Tangmo wudai dianquan falü zhidu zhi tantao" (A Discussion of the Legal System of *Dian* Rights in the Late Tang and Five Dynasties), *Henan caijing zhengfa University xuebao* (Journal of Henan University of Economics and Law) 28, no. 1 (2013): 159–167.

[4] The Tsinghua University Library collection contains 44,000 civil deeds. Hereinafter referred to as the "Tsinghua Collection of Deeds."

analyze the derivative rights and interests in detail, thus strengthening our understanding of *dian* rights and their benefits.

4.1 Tenancy with *Dian* Transaction: Rent or Interest

In the case of *dian* transactions, the *dian* seller obtains a loan by transferring all of the actual land control, transaction rights, and income disposal for an agreed-upon time and then pays interest on all of the land proceeds within this period.[5] At the end of the term, the seller can redeem the land on agreed-upon terms. Similarly, the rights to lease out the land *dian* sold by conditional sale was also an important land right. However, in the Song and Qing dynasties, the rights of the *dian* buyer to dispose of the land purchased by conditional sale differed, and the difference reflected the changes in the perception of the *dian* rights in different eras.

Restrictions on the Tenancy with Dian *During the Song*

"The *dian* transaction requires [the landowner] leaving the property" (*dianxu liye*) refers to a *dian* transaction in which the land should be transferred to the *dian* buyer from the *dian* seller for cultivation and management within the agreed term. It was the basic rule of *dian* transactions in the Song Dynasty, and the four Chinese characteristics express the essence of the *dian* rights simply and clearly. Since several studies have been conducted on this subject, there was no need to repeat the discussions here.[6] For the *dian* seller, this rule requires that he transfer the rights to manage the land and all the proceeds; however, the *dian* buyer's rights and interests were not clearly defined. For example, whether or not

[5] Long Denggao, Lin Zhan, and Peng Bo, "Dian yu qingdai diquan jiaoyi tixi" (Dian and Qing's Land Rights System), *China's Social Science* (Social Sciences in China), no. 5 (2013): 125–141. *Dian* transactions of real estate, such as houses, are similar and refer to a form of property transaction that involves the possession, use, and benefit of one's real estate. This book focuses on *dian* transactions of land but does not exclude real estate transactions.

[6] Li Rujun, "Cong 'minggong shupan qingmingji' kan songdai tianzahi maimai zhongde 'dian'" (The Song Dynasty's "dian" in the Sale of Lands and Houses from "Minggong shupan Qingmingji"), in Songdai guanzhen yanduhui (Song Dynasty's Official Regulations Study Semianr) ed., *Songdai shehui yu falü* (Society and Law in the Song Dynasty) (Taipei: dongda tushu gongsi, 2001), 305–325.

the *dian* buyer can lease out the land, particularly whether the land can be leased to the *dian* seller, was not clearly stipulated.

Nevertheless, in the Song Dynasty, some *dian* sellers already practiced "*dian* selling the land through self-tenancy" (*chudian zidian*). For example, in a case in the Southern Song Dynasty, Chaoxing's and Fu (Wusan)'s father, Yaxiu, "WuWuWu ***dian*** sold a piece of land of five ***mu***, three ***jiao***, and eleven ***bu*** to Chen Shuiyuan's father a long time ago; Wusan and his brother Chaoxing worked on the land as tenants and paid land rents every year without arrears." The brothers "again established a deed together and sold the above 'land root' to Chen Shuiyuan's father in the eighth year of the Jiading' reign (1215), with a clear seal on the deed; Chaoxing and his brother had been in a tenancy contract with Chen for more than 20 years. It was clearly written in the deed that the brothers agreed to sell the land owned by their late father, Yaxiu, to receive money. The father sold the land in a conditional sale in the first place, while the sons sold the land in an irrevocable sale after him." WuWuWuWuWuWu[7]

Obviously, Chen Shuiyuan's father obtained tenancy rights for the same piece of farmland by either conditional sale or sale. Further, his counterparty to this transaction could be either the father, Wu Yaxiu as the *dian* seller, the landowner (also the farmland seller), or the Wu brothers. From conditional sale to (irrevocable) sale, both transaction parties changed their *dian* contract to a lease. What distinguishes the process of a conditional sale from a sale was the treatment of the landownership document "farmland roots" (*tiangen*) or "farmland bones" (*tiangu*),[8] which the *dian* seller still retained in the Song Dynasty.

This case reflects both parties' rights to a *dian* land. Since the entire land rights have been transferred to the *dian* buyer, he was free to lease

[7] Zhongguo shehui kexueyuan lishi yanjiusuo songliaojin yanjiushi (Research Department of Song, Liao, Jin, and Yuan History, Institute of History, Chinese Academy of Social Sciences), ed., *Minggong shupan qingmingji* (Collections of Well-Crafted and Just Verdicts of Scholar-Bureaucrats in the Song Dynasty), *juan* 6, 181–182.

[8] For this important finding, see Dai Jianguo, "Songdai de mintian dianmai yu 'yitian laingzhu'" (The Song Dynasty's Civil Land Sales and the "One Land with Two Owners System"), *Lishi yanjiu* (Historical Research), no. 6 (2011): 99–117. It should be noted, however, that in the Song Dynasty, a "land bone" or a "land root" was not a subsoil rights of land in the Ming and Qing dynasties (although in some areas it was also called a land bone or a land root). In the Song Dynasty, land bones were only certificates of ownership kept in government records, and the *dian* seller did not receive the rights to the proceeds of the land during the agreed period, whereas in the Ming and Qing dynasties, the subsoil rights of the land was entitled to land rent.

the land to anyone, including the original *dian* seller. However, if a *dian* seller sells the land and rents it back to cultivate and manage, he then formally violates the rule that "the *dian* transaction requires leaving the property," which was mandatory in the Song Dynasty's *dian* transactions. Song Dynasty law stipulated that "in all land and house transactions, the original owner must leave his or her land and house properties after the transaction. Even if only parts of them were sold or sold by conditional sale, the original owner is not allowed to rent the land or house he sold himself" [应交易田宅, 并要离业, 虽割零典买亦不得自佃赁].[9] This provision meant that the *dian* buyer could not re-lease the land to the *dian* seller, depriving the *dian* buyer of the rights to lease the land—which contradicted the very nature of the *dian* sale of land. In fact, the form of transaction known as "*dian* selling the land through self-tenancy" (*chudian zidian*) was exercised by the *dian* buyer rather than the seller. This kind of transaction is, of course, the result of mutual agreement and may result from a request by the *dian* seller but was essentially a transfer of the rights to use the land by the *dian* buyer.

Although Song Dynasty law strictly prohibited any tenancy relations within the *dian* transaction, the land sellers and buyers developed correspondent ways of adaptation. The case of Xu Zizheng's and Yang Yan's land dispute was such an example. In 1215, Xu Zizheng *dian* purchased around seven *mu* of land from Yang Yan at 280 *qian* (280,000) of *huizi* (currency in the Southern Song Dynasty). Meanwhile, Yang Yan, the *dian* seller and landowner, made another tenancy contract with Xu Zizheng, the *dian* buyer, on the same piece of land as a tenant, agreeing to pay 30 *qian* to Xu per year without additional land rent. (When later Xu Zicheng and Yang Yan brought their dispute over the land to the court, the nature of their land transaction was questioned by the magistrate.) Prime facie, it seemed that Xu Zizheng, the *dian* buyer, was not in charge of land cultivation and management, so his transaction with Yang Yan did not seem to comply with the rules of *dian* transactions in the Song Dynasty. However, as Yang Yan and his son were still plowing the land and contributing to the rent and taxes, it was believed that "Yang Yan has only mortgaged the land to Zizheng, who just benefited from an increase in interest every year" [杨衍当来不过将此田抵当于子政处, 子政不过每岁利于增息而已].

9 *Songxingtong* (Song Criminal Code), collated by Xue Meiqing, *juan* 4, (Beijing: falü Press, 1999), 104.

The county magistrate then ruled: "Since Xu Zizheng has not paid agricultural taxes, and has not cultivated the land, he has not received any grains (which were considered as land proceeds). It is clear that Xu's and Yang's farmland transaction was a mortgage rather than a scrupulous *dian* (*zhengdian*)" [今既不曾受税，不曾管业，所以不曾收谷。其为抵当而非正典明矣].[10]

Regarding this case, today's scholar, Niu Jie, also regards it as a mortgage. Zheng Ding and Chai Rong agreed that the tenancy contract was a "fake" (*jiayue*).[11] However, from our perspective, the verdict of the county magistrate in the Song Dynasty and the present-day interpretation, according to the Song Dynasty's "regulations," may be justified, but the nature of the *dian* was not consistent with it. We will explain this in the following discussion of the Qing's *dian* transactions.

The *dian* buyer replacing the *dian* seller in the possession and management of the land ("possessing and managing the property," *guanye*), was a requirement of "*dian* selling the land by leaving the property" (*liye diantian*) in the Song Dynasty; the *dian* buyer receives the future income from the land ("receiving grain," *shougu*), and bears the tax on the land ("paying tax," *shoushui* that we will explain later). In the above-disputed case, the county magistrate argued that none of the three characteristics of a *dian* transaction, possession and management of property, collection of grain, and tax payment had occurred. Therefore, the land transaction between Xu Zizheng and Yang Yan was hardly a *dian* transaction but qualified as a mortgage transaction.

There were two differences between mortgages and *dian*. The first was whether the transaction was accompanied by the transfer of the land (property); in contrast to a *dian*, which requires "leaving the property," a mortgage does not deliver the property, meaning that control of the land remains with the original owner and there was no future redemption. Secondly, suppose the borrower loses the ability to repay. In that case, the mortgage ends the transaction with the delivery of the title,

[10] "Wu Shuzhai 'didang bu jiaoye'" (Wu Shuzhai "a mortgage does not require the payment of title"), *Minggong shupan qingmingji* (Collections of Well-Crafted and Just Verdicts of Scholar-Bureaucrats in the Song Dynasty), *juan* 6, 167.

[11] Niu Jie, "Lun songdai qiyue guanxi yu qiyuefa" (On Contractual Relations and Contract Law in the Song Dynasty), *Zhongzhou xuekan* (Academic Journal of Zhongzhou), no. 2 (2006): 181–184; Zheng Ding, Chai Rong, "Liangsong tudi jiaoyi zhong de ruogan falü wenti" (Some Legal Issues in the Land Transactions of the Two Song Dynasties), *Jianghai xuekan* (Jianghai Academic Journal), no. 6 (2002): 114–121.

while the *dian* retains the power of redemption of the *dian* seller, and the transaction continues automatically.

In other words, a mortgage would be accompanied by the eventual transfer of landownership, and there was no possibility of future redemption. For this reason, a mortgage was often referred to as an "unscrupulous mortgage" (*yidang*) and was discouraged by the Song government based on economic ethics. However, *dian* avoided the risk of the eventual transfer of property rights, thus protecting the disadvantaged, which was consistent with the moral and policy orientation of the traditional state. Therefore, it was called "scrupulous *dian*" (*zhengdian*). In addition, there were two other differences between mortgages and *dian*. The first is that a mortgage was a short-term loan, usually with monthly interest, while a *dian* was a long-term loan, which can last for one or two decades or even longer. The second difference is whether interest was incurred on the transaction, as a mortgage necessarily generates interest. At the same time, *dian* usually bears no interest because the interest on the loan was covered or replaced by the full annual proceeds of the land. Does the annual payment of 30 *qian* of *huizi* here equal interest?

In particular, two related transactions actually took place in the case of "*dian* selling the farmland through self-tenancy"—the *dian* and the tenancy—and the tenancy contract was not a false one or a fraud, but a transaction following the rules. First, the land was sold by conditional sale (*dian*). The price of this contract was 280 *qian* of *huizi*, and the *dian* buyer had the rights in rem to the land for an agreed term, which includes the rights to the use of the land. Then comes the lease on the land. The *dian* buyer leases out the land, but it happens to be leased to the *dian* seller for a monetary rent of 30 *qian* (30,000) of *huizi* per year. Therefore, this transaction consists of two types of transactions, "*dian*" and "tenancy," and was not related to "mortgage."

The interest on a *dian* transaction should be equal to the total proceeds of the land, not just the land rent. If the total annual return on the land was twice the land rent at the usual rate of 50%, its interest should be twice the land rent, which was 60 *qian* of *huizi*. Obviously, 30 *qian* of *huizi* was the land rent, not the interest on the loans. Namely, the total gain the *dian* buyer should receive in this transaction was much more than 30 *qian*. This is because if he had farmed the land himself, his gain would have been complete control of the land with the annual output of the land. If it was a mortgage, the *dian* buyer would have no control over the land.

Because of the close ties to their self-interest, landowners and money lenders in the Song Dynasty often had a better grasp of and more flexibility regarding *dian*, rents, and mortgages than the magistrate mentioned above. Since traders' needs vary greatly, it was the variety of approaches and financing instruments that help achieve their respective preferences and needs. In this case, the *dian* seller (also the landowner) needs to obtain a loan against the land but wants to receive the proceeds from the operation and labor on the land while also seeking to retain its ownership. At the same time, the *dian* buyer (also the moneylender) wants to obtain interest on capital through lending and acquire security and interest through control of the land without cultivating the land himself.

The rule that "the *dian* transaction requires [the landowner] leaving the property" (*dianxu liye*) refers to a scenario where the *dian* seller transfers actual control of the land to the *dian* buyer, including the rights to lease the land freely; as to whom the *dian* buyer leases the land from, this may also include the nominal owner, which was the *dian* seller at this time. By applying the two transactions of *dian* and tenancy, the *dian* buyer, Xu Zizheng, reaped the rent by leasing the *dian* land (*diantian chuzu*), while the *dian* seller retained ownership and earned revenues by renting the rights to cultivate the land. In this sense, avoiding the risk of ownership delivery and seeking to maximize the interests of both parties were the intrinsic motivations for creating the *dian* and the reason for the diversification of land rights transactions. By the Qing Dynasty, this cross-application was internalized into legal rules of *dian* transactions.

In fact, the Song government sometimes unconsciously approved of this self-tenancy, especially when it did not cause disputes. During the Zhenghe Period, in present-day Shaanxi Province, the landowners generally *dian* sold their land and could either redeem it or rent it from the current landowners (*dian* buyers) upon their return[12]; thus, the *dian*

[12] On October 23, 1114, the Ministry of Justice submitted a memorial: according to Qin Feng and other judges who were dispatched by the central court, "This is intended for herdsmen who came back to redeem the land. If the land had been *dian* sold to others and the original *dian* sellers wanted to redeem the land at the original price, it is allowed that the herdsmen raise horses on this land according to the law. If the landowners did not leave the land and rented the land as tenants, it is ordered that the original owners and tenants raised horses together. Accepted." See Xu Song, *Song huiyao jigao* (Song

buyers became the "current owners" and the original landowners became "tenants."

Types of Dian *Rentals and Their Benefits During the Qing*

During the Qing Dynasty, the development of *dian* transactions became more diverse. First, the *dian* buyers rarely cultivated the lands they had purchased by conditional sales but instead rented them out; the deeds of *dian* transactions also allowed the *dian* buyers to freely "recruit tenants for cultivation and collect rent and tax" [招佃耕作, 收租纳课].[13] Second, many of the *dian* lands were already in tenancy relationships. After taking over the land, the *dian* buyer maintained the same tenants, which was appropriately called "possession of tenancy" (*guandian*). For example, in 1711, Xu Eryuan of Fujian *dian* sold his land to the He family at the price of seven *taels* and five cents of silver; "his land was at the disposal of the He family for tenancy, property management, rent collection, and payment of money and grain."[14] Here, the possession of the tenant was expressed in the form of taking over the tenancy relationship. In fact, this situation already existed in the Song Dynasty,[15] and it may have been a common trend in the Yuan Dynasty. For example, the content of the "deed of purchase of land by conditional sale" (*dianmai tiandi qishi*) in the Yuan Dynasty was for the *dian* sale or sale in which tenancy relationships already existed. They read as follows:

Government Manuscript Compendium), *bing* (Soldiers) 21 (Beijing: Zhonghua Books), 7140.

[13] No. 86 "Yongtui gengtian cuodi qizi 永退耕田厝地契字" (Land Deed for Permanent Tenancy Rights of Arable Land and House) (1866), in Lin Zhen ed., *Taiwan sifa wuquan bian* (A Compilation of Taiwan Private Law Property Rights) (Taipei: datong Books, 1987), 305. This book is thereafter referred to as *Wuquan* (Property Rights).

[14] Fujian shifan University lishixi (Fujian Normal University History Department) ed., *Mingqing Fujian jingji qiyue wenshu xuanji* (Selected Economic Contracts of Fujian in the Ming and Qing Dynasties) (Beijing: People's Press, 1997), 16.

[15] In 1241, Wang Yizhi *dian* sold his house and land to Xu Kejian and was involved in disputes over the repeated sales of the same piece of land. Both parties went to court, and the final judgment was to "return the house to the original *dian* owner Xu Kejian, for management." See "Weng Haotang chongdie" (Weng Haotang "overlapping"), in *Minggong shupan qingmingji* (Collections of Well-Crafted and Just Verdicts of Scholar-Bureaucrats in the Song Dynasty), 302.

> "the place ... There are several sections of the late land that have been rented out."
> [口里口都姓口, 有已承分晚田若干段, 已出租]
> "[The lands] are cultivated by ... people, and each winter they pay a few *shi* of rice."
> [系口人耕作, 每冬交米若干石]
> "From the establishment of the deed, [I asked] the [*dian*] buyer of the land to offer tenancy to the tenants and manage the property."

The deed of *dian* transactions states that "the land will be redeemed within a few years (or three winters) in the form of paper money (*yuan-chao*), and if there is not enough paper money to redeem the land, the tenants will be kept and managed under the original agreement."[16] Of course, it was also fine for the *dian* buyer to recruit other tenants to manage the property. A deed of Taiwan in the Qing Dynasty was representative in this sense. It reads: "To the money owner who will be in charge, recruiting the tenants to cultivate the land, harvesting the grains, and paying the agricultural taxes, either by the original tenants or by the new tenants, is at the discretion of the *dian* buyer."[17]

As seen, the *dian* buyer had the rights to dispose of the farmland according to his will. In other cases, the land can be rented out to the *dian* seller. From the perspective of the *dian* seller, this was the so-called *dian* selling the land through self-tenancy (*chudian zidian*) or sharecropping the *dian* land (*dianzhong chudian zhidi*), which was widespread in the Qing Dynasty. Among the 39 cases of *dian* transactions recorded in the Qianlong *Xingke tiben*, 21 cases, or 53.8%, were "*dian* selling the land through self-tenancy."[18] As this practice was so widespread, people may not realize that two transactions had taken place

[16] "Gongsi beiyong dianmai tiandi qishi" (A Must for Public and Private Uses: Deed Types for Dian Transactions of Land), in *Xinbian shiwenlei juyao qizha qingqian waiji* (The New Series of Writings of Official Documents), *juan* 11 (reprinted copies in 1324, collected by China's National Library), 742.

[17] No. 24 "dianqizi" (Dian Deed) (December 1844), in *Wuquan* (Property Rights), 792.

[18] Zhongguo diyi lishi dang'anguan (China's No. 1 Archives), Zhongguo shehui kexueyuan lishi yanjiusuo (Institute of History, CASS), eds., *Qianlong xingke tiben zudian guanxi shiliao Qingdai dizu boxue xingtai* (The Documents of Tenancy Relationships in Grand Secretariat Memorials on Criminal Matters in Qianlong's Reign, and Types of Exploitation of Land Rents in the Qing Dynasty) (Beijing: Zhonghua Books, 1988), 207–302.

in the case of "*dian* selling the land through self-tenancy," but rather see it as one type of *dian*. The Qing government also fully endorsed it; no one would have considered it a counterfeit and an improper transaction, as in the Song Dynasty. In the Daoguang Period, a *dian* deed of Shanxi Province expressly stipulated that "the landowner of this place has leased and cultivated this piece of land" [此地地主租种]. (Whenever such words appeared on a deed, it marked the conclusion of such a transaction of *chudian zidian*.)

> Xin Bingguang, the deed holder of the *dian* land. Because of the inconvenience of use (shortage of money), now I am willing to make a deed with Wang Anbang, and *dian* sell a section of 18 *dui* of land on the southern head of my territory to him for property possession and cultivation. [I] made it clear with the middleman that the *dian* price is 10,000 *wen*, including the connected soil, trees, stones, and water, as well as the passage, rice land, and barren land. The labor's salary is 150 *wen* and the *dian* period is three years. I am afraid that only an oral promise is not enough proof, so I made this *dian* deed as evidence. The landowner will rent the land, and the annual rent for wheat is seven *dou*.
> The seventeenth year of the Daoguang reign
> The deed-maker:
> Xin Bingguang, and the middleman Yang Zuomei[19]

In the above quotation, the *dian* buyer "possessed and managed the land" (*guanye gengzhong*), while the landowner (also the *dian* seller) "rented and cultivated it" (*dizhu zuzhong*). The relationship between the two parties of the land was obviously a tenancy relationship. In fact, the practice of "*dian* selling the land through self-tenancy" (*chudian zidian*) had its inherent economic logic and rationality. To begin with, the *dian* sellers were usually poor borrowers who would probably not be able to make ends meet if there was no land to cultivate, let alone repay the loan. Just as a landowner in Jingle County, Shanxi Province, who *dian* sold his land through self-tenancy, said: "In previous years, I could survive by

19 "Li diandi tuwen qiren Xin Bingguang" (Xin Bingguang, the Deed Holder of the Land), July 1837, in Tsinghua Collection of Deeds, no. T2119.

renting and cultivating this land. Now that I am prohibited from cultivating the land that I have *dian* sold, I can hardly survive. How can I even redeem the land after the autumn?".[20]

However, if the *dian* sellers rented the land from the *dian* buyers and cultivated it, they could sustain their livelihoods by farming the land, and the *dian* buyers also received land rents, which was a win for both parties. Moreover, as the output of land increased in the Qing Dynasty, tenancy relationships became more developed. Most *dian* buyers in the Qing Dynasty rented out the *dian* lands, mostly to the *dian* sellers. In terms of *dian* buyers (also money lenders), the Qing state saw an increase in specialized financial institutions, such as out-of-town stores and native banks, which, similar to modern banks and other financial institutions, were often divorced from land operations and were not oriented toward acquiring land titles and farming but rather hoped to obtain loan proceeds through *dian* transactions.[21] Therefore, by leasing the *dian* land directly to the debtor and also the *dian* seller, there was no need to find a separate tenant farmer, thus reducing the cost of information search, negotiation, penalty costs for default, and the associated risks. It can be seen that the practice of "*dian* selling the land through self-tenancy" was beneficial to both parties and was a rational choice to reduce transaction costs and risks.

It is interesting to note that Song law did not allow a tenancy relationship between the *dian* buyer and the *dian* seller, meaning that the user rights contained in the *dian* was restricted. In the Qing Dynasty, it was

[20] Item 76, "Shanxi jingle xianmin sunqin dianzhong chudian zhidi" (Sun Qin Share-cropping the Dian land in Jingle County, Shanxi Province) (1764), in Zhongguo diyi lishi dang'anguan (China's No. 1 Archives), Zhongguo shehui kexueyuan lishi yanjiusuo (Institute of History, CASS) eds., *Qianlong xingke tiben zudian guanxi shiliao Qingdai dizu boxue xingtai* (The Documents of Tenancy Relationships in Grand Secretariat Memorials on Criminal Matters in Qianlong's Reign, and Types of Exploitation of Land Rents in the Qing Dynasty), 236.

[21] In Wuning County, Jiangxi Province, Shu Jiande ran a goods store to make a living. In 1749, Shu Yunhui, who owed the goods on credit, *dian* sold his land for 2 *mu* and 9 *fen* at the price of 20 taels (to Shu Jiande). The land would still be cultivated by Yunhui, who paid 6 *dan* of rent per year. The store owner (Shu Jiande) did not farm himself. See Zhongguo diyi lishi dang'anguan (China's No. 1 Archives), Zhongguo shehui kexueyuan lishi yanjiusuo (Institute of History, CASS), eds., *Qianlong xingke tiben zudian guanxi shiliao Qingdai dizu boxue xingtai* (The Documents of Tenancy Relationships in Grand Secretariat Memorials on Criminal Matters in Qianlong's Reign, and Types of Exploitation of Land Rents in the Qing Dynasty) 151–153.

prevalent for tenancy relations to occur between the *dian* buyer and the *dian* seller, but this led to another misunderstanding. As the *dian* buyer rented out the land to the *dian* seller, the annual interest was ostensibly reflected in the land rent. Moreover, there were many old sayings such as "silver is not counted as interest and the land is not counted as rent" [银不计利, 田不计租], or "rent is collected against interest" [收租抵利].[22] Some may wonder: was "*dian* selling the land through self-tenancy" a transaction between land rent and interest?

Some scholars regard the "balancing of rent and interest" (*zuxi xiangdi*) as the core of the *dian*. But if we go back to the Song Dynasty's rule of "the *dian* transaction requires leaving the property" (*dianxu liye*), that is, if the dian *buyer* does not rent out the land but cultivates it himself, then all he gets was the profit. Was that so? It is where the problem lies, so let me try to interpret it. Suppose the annual interest payable by the landowner (*dian* seller) on the funds is P, and the yearly total return on the land received by the silver owner (*dian* buyer) is Y. When the *dian* buyer leases out the land, he receives an investment income of land rent of R, and when the tenant farmer cultivates the land, he receives a labor and management income of M. When the *dian* buyer cultivates and manages the land himself, the annual interest on the capital P equals the total annual return on the land Y, which is $P = Y$.

It was clear in the Song Dynasty. After the *dian* transaction of land in the Song Dynasty, the *dian* seller could no longer cultivate it, but the *dian* buyer cultivated it. However, when the *dian* buyer did not cultivate it himself but exercised his *dian* rights to rent out the land, the entire annual land income became shared between the *dian* buyer and

[22] In 1874, Zhao Qinglin *dian* purchased a piece of land, and the deed read: "allowing Qinglin to cultivate and manage the property and granting other tenants to offset the interest," "this is silver without calculating the profit and land without calculating the rent" (此系银不计利, 田不计租). This deed is named "Tongzhi shisannian dongguan zhangjiarun dangchang Tianqi 同治十三年东莞张家闰当尝田契" (A Dian Land Deed of Zhang Jiarun in Dongguan County in the Thirteenth Year of the Tongzhi Reign), See *Qingdai Guangdong tudi qiyue wenshu huibian* (A Compilation of Land Deeds in Guangdong Province during the Qing Dynasty) (Jinan: qilu shushe, 2014), 28. Zhao Hengrun of Taiwan inherited property from his grandfather, and *dian* sold it to Lin Benyuan at the price of 900 *dayuan* for three years. "If [I] do not have enough money to pay back, I still allow the silver owner to recruit tenants to cultivate and collect rent against the profit" See No. 25 "Jinqi gengdian qizi 尽起耕典契字" (A Deed of Dian Land for Cultivation) (November 1875), in *Wuquan* (Property Rights), 794.

the tenant farmer, with the proceeds of labor and management going to the tenant farmer (M) and the *dian* buyer gaining the land rent (R).

Prime facie, P = R. However, this is an illusion created by the fact that the *dian* buyer receives only the land rent R, as the *dian* buyer cedes the rights to cultivate the land and its harvest. Obviously, here.

(a) $P = Y = M + R$

If half of the land proceeds will be paid as land rent at the usual land rent rate of 50%, M = R. Then, in the case of the Song Dynasty cited above, the land rent was 30 *qianwen* (thousand coins), so the interest should be 60 *qianwen*.

(b) $P = Y = 2R$

Suppose the tenant of the land is the *dian* seller. In that case, he receives M and pays the *dian* buyer a rent of R. If the *dian* buyer takes back the rights to use the land and manages it himself instead of renting it out, he receives all the proceeds from the operation of the land Y. It can be seen that it is not only the rent that is exchanged for capital interest, which means P does not equal R.

The essence of *dian* did not change. In the Song Dynasty, "*dian* selling the land by leaving the property" (*liye diantian*) was what was usually referred to as the "possession of the land" (*guanye*) in the Qing Dynasty. It meant taking over control of the farm and managing the land. This "possession of the land" was expressed in the form of "possession and management of tenancy" (*guandian*) over the tenant relationship, that is, to take charge of the tenant and his management of the land and to share all the proceeds of the land Y with the tenant. Thus, the *dian* buyer and the tenant farmer received R and M, respectively. It leads to the following:

1. According to the Song Dynasty's rule that "the *dian* transaction requires leaving the property," a *dian* land was a transfer of all land rights and its total output Y for an agreed term; however, it was not understood that Y could be decomposed into M + R, and the transfer of M was the rights of the *dian* buyer. Alternatively, when a tenancy relationship occurs on *dian* land, its entire income decomposes into operating income and investment income, in which the tenant farmer receives the operating income and the *dian* buyer receives the pure investment income.

For example, in Qing Taiwan, Cao Daishi and Cao Jinzong's grandfather *dian* purchased two pieces of land. Due to poor harvests, debts, and the lack of silver, he was willing to transfer it to Luo Qiying at the price of 820 *yuan* of silver (*foyin*). The deed read:

I will leave it up to the *dian* buyer to provide his own labor and recruit tenant farmers to cultivate the land for rent and then pay the rent against the profit. I would not dare say anything to prevent any trouble. If the price of land increases a hundredfold in the future, it will be a great blessing for the *dian* buyer, and I dare not say anything about redemption.[23]

This amount of 820 *yuan* of silver was a big investment for Luo Qiying, which can be used to recruit tenant farmers and improve the soil. The return on the investment was the future rent, which could "increase a hundredfold" or fail like Cao's, the owner, which was the risk of investment. The so-called rent against profit (*nazu dili*) was an investment by the *dian* buyer. He invested part of his rights in the land—the rights to use the land—but not all of his rights, and he gained a profit. The transfer of all the land rights during the agreed terms was the transfer of *dian* and was also the acquisition of the principal amount of the loan. We will discuss this below.

2. The *dian* buyer leases the land; he still had the rights to control and dispose of the land. In fact, M can be considered an opportunity cost to the *dian* buyer, who cannot engage in other activities to earn another income if he operates the land himself. After leasing out the land, the *dian* buyer could break away from the farm operation and engage in other business activities, such as commerce and industry, to generate profit. Many *dian* buyers (also lenders) in the Qing Dynasty were non-native merchants and even specialized lenders and lending institutions.
3. Further, when a tenant farmer acquired the rights to use the land to establish his own family farm, the full benefit was usually more than twice the land rent, as the tenant farmer also had additional benefits

[23] No. 43 "Qigeng zhuandian tianyuan zi 起耕转典田园字" (A Deed for Dian Transfer of Land and Yard) (November 1897), in *Wuquan* (Property Rights), 822–823.

from residual control and residual claims on the family farm, as well as risk premium benefits.[24]

Therefore, in general, the tenant farmer would receive more than or equal to the land rent: $M \geq R$. And the interest rate on the loan of *dian* was usually greater than or equal to two times the land rent, which is.

(a) $P = Y = R + M \geq 2R$

Breakdown of the Rights and Benefits of the Dian *Buyer*

The rights and benefits of the *dian* buyer would include the following three related components:

1. Establishing an individual family farm (by the *dian* buyer) with the rights to operate the land and receive all the proceeds from the land was called the operating income.
2. Leasing out the land use rights therein and receiving the investment income was called future land rent.
3. Exercising the security correct function of the *dian* land and receiving cash by transfers or mortgage was called the realization of future proceeds or transfer across time.

The third right of a security interest was derived or subdivided from the first right of *dian*. Since the *dian* buyer acquires complete control and management of the land, when he needs cash, he can realize the future proceeds through a transfer or mortgage, thus realizing across-term transfers with the right of *dian*. It was equivalent to a security interest, while the right of land use cannot be used to exercise a transfer or mortgage. Besides, the third right was recognized in the Song Dynasty[25] and became

[24] Long Denggao, Pengbo, "Jinshi diannong de jingying xingzhi yu shouyi bijiao" (A Comparison of the Nature of Business and Earnings of Tenant Farmers in Modern Times), *Jingji yanjiu* (Economic Research Journal), no. 1 (2010): 138–147.

[25] For example, in the Southern Song Dynasty, "Zeng Qi has originally *dian* purchased a piece of land from Hu Yuangui. As the term expired, he transferred the land to Chen Zeng" (曾沂元典胡元珪田，年限已满，遂将转典与陈增), see "Zeng Qi su Chen Zeng qudian weijin jiaqian 曾沂诉陈增取典田未尽价钱" (Zeng Qi Sued Chen Zeng for Taking

more common in the Qing Dynasty, giving rise to multiple transfers (see later). It was important to emphasize that even after the *dian* buyer leased out the land, he still had the right to transfer it. However, even if the *dian* buyer transferred or mortgaged the land, the original tenant farmers could continue cultivating the land. Thus, the previous scholarship considered the *dian* transaction in the Qing Dynasty as a "balancing of rent and interest," which actually ignored the proceeds other than land rent brought about by the exercise of the security right by the *dian* buyer.

Suppose we review the process of a *dian* transaction from the perspective of the modern concept of property rights, followed by *dian* selling the land. In that case, the *dian* seller actually releases other property rights from the "right over full ownership" of the land, which was the "right over the property of another." "Other property rights" of the land include the right to rent, mortgage, and pawn. It can be seen that the right of *dian* included but was not limited to the right to use. If we equate the right of *dian* with the right to use, we ignore that the right to use did not have the function of a mortgage or pawn.

Regarding the development of *dian* rights and their nature, the use rights released by *dian* lands and their transactions were relatively limited in the Song Dynasty but more substantial in the Qing Dynasty. Since the right of land was divisible, in the type of "*dian* selling the land through self-tenancy" (*chudian zizhong*), the *dian* seller retained the ownership right (self-interest) and rented back the user right; accordingly, the *dian* buyer acquired other property rights and released the user rights for rent. In other words, the property owner (ownership) released other property rights to the *dian* buyer through a *dian* transaction within an agreed-upon term. Among other property rights were usufruct rights, including the right to use, and security rights that can be used for transfers or mortgages.

Here, other rights were separated from self-ownership, and use rights were separated from other rights in Rem. The three can be independent and practically interrelated, sharing land property rights and benefits at various levels or times. However, when rights over the property of another were separated from property rights, what remains of self-ownership? The self-ownership rights still had the corresponding rights, such as being

the Dian Land Without Paying the Required Amount of Money), in *Minggong shupan qingmingji* (Collections of Well-Crafted and Just Verdicts of Scholar-Bureaucrats in the Song Dynasty), *juan* 4, 104.

sold. For example, a case in Shanghe County, Shandong Province, in the Qing Dynasty illustrates this point: "When a landowner *dian* sold a piece of land or a house in the countryside to a *dian* buyer [within an agreed term], it was not considered a fraud [if the landowner sold this same piece of land to a third party in an irrevocable sale] before the term ended, as long as it was explained to the original *dian* buyer" [乡间典当田房, 没满年限, 只要向原典主说明, 就算不得朦混].[26] That means the landowner could resell the land, and the *dian* relationship continued. When the *dian* period expires, the new landowner (buyer) redeems the land from the original *dian* buyer.[27] Further, when the landowner sold his title, the *dian* buyer had the "first right of refusal" (*xianmaiquan*).[28] This was out of respect for the rights of *dian* and to reduce the potential for trouble caused by too many parties to the transaction.

In summary, tenancy (including rent-deposit, *yazu*) was a transaction of the right to use, sale (revocable sale and irrevocable sale) was a transaction of the right of ownership, and *dian* was a transaction of the right

[26] Zhongguo diyi lishi dang'anguan (China's No. 1 Archives), Zhongguo shehui kexueyuan lishi yanjiusuo (Institute of History, CASS), eds., *Qianlong xingke tiben zudian guanxi shiliao Qingdai dizu boxue xingtai* (The Documents of Tenancy Relationships in Grand Secretariat Memorials on Criminal Matters in Qianlong's Reign, and Types of Exploitation of Land Rents in the Qing Dynasty), 285.

[27] In 1727, Qi County, Henan Province, Yu Kechen *dian* purchased Han Yiyuan's land of one *qing* and sixty *mu* for farming, at the price of 42 taels of silver, in an agreed term of ten years. In 1734, Han Yiyuan "sold this piece of land to Han Yunji. But Yu Kechen, who had *dian* purchased it, did not allow Han Yiyun to redeem it, as the term limit had not yet expired." It was not until 1737 that Han Yunji finally redeemed the land from Yu Kechen. See "Henan qixian Han YIyuan shuhui diandi lingxin chumai" (Han Yiyuan redeemed his land and sold it separately in Qi County, Henan Province), in Zhongguo diyi lishi dang'anguan (China's No. 1 Archives), Zhongguo shehui kexueyuan lishi yanjiusuo (Institute of History, CASS) eds., *Qianlong xingke tiben zudian guanxi shiliao Qingdai dizu boxue xingtai* (The Documents of Tenancy Relationships in Grand Secretariat Memorials on Criminal Matters in Qianlong's Reign, and Types of Exploitation of Land Rents in the Qing Dynasty) (1737), 207–209.

[28] No. 69 "Hunan hengshanxian Wen Feiqun jiang tianzhong jiudan wudou dianmai yu shengyuan dizhu" (Wen Feiqun sold nine dan and five dou of land to the scholar landlord in Hengshan County, Hunan Province), see Zhongguo diyi lishi dang'anguan (China's No. 1 Archives), Zhongguo shehui kexueyuan lishi yanjiusuo (Institute of History, CASS) eds., *Qianlong xingke tiben zudian guanxi shiliao Qingdai dizu boxue xingtai* (The Documents of Tenancy Relationships in Grand Secretariat Memorials on Criminal Matters in Qianlong's Reign, and Types of Exploitation of Land Rents in the Qing Dynasty) (1733), 219–222.

of land between tenancy and sale. However, the *dian* was neither a transaction of use nor a transaction of ownership and can be regarded as a transaction of limited property rights (right over the property of another). By entering the land market in its own form, the canon promoted the stratification of land rights and their transactions and the development of a rich and diverse system of land rights transactions.

4.2 Changes in Farmland Taxes and Transaction Taxes

In the Song Dynasty, the provision "the *dian* transaction requires leaving the property" had mandatory correspondent procedures: both parties to the *dian* transaction had to go to the local court for the relevant procedures, including the payment of transaction tax—that is, the deed tax (*qishui*); and the transfer of tax payment to the *dian* buyer—in order to complete the *dian* seller's "leaving the property" (*liye*) procedure. However, in the Qing Dynasty, the situation was very different.

Transfer of Farmland Tax and Property

During the Song Dynasty, it was stipulated that a *dian* transaction was like the purchase or sale of land, which required the transfer of the farmland tax and service. After the farmland transfer, the *dian* buyer was responsible for the land tax, called the "transfer of tax and service" (*tuige shuifu*). In this respect, there was no difference between a *dian* and a sale.

> In the law, all the *dian* transactions of land and houses must [have the landowners] leave the property, and all the sales of land and houses; regarding the tax collection, [one should] transfer the property at the court and collect tax and rent. This law must be followed, which is the valid [process] of a ***dian* transaction.**[29]

In the dian, like the sale, taxes and property must be transferred at the time of the transaction; however, at the time of redemption, the taxes and property of the land revert to the original. As the records state, "If

[29] "Wu Shuzhai 'didang bujiaoye' 吴恕斋 '抵当不交业'" (Wu Shuzhai, "Mortgaging without proper transfer"), in *Minggong shupan qingmingji* (Collections of Well-Crafted and Just Verdicts of Scholar-Bureaucrats in the Song Dynasty), *juan* 6, 167.

the property is sold by conditional sale, it is to be returned at the time of redemption on another day" [如系典业, 即候他日收赎之日, 却令归并].[30] The procedures for the *dian* of land were more complicated. For example, the regulation of Shaoxing in the year 1145 required that "when a person or household *dian* sold his land and house, it was allowed to have an account to record the hectarage, quality of land, the original land rent and tax, and the amount of money for service, all of which were equally taken and recorded, and the case was received in the land inventory on the same day before the deed was sealed."[31] In the Yuan Dynasty, "the deed format to purchase a piece of land by sale or conditional sale" (*dianmai tiandi qishi*) contained deed formats for both sale and conditional sale: "all the red deeds should be submitted to the court with the official seal. The former property is under the 厶 household and is now transferred with its rent and taxes. It is permitted and, therefore, issued. The agreed contract is as above, and this is used as evidence. Sincerely."[32]

Despite the transfer of taxes, the *dian* seller retained ownership of the land. The retention of landownership thus distinguishes between two types of transactions: *dian* and sale. During the Song Dynasty, it was stipulated that the *dian* buyer would pay the taxes. However, if the *dian* buyer fled the land or evaded the taxes, the original owner of the land would still pay.[33] This placed joint liability and ultimate obligation on the

[30] "Shihuo qishi zhi qisan" (Food and Commodities, 70–73), in *Song huiyao jigao* (Song Government Manuscript Compendium), 6.

[31] "Shihuo liuyi zhi liusi" (Food and Commodities, 60–61), in *Song huiyao jigao* (Song Government Manuscript Compendium), 5905. The *dian* seller not only needed to transfer land tax, but also had to register the *dian* buyer in the household. "The people who are in a *dian* transaction have been registered in the household, and as for the taxes, there is no difference from the landowner" (见典之人已编于籍, 至于差税, 与主不殊), **in "Shihuo liuyi zhi wuliu" (Food and Commodities, 61–56), in** *Song huiyao jigao* (Song Government Manuscript Compendium), 5901. During the Song Dynasty, the household system was implemented, and the main households (*zhuhu*) were divided into five classes according to the amount of land they possessed, and taxes were levied accordingly. This means that the secondary households (*kehu*) may change into the main households if they *dian* purchased lands; the number of *dian* lands may also change the rank and corresponding tax burden among the five classes of main households.

[32] "Gongsi beiyong dianmai tiandi qishi" (A Must for Public and Private Uses: Deed Types for Dian Transactions of Land), in *Xinbian shiwenlei juyao qizha qingqian waiji* (The New Series of Writings of Official Documents), *juan* 11, 742.

[33] "[I would like to] request that the land should be *dian* sold to people for a certain number of years, and if the *dian* buyer fails to pay the tax and escapes, the

owner of the land (the *dian* seller) and also indicates that while the *dian* buyer contributed the taxes, the *dian* seller bore the ultimate risk. It was both unreasonable and difficult to operate. Except for the longer period, the transfer of the taxation of the *dian* land was reasonable. However, the term limit for *dian* was usually short, three to five years.

Of the 136 deeds with a term in the Ming and Qing dynasty Fujian land rights transactions database (*Mingqing Fujian diquan jiaoyi shujuku*), [34] the average term was 5.7 years, which can be considered an extended redemption period (deeds that survive today usually have a longer redemption period, and short-term ones have not generally survived). During the Republican Period in southern Jiangxi, "the period of redemption ranged from one to three years, and there were very few cases of more than three years [there were also cases of the indefinite period."[35] After a *dian* sale, the delivery of taxes and material resources could often be delayed. If the taxes were paid in the second year after the *dian* transaction, and then the land and its tax payment had to be returned in the third year, this obviously added to the burden. If the landowner redeemed the land after two or three years, why should such a transaction of *dian* go through the government and add to the trouble? As long as the *dian* transaction was sufficiently creditable, both the *dian* sellers and buyers would try to avoid the government's tax collection and procedural control. In addition, in the Qing Dynasty, practices of transferring (*zhuandian*), adding (*tiandian*), and price add-on (*jiazhao*) were quite common. If every transaction had to go through the government for delivery and taxation, and the original owner had to go to the government for resuming (*guibing*) at the end of the transaction, it was complicated and easily confused many traders.

tax will be paid regardless of the number of years that have not yet expired, and the landowner (*dian* seller) should be ordered to pay the tax." See "Shihuo liuyi zhi wuqi" (Food and Commodities, 61–57), in *Song huiyao jigao* (Song Government Manuscript Compendium), 5902.

[34] The database is established based on Fujian shifan University lishixi (Fujian Normal University History Department) ed., *Mingqing Fujian jingji qiyue wenshu xuanji* (Selected Economic Contracts of Fujian in the Ming and Qing Dynasties), the research group members include Peng Kaixiang, Chen Zhiwu, and others.

[35] Qian Nanjing guomin zhengfu sifa xingzhengbu (Former Ministry of Justice and Administration, Nanjing National Government) ed., *Minshi xiguan diaocha baogaolu (1930)* (Civil Custom Survey Report Book, 1930) (Beijing: Zhongguo zhengfa University Press, 2000), 246. Referred as *Minshi xiguan* (Civil Customs) thereafter.

Therefore, the regulations of *dian* in the Qing Dynasty were more consistent with the actual and private needs. In the Qing Dynasty, both parties to a *dian* land were not usually required to transfer the land tax, let alone transfer of the ownership (*guohu*), and were only required to do so when the land was sold from a *dian* sale to a sale.[36] This was generally the case with all local *dian* deeds, and some "additionally established a grain retention certificate, stating that the grain was retained for ten or twenty years." However, during this period, "the seller may still claim redemption." This grain retention certificate was equivalent to a redemption certificate. In fact, it did not matter which party paid the land tax; both parties could negotiate. For example, in Le'an County, Jiangxi Province, it was stipulated that "for the land that has been *dian* sold, grain to the original owner or the *dian* buyer to submit, subject to the approval of the contract." [37] This shows that the attribution of property ownership and the final control of the land were key. However, the sale contract generally specifies in some form the transfer of taxes, as was the case with the Ming and Qing dynasty deeds in the Tsinghua University collection.

Dian *Transaction Tax*

The number of land transactions was much larger than that of general commodities, so the government naturally did not easily let go of the opportunity to levy taxes. In the Song Dynasty, the transaction procedures

[36] For example, *Qinding hubu zeli* (Imperially commissioned regulations and precedents of the Ministry of Revenue), *juan* 10. It was stipulated that "If the original landowner is unable to redeem the land, then it is at the disposal of the *dian* buyer for taxation, property transfer, and farming." In 1909, "Fengsheng dufuxian wei zhengdun tianfang qishui zhi shiyu fulu xianding banfa sitiao" (The Four Methods issued by the Fengtian Provincial Governon for the Rectification of the Deeds of Lands, Houses, and Taxes) stipulated that "In accordance with the provincial tax deed regulations, the lands and houses that have been *dian* sold for more than 20 years are to be sold out in irrevocable sales and allowed to be transferred to the *dian* buyer in terms of tax and property." This means that the general *dian* deeds did not need to go through the tax and property transfer. See *Shengjing shibao* (Shengjing daily), August 20, 1909. This is quoted from Minami Manshū Tetsudō Kabushiki Kaisha (Investigation Division, South Manchuria Railway Co.), "Ten Ten kanshū, Foroku" (Customary Practices of Dian, Appendix), *Kisaki-hen dai ni-kan furoku* (Report on the Survey of Old Manchurian Customs) (Tokyo: Kabushikigaisha shūei-sha, 1913), 13.

[37] *Minshi xiguan* (Civil Customs), 205, 257.

for *dian* and sale were basically the same. The parties to a *dian* transaction had to submit documents with seals to the local government, apply for a contract, and pay the transaction tax. In 969, "[the local government] began collecting deed tax from people. It stipulated that people must pay the deed tax for *dian* selling their land and houses" [始收民印契钱, 令民典卖田宅, 输钱印契税].[38] At this time, the deed tax was levied at 2%, increasing to 4% and then 6% in the middle of the Northern Song Dynasty; it rose to 10% in the Southern Song Dynasty under Emperor Xiaozong.[39] However, the redeemability and other features of the *dian* made it easy to avoid government regulation and taxation. According to the records:

> "Rich families usually did not pay the deed tax according to the tax rate when they *dian* sold their lands and houses. The government hoped to finish the procedures for transferring the property rights, but there was no way to investigate... The county then requested the real estate red deed and the three-colored official books, which were the summer tax book, the autumn seedling book, and the resources book, requiring that no one is allowed to pay taxes without first going through the procedures of transferring the property rights."[40]

By the Yuan Dynasty, the sale of lands and houses was also strictly regulated, and the procedures were complicated. "Where there is a sale of land and houses, according to the rules, the relatives, neighbors, or guarantors, and others, were required to make a deed with signatures and to go to the local government to pay taxes."

These government regulations were mainly for taxation purposes, and the parties to such transactions also sought to avoid taxes. Since private loans and mortgages were not subject to taxation, many land and house transactions were *dian* transactions under the guise of mortgages. For example, in the Yuan Dynasty, "there are many cases where the buyers

[38] Ma Duanlin, "Zhengque kaoliu" (No. 6 Examination of Tax Collection), in *Wenxian tongkao* (Comprehensive Examination of Literature), *juan* 19 (Beijing: Zhonghua Books, 2011), 187.

[39] Jin Liang, Yang Dachun, "Zhongguo gudai qishui zhidu tanxi" (An Analysis of the Ancient Legal System of Deed Tax in China), *Jiangxi shehui kexue* (Jiangxi Social Sciences), no. 11 (2004): 99–102.

[40] "Shihuo sanwu zhi yiliu" (Food and Commodities, 35–16), in *Song huiyao jigao* (Song Government Manuscript Compendium), 5416.

and sellers who sell their lands and houses, for fear of paying tax, fabricate and refuse to write the deeds as required. Instead, they often write such deeds as pledges of the house in the name of borrowing money. Such vague writing often invokes litigation."[41] Perhaps it was because *dian* transactions were taxable that the official documents of the Song Dynasty characterized "*dian*" as "valid *dian*" (*zhengdian*) and, like "sale" (*mai*), it was known as "proper trade" (*zhenghang jiaoyi*); since mortgage (*didang*) (usually usury) tended to cause vulnerable peasants to lose their landownership, the government disparaged it as "invalid mortgage" (*yidang*).[42] The Chinese character "*yi*" refers to something biased or distorted.

The Song government responded to private tax avoidance with both soft and hard measures. On the one hand, the government repeatedly extended the time limit for filing deeds, from 1 to 2 months to one hundred days in the Northern Song Dynasty and even to 6 months in the early Southern Song Dynasty; on the other hand, the government also required that if the tax were not paid within the time limit, it would be doubled, the so-called double tax (*beishui*), and the penalty would be increased to the point of forfeiture of the property.[43] In order to avoid late payment of the "double tax," many people simply traded using white deeds and did not submit the deeds to the government.[44] However,

[41] "Tianzhai·dianmai jiu" (No. 9, Land and House, Dian Transaction), in *Dayuan shengzheng guochao dianzhang hubu* (Statutes of the Yuan dynasty, Ministry of Revenue), *juan* 5 (Beijing: Zhongguo guangbo dianshi Press, 1998), 49.

[42] Volume 6 contains the text of Ye Yanfeng's judgment on "*yidang*" (invalid mortgage), in *Minggong shupan qingmingji* (Collections of Well-Crafted and Just Verdicts of Scholar-Bureaucrats in the Song Dynasty), 170. It is recorded that "Should all places of people's land and houses, where there is a *dian* transaction and must be done in a valid way. [Both parties] should clearly establish deeds, pay taxes on time, and not to set the monthly interest, gaining money through valid mortgage." See "Shihuo sanqi zhi eryi" (Food and Commodities 37–12), *Song huiyao jigao* (Song Government Manuscript Compendium), 5454.

[43] Gao Nan, *Songdai minjian caichan jiufen yu susong wenti yanjiu* (Study on Civil Property Disputes and Litigation in Song Dynasty) (Kunming: Yunnan University Press, 2009), 44–46.

[44] "Shihuo liuyi zhi wuba" (Food and Commodities 61–58), in *Song huiyao jigao* (Song Government Manuscript Compendium), 5903.

for private transactions of white deeds, the Southern Song government requested a "white deed tax" (*baiqi shuiqian*).[45]

Regarding the *dian* transaction, the subsequent or related transactions (including additions, transfers, sales, and redemptions) were also more complicated regarding procedures and taxes. In the case of addition (*tiandian*), where the *dian* seller requested more money from the *dian* buyer, as the *dian* price increased, this increase had to be taxed; when a *dian* transaction turned into a sale, the price was also increased, and it had to be taxed again.[46] It is worth noting that the redemption process (*huishu*) could also require the payment of taxes, as indicated by the Southern Song government's revenue records: "the owner of a certain piece of land paid the price for the redemption of it."[47] The sale and redemption constituted a single *dian* transaction but required two tax payments. The reason lay in that since the *dian* transaction had to go through the government, the redemption naturally had to be approved by the government, and it was logical and "reasonable" to pay the tax on the redemption. Accordingly, the *dian* transfer was also taxable because it could be regarded as another *dian* transaction. Although we have not found any explicit regulations from the Song Dynasty, this was the case in the late Qing Dynasty when Emperor Xuantong reformed the *dian* tax system: "In cases of transfer of *dian*, taxes should be paid separately according to the regulations."[48] It is evident that the government was trying hard to collect taxes, and the people were not satisfied with it.

[45] Wei Tian'an, "Songdai de qiyue" (Deed Tax in the Song Dynasty), *Zhongzhou xuekan* (Academic Journal of Zhongzhou), no. 3 (2009): 19–201.

[46] In August 1028, an imperial edict was issued: "After the tax If the amount of *dian* money is added to the deed, or if the *dian* transaction has become a sale, according to the rules of the Beijing Commercial Tax Court, the tax is collected only according to the money added and bought, and the deed is stamped before the deed is posted." See "Shihuo liuyi zhi wujiu" (Food and Commodities 61–59), *Song huiyao jigao* (Song Government Manuscript Compendium), 5904.

[47] Xie Shenfu, "Jingzongzhi tidianxingyusi shen qifa shouzhi zongzhi qianwu zhang" (Additional Miscellaneous Taxes in Song Dynasty·The Department of Criminal Justice Applied for and Proposed a Total Account of Receiving and Spending of the Miscellaneous Taxes), in *Qingyuan tiaofa shilei* (The Law Code of the Qingyuan Reign), *juan* 30 (Harbin: Heilongjiang People's Press, 2002), 459.

[48] *Shengjing shibao* (Shengjing Daily), August 20, 1909, which is quoted from "Ten kanshū, Foroku" (Customary Practices of Dian, Appendix), *Kisaki-hen dai ni-kan furoku* (Report on the Survey of Old Manchurian Customs), 13.

In fact, the payment of the deed tax of the *dian*, the seller's offer of the *dian*, and even the redemption had to be processed by the local government, and these cumbersome procedures were contrary to the transaction characteristics of the *dian*. Since the *dian* seller could redeem the land after 3 or 5 years (a short period), there was no need to go through the government. However, to secure tax revenue, the state required that the relevant procedures be carried out at the government office, resulting in high collection costs. The Yuan Dynasty inherited the system from the Song Dynasty, which was probably still the case in the Ming Dynasty.[49] This situation changed during the Qing Dynasty. The Qing state initially followed the Ming law and required the payment of the *dian* tax,[50] but in the thirteenth year of the Yongzheng era (1735), it was abolished.

> "The *dian* transaction with a revocable deed is a temporary and private loan and is originally not being taxed as sales. In the future, for the parties to a *dian* transaction, there is no need to submit the deed, get sealed, or pay taxes by silver, and they can transact at their convenience."[51]

These two sentences reveal the debt character of the *dian*, which was not materially different from ordinary transactions such as borrowing, land mortgages, and rent deposits, and there was no transaction tax on lending transactions. In 1759, the Ministry of Finance (*hubu*) regulated that: "where the private *dian* transactions of houses with revocable deeds, all [are] exempt from their taxes." This example was accepted into law in 1761. In 1770, the Ministry of Finance agreed on the following rules:

[49] Bian Li argues that in the Ming period, there was no specific and clear regulation on the pledging and sale of land and houses, tax deeds, or the text of the sale deeds. Bian Li, "Mingqing diandang he jiedai falü guifan de tiaozheng yu xiangcun shehui de wending" (The Adjustment of Pawning and Lending Laws and the Stability of Rural Society in the Ming and Qing Dynasties), *Zhongguo nongshi* (Agricultural History of China), no. 4 (2005): 66–75.

[50] *Daqing lüli* (Qing Law Code) followed the text of the third year of the Shunzhi reign (1646). The contents of "dianmai tianzhai" (Dian Transactions of Lands and Houses) almost exactly copied the "hulü yi·tianzhai·dianmai tianzhai" (Laws of the Ministry of Revenue·Houses and Lands·Dian Transactions of Lands and Houses) in *Daminglu jijie fulu* (Ming Law Code), *juan* 5. See *Daqing lüli*, collated by Huai Xiaofeng (Beijing: falü Press, 1999), 55.

[51] Kun Gang, "Hubu zafu jinli" (The Ministry of Revenue, Miscellaneous Taxes, Prohibitions), in *Daqing huidian shili* (The Collected Institutes and Precedents of the Great Qing), *juan* 247 (Taipei: Xinwenfeng chuban gufen youxian gongsi, 1978), 8365.

"In the future, when the banner and civil people *dian* sold their lands and houses, the years written on the deeds should be uniformly three, five, and even 10 years; still under the old rules, all [were] tax-free."[52] On the one hand, this was an initiative to benefit the people. On the other hand, it shows that the essential characteristics of *dian* transactions, especially the difference between *dian* and sale, were fully understood during this period.

Although the Qianlong emperor issued a decree on tax exemptions for the *dian* fields, the local governments intentionally or unintentionally delayed the process because it was a considerable source of income for them. This was the case in Fujian Province, and the governor had to give strict orders:

> "As the officials are mostly idle, the notice is issued to inform the public. Although it is required that the notices be posted in public, half of them are not hung, so civilians have no way to know about them. Now that *dian* transactions with revocable deeds do not require tax payment, tax officials are not happy to hear this. Some officials may hide the information on purpose and prevent the emperor's benevolence from reaching out to the public. Therefore, this is a special publication of the notice for promulgation with earnest orders."[53]

The Fujian governor strongly urged the local officials to put up notices to exempt the deeds from taxation, which shows that the "tax exemption for *dian* lands" (*diantian mianshui*) was implemented nationwide during the Qianlong Dynasty. There were indeed few records of deed taxes in the Qing Dynasty.

It is unclear when the "tax exemption for *dian* lands" was implemented in the Qing Dynasty, but it probably lasted in most areas until the end of Guangxu. Before rectifying the tax deeds of lands and houses in the first year of Xuantong (1909), "no tax was charged on deeds that were less than 20 years" [其未满20年之典契, 向不收税]. However, the new tax system was established at this time, and in the first year of Xuantong,

52 Ma Jianshi, Yang Yuchang eds., "Hubu zhailü" (The Ministry of Revenue, House laws), in *Daqing luli tongkao jiaozhu* (A General Examination of Statutes and Sub-statutes of the Great Qing), *juan* 9 (Beijing: Zhongguo zhengfa University Press, 1992), 437.

53 Kong Zhaoming ed., *Fujian shengli·tianzhai li·dianye mianshui* (Fujian Province Example, Examples of Lands and Houses, The Tax Exemption for *Dian* Properties) (Taipei: datong Books, 1987), 441.

the tax for *dian* lands was unified to 6 cents (*fen*) for one tael of *dian* price.[54] Most provinces, where the new tax rate was actually low, took the opportunity to raise it this time, such as Jilin and Zhili.[55] Under the fiscal crisis of the late Qing Dynasty, tax collection was pervasive, and even transfers of *dian* were taxed.

Compared with the general transactions, the transaction amount of the *dian* land was not insignificant, and the tax amount was also considerable. For example, in 1911, Wen Guiqing established a *dian* deed, and the *dian* price was 2600 *diao*. The Fengtian fenghuangting taxed six *fen* on every tael of silver of the *dian* price and collected a total of 17 taels, three *qian*, two *fen*, eight *li*.[56] The scale of this transaction and the *dian* tax were quite representative. Half of this collection of *dian* taxes went to the central government, and the local government kept half. Both the central and local governments actively collected the *dian* tax. Since local governments were very dependent on taxes, it is possible that some local governments in the late Qing Dynasty also collected the deed tax. For example, in May 1864, a "license" from Taiwan County shows that Liu Kuai, a landowner, *dian* sold his land to Huang Huang for 1 year in 1863, receiving 30% of the proceeds [受种三分]. Huang Huang paid 66 taels of silver for the deed and one tael of nine *qian* and eight *fen* for the

[54] According to *Dongsansheng zhenglue* (The Political Strategy of the Three Eastern Provinces), there was still no taxation in the 33rd year of the Guangxu's reign (1907). It was only in the "Tax and Deed Regulations" (*shuiqi zhangcheng*) of that year that the tax on deeds was stipulated, the purpose of which was **"fear of treacherous people to use sale as *dian* transaction to avoid the tax. So the tax rate was set at six *fen*, the *dian* seller will still pay half of the tax at the time of redemption."** See "Ten Ten kanshū, Foroku" (Customary Practices of Dian, Appendix), *Kisaki-hen dai ni-kan furoku* (Report on the Survey of Old Manchurian Customs) (Tokyo: Kabushikigaisha shūei-sha, 1913), 10.

[55] "Zhuojia shiban shuiqi zhangcheng" (Regulations on Additions of Deed Taxes), "lands and houses in *dian* transactions should be levied *dian* tax. However, there are provinces whose *dian* tax was reduced by half of the sale tax, and there are other provinces that levy taxes on lands and houses in *dian* transactions as that of sale tax." This was the same as in Jilin Province. The *dian* tax was reduced to three *fen* due to civil complaints, but was later unified. See *Jilin guanbao* (Jilin Official Journal), vol. 26, which is quoted from "Ten Ten kanshū, Foroku" (Customary Practices of Dian, Appendix), *Kisaki-hen dai ni-kan furoku* (Report on the Survey of Old Manchurian Customs) (Tokyo: Kabushikigaisha shūei-sha, 1913), 15–16.

[56] "Ten Ten kanshū, Foroku" (Customary Practices of Dian, Appendix), *Kisaki-hen dai ni-kan furoku* (Report on the Survey of Old Manchurian Customs) (Tokyo: Kabushikigaisha shūei-sha, 1913), 15–16.

tax.[57] The deed tax here was precisely 3%, which was half of the tax on the sale of land.

Although the Qing government waived the tax on the deed of *dian* for a long time, it still issued standard *dian* deeds. "The standard deeds were sent to the paperwork stores to be bought by the people," so that they did not have to go to the county offices to purchase them.[58] Most *dian* sellers and buyers used these deeds with their private seals or fingerprints, and officials rarely certified or collected taxes on them. A survey of local customs during the Republican Period confirms this. For example, in Yangshan County, Jiangsu Province, "where a *dian* transaction of real estate is agreed upon through the middleman, only a private contract is made, no tax or official deed is made." In the Republican Period, "there were new rules for the *dian* taxation. However, since the old rules have been in place for a long time, it was difficult to implement the new regulations."[59] As there was no tax on *dian* transactions before the late Qing Dynasty and no need to go to the government for processing, people found it hard to accept the new practices. However, since white deeds without the official seal had a lower legal effect in disputes, while red

[57] In Taiwan, "in a *dian* transaction of land and house, one should be taxed in accordance with the regulations, and receive the deed as evidence. Violators would be confiscated half of the *dian* price as a penalty and are required to pay back all the taxes. This has long been practiced as the norm." Since the official deed of Taiwan County had been used up to this time, the local government temporarily used "license" instead. "Once the renewal of the deed has been issued, the deed received will be sent to the accounting office; the tax will be filled in with the same number as before and attached to the end of the deed. The deed will then be given to the transaction parties as evidence of possession. The previous certificates will be canceled and destroyed." **See "No. 30 zhizhao" (No. 30 Licenses) (The eighth day of the fifth lunar month of the third year of Tongzhi), in *Wuquan* (Property Rights), 902–803.**

[58] Suzhou zhoushi wenshu (Suzhou Zhou's Paper) records that in 1735, "Jiangnan Jiangsu dengchu chengxuan buzhengsi wei qingdu tianfang shuiyin dengshi" (Provincial Administration Commission of Jiangnan, Jiangsu, and other places, for the Request of Reducing the Taxes of Lands and Houses) (1735), quoted from Takeshi Hamashita and Mio Kishimoto eds., *Dongyang wenhua yanjiusuo suocang Zhongguo tudi wenshu mulu jieshuo* (Explanation, Catalog of Chinese Land Documents stored in Oriental Culture Research Institute), vol.1 (Tokyo: Oriental Culture Research Institute, Tokyo University, 1983), 63.

[59] *Minshi xiguan* (Civil Customs), 213.

deeds with the official seal were legally stronger, red deeds with the official seal were often found in folk documents.[60] To apply for the official deed, one needs to pay a fee. For example, Fuzhou Prefecture "established the official deed of the *dian* land according to the ministry's orders." At the end of the official deed form, it stated that "each deed is sold for five *wen* and the Department of Law (*jiesi*) charges for the cost of oil and paper; it will not take more than necessary, which will be a burden to the ordinary people."[61] In Fengtian, at the end of the Qing Dynasty, the labor cost of each deed was six *qian*.[62]

To sum up, the Qing state was freer and simpler than the Song state in *dian* transactions. The Qing government did not levy transaction taxes for a long time, nor did it require the transfer of property rights to the government, leaving it to the private sector to trade voluntarily. In the middle of the Qianlong's reign, after a period of discussion and pilot schemes, the government approved the civil *dian* deed form and never fully restored the "contract" form of deed pervasive in the Song Dynasty. The Song dynasty's practices of making deeds at the government level, transferring land tax and property rights, and paying transaction tax complemented each other. Moreover, the local government kept a copy of the contract deed for purposes of tax collection. Since there was no need to pay transaction tax in the Qing Dynasty, the local government no longer kept the contract deed.

The Qing regulations were also more in line with the characteristics of *dian* transactions. The redeeming feature of the *dian* was that the transaction evaded government control and taxation. Since the land property would be returned to its original owner after a certain period (for example, 3–5 years), both parties to the transaction would have tried to circumvent the government's tedious procedures and traded on their

[60] Nearly 2,000 copies of the Shanxi *dian* deeds in the Tsinghua University collection have been compiled, including 61 red deeds from before 1909.

[61] Fujian shifan University lishixi (Fujian Normal University History Department), ed., *Mingqing Fujian jingji qiyue wenshu xuanji* (Beijing: People's Press, 1997), 1–2.

[62] "This tax should be filled out and issued with a license, and each sheet should be charged with 6 *qian* of silver, with 3 *qian* as the paper capital (labor) capital, and 3 *qian* as a reward for the clerk who undertakes the work. ... All the deeds that have been taxed should be attached a license and a seal on the perforation." *Shengjing shibao* (Shengjing daily), August 20, 1909, which is quoted from "Ten Ten kanshū, Foroku" (Customary Practices of Dian, Appendix), *Kisaki-hen dai ni-kan furoku* (Report on the Survey of Old Manchurian Customs) (Tokyo: Kabushikigaisha shūei-sha, 1913), 13.

own. If the Qing state had imposed a transaction tax like the Song state, the local government would have had to take corresponding measures to deal with the tax avoidance behavior, which would have led to high collection costs. The subsequent procedures for the related *dian* field transactions (including additions, transfers, sales from *dian* transactions, and redemptions) would have been more complicated.

These changes reflect the more liberal nature of private *dian* transactions in the Qing Dynasty and the more accurate understanding of the substance of the *dian* by the Qing people. The Song Dynasty's practices of making deeds at the government level and transferring the land tax and property rights, as well as the *dian* taxes imposed by the late Qing government, were driven by the state's tax interests. However, these caused much inconvenience to both parties to the transaction and restricted re-transactions, such as renting and *dian* transferring.

4.3 Types of *Dian* Deeds: from "Contract" to "Single Deed"

Correspondingly, the types of *dian* **deeds in the Song and Qing dynasties were also very different. The** *dian* **deeds in the Song Dynasty were in the form of "contracts," while the Qing people commonly used single deeds (*danqi*). The change in the form of the deed reflects the difference in the understanding of** *dian* **transactions in different eras. However, little research has been done on this issue, and there were few studies to reveal the reason behind this change.**[63]

Deeds and the Redemption of the Dian

The salient feature of the *dian* transaction was the redemption of the land after the agreed-upon term at the original price. In the Song Dynasty, the *dian* transaction took the form of "matched deeds in the two identical contracts" (*heqi tongyue*), with each party holding a certificate that could be coupled up like a tiger talisman when the *dian* seller redeemed the land from the *dian* buyer. The form of the "matched deed to form the same

[63] Yu Jiang, "'Qiyue' yu 'hetong' zhibian—yi qigndai qiyue wenshu wei chufadian" (The Identification of "Contracts" and "Contracts"—The Qing Dynasty Contract Documents as a Starting Point), *China's Social Science* (Social Sciences in China), no,6 (2003): 134–149.

contract" could reduce the occurrence of disputes, and its style was similar to that of the modern contract, which has a seal on the perforation.[64] In the Song Dynasty, it was stipulated by Song Taizu that: "In the case of a *dian* transaction of lands and houses, a contract deed is used, and the lender (*dian* buyer) and the landowner (*dian* seller) to a transaction keep half of it respectively. It is a common practice worldwide and is known to everyone." The rule lasted until the Song Dynasty.[65]

In order to reduce disputes over land transactions, the government of the Northern Song even issued a quadruplicate sheet (*siliandan*) in 1022.[66] The Song State also stipulated that the ***dian*** seller and the ***dian*** buyer must go to the government together and ask for the purchase of the standard deed contract, filling in the amount of the transaction and the agreed period, and then proceeding on the spot.[67] The Yuan state inherited from the Southern Song and also made provisions for *dian* transactions:

> "In the case of a *dian* transaction, in addition to meeting to exchange the documents, [the seller and buyer] must write a deed and a contract on two pieces of paper. They must sign both of them and pay taxes at the local

[64] Zhang Chuanxi, *Qiyue shi maidiquan yanjiu* (A Study of the Contractual History of Land Purchase Vouchers) (Beijing: Zhonghua Books, 2008), 40–53.

[65] Puyang "dianmai yuanwu jiwu qiyue nanyi qushu" (It was difficult to redeem a house without a *dian* deed), in *Minggong shupan qingmingji* (Collections of Well-Crafted and Just Verdicts of Scholar-Bureaucrats in the Song Dynasty), 149.

[66] "Should sell the houses and lands on invalid mortgages and make four copies of the contract deed: one for the buyer, one for the seller, one for the commercial tax institute, and one for the county court." See "Shihuo liuyi zhi wuqi" (Food and Commodities, 61–57), in *Song huiyao jigao* (Song Government Manuscript Compendium), 5902. In the Southern Song Dynasty, a distinction was made between the official issue of the original deed and the copy of the contract, which was different from the contract deed of the Northern Song Dynasty, where both parties had the same status. It was stipulated that "in a *dian* transaction of house and land, according to the law, there should be an official deed and a contract deed. The *dian* seller and buyer each hold one of them as evidence of redemption." See "Shihuo liuyi zhi liusi" (Food and Commodities, 61–64), in *Song huiyao jigao* (Song Government Manuscript Compendium), 5905.

[67] "In a *dian* transaction, the *dian* seller should go with the *dian* buyer to the court to request the purchase of the official deed, and to fill out the general contract deed, with the amount of money, the number of years, and the very person who takes the responsibility. All fees and taxes should be paid at the court." See "Shihuo liuyi zhi liusi" (Food and Commodities, 61–64), in *Song huiyao jigao* (Song Government Manuscript Compendium), 5905.

> court. The *dian* buyer shall take possession of the original deed, and the *dian* seller shall take possession of the contract. Although the term might be long, the land can be redeemed with a deed. This is to eliminate the disadvantage of possible litigation."[68]

In order to facilitate future redemption, the parties to the *dian* transaction adopted "two identical contracts of matched deeds" (*heqi tongyue*), which reflected the characteristics of a *dian* transaction, that is, redeemability. It is the essential difference from a sale, as the *dian* buyer does not have the right to dispose of the property and must return the land at the original price at the end of the contract.

During the Ming and Qing dynasties, *dian* transactions usually no longer required such a complicated contract format. For example, the "pawn land deeds" (*dangtianqi*) and "pawn house deeds" (*dangwuqi*) of that time, as cited in Chen Jiru's *Chidu shuangyu* [尺牍双鱼] of the Ming Dynasty, were both single deeds.[69] However, the "contract" of using a house for security can still be seen from time to time in Chinese materials. For instance, in the 33rd year of the Wanli reign (1605), the "house contract *dian* purchased by Hong Jiayong" in Qimen County, Huizhou Prefecture, stated that "this contract is established on two pieces of paper, and each party holds one piece of paper for records."[70] In the late Qing and Republican periods, the "contract" form can still be found in the civil customs of China.[71]

68 "Tianling, dianmai tianchan shili" (The Land Order-Cases of Sales of Property), *Dayuan tongzhi tiaoge* (Comprehensive Regulations of the Great Yuan Dynasty), *juan* 16, collated by Guo Chengwei (Beijing: falü Press, 2000), 206.

69 Chen Jiru, "Chidu shuangyu" (Paired Carp (Personal Correspondence)), quoted from Zhang Chuanxi ed., *Zhongguo lisdai qiyue huibian kaoshi* (Examinations of the Compilation of Chinese Deeds of Each Dynasty), vol. 2 (Beijing: Beijing University Press, 1995), 1029–1030.

70 Zhang Chuanxi, *Qiyue shi maidiquan yanjiu* (A study of the contractual history of land purchase vouchers), vol.2 (Beijing: Zhonghua Books, 2008), 1026. The Qing deeds collected in this book are all single deeds. The 20 "contracts" of the Qing collected in this book are not *dian* deeds.

71 In Kunshan County, a the time a deed of *dian* was established, a receipt of redemption would be issued. "The word 'contract' was written on both the *dian* deed and the receipt, which serves as evidence as upper deed and lower deed." **When the *dian* seller redeemed the property at the original price, he should deliver the receipt to the *dian* buyer and take back the *dian* deed or destroy it.** See *Minshi xiguan* (Civil Customs), 203. In Jinshan County, in a revocable sale (*huodian*), there were two set of deeds. The

It is difficult to verify when the "contract" form of the deed ceased to be the strictly standard format, but the problems reflected in the changing format of the deed were intriguing. During the Qianlong's reign, local and central governmental exploration and discussion on the "contract" format provided a rare case study. In the 25th year of Qianlong's reign (1760), the Fujian governor attempted to restore contractual deeds by issuing a "pair of deeds" (*duiqi*) in the form of coupled upper and lower deeds, but this local regulation was ultimately not effectively implemented.

> "Now the upper-and-lower contract deed form is promulgated. [One should] write the number of acres of land, location, amount of grain, the amount of rent, price of silver, and the length of the term clearly one by one [on the contract deed]. If the property is a *dian* property, the contract should include both an upper and a lower deed, written by one hand. The middleman should sign on the spot. In the junction of upper and lower deeds, the words "upper-and-lower *dian* deed contract" should be written in large letters. Then the contract is split in half, with the *dian* buyer holding the upper deed and the *dian* seller holding the lower deed, each holding a piece of paper as evidence so that when the *dian* seller (original owner) holds the lower deed to redeem the land from the *dian* buyer, he should take back the upper deed."[72]

The above case was almost the same as the Song Dynasty contract form, except that the "left and right contract" (*zuoyou hetong*) deed may be replaced by a "contract of upper and lower" (*hetong shangxia*) deed.

However, this type of contract deed was not heeded by ordinary people, and the Fujian governor's attempt was not successful. The government's implementation of the "pair of deeds" contract in Fujian was intended to eliminate disputes in *dian* transactions and to facilitate

dian seller established the main deed (*zhengqi*) and gave it to the *dian* buyer; while the *dian* buyer made another sub-deed (*fuqi*), and offered it to the seller, for the future land redemption. See *Minshi xiguan* (Civil Customs), 194; in Changan County, Shaanxi Province, "in a civil *dian* transaction of land, the *dian* seller establishes two copies of deeds, and writes '*qifeng*' (peforation) at the end of the date. The text says that the local contract contains two copies of papers, and each party to a transaction holds one copy of contract; later when the *dian* seller redeems the land from the *dian* buyer, he then uses the contract as proof." See *Minshi xiguan* (Civil Customs), 363.

[72] Kong Zhaoming ed., *Fujian shengl i· tianzhai li · dianmai qishi* (Fujian Province Example, Examples of Lands and Houses, Deed Types of Dian Transactions), 443.

"the *dian* seller holding the lower deed for redemption" [典产者仍得执下契以取赎], but in fact, it did not work. In 1783, the Fujian governor investigated the implementation of the above provisions and found that:

> "If the *dian* buyer fabricates a sale deed, how can [we] guarantee that the original *dian* seller does not falsify the contract? Suppose that in the case where the seller converts the sale of his land from a conditional sale to an irrevocable sale or the previous corresponding [*dian*] deed has not been destroyed [after the seller changes the *dian* transaction of land to an irrevocable sale], the original *dian* seller insisted on the redemption. The old middleman has passed away, and there is no evidence of the matter, which leads to total confusion. Our anticipation of removing one disadvantage actually gives rise to a new disadvantage. It seems better to follow people's conveniences and allow them to trade by themselves. There is no need to set up corresponding deeds that might trigger new disputes."

New problems may also arise, especially if the original owner fabricates the deed privately and alters it.[73] Therefore, this reform to the deed form ended up returning to the pre-existing civil custom of single deeds.

The Qing central government also debated the form of the deed. In the 29th year of the Qianlong reign (1764), Jiang Bing, an assistant minister of the Ministry of War, submitted a report on civil

[73] "These insidious people's tricks are full of loopholes. The original landowner, by virtue of holding one copy of the deed from the deed pairs, fabricates the deed by reducing the years of the agreed term, or rewriting the *dian* price of silver as low, in an attempt to extort; until the prosecution, the two parties each has his own opinion. Or due to the death of the original witness (middleman), there is no proof of the transaction. As it is still easy to confuse the true and false, it is necessary to prevent its drawbacks. How should we try to identify these tricks, especially to prevent the original landowners, who hold one copy of the deed from the deed pairs, from fabricating the deeds by reducing the years and price? This is what we cannot guarantee. However, there is a slight distinction between the original writing and the imitation of the writing when one tries to fabricate the deed. But it is still difficult to identify all the devilish tricks. Please do as suggested, and it could be easier to eliminate the disadvantage." See Kong Zhaoming ed., *Fujian shengli · tianzhai li · minjian huodian chanye wuyong sheli duiqi* (Fujian Province Example, Examples of Lands and Houses, to promote the civil *dian* transaction, it is not necessary to establish the pair of deeds), 449. This situation may occur, but it should not be the main reason. A similar situation occurred in the Song Dynasty, where "[people] intend to be greedy, increase the number of transactions of money, or change the year of the yuan dian, or a wide range of boundaries. All sorts of foul play, each resulting in a complaint." See "Shihuo liuyi zhi liusi" (Food and Commodities, 61–64), *Song huiyao jigao* (Song Government Manuscript Compendium), 5905.

deeds, suggesting that "two separate deeds—one main deed and one vice-principal deed—should be established. [The buyer and seller] take possession of one deed, respectively." However, the Ministry of Finance considered it unnecessary because "The deed of *dian* has always been kept and held by the *dian* buyer. The evidence of a middleman in the deed is clear, and the deed is clearly signed, sufficient as a certificate of trust, and there is no need to create a duplicate deed to eliminate the mischief."[74]

This case shows that the form of single deed prevailing in folk practice was simple and convenient; its information and content were sufficient to form the credit and legal effect of the transaction. Therefore, improving the market mechanism was an important reason for simplifying the deed form in the Qing Dynasty. In addition, in the Qing, the distinction between the rules of the transactions of *dian* and sale was already fully and socially accepted. Hence, it was not necessary to distinguish them by deed form.

Single Deeds and Transactions

The second reason for the change in the deed was that various subsequent transactions in the Qing Dynasty were becoming more frequent, and the contractual deed was rather inconvenient. In contrast, the single deed was more suitable for subsequent transactions such as transfers of *dian*. In the case of a single deed, whether the debtor (*dian* seller) renewed the deed or added to it, or the creditor (*dian* buyer) transferred the deed, it was only necessary to add a note on the single deed paper stating "*dian* transfer at the original price recorded in the contract" [原约原价转典] or "the original price of silver" [元银元价] to transfer the deed, which was easy to do.[75] However, in the case of a contract deed, a subsequent

[74] Kong Zhaoming ed., *Fujian shengli · tianzhai li · minjian huodian chanye wuyong sheli duiqi* (Fujian Province Example, Examples of Lands and Houses, to promote the civil *dian* transaction, it is not necessary to establish the pair of deeds), 449–450.

[75] In 1874,"On the sixth day of the tenth month of the third year of the Tongzhi era, [Ji Weili's] *dian* land was transferred to Ji Yinglong at the original price recorded in the previous deed"; and in 1878, "On the fourth day of the fourth month of the fourth year of the Guangxu reign, [Ji Weili] transferred the *dian* land to Liu Gengsan at the original price of the previous *dian* deed," in "Lixie dangchang qiren Ji Weili" (Ji Weili, the Deed Holder) (1857), in *The Tsinghua Collection of Deeds*, not yet numbered. In 18,570, Ji Xingnan "transferred the land to Li, with the middleman, at the original price of the

transfer was likely to require a new deed, as it was a new *dian* transaction. In particular, according to the regulations of the Song Dynasty, each *dian* transaction was subject to delivery and taxation procedures according to available sources, while in the Qing Dynasty, single deeds were more convenient. For example, a land deed of Shanxi Province in the Qing Dynasty, "A *Dian* Transfer Deed made by Duan Qingzhen," recorded that the piece of land he had *dian* purchased had been transferred five times during the 65 years from 1839 to 1904. All of them were annotated on the original deed as follows:

> In the nineteenth year of the Daoguang's reign (1839), "a deed is established to transfer the *dian* land to Wu Lü zhong to cultivate, at the price of 160 taels of silver".
> In the twenty-sixth year of the Daoguang's reign (1846), "Wu Erliang transferred the land to *Sanhebao* at the original *dian* price".
> In the twenty-eighth year of the Daoguang's reign (1848), "*Sanhexin* transferred the land to Li Tinghui for farming through the middleman Wu Chengning. The land will be redeemed regardless of the term when Duan pays silver".
> In the ninth year of the Xianfeng's reign (1859), "Li Tinghui transferred the land to Li Tianyu for farming at the original *dian* price".
> In the thirtieth year of the Guangxu reign (1904), "Li Tinghui transferred parts of the land to Family Yang and Family Li".[76]

As seen from the deeds, the handwriting of each transfer was different. The first three transfers were made only 7 years and 2 years apart. If the contract deeds of the Song Dynasty were used at that time, each transfer would have required a separate deed from the previous deeds of *dian*, which was a tedious and complicated procedure and prone to forgery.[77] In the case of a single deed, the transfer could be done several times, and

previous deed," in "li dangchangren Ji Xingnan" (Ji Xingnan, The Deed Holder) (1860), in *The Tsinghua Collection of Deeds*, not yet numbered.

[76] The Tsinghua Collection of Deeds, no. T0964.

[77] It is recorded that "from 1167 to 1177, Fan Shen *dian* sold his house to Ding Yi and charged three times at the total price of 192 *guan*. Ding Yi's family member Ding Shuxian paid twice, respectively in 1204 and 1205, and the total amount of payment was 182 *guan*. The Ding family then transferred the land to Ding Bowei for cultivation and possession." See "Huhunmen qushu" (Household marriage, redemption), in *Minggong shupan qingmingji* (Collections of Well-Crafted and Just Verdicts of Scholar-Bureaucrats in the Song Dynasty), *juan* 9, 321–322.

the addition of the *dian* and the supplementary payment (*zhaojia*) could be done again and again until it was changed from a *dian* transaction to a sale. The *dian* seller and the *dian* buyer only needed to mark the original deed. If each time a new deed was made, the transaction costs would increase; if each transaction had to go to the county government office for processing and paying taxes, it was even more laborious and costly.

In another case of additions (*tiandian*), for example, in "Wuzhuan's *dian* land deed" [吴砖典地契] made in the sixth year of the Xianfeng's reign (1856), the *dian* price was 50 *dayuan*. At the end of the deed, it was written that "in the first month of the second year of Tongzhi, ten *dayuan* of silver were added to this *dian* transaction. Indicated at the deed end." In a *dian* deed established in 1849, a note was added to the 11 dayuan: "it was again indicated that two *yuan* and five *jiao* of silver were added by borrowing in 1865."[78] These diversified types of related transactions were all manifestations of the development of *dian* rights. Since these diverse types of transactions were not yet common in the Song Dynasty, the rules of the *dian* did not need to be taken into account; in the Qing Dynasty, the types of transactions of the *dian* became increasingly abundant, and new practices and rules needed to be formed accordingly (Fig. 4.1).

This was also the case with the supplementary payment (*zhaojia*) of the *dian*. In the twenty-third year of the Jiaqing's reign (1818), a white deed of the *dian* land contained the following.

> I, Han Licao, establish the *dian* deed of flatland. Because of the shortage of money, today, [I have] this flat land in the west of the village, an area of one *mu* one *fen* two *li*, facing north to south. The area is clearly defined from the east to Nan Xipeng's, from the west to Han Lijie's, from the south to a path, and from the north to Nan Fuduo's. The deed is made to *dian* transfer the land to Nan Fuduo for farming. [I] spoke clearly to the middleman that the price at the time was 20 taels of silver for three years. The money is paid on the same day the land is transferred with no arrears. [I am afraid] I cannot prove it by my words, so I make a contract to keep records.
> September 26, the twenty-third year of the Jiangqing's reign (1818)
> Deed maker: Han Licao

[78] "Wuzhuan diandiqi" (A Dian Deed of Land by Wu Zhuan) (1856); "Li taidian shuizu yinzi" (A Deed of shuizuyin) (1849), Taipei: "Zhongyanyuan" fusinina tushuguan (Fusinian Library, Academia Sinica), not yet numbered.

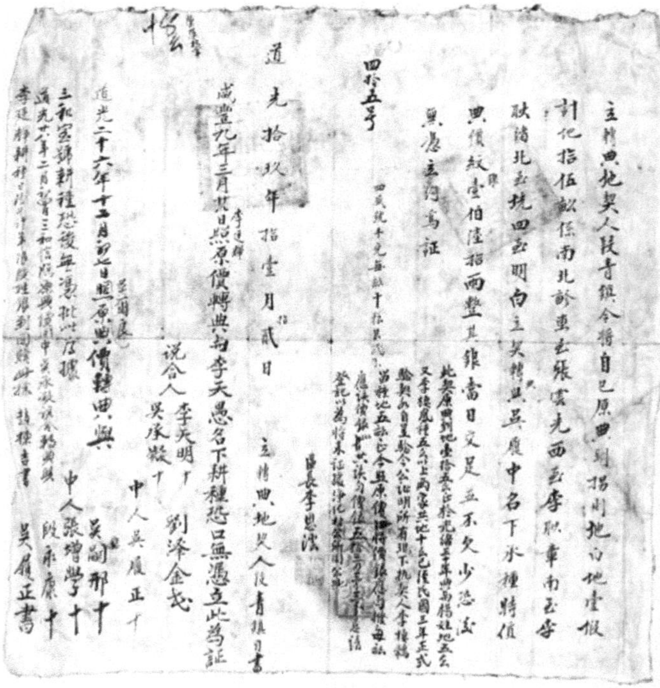

Fig. 4.1 Shanxi Farmland Deed Sample of the Qing Dynasty, "A *Dian* Transfer Deed Made By Duan Qingzhen." *Source* Tsinghua University Collection of Farmland Deeds, number: T0964

Middlemen: Nan Fumei, Han Chaohuan[79]
Subsequent notes: as fair exchange [后批南若公平兑]
Added 5000 *wen* through the original middleman on December 30th, the first year of the Daoguang's reign (1821)

In this deed, the land was *dian* sold in the twenty-third year of the Jiaqing's reign, and the agreed term of 3 years expired in 1821. Since the deed was automatically renewed, the *dian* seller requested an add-on

[79] "Lidian pingdi wen yueren Han Licao" (The Deed Maker of the Flatland Han Licao) (1818), *the Tsinghua Collection of Deeds*, not yet numbered at this time.

of 5000 *wen*. If the amount of add-on became equal to the sale price, it was possible that the *dian* seller would sell his land in a sale instead of a conditional sale.[80] A price add-on was one part of a *dian* transaction, and its alternative was similar to an installment payment.

In order to adapt to the development of *dian* rights, the Qing state changed the format of "contract" to "single deeds." Based on the folk customs of the countryside, the Qing government finally established a single-deed system after central and local government debates, reforms pilots, and a large number of investigations and surveys. This was recorded in the above case of Fujian: "according to Fuzhou and other nine prefectures and two sub-prefectures, [the governor should survey and consider the contract types] each according to the local circumstance and submit a detailed reply to [the central court]." The contract was piloted for more than 20 years, but the final choice was to respect the customs of the people, "Please obey the convenience of the people and allow them to trade on their own." This phrase was very important and reflects the government's basic orientation toward private land transactions—free trade and respect for private customs and local practices, including *dian*.

In the case of the *Xingke tiben*, when the two sides of the transaction conflicted, the magistrate, who was the arbiter, mostly had to conduct field investigations and base his verdict on local customs. This was the third reason for the change in the form of deeds, namely, the weakening of the government's control over private transactions.[81] As in the Song and Yuan dynasties, both parties to the transaction had to "visit the government to receive the contract deed" [当官收领] and pay the taxes, which was not usually required in the Qing Dynasty. Or, the Song state strictly

[80] In 1829, the Liu family *dian* sold the ancestral land of four *duan* and seven *ri* to the Sanguan temple at the Fenghuangshan for cultivation at the price of 3150 *diao*. In 1835, the Liu family requested add-on money of 150 *diao*, and another 100 *diao* in 1836. In 1837, the Liu family requested final add-on money of 400 *diao*. The price of the dian plus three add-ons, meant the irrevocable sale price was 3800 *diao*. See "Ten Ten kanshū, Foroku" (Customary Practices of Dian, Appendix), *Kisaki-hen dai ni-kan furoku* (Report on the Survey of Old Manchurian Customs) 63.

[81] The Qing Dynasty's control over the private economy was largely relaxed after its rule was firmly established, see Long Denggao, "Lishi shang Zhonggou minjian jingji de ziyou zhuyi pusu chuantong" (The Simple Tradition of Liberalism in Chinese Civil Economy), *Sixiang zhanxian* (Thinking), no. 3 (2012): 84–91.

required an official contract deed record, driven by the government's economic interests.

4.4 Conclusions

Finally, we summarize this chapter, first, on the origin and derivative rights of the *dian*.

To begin with, in the Song Dynasty, the rule that "the *dian* transaction requires leaving the property" (*dianxu liye*) reveals a process where the *dian* seller transferred the right to manage and dispose of the land to the *dian* buyer, retaining only the landownership document "land roots" (*tiangen*) or "land bones"; the *dian* buyer thus received all the proceeds of land management for an agreed term. That was the original right of *dian* rights.

Furthermore, the derivative rights and diverse expressions of the *dian* were mainly in the disposition of the right to use the *dian* land; the different misconceptions of the Song and Qing dynasties and the present-day researchers were all related to this. The lease of *dian* land was a right included in or necessarily derived from the right to manage and dispose of the land acquired by the *dian* buyer. Relying on the tenancy relationship, the expression of *dian* land transactions in the Qing Dynasty was more liberal and diverse. The *dian* buyer did not necessarily cultivate the land himself but could obtain land rent by renting out the *dian* land, which was appropriately referred to as "possession of the tenancy" (*guandian*). The *dian* buyer could either rent out the land to a third party, which was called "to invite tenants to cultivate the land and collect rents from them" (*zhaodian gengzuo, shouzu nake*), or maintain the original land tenancy relationship or rent out the land to the *dian* seller, which was called "*dian* selling the land through self-tenancy" (*chudian zidian*).

The sharecropping of *dian* land allowed the *dian* seller to satisfy his financing needs by *dian* selling the land and to maintain his income by renting and cultivating this same piece of land, and the *dian* buyer did not need to find another tenant at his own expense. However, as the land was still cultivated by the landowner who had *dian* sold the land, it was apparently a violation of the Song Dynasty stipulation: "the *dian* transaction requires [the landowner] leaving the property" rule (*dianxu liye*), which was regarded as a violation by today's researchers. Nonetheless, in fact, the self-tenancy was under the rules of *dian* rights transactions. It reflected the *dian* buyer's right to control and use the *dian* land, including the free trade of land user rights.

The development of tenancy in *dian* transactions in the Qing Dynasty was a phenomenon of the Song Dynasty but gave rise to another misunderstanding. The "balancing of rent and interest" (*zuxi xiangdi*), "collection of rent against interest" (*shouzu dili*), and "silver without interest calculation and land without rent calculation" (*yinbu jili, tianbu jizu*) can be found in the deeds of *dian* make the *dian* transactions seem to be a trade between interest and rent. However, suppose we return to the first conclusion. In that case, we will see that such descriptions actually refer to transfers of the operation of the land and its income to the tenants by the *dian* buyer, who had the pure investment income of the land rent; the *dian* buyer could also get rid of the land operation and engage in commercial and industrial activities and get another source of income. In other words, the *dian* buyer received the rights and benefits to which he was entitled. Whether the *dian* buyer (the creditor) leased out the land to the *dian* seller (the original landowner and debtor), leased it to a new third-party tenant, or maintained a tenancy relationship with the existing tenants, it shows that the three parties, the landowner, the *dian* buyer, and the tenant, constructed a pattern to share land rights through market transactions.

Moreover, the *dian* buyer could also exercise the function of the security right and realize the future proceeds of the *dian* field by transferring or mortgaging it to meet his own financing needs, a way to achieve an intertemporal transfer of current and forward proceeds. It also derives from the first right.

Second, the above clarification of misconceptions shows that a *dian* transaction was not an ownership transaction. Moreover, the developed tenancy relationship of *dian* lands in the Qing Dynasty could also easily lead to the misconception that the *dian* right was a transaction of the user right. However, based on the first and third *dian* rights, it is clear that the rights and benefits of the *dian* far exceeded the right of use. In modern terminology, a *dian* was a limited right of property (other rights), including both usufruct and security, and the right of use was only a part of the usufruct.

In summary, the *dian* buyer could dispose of the *dian* land according to his own needs and preferences; he could cultivate it himself for operating income, rent it out for investment income, or transfer it or mortgage it for future income. All these types of *dian* rights not only satisfied the diverse needs and preferences of both parties to the transaction and expanded their choice but also contributed to the development of land property rights and land rights transactions in the Qing Dynasty, together with new types of land rights and transactions such as top-soil right, rent deposits, and revocable sales.

Third, the policies and regulations of the Song and Qing dynasties regarding *dian* transactions differed. In line with the regulations of "*dian* selling the land by leaving the property" (*liye diantian*), the Song Dynasty government imposed mandatory procedures, including the transfer of property rights, payment of transaction tax, and the making of the *dian* deed. Correspondingly, the Song state adopted the contractual form of deeds so that, on the one hand, it was convenient for the landowner to redeem the land by verifying the inscribed deeds. On the other hand, it was easy for the government to keep the certificates to facilitate tax collection. Because of their high value, the government spared no effort in regulating the taxation of *dian*. However, its transaction characteristics made it easy for people to avoid the government's supervision and taxation, thus pushing up the cost of tax collection.

In the Qing Dynasty, the *dian* transaction was freer and more convenient. From the Yongzheng reign onwards, the Qing government exempted the *dian* tax until the end of the Qing; moreover, either party to the transaction or even a third party could pay the land tax; further, there was no mandatory processing by the government and no requirement to transfer the property rights. Accordingly, the contractual form of the deed was changed to a single-deed form. The single-deed form was adapted to the subsequent transactions of *dian* land in the Qing, such as the transfer of the land or the continuation of the agreement between the two parties to add payment and even irrevocably sell the land. In the Qing, both parties to the transaction only needed to indicate the original *dian* deed, so the single-deed form was more convenient than the contractual deed.

All these phenomena and differences do not exist in isolation but were interrelated and compatible with an internal logic. The explanatory framework of this chapter not only clarifies the misconceptions but also reveals the differences and characteristics of the evolution of canonical rights and more deeply grasps and argues the nature and rights of ***dian***, thus helping the researchers to understand the property rights and transactions of traditional Chinese land more comprehensively.

CHAPTER 5

An Examination and Interpretation of Farmland Rights Distribution

The proportion of farmland occupied by landlords and rich peasants was an important indicator of the distribution of land rights in the modern era and a basis for understanding China's land property system and modern economy. However, there has been a lack of convincing primary data on land issues in modern China. In the 1940s and 1950s, an informative nationwide survey was conducted for land reforms under the leadership of the Chinese Communist Party. Although accurate national data were not published then, this land survey laid some foundation for subsequent statistical work. This chapter examines the proportion of land held by the top 10% of the wealthy rural class on the eve of the Land Reform Movement, based on the data collected by the land reform survey while referring to survey data from the Republican Period. According to our study, the accuracy of the data from the southern provinces was around 30% (±5%), while the data from the northern provinces was well below this level. Moreover, the actual comprehensive data was even lower than the level presented by this data if the occupation status of land rights

This chapter was originally published in *Dongnan xueshu* (Southeast Academic Research), no. 4 (2018). We are grateful for the work done by Ding Qian, Ding Mengmeng, Wang Ming, and Zhao Liang in the past 10 years.

D. Long and X. Chi, *The Institutions of Land Property Rights in China*, Palgrave Studies in Economic History,
https://doi.org/10.1007/978-981-97-5112-9_5

such as top-soil right, permanent tenancy rights, and common land was considered. This chapter argues that previous studies have exaggerated the phenomenon and trend of land concentration in modern China, and one of the crucial reasons for this exaggeration was the neglect of the role played by the negative feedback mechanisms that inhibited and hedged against the concentration of land rights.

5.1 Origin and Solution of the Issue

Reflection on the Traditional View and Data

It has long been the tendency to blame private ownership when evaluating the Chinese land system in the historical period. It was generally believed that private ownership of land triggers land annexation and concentration, thus causing peasants to lose their land; the bankruptcy and exile of peasants, in turn, brought social unrest and disorder to the existing economic order, eventually leading to social revolution. Private ownership has also been regarded as the fundamental cause of economic backwardness and the outbreak of revolution in the modern era. "Landlords and rich peasants, who accounted for about 10% of the population, occupied 70–80% of the total land." This unsubstantiated political slogan from the "Report on Land Reform Issues" (*Guanyu tudi gaige wenti de baogao*) was later incorporated into textbooks and therefore laid the foundation for a deep-rooted and widespread impression that there was a marked concentration of land in the Republican Era. It was not until the 1980s and 1990s that Chinese scholars began reflecting on and testing the fundamental notion that modern China's landholdings were uneven. As a result, landlords and rich peasants' previous land concentration rates of 70–80% have been revised to 50% of China's total land.[1]

[1] Scholars have expressed this only slightly differently. See Zhang Youyi, "Ben shiji ersanshi niandai woguo diquan fenpei de zai guji" (Re-estimation of the Distribution of Land Rights in China in the 1920s and 1930s), *China's Social Science* (Social Sciences in China), no. 2 (1988): 3–10; Guo Dehong, "Jiu Zhongguo tudi zhanyou zhuangkuang ji fahzan qushi" (Land Occupation Status and Development Trend in Old China), *China's Social Science* (Social Sciences in China), no. 4 (1989): 199–212; Wu Tingyu, "Jiu Zhongguo dizhu funong zhanyou duoshao tudi" (How Much Land the Landlords and Rich Peasants Occupied in Old China), *Shixue jikan* (Collected Papers of History Studies), no. 1 (1998): 57–62; Gao Wangling, *Zudian guanxi xinlun: dizhu, nongmin he dizu* (A New Theory of Tenancy Relations: Landlord, Peasant and Rent), Shanghai: Shanghai shudian Press, 2005.

The Land Reform of 1949–1952 supported the basic judgment on land concentration in modern China. As shown in the article "The Great Victory of the Land Reforms" (*Tudi gaige de weida shengli*), which recorded landholdings by class on the eve of the land reforms, landlords and rich peasants, who accounted for 9.4% of the population, occupied about 51.9% of the total land (as shown in Table 5.1). Almost all researchers of the Land Reform have cited this data as the most important reference. However, most of those who cited it have ignored the notes in the table, which read:

> The number of households, population, and total arable land was calculated based on the information from the 1950 annual report on agricultural production. The figures for each class were extrapolated from the proportion of each class in each region before the Land Reforms. The figures for each class differ from those published in the past and are for internal reference only.
> Each class before the Land Reforms refers to the class composition three years before the Land Reforms. (For example, the land sale by the landowner in 1949 would not change his class composition.)

It was difficult for the then-nascent regime to obtain accurate data on arable land and population in 1950, and the data on the various classes before Land Reform could only be a generalized estimate, so it was deliberately stated that the data was an estimation for "internal reference only." In other words, this data was not a statistical result based on a comprehensive survey of land reforms but more of an extrapolation. However, subsequent researchers have treated this data as actual land reform statistics, which was problematic.

Is there any survey on land reforms? In 1980, the National Bureau of Statistics published "National Arable Land Holdings by Class at the End of the Land Reforms" (*Quanguo tudi gaige jieshu shi ge jieji zhanyou gengdi qingkuang*), concluding that landlords and rich peasants, who accounted for 7.9% of the population, held 8.6% of the country's land. However, this figure was only calculated based on data from a survey of the income and expenditure of more than 15,000 peasant households in 23 provinces and autonomous regions in 1954.[2] This means

[2] After the Land Reform, the number and proportion of landlords should be much lower than before the Land Reform, because a large number of landlords were executed

Table 5.1 Arable land occupied by various classes before the land reforms. *Source* "Tudi gaige de weida shengli" [The Great Victory of Land Reforms], *1949–1952 nian Zhonghua renmin gongheguo jingji dang'an* [Economic Records of the People's Republic of China 1949–1952]

	Number of households (wanhu, *10,000 households)*		*Population* (wanren, *10,000)*		*Arable land*			
	Total	*Percentage of total*	*Total*	*Percentage of total*	*Total* (wanmu)	*Percentage of total*	*Average per house-hold* (mu)	*Average per person* (mu)
Total	10,554	100.00	46,059	100.00	150,534	100.00	14.26	3.27
Poor and hired peasants	6062	57.44	24,123	52.37	21,503	14.28	3.55	0.89
Middle peasants	3081	29.20	15,260	33.13	46,577	30.94	15.12	3.05
Rich peasants	325	3.08	2144	4.66	20,566	13.66	63.24	9.59
Landlords	400	3.79	2188	4.75	57,588	38.26	144.11	26.32
Others	686	6.49	2344	5.09	4300	2.86	6.87	1.83

that survey-based statistics may not have been aggregated nationally or at least not published, after the end of the Land Reform. The National Bureau of Statistics used this sample survey data until 1980. Data for some provinces were also mostly estimated from sample surveys or extrapolations.[3] Admittedly, under the conditions of backward information

as bullies during the movement. This was a small sample data, with an average sample size of only 652 households per province, of which about 56 were landlords and rich peasants. See Guojia tongjiju (National Bureau of Statistics), ed., *Zhongguo sanshi nian quanguo nongye tongji ziliao (1949–1979)* [National Agricultural Statistics for Thirty Years in China (1949–1979)], March 1980.

[3] For example, the summative material of the Land Reform Committee of the Central-South Region in September 1952 was based on the data from 100 townships surveyed. The survey showed that landowners, who accounted for 6.5% of the population, held 43% of the land, and rich peasants, who accounted for 3.6%, held 7.2%. The combined share was more than 50.2%. Of course, the data for these 100 townships should be true, but it was hardly representative of the Central-South region. In fact, the percentage of tenant

technology at that time, many local data on townships, counties, and regions were handwritten materials, and the statistical summary was not easy.

Testing Approach

It appears that survey-based work has been conducted on land reforms, but there has been a lack of compilation of land data for certain provinces and for China as a whole. Therefore, statisticians at the time obtained data by extrapolation. Nonetheless, national Land Reform still provided rich and reliable data and laid the foundation for our subsequent statistical and examination work. There were four aspects of land reform data in this section that need to be explained.

First, some informative data on certain provinces and land reform zones was published in the land reform survey, such as the total land statistics in Guanzhong (the Weihe Plain), Guangdong, Fujian, Anhui, Zhejiang, Southern Jiangsu, and East China (*huadong*). Data from these provinces and areas is critical to capture the national level accurately.

Second, some provinces did not publish statistics on land but published the amount of land "confiscated (*moshou*) and expropriated (*zhengshou*)" as a great achievement of the Land Reform. According to the "Outline of China's Land Law" (*Zhongguo tudifa dagang*) in October 1947, "all land of landlords and all common land in the countryside shall be confiscated"; the surplus land of the rich peasants, which was land for rent, was to be expropriated. Therefore, the land "confiscated and expropriated" can be regarded as the amount of rented land, and thus the tenancy rate can be calculated. We can also roughly calculate the percentage of land held by landlords and rich peasants based on this data. During the Land Reform period, the CCP cadres usually confiscated more than 90% of the landowners' land and most of the common land and expropriated about 10% of the rich peasants' land. However, from the data below, the amount of land confiscated and expropriated was often higher than the total amount of land added above.

Third, by referring to statistics from the Republican Period, estimates can be made for other provinces and regions that lack compiled data

farmers in Henan, Hubei, and Guangxi in the Central-South region was lower. There was reason to believe that this survey was not a random sample but may have been selective.

from land reform surveys. Because of the significant geographical variation in land tenure status and the wide variety of regional research findings and estimates, only statistics sufficient to reflect the region's overall level were considered in this chapter. Since most of the data from the Republican Period were not accurate or detailed survey data and the sample size was limited, we can only view them in a general way for reference. For example, by collating the data from the northern provinces, we were able to come to a basic understanding that, compared with the southern provinces, the northern subsistence farmers (*zigengnong*) dominated, with a meager share of tenant peasants.

In addition, it was important to note the inconsistency of the statistics. The division of subsistence farmers, semi-subsistence farmers (*ban zigengnong*), and tenant farmers was fluid, and there was neither a set nor an absolute standard. Tenant peasants and hired peasants with no land of their own were rare. In the southern provinces, where land rights and farming patterns were more diverse, the definition of tenant peasants and subsistence farmers was more flexible. Those peasants might rent more land in some years (as tenants) or rent no land or less in other years (as subsistence farmers). They even leased the land out (as landlords). The types of farmland tenancy were also so diverse that the classification of peasant status was complex. There were "landlords and tenant farmers," "semi-landlords and tenant farmers," "subsistence farmers and tenant farmers," and so on. These complex farmland tenure phenomena make statistics difficult and the data itself inaccurate. For example, the difference between the three government statistics for 1934 was considerable.

Finally, while examining landownership status by province and district, it is also necessary to consider the status of land rights possession. Although the right of possession or the user right other than landownership cannot usually be presented in statistics, they cannot be disregarded. If 70% of the land rights of a piece of land do not belong to the landowner, then the appearance and the substance of the so-called farmland concentration were very different. This is reflected in the following revisions.

The first was to revise the ownership of common land. The proportion of common land such as clan land (*zutian*), temple land (*simiao tian*), and school land (*xuetian*) is high in some areas, and detailed statistics were kept on these common lands during the Land Reforms. Since these common lands were not the private lands of the landlords, they were the property of legal persons. Therefore, it was not appropriate to emphasize the high proportion of land owned by landowners by saying that "landowners possessed land and controlled common land" in the Land Reforms records.

The second revision level was to consider the top-soil right. Top-soil right was generally not included in the ownership statistics, but as a property right, top-soil right had comparable or even greater land rights than subsoil rights. After considering the top-soil right, we found a reduction in the Gini coefficient with a correction strength of 0.31 on average in our calculations using three materials from the East China Military Affairs Commission (*Huadong junzheng weiyuanhui*).

The third revision level considers "absentee landowners" (*waidi yezhu*). This factor profoundly affects some of the macro material and almost all of the small sample survey material. "Absentee landlords" tend to live in cities or outside the village. This phenomenon was most pronounced in more urbanized areas such as Jiangnan. In modern Guangdong and Fujian, more overseas Chinese bought farmland and property in their hometowns. They invested in their hometowns and provided for their families with their hard-earned money, but most of them and their next generation often lived outside China, equivalent to "absentee landowners." They invested in agricultural land and mostly owned the right to subsoil field rights. In this way, not only did "absentee landowners" not reinforce the inequality of land ownership, but they made the distribution of land rights relatively even.

Therefore, this chapter takes the Land Reform Survey as the basis and thus verifies other statistics and considers the reasonable parts of other statistics. Based on the corrected data, this chapter then attempts to make a basic description and judgment of the land occupation status of China's eastern and central provinces during the Republican Period, especially on the eve of the founding of the PRC (Fig. 5.1).

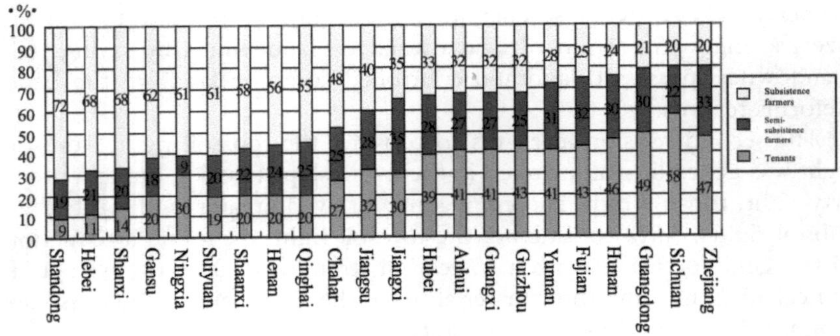

Fig. 5.1 Distribution of tenants in provinces, 1934. *Source* Guomin zhengfu zhujichu tongjiju [The Bureau of Statistics, Office of the Comptroller of the National Government], ed., *Zhongguo zudian zhidu zhi tongji fenxi* [Statistical Analysis of the Tenancy System in China], p. 8

5.2 Subregional Examination

East China

East China[4] has the highest degree of economic development in modern China, and its land occupation situation is relatively complicated. According to statistics from the Republican Period, Zhejiang, Anhui, and southern Jiangsu were among the regions with more severe land occupation inequalities. Fortunately, the East China Military Affairs Commission and these provinces published relatively accurate survey statistics.

As shown in Fig. 5.2, landlords and rich peasants in Zhejiang occupied 27% of the total land, middle peasants 32.4%, and poor peasants 17.6%. In addition, common land in Zhejiang accounted for 16.3% of the total. However, regarding the rate of tenancy and the ratio of tenant farmers in the Republican Period, Zhejiang still ranked first in China. In 1934, the percentage of land leased by peasants in Zhejiang reached 51%, higher than the average tenancy rate of 47% (for 15 provinces). In

[4] Shandong, the province with the highest share of subsistence farmers in the country, was included in the northern category. Data on land reforms was also available for Fujian, which was very similar to Guangdong and was merged into a separate discussion in the next section. Therefore, "East China" in this section refers only to Zhejiang, Jiangsu, and Anhui provinces.

terms of farming patterns, in 1936, 20% of the total number of peasants in Zhejiang were subsistence farmers, and 47% were tenants. It was noteworthy that neither this nominal tenancy rate nor the tenant rate considers 16.3% of common land.

In the land reform area of southern Jiangsu, as shown in Table 5.2, 6.2% of the landlords and rich peasants occupied 35.3% of the total land, while the common land accounted for 5.9%. The land reforms in southern Jiangsu confiscated 10.418 million *mu* of land, accounting for 43%[5] of the total arable land, which was slightly higher than the sum of the land owned by landlords, rich peasants, industrialists and businessmen, and common land, which accounted for 42.3% of the total.[6] According to the

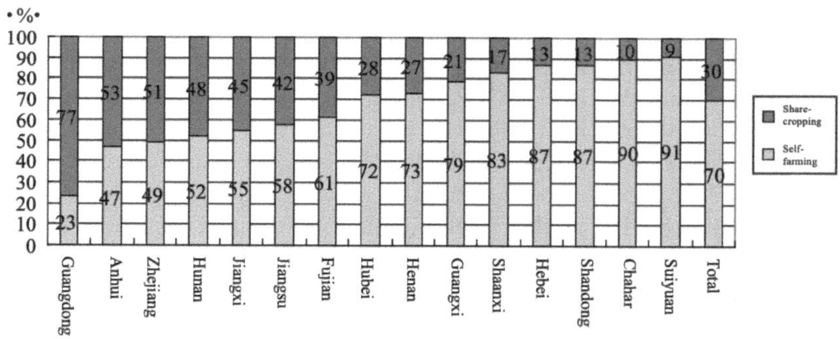

Fig. 5.2 Land under owner-farming and sharecropping in provinces, 1934. *Source* Tudi weiyuanhui [Land Commission], ed., *Quanguo tudi diaocha baogao gangyao* [Outline of the National Land Survey Report], p. 36. Figures in the original text have been rounded off

[5] Southern Jiangsu punished 14,413 unscrupulous landowners. Confiscation and expropriation of land accounted for 43% of the total. Landowners' land was reduced by 90% and rich farmers' by 10%. See Xu Hui, Wu Yuqin, "Sunan diqu tudi gaige yundong shulue" (A Brief Description of the Land Reforms Movement in Southern Jiangsu Province), *Xuehai* (Sea of Learning), no. 3 (1996).

[6] The 1950 Land Reform Law of the People's Republic of China stipulates that during the land reforms, revolutionary soldiers, families of martyrs, workers, employees, freelancers, peddlers, and those who rent out a small amount of land because they are engaged in other occupations or lack of labor shall not be treated as landlords. If the land exceeds the standard, the land in excess will be expropriated. If the land was indeed purchased by the landowner by his own labor, or if the widow, widower, orphan, or

data from Jiangsu Province in 1937, 39% of the total farming households in Jiangsu were subsistence farmers, and 34% were tenant farmers.[7]

According to the survey of land reforms in Anhui Province, the agricultural population of the province was 27.11 million, with 6.31 million households. Among them, 4.28% of the agricultural population were landlords, semi-landlords, and rich peasants, with 270,000 households occupying 32.53% of the total land. There were 5.309 million poor peasant households and 366,000 hired peasant households, which together accounted for more than half of the total number of households and occupied 19.4% of the total land.[8] Comparing the composition of farming households in Anhui Province in the Republican Period, taking the number from the year 1936 (the variation was greater in 1937), then in the 1930s, Anhui Province, subsistence farmers accounted for 35% of the total agricultural population and tenant farmers accounted for 37%.

According to the statistics of the results of land reforms in East China (now Jiangsu, Shanghai, Zhejiang, Anhui, Fujian, and Shandong provinces), as shown in Table 5.3, landlords, rich peasants, and semi-landlords/rich peasants accounted for 7.16% of the total population and occupied 33.38% of the total land; the middle and poor peasants, who accounted for 82.1% of the total population, occupied 51.66% of the total land. In addition, common land accounted for 10.32%. However, the table does not include data for Shandong, even though landlords and rich peasants in Shandong held the lowest share of land.

The result of land reforms in East China is based on the statistics of 65 million people, which is roughly close to the survey data of the entire population of this area. In terms of the data on the percentage of landowners and rich peasants occupying land, landowners and rich peasants in Fujian Province occupied 18% of all land, those in Zhejiang Province occupied 27%, and those in Anhui Province occupied 32.5%. The percentage of landowners and rich peasants in total farmland in all three provinces is below average and only slightly higher in southern

disabled person depends on the land for his livelihood, the land will be taken care of even if it exceeds 200%.

[7] Mo Hongwei's data was slightly different from *Sunan tudi gaige wenxian* (Literature on Land Reforms in Southern Jiangsu). See Mo Hongwei, *Sunan tudi gaige yanjiu* (A Study of Land Reforms in Southern Jiangsu) (Hefei gongye University Press, 2007).

[8] Xu Wei, "Jiefang chuqi Anhui de tudi gaige" (Land Reforms in Anhui at the Beginning of Liberation), *Xueshu tansuo* (Academic Exploration), no. 12 (2011).

Table 5.2 Changes in landholdings by classes before and after the land reforms, Zhejiang. *Sources* Zhejiang sheng tudi gaige weiyuanhui [Zhejiang Land Reforms Committee], *Compilation of Land Reforms Documents* (Tudi gaige wenxian huibian), 1953, JT35

Period	*Before land reform*		*After land reform*		*Comparison before and after land reform*	
Number and percentage of land (*mu*)	*Amount of lands* (mu)	%	*Amount of lands* (mu)	%	*Increase*	*Decrease*
Landowners	5,663,524	20.6	834,772	2.7		4,828,752
Semi-landlord rich peasants	282,584	1.03	124,923	0.4		157,061
Rich peasants	1,484,373	5.4	1,222,945	4		261,428
Middle peasants	8,888,239	32.4	12,121,857	40	3,233,618	
Poor peasants	4,749,286	17.6	13,061,384	41.5	8,312,098	
Hired peasants	107,093	0.39	1,098,431	3.6	991,338	
Small land renters	669,365	2.4	481,262	1.6		188,103
Large tenant farmer	87,607	0.32	202,198	0.6	114,591	
Industrial and commercial capitalists	169,140	0.62	25,554	0.08		143,586
Others	824,177	3	1,371,107	3.8	546,930	
Public land	4,480,794	16.3	544,479	1.8		3,936,315
Total	27,406,182		31,088,912		3,682,730	

Notes (1) This table was based on the materials of the nine prefectures of Jiaxing, Ningbo, Quzhou, Wenzhou, Lishui, Taizhou, Jinhua, Lin'an, Shaoxing, and the subordinate county of Hang County. Among them, 18 townships in Jiaxing, six townships in Jinhua, 15 townships in Weizhou, 54 townships in Taizhou, and one county in Wenzhou, Yuhuan, were still missing. (2) The additional figures after the land reforms were the "undocumented fields" (*heitian*) identified during the land reforms

Table 5.3 Household sizes, population, and farmland occupied by classes before land reforms in 1722 townships of 20 counties in Jiangsu. *Sources* Mo Hongwei, *Sunan tudi gaige yanjiu* [Study on Land Reforms in Southern Jiangsu] (Hefei: Hefei gongye daxue chubanshe, 2007), 15

Items	*Households as a percentage of the total population*	*Population as a percentage of the total population*	*Percentage of occupied land to total land*
Landowners	2.50	3.18	28.32
Public land	1.66	0.07	5.91
Industrial and commercial capitalists	0.65	0.72	1.07
Small land renters	3.85	2.90	3.68
Rich farmers	2.23	3.05	7.01
Middle peasants	30.16	34.11	31.63
Poor peasants	51.90	50.21	20.88
Hired peasants	3.36	2.37	0.44
Others	3.69	3.39	1.06
Total	100.00	100.00	100.00

Jiangsu. Suppose we refer to the composition of tenants in Suzhou, Zhejiang, and Anhui provinces and take the numbers collected in 1936. In that case, we can see that the subsistence farmers in East China accounted for 33.3% of the total population, and the tenants accounted for 39.7%.

Three prominent factors influenced the distribution of land rights in Zhejiang, southern Jiangsu, and southern Anhui provinces. First, the high development of top-soil right in the region meant that most tenants possessed lands with property attributes; second, southern Jiangsu, northern Zhejiang, and western Zhejiang were the most urbanized areas in modern China. The unequal possession of land rights was exaggerated by the high proportion of absentee landowners, who were not local and had special rent bursaries (*zuzhan*) to collect land rent for them; third, the percentage of corporate property rights such as common land to all land in East China was 10.3%, and 16.3% in Zhejiang Province, which was quite high. Regarding top-soil right and absentee landowners, this chapter lacks specific data to correct them for now; however, it was certain that the data for Zhejiang, Southern Jiangsu, Anhui, and the whole of East China roughly reflect the level of unequal landownership, but the unequal land rights possession was also exaggerated (Figs. 5.3, 5.4, 5.5, 5.6 and Tables 5.4, 5.5, 5.6).

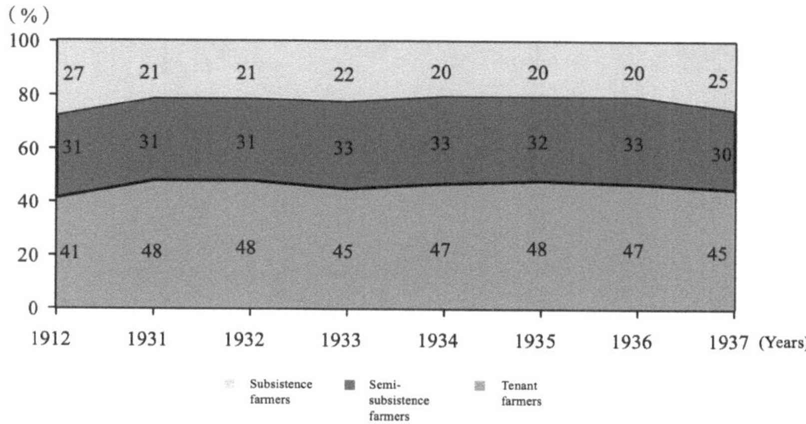

Fig. 5.3 Classification and distribution of farmers in Zhejiang, 1912–37

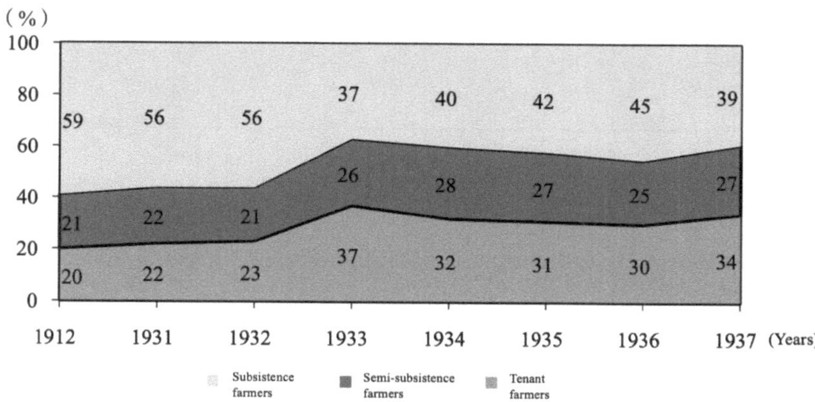

Fig. 5.4 Classification and distribution of farmers in Jiangsu, 1912–37. *Source* Mo Hongwei, *Sunan tudi gaige yanjiu* [A Study of Land Reforms in Southern Jiangsu] (Hefei gongye daxue chubanshe, 2007), 15

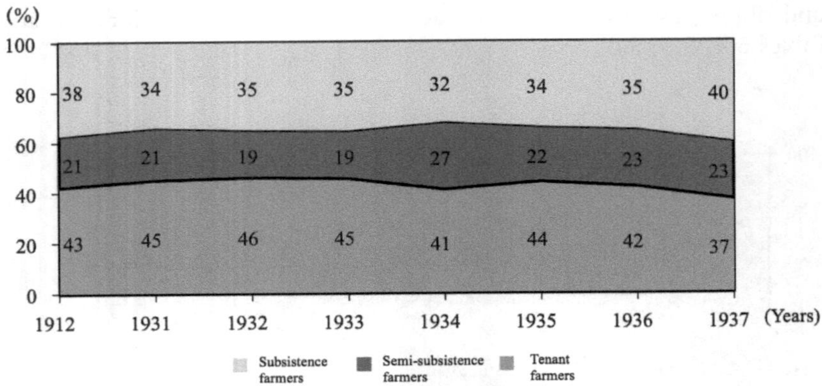

Fig. 5.5 Classification and distribution of farmers in Jiangsu, 1912–37

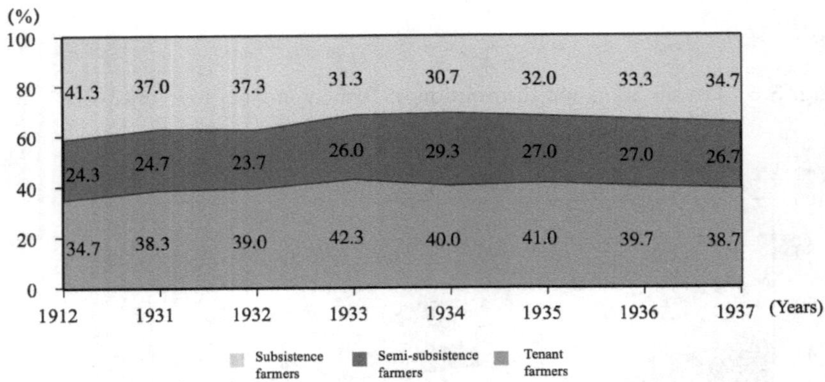

Fig. 5.6 Mean value of tenant farmer distribution in Jiangsu, Zhejiang, and Anhui, 1912–37

Coastal Region of Southeast China

Regarding the uneven distribution of land rights in Guangdong and Fujian provinces, the relevant political literature emphasizes that landowners owned a high proportion of farmland and controlled a high proportion of common land. For example, landowners in Fujian owned and controlled 48% of the total farmland in the province, and landowners

Table 5.4 Statistics for farmland occupation by classes in East China before land reforms. *Sources* Land reforms committee of the East China Military Commission, *Statistics on the Results of Land Reforms in East China* (Huadongqu tudi gaige chengguo tongji), 1952, JT45

Classes	*Number of households*	*Percentage of total households*	*Population*	*Percentage of total households*	*Land* (shimu)		
					Amount of land (mu)	*Percentage of total land*	*Amount of land occupied per capita*
Landlords	485,428	3.07	2,612,643	4.00	37,265,955	26.17	14.26
Semi-landlord rich peasants	50,924	0.32	271,102	0.41	1,952,643	1.37	7.20
Rich peasants	306,061	1.94	1,794,629	2.75	8,321,252	5.84	4.64
Industrialists and businessmen	59,326	0.38	314,397	0.48	443,406	0.31	1.41
Small land renters	375,009	2.37	1,110,337	1.70	3,639,184	2.56	3.28
Middle peasants	5,173,128	32.72	23,783,996	36.40	47,918,594	33.65	2.01
Poor peasants	7,612,914	48.15	29,863,778	45.71	25,644,368	18.01	0.86
Hired peasants	784,635	4.96	2,087,140	3.19	700,931	0.49	0.34
Craft workers	69,464	0.44	258,104	0.40	50,081	0.03	0.19
Other classes	893,999	5.65	3,243,537	4.96	1,786,887	1.25	0.55
Public land					14,696,522	10.32	
Total	15,810,888	100.00	65,339,663	100.00	142,419,824	100.00	2.18

Notes Other classes include freelancers, religious professionals, the poor, vagrants, small traders, and those living in debt

Table 5.5 Landholding by classes on the eve of land reforms in Fujian Province. *Sources* Land Reforms Committee of Fujian Provincial People's Government (Fujiansheng renmin zhengfu tudi gaige weiyuanhui), ed., *Compilation of Documents on Land Reforms in Fujian Province* (*Fujiansheng tudi gaige wenxian huibian*), 1953

Classes	*Total number of households*	*Total population*	*(a) Total land (before land reforms)*	*(b) Number of households whose land was confiscated and expropriated*	*b/a: %*	*Population whose land was confiscated and expropriated*
Landowners	63,105	368,364	2,753,304.41	63,105	100.00	368,364
Industrialists and businessmen	27,818	172,553	136,949.33	18,161	65.37	98,850
Semi-landlord rich peasants	11,332	62,623	314,477.69	10,497	92.37	53,259
Rich farmer	39,014	236,229	728,812.87	16,250	41.43	92,484
Small land renters	68,543	214,500	509,177.51	28,824	42.08	78,665
Public land			5,936,632.13			
Those who live in debt and profit	1772	7461	11,221.77	504	28.42	1792

Notes b/a number of confiscated households as a percentage of that class, and the proportion of confiscated classes in the province

Table 5.6 Farmland occupation by class before and after land reforms in 2516 townships of 41 counties in Guanzhong Region. *Sources* Shanxi sheng nognmin xiehui bangongshi [Shaanxi Provincial Peasant Association Office], "Guanzhong tugaiqu 41 xian(shi) 2516 xiang tugai qianhou ge jieceng tudi zhanyou tongji biao" [Statistical Table of Land Occupation by Classes before and after Land Reforms in 2516 Townships of 41 Counties (Cities) in Guanzhong Agrarian Reforms Area], August 1951, Shaanxi Provincial Archives no.123-24-42, quoted from He Jun, "20 shiji 50 niandai chu guanzhong nongcun de tudi gaige" [Agrarian Reforms in Rural Guanzhong in the Early 1950s], *Zhongguo nongshi* [Chinese Agricultural History], no.2 (2006): 115–124

		Landlords	*Semi-landlord rich peasants*	*Rich peasants*	*Small renters*	*Middle peasants*	*Poor peasants*	*Hired peasants*
Land occupation before Land Reforms	Total	2,152,583	252,800	1,148,098	841,065	5,161,053	6,997,214	575,209
	%	7.8	0.9	4.2	3	54	24.8	2.1
	Per capita	11.6	24.2	7.8	6.8	4.7	2.6	1.32
Land occupation after Land Reforms	Total	463,608	131,375	1,131,781	666,602	5,715,283	8,541,441	1,298,079
	%	1.62	0.47	3.95	2.35	55.5	30.2	4.6
	Per capita	2.5	12.9	7.1	5.4	4.8	3.3	3.0

Notes (1) There were 2,982,182.21 *mu* more land after the Land Reforms, which were "unregistered land" (*heidi*); (2) there were a total of 2522 townships in the Guanzhong land reform area, of which Weinan lacks six townships' statistics

in Guangdong possessed an even higher percentage of land. However, since the common lands were corporate property rights, they could not generally be taken for individuals.

According to the Guangdong Land Reform Commission, landlords in Guangdong accounted for 5.8% of the total number of households and 8% of the total population, occupying 26.9% of the land; rich peasants accounted for 2.3% of the total number of households, 3.9% of the total population, and possessed 5.5% of the total land. The middle peasants accounted for 21.5% of the total number of households, 27% of the total population, and 18.5% of the land. The poor peasants accounted for 56.7% of the total households, 50.3% of the total population, and 11.6%

of the total landholdings. Among them, 33% of the total farmland was common land (*gongchangtian*). Other small renters and traders accounted for 13.7% of the total number of households, 10.8% of the total population, and occupied 4.6% of the land.[9] On the eve of the land reforms, landlords and rich peasants in Guangdong accounted for 32.4% of the total population; the percentage of tenant peasants was high, reaching 43–58% in the 1930s, while the proportion of subsistence farmers was low, ranging from 17 to 25%. The farmland for lease was mainly public, accounting for 33% of the total land.

According to the Fujian statistics on land, the total amount of farmland in Fujian province was around 20,391,005 *mu*, of which 2,753,304 *mu* was occupied by landlords, accounting for 13.5% of the total land. The semi-landlords and rich peasants occupied 314,478 *mu*, rich peasants occupied 728,813 *mu*, industrial and commercial workers occupied 136,949 *mu*, small renters occupied 509,178 *mu*, debtors (*zhaili shenghuo zhe*) occupied 11,222 *mu*, and other farmland accounted for 367,536 *mu*.[10] Thus, the landlords and rich peasants in Guangdong occupied a total of 3,796,595 *mu* of land, accounting for 18.6% of the total land; among them, there were 5,936,632 *mu* of common land, accounting for 29.1% of the total land; the middle peasants and poor peasants together occupied 9,582,894 *mu* of land, accounting for 47% of the total land (Figs. 5.7, 5.8).

Among the three datasets in 1934, Guangdong had the highest share of tenant peasants and the lowest share of subsistence farmers in China. The high land tenancy rates in Guangdong and Fujian provinces were mainly due to the high proportion of common land in the land reform

[9] Overseas Chinese and industrial and commercial households. Most urban industrial and commercial households owned land. Grain production in Guangdong, which was 8.25 million tons in 1934 and 7.235 million tons in 1949, fell by 12.3% in 1949. Guangdong confiscated and expropriated 23 million *mu* of land. See Shen Jinsheng, "Guangdong sheng tudi gaige yundong gaishu" (Overview of the Land Reforms Movement in Guangdong Province), in Zhonggong Guangdong sheng dangshi yanjiushi (Party History Research Office of the CPC Guangdong Provincial Committee) ed., *Guangdong dangshi ziliao* (Guangdong Party History Materials), vol. 27, Guangzhou: Guangdong People's Press, 1995, 278–304.

[10] Fujian sheng renmin zhengfu tudi gaige weiyuanhui (Land Reforms Committee of Fujian Provincial People's Government), *Fujian sheng tudi gaige wenxian huibian* (Compilation of Documents on Land Reforms in Fujian Province), 1953.

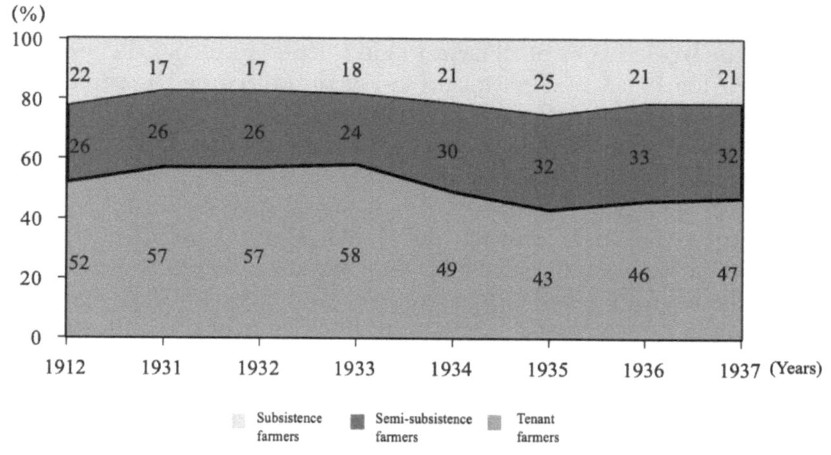

Fig. 5.7 Classification and distribution of farmers in Guangdong, 1912–37. *Source* Zheng Linkuan and Huang Chunwei, "Statistical Analysis of the Tenancy System in Fujian Province" (*Fujiansheng zudian zhidu zhi tongji fenxi*), *Agricultural Economic Research Series* (*nongye jignji yanjiu congshu*), no.4, Survey Office of the Agricultural Improvement Department of Fujian Province (Fujiansheng nongye gaijinchu diaochashi), 1946

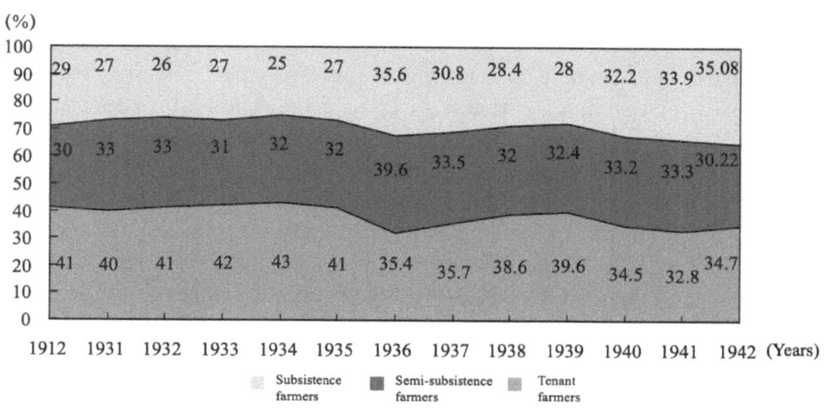

Fig. 5.8 Classification and distribution of farmers in Fujian, 1912–42

surveys. According to land reform statistics, common land in Guangdong accounted for 33% of all farmland in the province, and the province accounted for 29.1% of all farmland in Fujian, exceeding the percentage of land held by landlords and wealthy peasants in the province. In other words, only about 70% of the farmland in Guangdong and Fujian was in private possession. According to Zhang Yan's study of clan fields, the average percentage of common lands in eight areas in western Fujian and northern Fujian accounted for 54.74% of the arable land area.[11] According to a survey by Chen Han-sheng and others, the percentage of clan fields in a county in Guangdong also reached 50% of the total arable land. As a corporate property right, the clan field also mitigated the uneven distribution of land rights to some extent. However, the typical tenancy rate in Guangdong was not so high if we disregard the tenancy relationship in clan fields. Of course, common lands were both rented and rotated by clan members.

In Fujian and Guangdong provinces, the trade of the top-soil right was quite common; the so-called tenant peasants were peasants who possessed some property rights on their fields other than ownership rights. For example, there were many tidal flats (*shatian*) in Guangdong, and the sub-sand rights (*shaguquan*) alone accounted for 10% of the total farmland in the province. The fertility of tidal lands was largely dependent on tenant peasants' investment of work capital, whose land returns from top-soil right were often higher than those from field bottom rights. Thus, although the land owned by tenant peasants was small, they held a large amount of top-soil right, so it cannot be said that the high proportion of tenant peasants meant an uneven possession of land rights.

In the coastal provinces, a large number of Chinese traveled, struggled overseas to earn money, and then purchased land and property in their hometowns. Therefore, in the 1950s, many overseas Chinese were classified as "landlords" according to the land reform policy. Since local officials such as Ye Jianying and Fang Fang understood the situation of the overseas Chinese, they delayed the implementation of the land reform policy. Still, after the arrival of non-local officials, they started to implement the land reforms forcefully.

[11] Zhang Yan, "Guanyu Qingdai zutian fenbu de chubu kaocha" (A Preliminary Examination on the Distribution of Clan Fields in the Qing Dynasty), *Zhongguo jingjishi yanjiu* (Researches in Chinese Economic History), no,1 (1991).

The high proportion of nominal tenant peasants was caused by the right to top-soil, clan land, and farmland owned by absentee landowners such as overseas Chinese. Guangdong had the highest proportion of nominal tenant peasants in China, still at 47% in 1937, while its subsistence farmers accounted for only 21%. In Fujian, if we take the adjusted data for 1937, the tenant peasants accounted for 35.7% of the total population, and the subsistence farmers accounted for 38%.[12] If we calculate the average values of the original cadastral data for Guangdong and Fujian, we can see that the share of subsistence farmers in the two provinces was 23.5% of the population and that of nominal tenant peasants was 44.5% of the total population. If we suppose all the landowners' land was rented out, the typical tenancy rate was 13.5% in Fujian and 26.9% in Guangdong, both of which were relatively low.

Central and South Regions

China's central and south regions include Jiangxi, Hubei, Hunan, Guangxi, Henan, and Guangdong provinces. As the case of Guangdong has been discussed in the previous section and the case of Henan will be discussed in the part on northern provinces, we will only focus on Jiangxi, Hubei, Hunan, and Guangxi provinces in this section.

During the Land Reform Movement, a total of 13,368,734 *mu* of farmland was confiscated and expropriated in Jiangxi Province, accounting for 35.3% of the total land in the land reformed areas of the province, from which we can calculate that the nominal tenancy rate in Jiangxi was 35.3%.[13] If public farmland was counted as 15%, the typical tenancy rate was 20.3%. Thus, the landowners in Jiangxi occupied 20.3% of the land, and the rich peasants occupied 7.2%, which means that the

[12] The data for 1936 and 1937 were adjusted by Zheng Linkuan, Huang Chunwei, and others.

[13] Zhang Guozhen, "Jiangxi sheng tudi gaige yundong de weida chengjiu" (The Great Achievements of the Land Reforms Movement in Jiangxi Province), *1949–1952 Zhonghua renmin gongheguo jignji dang'an ziliao xuanbian nongcun jingji tizhi juan* (Selected Materials from the Economic Archives of the People's Republic of China 1949–1952-Volume on Rural Economic System.), Beijing: Shehuikexue wenxian Press, 1992, 404–502.

landowners and rich peasants in Jiangxi occupied about 27.5% of the total land.[14]

According to statistics, the number of landlords in Guangxi accounted for 7.2% of the total population, and their possession of land and control of common land accounted for 36.5% of all the land; rich peasants occupied 4.6% of the land.[15] If the common land was counted as 15%, the landlords and rich peasants in Guangxi occupied 26.1% of all the land.

According to 1949 statistics, the total arable land in Hubei Province was 56.14 million *mu* (3,742,500 ha), and 11.83 million *mu* of farmland was expropriated during the land reforms, accounting for 21% of its arable land. The proportion of common land seems too high if we take the 10% estimated by the Central and Southern District Land Reform Committee (*Zhongnanqu tudi gaige weiyuanhui*); we use 5% to calculate the typical tenancy rate in Hubei Province, which was about 16%.

Common lands (clan fields, temples, churches, schools, and communities) were common in the central-southern regions. Specifically, in Hunan and Guangxi provinces, common land accounted for 15–20% of the land in their provinces, in Jiangxi, 15%, in Hubei, 10%, in Guangdong, 30%, and in some counties up to 60%.[16] The actual proportion of common land in Guangdong was as high as 33%, while in Henan it should have been lower. If the percentage of common land in the central-southern regions was calculated at 15%, the proportion of landowners occupying land in the region was 28%; landowners and rich peasants, who account for 10.1% of the population, occupied about 35.2% of the land. However, due to the prevalence of permanent tenancy and the widespread trading of top-soil right in this area, the land share data do not fully reflect the actual land rights possessed by tenant peasants (Figs. 5.9, 5.10, 5.11, 5.12).

[14] According to the data of Republican China, the tenancy rate in Jiangxi in 1934 was 40%, the proportion of tenant farmers in 1934 was 30%, and in 1934–1937 it was 30–40%. The proportion of land leased in 1934 was 45%, and if at least 10% of the public land leased was excluded, the proportion of actual land leased was 35%. Hunan had a total of 51 million *mu* of land.

[15] *Guangxi sheng tudi gaige jiben qingkuang zongjie* (Summary of the Basic Situation of Land Reforms in Guangxi Province), 1952.

[16] Zhongnan tudi gaige weiyuanhui diaoyanchu (Central and South Land Reforms Commission Investigation Division), ed., *Zhongnan qu gesheng nongcun teshu tudi wenti diaocha* (Survey on Special Rural Land Issues in the Provinces of Central and South Region), November 17, 1950.

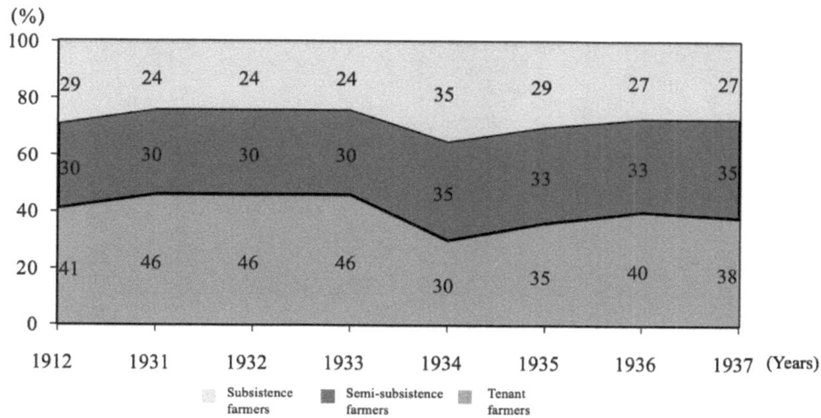

Fig. 5.9 Classification and distribution of farmers in Jiangxi, 1912–37

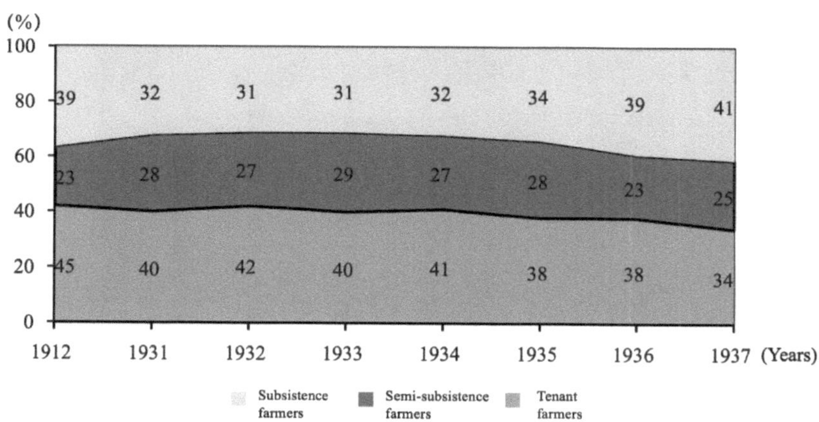

Fig. 5.10 Classification and distribution of farmers in Guangxi, 1912–37

Northern Provinces

Land reforms in the northern provinces took a long time, but detailed survey data have not been fully disclosed. Among the northern provinces in the Republican Period, Shaanxi had the highest degree of inequality in

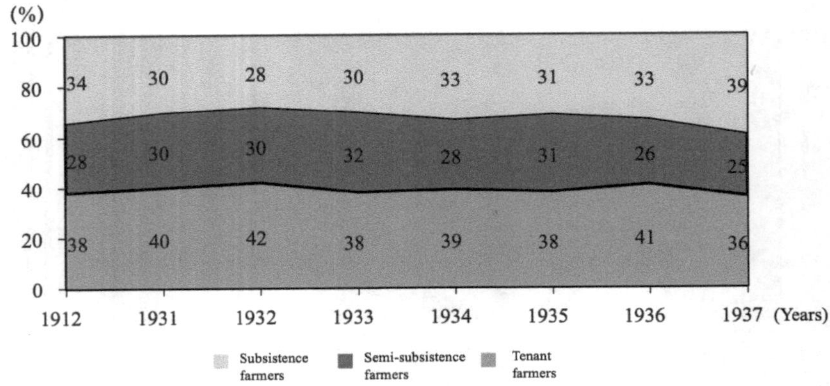

Fig. 5.11 Classification and distribution of farmers in Hubei, 1912–37

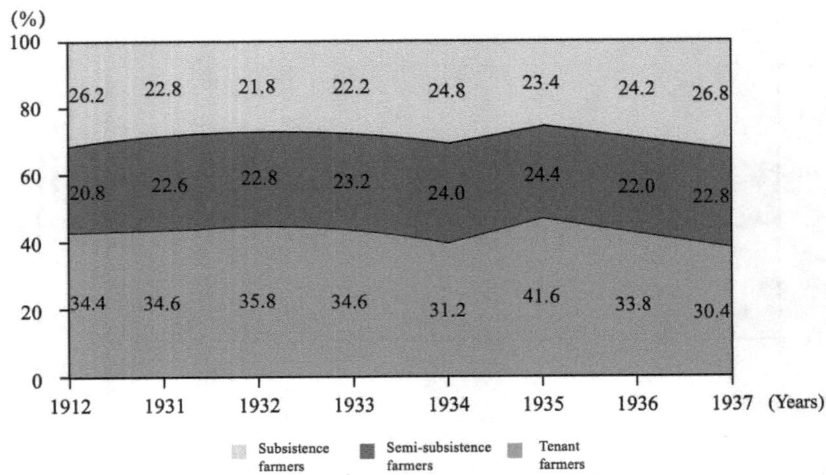

Fig. 5.12 Classification and distribution of farmers in Jiangxi, Hubei, Hunan, and Guangxi, 1912–37

land rights, but Guanzhong also had a proverb that "there are no landlords in Guanzhong" (*Guanzhong wu dizhu*). In the 1950s, there were 41 counties in the land reform area of Guanzhong, accounting for half of the

Shaanxi province, but its population was far more than half. According to the survey data on land reforms in Guanzhong, as shown in Table 5.7, landlords and rich peasants occupied only 12.9% of all land, while middle and poor peasants occupied 78.8%.[17]

In addition, a survey on land reforms in Shaanxi, Gansu, Ningxia, and Xinjiang showed that "landlords and rich peasants accounted for 7% of the total number of peasant households and occupied 35% of the arable land." The middle and poor peasants accounted for 94% of the total number of peasant households and 64% of the arable land. In three provinces, Hebei, Shandong, and Suiyuan, "rich landowners accounted for 6% of the total number of peasant households and occupied 27% of the arable land. The middle and poor peasants accounted for 88% of the total number of peasant households and 71% of the arable land."

Referring to the various statistical data from the Republican Period, the land distribution status in North China was relatively even, with Shaanxi being the only region with a high degree of land rights inequality. However, based on the above, we can also roughly infer that the proportion of land held by poor and hired peasants in those sample data on land reforms was high. The real state of land rights distribution in most northern provinces should be closer to the condition in Guanzhong.

According to various statistics from the Republican Period, North China had a higher proportion of subsistence farmers and a lower proportion of tenant peasants than South China. In 1930, the share of tenant peasants in the south was between 32 and 57%, and the share of subsistence farmers was between 22 and 39% (Fujian's case was different), while the share of tenant peasants in the north was between 9 and 29%, and the share of subsistence farmers was as high as 58–72%. In 1937, the share of tenant peasants in South China was between 36 and 52%, and that of subsistence farmers was between 21 and 40%, while the share of tenant peasants in North China was only between 10 and 19%, and that of subsistence farmers was as high as between 58 and 75%. Such a high proportion of subsistence farmers and a low proportion of tenant peasants reflected

[17] The change in land rights after the land reforms was not significant for most peasants, as the land per capita of landlords and rich peasants decreased significantly, but the land per capita of poor peasants increased by only 0.7 *mu*. However, the social effect of "equalizing the land" (*jun tiandi*) and "those who cultivate have their own land" (*gengzhe you qitian*) was basically achieved.

Table 5.7 Landholdings of the top 10% of the wealthy class in 1949

Regions	*Share of landowners and wealthy farmers*	*Tenancy rate*
Fujian	18%	45.47%* (nominal) 16% (typical)
Guangdong	32%	46.5%* (nominal) 16.5% (typical)
Zhejiang	27%	39.75%* (nominal) 24.75% (typical)
Sunan	35.33%*	38.3% (nominal) 32.3% (typical)
Anhui	32.5%	38.59%* (nominal)
Jiangxi	27.5%	37%* (nominal) 22% (typical)
Guangxi	26.1%	40%* (nominal) 25% (typical)
Hunan		48%* (nominal) 33% (typical)
Hubei		21% (nominal) 11% (typical)
Hebei	27% (sample data, biased high)	25.25%* (nominal)
Shandong	27% (sample data, biased high)	
Guanzhong	12.9%	

Notes (1) Nominal tenancy rate refers to the rental rate of all land, including public land, etc. In this table, the share of confiscated land is usually regarded as the nominal tenancy rate. (2) The typical tenancy rate refers to the rental rate of the land of rich landowners, which was calculated by subtracting the amount of public land rented from the nominal tenancy. In the central and southern regions, public land (clan fields, temples, churches, schools, and groups) accounted for 15–20% in Hunan and Guangxi, 15% in Jiangxi, and 10% in Hubei, 30% in Guangdong, and up to 60% in individual counties. See Zhongnan tudi gaige weiyuanhui diaoyanchu [Research Division of the Central-South Land Reforms Committee], ed., ***Zhongnan qu gesheng nongcun teshu tudi wenti diaocha*** [Survey on Special Land Problems in Rural Areas of the Provinces of the Central-South Region], November 17, 1950. Except for Guangdong, the share of public land in other provinces seems to be overestimated. (3) For data on the proportion of confiscated and expropriated land, see Mo Hongwei and Zhang Chengjie, ***Xinqu nongcun de tudi gaige*** [Agrarian Reforms in the Rural Areas of the New District], Nanjing: Jiangsu University Press, 2009.

that landholding in North China was much less unequal than in South China.

According to the "Outline of the National Cadastral Report" (*Quanguo tudi diaocha baogao gangyao*), in 1934, the average share of subsistence farmers in North China was 70.2%, fluctuating between 61.3% and 80.5% in all types of land occupation patterns. In Shaanxi and Henan, the proportion of subsistence farmers was slightly over 60%, while the proportion of those in Hebei, Shandong, and Shanxi was over 71%. However, the share of subsistence farmers in the south was 34.8% on average, about half that in the north. According to "Statistical Analysis of the Tenant System in China" (*Zhongguo zudian zhidu zhi tongji fenxi*), the proportion of subsistence farmers in all northern provinces exceeded 55% (except Chahar). In Henan and Shaanxi, the proportion of subsistence farmers was lower, between 56 and 58%; in Shanxi, Hebei, and Shandong, the proportion was higher, between 68 and 72%. The corresponding share of tenant peasants in Henan and Shaanxi was 20%, while that of those in Shanxi, Hebei, and Shandong ranged from 9 to 14%. The cases of Hubei and Guangxi were similar to those of the north, with slightly higher land tenure inequality than that in Henan and Shaanxi.

Based on the data from 1936 and 1937, the tenant peasants in the north accounted for about 16%, and the subsistence farmers accounted for about 63%. Shandong, Hebei, and Shanxi had the highest proportion of subsistence farmers.[18] By 1934, the provinces with high land tenancy rates were Suiyuan (91%), Chahar (90%), Hebei (87%), Shandong (87%), Shaanxi (83%), and Henan (72%). The combined calculation shows that the tenancy rate in the North was about 14.9% (Figs. 5.13, 5.14, 5.15).

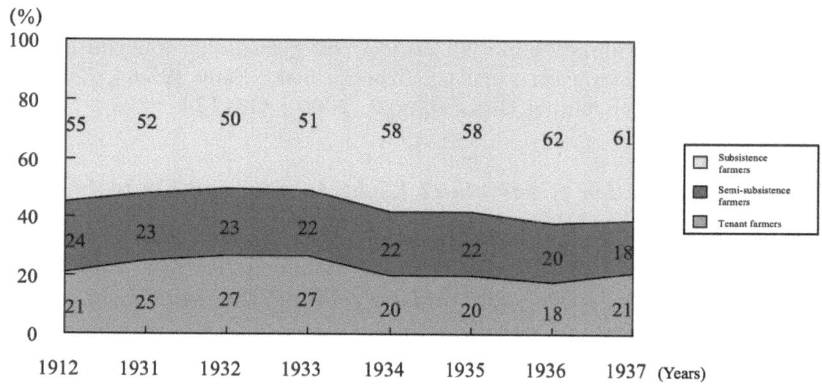

Fig. 5.13 Classification and distribution of farmers in Shaanxi, 1912–37

[18] In fact, about 5% of the rural population cannot be classified into these three categories but belongs to other classes, including industrialists and businessmen, small renters, and others.

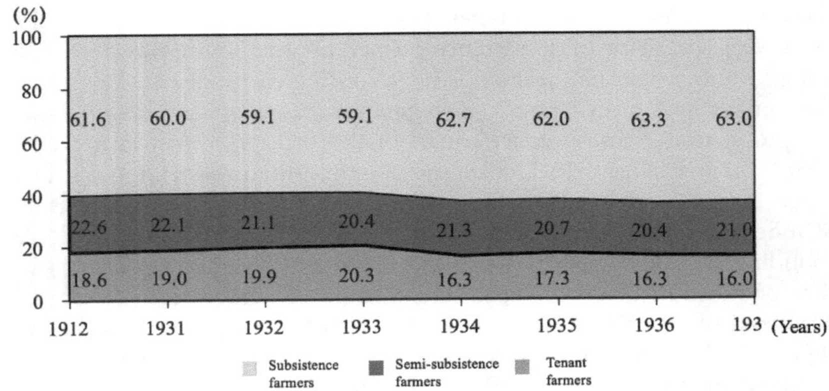

Fig. 5.14 Classification and distribution of farmers in Hebei, Shandong, Shanxi, and Shaanxi, 1912–37. *Notes* (1) 2,982,182.21 *mu* of unregistered land were identified after the land reforms. (2) There were 2522 townships in the Guanzhong land reform area, of which Weinan lacks statistics for six townships. *Source* See Shaanxi Provincial Peasants' Association Office System (*Shaanxisheng nongmin xiehui bangongshi*), "Statistics of Land Possession by Classes before and after Land Reforms in 2516 Townships in 41 counties (cities) of Guanzhong Agrarian Reforms Area" (*Guanyu tugaiqu 41 xian (shi) 2516 xiang tugai qianhou ge jieceng tudi zhanyou tongji biao*), 1951, Shaanxi Provincial Archives, 123-24-42, cited from He Jun, "20 shiji 50 niandai chu guanzhong nongcun de tudi gaige" [Agrarian Reforms in Rural Guanzhong in the Early 1950s], *Zhongguo nongshi* [Chinese Agricultural History], no.2 (2006): 115–124

Overall Distribution of Farmland Rights in East and Central China

The above is an examination of the land occupation status of the eastern and central regions of China. The primary data are shown in Table 5.7.

According to the survey data on land reforms, the proportion of land held by landowners and rich peasants in the southern provinces ranges from 18 to 35.5%, and the Gini coefficient was not high. The proportion of land held by wealthy landowners in the northern provinces was much lower than that in the south, and the Gini coefficient was relatively low. Therefore, it is difficult to derive a national average value of the proportion of land held by wealthy landowners and farmers. However, the data in the south are basically accurate, about 30% ± 5%, with the lowest in Fujian, only 18%. There were few survey data points in the north and,

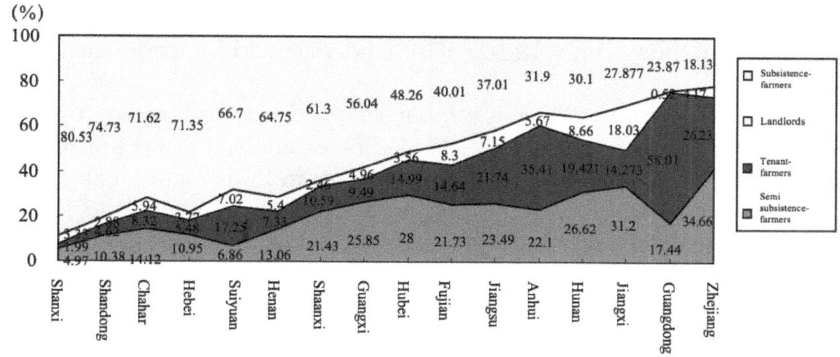

Fig. 5.15 Patterns of households with farmland rights by province, 1934. *Notes* This chart summarizes the ten categories of land rights forms, i.e., landlord and subsistence farmer, landlord and subsistence farmer and tenant farmer, and landlord and tenant farmer were classified as "landlord"; Tenant farmers and hired farmers were classified as "tenant farmers"; Since the proportion of hired farmers and other categories is tiny, they were also classified as "tenant farmers," while the remaining two categories, namely subsistence farmers and subsistence farmers and sharecroppers (semi-subsistence farmers), remain unchanged. *Sources* Tudi weiyuanhui [Land Commission], *Quanguo tudi diaocha baogao gangyao* [Outline of the National Cadastral Report], p. 34

at present, only data on the central land reform areas, where the proportion of land held by landowners and rich farmers was less than 13%. If we were to take a rough figure, we infer that the proportion of land held by wealthy landowners in the north was about 20%.

This ratio is not consistent with the political slogan that "the landlords and rich peasants occupy the largest amount of land," but it also does not indicate that the amount of land per capita was more even in China at the time. There were still wide gaps regarding the amount of land held by landlords and poor peasants, and in some areas the phenomenon of "the rich having thousands of *mu* of land and the poor having no place to stand" still existed. The distribution of land rights among provinces can be roughly divided into three categories, as follows:

The first type was the northern provinces, which have equal land rights. Overall, the northern provinces were dominated by subsistence farmers and had a low share of tenant peasants. Shandong, Hebei, and Shanxi had the highest share of subsistence farmers; the next highest share of subsistence farmers was recorded in Shaanxi and Henan provinces; moreover, in Guanzhong, only 12.9% of all land was held by landowners and rich peasants.

The second type was the southeastern provinces, where landowners and wealthy peasants occupy less land. For example, the proportion of land occupied by landowners and rich peasants in Fujian and Guangdong was 18% and 32%, respectively. The high share of common land led to a high nominal tenancy rate. Similarly, the percentage of land held by landowners and wealthy peasants in Hubei and Guangxi was also low.

The third type was the middle and lower reaches of the Yangtze River, where tenant peasants had stronger land rights. The proportion of land held by rich landowners in Zhejiang was 27%, in Anhui 32.5%, and in southern Jiangsu up to 35.3%. From this, it can be seen that the average share of land held by landowners and rich peasants in East China was 33.38%, and the nominal share of tenant peasants was high. Further, because of the widespread transaction of top-soil right, poor peasants also possessed the right of land instead of real ownership rights. The statistics for Jiangxi and Hunan were not comprehensive, but the nominal tenancy rate in Hunan should be higher than 27.5% in Jiangxi. Since permanent tenancy rights were more common in these regions and top-soil right were frequently circulated, the inequality of their land rights possession should be lower than the statistical data (Fig. 5.15, 5.16, 5.17).

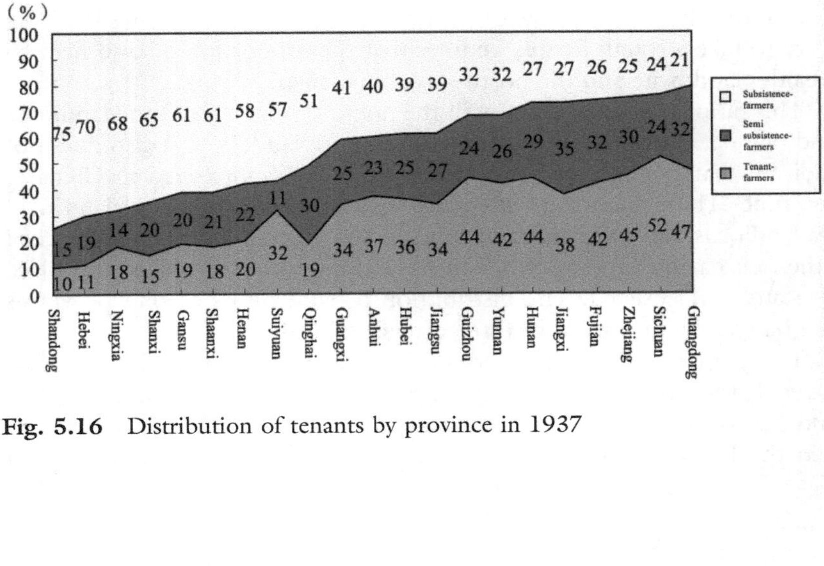

Fig. 5.16 Distribution of tenants by province in 1937

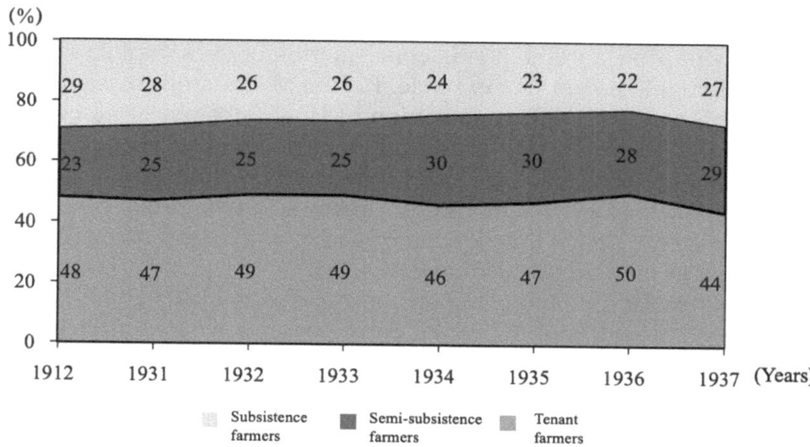

Fig. 5.17 Classification and distribution of farmers in Hunan, 1912–37

5.3 Feedback Mechanism of Farmland Concentration

China's rural economy collapsed in the modern era, and the invasion of the imperialist powers further weakened it.[19] In the past, it was common to blame modern China's problems on land annexation and even exaggerate the extent of farmland concentration. However, as Fang Xing points out, China during the Qing Era did not show a trend of farmland concentration.[20] Nor did the Republican Era. From 1931 to 1937, the average value of the national share of subsistence farmers remained more or less the same: 45% in 1931, 46% in 1934, and still 46% in

[19] It should be noted that in the era of a shortage economy, peasants were generally unable to live at a subsistence level; especially with the recent economic collapse, peasants became poorer. However, the root cause of peasant poverty does not lie in land inequality. Against the background of the overall scarcity of land resources, further equalization of land cannot fundamentally solve the problem of the small amount of additional land per capita. The fundamental solution lies in urbanization and industrialization, reducing the rural population and increasing labor productivity and land output.

[20] Fang Xing, "Qingdai diannong de zhongnong hua" (The Middle Peasantization of Tenant Farmers in the Qing Dynasty), *Zhongguo xueshu* (China Scholarship), vol.2, Beijing: Shangwu yinshuguan, 2000.

1937.[21] Regarding the number of farm households in each form, China also does not show a trend of land concentration or even local or specific periods of fragmentation. For example, Ramon Myers' study of Shandong and Hebei showed that the distribution of land there was more even in 1930 than in 1880.[22] Thus, the phenomenon of land concentration in modern China has clearly been exaggerated. Many complex factors have contributed to the misperceptions of the past, but an important one lies in the neglect of the negative feedback mechanism on the land concentration that existed in the traditional Chinese system.

Prime facie, land mobility, transactions, and sales would result in rich people owning more land. However, corresponding hedging mechanisms existed in traditional Chinese society to counteract land concentration. The so-called negative feedback mechanisms were of the following three kinds:

The first was the system of equal inheritance. For example, suppose a Chinese peasant has two sons and 100 *mu* of land. When the two sons grow into adults, each will inherit 50 *mu* of farmland from their fathers; later, when the third generation of four grandchildren (hypothetical) divides the land again, it will be 25 *mu* per person. In this way, land holdings were dispersed. Peasants with more land will have more offspring, while those with less land will have fewer children because they don't have enough land to sustain population reproduction. As a result, the system of equal inheritance promoted the division of family property among large families and tended to disperse landholdings.

Due to the practice of primogeniture in some parts of Europe and Japan, the trajectory of its historical transition presents a different picture. In the past, many people attributed the differences between China and the West to "cultural determinism," believing that the Chinese culture was centralized and authoritarian and should practice primogeniture, while Western Europe was more democratic and equal and should implement

[21] The year 1912 marked the change of regime in China, and the data was for reference only.

[22] Ramon Hawley Myers (Ma Ruomeng), *Zhongguo nongmin jingji—Hebei he Shandong de nongye fahzan* (The Chinese Peasant Economy: Agricultural Development in Hopei and Shantung, 1890–1949), translated by Shi Jiangyun (Nanjing: Jiangsu People's Press, 1999), 257. In the 1930s, the share of subsistence farmers was 71.35% in Hebei and 71.73% in Shandong (*Zhongguo nongmin jingji*, 338). The disappearance of large landowners and the small change in landless farmers brought a large number of farmers into the intermediate category.

equal inheritance.[23] However, it was the property rights system and business model that were at the root of the creation, differences, and long-term continuation of the inheritance system.[24]

Second, diversified types of land rights transactions, including various redemption mechanisms, have effectively offset the trend of land concentration. If only a single form of property rights delivery existed in traditional China, such as land sales, it might easily have led to land concentration. However, the types of land rights transactions in traditional Chinese society were very diverse, and peasants could choose from a variety of types of land transactions such as tenancy, pawn, and mortgage; more importantly, the redemption mechanisms of *dian* (conditional sales) and *huomai* (revocable sales) also effectively prevented the eventual transfer of land titles. In fact, the more diversified the transaction format, the more likely it was that systemic risk will be reduced. It was basic, if often forgotten, logic.

Third, the independent operation of individual peasant households was viable and competitive. When a wealthy landowner (or rich peasant) owns a lot of land, if he only hired laborers to operate the land, it was difficult for him to compete with the individual peasant household for small land operations. Under the prevailing technological conditions, large-scale hired labor operations were less effective.[25] Therefore, when the rich peasants owned more land, they still had to release their land rights, such as the right to use and possess, in the form of rent deposits, permanent tenancy, and top-soil right, in order to gain more income; this also alleviated the unequal possession of land rights to a certain extent.

[23] Many people blame China's long history for many of the Chinese problems. They first ignore the basic fact that today's China, after a century of revolution, was very different, if not completely opposite, from the traditional period. Second, China's traditional culture was also diverse. Finally, contemporary China was in a state of flux, and many traditional cultures have become less and less binding. The China of 40 years ago was a far cry from today. We cannot always blame our ancestors for the present problems.

[24] In contrast to China's individual household operation and private property rights of land, the agricultural and pastoral farming model of Western European manors was highly integral and indivisible; its corporate property rights were also indivisible. See Chapter 8, first section, for details.

[25] Long Denggao, Pengbo, "Jinshi diannong de jignying xignzhi yu shouyi bijiao" (A Comparison of the Nature of Business and Earnings of Tenant Farmers in Modern Times), *Jingji yanjiu* (Economic Research Journal), no. 1 (2010): 138–147.

Fourth, corporate property rights and two-layered land rights were also negative feedback mechanisms for land concentration. The top-soil right of land enabled the lower- and middle-class peasants to have the right to occupy land, thus reducing the Gini coefficient of land occupation. Further, corporate landownership such as clan land, temple land, school land, association land (*huitian*), and community land reduced the inequality of private land occupation to a certain extent. For example, the share of clan land in Guangdong and Fujian could be around 30%. In this way, the inequality limit in private landholdings (even if all of it was held by the wealthiest class) did not exceed 70%.

Fifth was state restraint. The state imposes explicit constraints on bureaucratic power that may trigger land annexation. For example, the rule that bureaucrats were not allowed to purchase land and property within their jurisdiction was a binding institutional arrangement by the principal (the emperor) to the agent (the bureaucrat) against incentive incompatibility. However, this restrained "tendency toward land concentration" may have emerged from its "cage" during the modern warlord conflict. As the modern land rights market was subject to violence and encroachment by the powers, localized land annexation may have intensified.

Sixth was the impact of natural and man-made disasters, especially war. During wartime, people usually abandon their landholdings because they have lower expectations of controlling current versus future returns. For example, during the anti-Japanese war period, there was a significant scattering of land in some areas, and the price of subsoil rights fell in the Jiangnan region (Figs. 5.18, 5.19).[26]

[26] Sui Fumin, "20 shiji 30–40 niandai baoding 11 ge cun diquan fenpei de zai tantao" (Re-examination of the Distribution of Land Rights in 11 Villages in Baoding in the 1930s and 1940s), *Zhongguo jingjishi yanjiu* (Researches in Chinese Economic History), no. 3 (2014): 150–166.

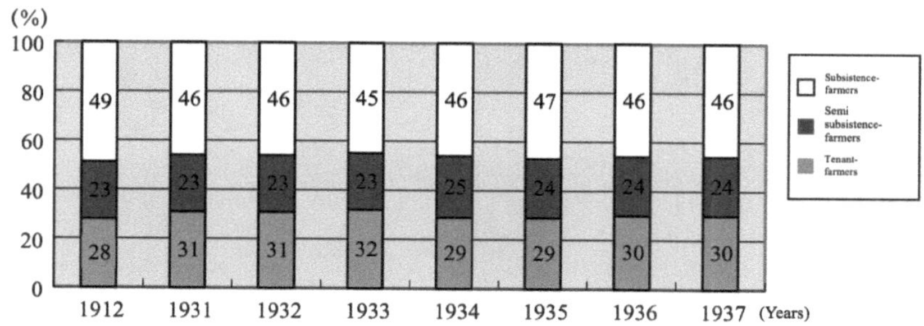

Fig. 5.18 Changes in shares of tenants from 1912 to 1937 (total farm households)

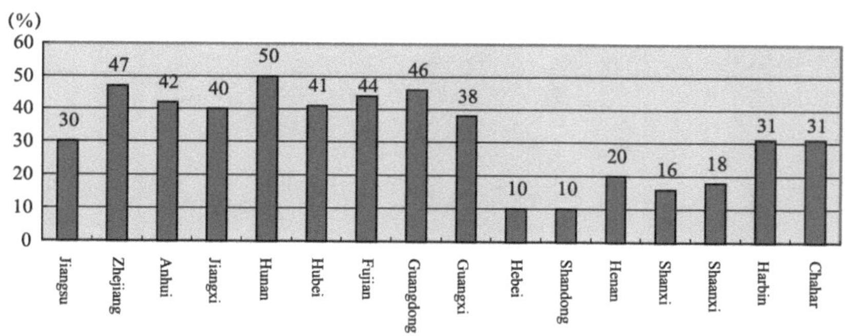

Fig. 5.19 Tenancy rates by province

CHAPTER 6

Farmland Transaction and Peasant Household Operation

Chinese traditional economics had two basic features compared to Western European societies: the trading of land rights and the operation of family farms. These two factors provide a unique development path for China's traditional agricultural economy.

6.1 Farmland Rights Transactions and Family Farms

In China's traditional economy, land property rights and diverse transactional systems enabled landless peasants to establish family farms and operate them independently. According to prior theories, "subsistence farming optimal" and "average land rights" do not take into account the dynamic nature of the market and ignore the fact that peasants can choose to trade land according to their risk preferences and at different price points in a variety of land rights transactions. Specifically, in the traditional economy, peasants could acquire land use rights by leasing the land; they could also obtain stronger control over the land by rent-depositing (*yazu*); and they could acquire other rights and interests such as *dian* rights, top-soil right, and permanent tenancy rights. In other words, the right to dispose of, benefit from, and trade in the land could be freely

D. Long and X. Chi, *The Institutions of Land Property Rights in China*, Palgrave Studies in Economic History,
https://doi.org/10.1007/978-981-97-5112-9_6

traded without conflicting with landownership. Therefore, the diversification and differentiation of traditional land transactions could meet the needs of peasants with different orientations while reducing transaction costs and systemic risks and stimulating and facilitating land circulations and resource allocations. It has been argued that trading land rights tends to trigger land annexation.

However, in fact, the land rights market has its own negative feedback mechanism, as it protects the rights and interests of vulnerable groups through the redemption mechanism, delays the transfer of landownership, and provides peasants with the possibility to overcome the hardship and restore and re-establish independent farm operations, forming a hedging factor for land rights concentration. Thus, individual peasant households have maintained competitiveness through these types of land transactions and redemption mechanisms even under traditional technological conditions and have become an integral part of the traditional Chinese economy.

Tenancy System and Family Farms: A Case Study

What did a family farm mean for peasants? In the past, textbooks and people had the impression that tenant farmers were as vulnerable as hired farmers. However, there were also middle sharecroppers (*dian zhongnong*), large sharecroppers (*da diannong*), and rich sharecroppers (*dian funong*), and there was a qualitative difference between sharecroppers and hired farmers. Although a tenant farmer did not necessarily own the land, when he built his own farm by acquiring land from the market through tenancy, rent-depositing, *dian* transactions, and purchasing topsoil right, he became a peasant entrepreneur with "residual control" and "residual claim" over his farm, meaning that he controlled and acquired the rights and interests beyond the contractual provisions.

Tenancy agreements usually required that the tenant farmer pay 50% of the rent to the landlord, which was approximately one season's crop. Generally, the tenant farmer cultivated two seasons, and the second harvest was not subject to rent and was at the disposal of the tenant farmer. (Of course, to maintain a good owner-tenant relationship, the tenant farmer usually chooses to give two rice fish to the owner as gifts, which was called "residual control.") As a peasant entrepreneur, the tenant farmer received the operation, investment, and risk income. However, because of the uncertainty of climate, harvest, and market, the tenant farmer had to make judgments and decisions about the uncertainty of the future and had the burden of the risky income, while the hired farmer received only the labor income, the wage; moreover, the hired worker did not bear the risk and had no business income.

When a tenant farmer built his farm, he gained entrepreneurial wealth. Consequently, the farm owner or peasant entrepreneur received operating income, and the landowner, including the owner of top-soil right, received property income, contributing to the preservation of traditional social stability. In this way, most tenant farmers became "middle class," a "middle class in the era of a shortage economy."

Each type of land rights transaction played a role for individual family farms and increased their economic efficiency. In the case of the rent deposit system, for example, intellectuals in the Republican Era believed that the prepayment of deposits by tenant farmers increased their exploitation. They therefore demanded the prohibition of the rent deposit system. However, they failed to understand the economic logic of the system, which had three functions: first, a base deposit as a security for land rent; second, a stable tenant deposit as a long-term distribution of the proceeds of land improvement; and third, a discounted deposit as an intertemporal substitute for land rent income. With different functional types, the three institutional variables, namely, the amount of rent, the duration of the tenancy contract, and the actual rent rate, show a substitution relationship.[1]

In the past, academics always made moral judgments about landlords, lamenting that they were cruel and exploitative, especially Chinese landlords. However, if we look at it from the perspective of paying rent at a later time, were traditional landlords more merciful than current landlords? In real life, we must pay rent or deposit in advance for renting a house, but in the past, land tenants paid rent only after there was a harvest from the leased land. In fact, post-payment of rent was a realization of the tenant farmer's labor and operation, enabling the tenant farmer to use his labor while the landlord took the risk. So, a tenancy is, in fact, a combination of land and labor.

The form of paying part of the rent in advance or the whole rent was the "rent deposit," which was common after the Song dynasty, especially

[1] He Guoqing, "Chuantong nongdi yazuzhi duochong gongneng de zhidu jignjixue yanjiu" (An Institutional Economics Study of the Multiple Functions of the Traditional Farmland Tenancy System), Master thesis, Tsinghua University, 2012.

during the Ming and Qing dynasties. The rent deposit was an option for the landowner and the tenant farmer to meet their individual needs. The landowner, who would not receive the rent until after next year's harvest, would be cashing in on the future rent if he could get a portion of the rent upfront. In particular, if the landowner needed cash urgently, he could raise the rent and reduce the future rent accordingly. For example, a Taiwan tenancy deed from the reign of Xianfeng, "Establishing a document for recruiting tenant farmers to farm" (*Li zhaodian geng zi* 立招佃耕字), reads:

> [The native landowner] "could not afford his daily living and had debts to others, so he leased the land to tenants for cultivation to deduct the interest. However, it was still difficult to repay the loan. As there was no way to repay the loan, he re-contracted the field to other tenants. He borrowed extra silver." The landowner, the middleman, and the new tenants "agreed on three sides that the deposited silver should be more and the rent for the field should be less.[2]

From the material, it seems that the indigenous field owner was in urgent need of cash to pay off his debts due to difficulties in life, so he took back the rented out lands and recruited tenants with a higher deposit, named "rocky land silver" (*qidiyin*碛地银). The two parties and the agent negotiated on three sides that the deposit should be higher so that the future rent of the land could be less. For those who could afford it, the "deposit" was a cash purchase of tenancy rights and therefore stronger control. Thus, the deposit was a way to satisfy the needs of both owners and tenants.

Second, the deposit was a security for the tenant farmer's right to use the land. As long as the tenant did not default on the rent, the landowner could not withdraw the tenancy in default; for the landowner, the deposit was a risk deposit, and if the tenant reneged on the rent, the landowner could deduct it from the deposit.

Third, the rent deposit was a kind of selection by tenant farmers. The landowners usually chose capable and wealthy tenant farmers or good cultivators because they could guarantee high land output and rent

[2] Liu Zemin ed., *Pingpu baishe guwenshu* (Pingpu Baishe Ancient Documents), Taipei: "Guoshiguan" Taiwan wenxian guan, 2002, 127.

payments, and no one was willing to hand over fertile land to a lazy dilettante. As a result, the land was increasingly concentrated in the hands of capable or wealthy farmers, who increased the yield and thus the land's total output. As shown in another source:

> "The land in Dongfeng County (Fengtian Province) was fertile, but most landlords lived in other counties and could not manage the land themselves. Therefore, if the landlords did not select the tenants and recruited the poor ones by mistake, the poor tenants defaulted on the rent, and it was difficult for the landlords to claim the rent." Therefore, the amount of deposit ranged from one hundred to ten *yuan* per *shang*. The landowner paid interest (ranging from about two to three *shi* of grain per hundred *yuan* per year), which was deducted from the amount of rent. "If the tenants were not well-off, they could not afford to pay the rent. In this way, the landlord would not mistakenly recruit poor tenants."[3]

Landowners needed to select tenants carefully, and deposits were a way to test the tenants' credit, ability, and financial resources; a tenant farmer who couldn't pay the deposit wasn't likely to be an able cultivator. Accordingly, the rent deposit system served to screen and incentivize labor and business ability. Ultimately, land became more concentrated in the hands of able farmers, thereby improving the use of scarce resources.

A farmer's household asset portfolio could be mediated through the intertemporal function of land rights transactions in a rent deposits system. Under the standard rent-deposit system, farmers had to pay a deposit named "approval head silver" (*pitouyin*批头银) or "approval gift silver" (*piliyin*批礼银) to the landowner before they could farm the land. They would then have to pay annual rents to the landowner after that. The "deposit" here was equivalent to a risk deposit to ensure the collection of future rents, as farmers were becoming more and more delinquent in paying rent to the landlord.[4]

When a tenant transferred the right to cultivate the land to another cultivator (*gengfu*耕夫), the cultivator also had to pay the tenant the

[3] Nanjing guomin zhengfu sifa xingzhengbu (Ministry of Justice and Administration, Nanjing National Government), ed., *Minshi xiguan diaocha baogao lu* (Report on the Investigation of Civil Customs), vol.2, 761.

[4] Thomas M. Bouye, *Manslaughter, Markets, and Moral Economy: Violent Disputes over Property Rights in Eighteenth-Century* China (New York: Cambridge University Press, 2000).

"deposit silver" (*dinggeng yin* 顶耕银), which was the "rent deposit system" in the tenant-right or top-soil-right tenancy relationship. For example, Huang Chengyun sold a piece of land that yielded eight *dou* of rice to Guo for 95 taels and five *qian* during the Kangxi period and agreed to redeem it for the original price in 1745. After two or three decades, Guo transferred the land to An Xi at the price of 10 taels five *qian* as a deposit; by 1726, An Xi retired from farming due to old age and weakness, and Guo transferred the land to Zhu. Zhu gave five taels of silver to Guo as *pitouyin* and paid the Huang family the silver of deposit at the price of 10 taels of 5 *qian*. In 1754, Huang Chengyun wanted to redeem the land for his own cultivation but had a conflict with the tenant Zhu. In the end, the local magistrate ruled that the landowner, Huang Chengyi, should return the deposit to the tenant, Zhu, and Guo should return the *pitouyin* (deposit) to Zhu (*Xingke tiben*, no.184).

Institutional Arrangement of Farmland Transactions: A Case of Redemption

Redemption mechanisms in farmland transactions can delay the transfer of land rights. For example, traditional land transactions, including *dian*, revocable sale, and rent deposits, can be redeemed to avoid the eventual transfer of land properties, although the target of redeeming differs. Therefore, the civil practices and legal provisions of land rights transactions not only preserved the landownership of farmers but also protected vulnerable groups and provided the possibility for farmers to overcome their difficulties and restore and re-establish the independent operation of their farms, thus effectively reducing the sale of landownership. This was a hedge against the concentration of land rights, a "negative feedback mechanism." In traditional society, practices such as "supplementary payment" (*zhaojia*) and "happy gift silver" (*xiliyin*) could also be regarded as relief for landless farmers to some extent.

Concerning the redemption of transactions in the form of *dian*, rent deposits, and revocable sales, some scholars argue that such mechanisms affect efficiency. However, this chapter, after digging into the original land deeds of Shanxi in the Tsinghua University collection and analyzing the *dian* transactions in the modern land market, finds that the redemption mechanism of *dian* at the original selling price exhibited complex and diverse types, not exclusively the "original price" of the initial transaction. There were at least five ways in which the parties to a transaction could negotiate a return on investment or loss of interest, ensuring the rights and interests of the *dian* buyer (*chengdianren*) and the incentive to invest while allowing the *dian* seller (*chudianren*) flexibility to respond to different levels of demand. This mechanism ensured clear property rights, maintained investment in agricultural production at an effective level, and optimized resource allocation.

The mechanism to "redeem the land at the original price" in traditional Chinese *dian* transactions was quite different from what it implies. In fact, there were at least five ways in which the parties to a transaction could resolve many issues, such as return on investment or loss of interest, through negotiation:

1. Early redemption within the period: The *dian* seller should pay the default fee or the related interest on the price to compensate for the loss of land revenue of the *dian* buyer because the period has not yet expired.
2. Redemption after supplementary payment (*zhaojia*) outside of the period: the *dian* seller should include the added payment in the redemption price when redeeming.
3. When the *dian* buyer increases the long-term investment, the *dian* seller must compensate for the investment and return when redeeming.
4. When the *dian* buyer needs financing, he may transfer the property that he *dian* purchased at the original price or at a lower price to realize it.
5. When the *dian* seller has limited financial resources, he may redeem the land in part or in installments.

In these cases, the redemption price could be higher or lower than the initial *dian* price. These different scenarios of redemption price requirements ensured the interest and investment of the *dian* buyer while allowing the *dian* buyer the flexibility to respond to different levels of demand.

Such a redemption mechanism strongly refutes the notion that *dian* transactions were inefficient. First, the five redemption routes above eliminate the challenge that *dian* transactions do not guarantee investment in the land; second, a mature market for *dian* circulations reduces the transaction costs of *dian*; finally, this redemption mechanism offers fixed expectations on both sides of the transaction and does not lead to the allocation of resources to inefficient producers or hinder land expansion; rather, through the *dian* transaction, efficient laborers can expand their operations.

In addition, different means of land trading, such as *dian*, rent deposit, *taijie* (loan through the land as collateral), revocable sale, and irrevocable sale, work together to create a multi-level and diversified transaction system. There was a focus and preference for each of these types of trading. An individual form has a high-risk preference and a protection preference, but when they were combined, they reduce systemic risk. Farmers can choose according to their needs and circumstances and, to a certain extent, can transfer over time. In addition, this lowers the barrier for farmers to enter the land rights market for financing or acquiring land rights in Rem for production, enabling them to optimize resource allocation in various situations and improve economic efficiency.

Individual family farms have had a significant impact on Chinese society. Tenant farmers built their farms through transactions such as tenancy, rent deposits, *dian*, and top-soil right, earning operating income, investment income, risky returns, and being entrepreneurial. As a result, the peasant "middle class" in traditional Chinese society included landowners who received property income and farm owners (peasant entrepreneurs) who received business income, demonstrating the resilience of the family business over time and the long-term stability of Chinese society. However, purely hired farmers, who couldn't afford a wife or children, accounted for only 2–3% of the agricultural population. It was also the divisibility, low threshold, easy replication, and easy recovery of the individual peasant household that dissuaded from the modernization of large farms or hired farms and led to the divergent development paths taken by China and Western Europe.

6.2 Subsistence Farming with Optimal Farmland Rights

Traditionally, classical economics considers the subsistence farmer optimal, as demonstrated by Arthur Cecil Pigou's (1877–1959) "inefficiency of tenant agriculture." The so-called subsistence farming optimum means, strictly speaking, that farmers should not take land, capital, and labor from the market. Instead, they should cultivate their land. Nevertheless, in the reflection about average land rights, it can be seen that assuming the initial state, all farmers were subsistence farmers with equal fields per capita; when factors of production were actively traded, the equilibrium of subsistence farmers was broken quickly; when trade was not smooth, it causes resource misallocation and waste.

Notion of "Subsistence Farming Optimum"

The theory of the optimality of subsistence farming is a claim for a specific historical period, a static view, and an idealized argument. In light of the changing composition of farming families and their varying farming abilities, if all farmers could only cultivate their land, it would make resource allocation inefficient. In Jiangxi province in the Qing dynasty, the example of the peasant family with four sons illustrates this principle. When the boys were young, the family could not cultivate the land alone, so renting or selling the land was a rational option. A few years later, when all four sons grew up and the peasant's land was not enough, he needed to acquire land from the market to realize an effective combination of labor and land. In other words, only through the market can the factors of production reach an equilibrium state of dynamic allocation. All farmers would be obliged to own land, just as all businesses would be obliged to own offices and factories. Not only would this be absurd in theory, but it would also raise the barrier for people, especially young people, to start their own businesses. When farmers can establish their family farms, even if they only have rights to use or occupy the land, then the threshold for establishing a family farm is lowered for most farmers, especially those experiencing financial issues. Only when landownership, occupation, use, and cultivation rights were accessible to the market will there be a sound market for land rights to allocate resources.

It has been argued by some scholars that farmers must, or even can only, control ownership of land; controlling the right to occupy and use land is considered inferior. This kind of emotional demand is understandable but does not stand up to academic logic and historical evidence. Land rights were divided into ownership, possession, and use rights, and use rights can be further divided into cultivation rights and others. Suppose farmers can choose to have access to a certain level of land rights according to their preferences. In that case, it lowers the threshold, increases the diversity of choices, and reduces the risk, which is more beneficial to farmers, isn't it?

Moreover, the theory of subsistence farming optimality implies that each farming household operates in a constant, self-sufficient state. However, farming households cannot achieve self-sufficiency without external factors. Only by accessing the market for land rights can farmers fulfill their needs for financing, realize future earnings, and survive difficult times.

One of the theoretical foundations of the optimal theory of the subsistence farmer is the theory of exploiting tenant farmers and of the inefficiency of tenant farmers. These theories hold that once farmers rent land, landlords exploit them, which leads to social inequity and injustice, as shown by Pigou's "inefficiency of tenant agriculture." Pigou argues that there were three main reasons for the inefficiency:

1. Tenant farmers produce substantially less than subsistence farmers. However, Buck's empirical analysis shows that subsistence farmers produced 100–101 and sharecroppers produced 103–104.
2. The shorter the tenancy period, the lower the tenant farmer's productivity. The statistical yearbook of 1936 shows that the period of shared tenancy was shorter than the period of fixed-rent tenancy, and the rent was slightly higher. There were two reasons for the difference. One is that short-term contracts cost more, just as short-term rent contracts were more expensive. Second, under short-term tenancy, the maintenance of the land was mainly settled by the landlord's investment. This is also the difference between a shared tenancy and a fixed-rent tenancy, which has been solved by Steven N. S. Cheung's theory of sharecropping. The two were different options, and there is no superiority or inferiority.
3. In terms of inputs such as land improvement, tenant farmers have lower inputs than subsistence farmers. However, the essence of the difference is not whether landlords or tenant farmers invest in land improvements. As discussed in the first section of this chapter, the future benefits of tenant farmers' inputs into water and fertility were guaranteed and can be realized through the market. Therefore, under the system of permanent tenancy and field rights, land inputs were essentially borne by the tenant farmer. In fact, the total value of non-land assets is roughly the same for homesteads and tenant farms and can be higher for tenant farms.

The tenancy system in traditional China was relatively well-developed and broadly divided into the following types:

Shared tenancy: The tenant farmer's own means of production were incomplete.
Fixed-rent tenancy: The tenant farmer was completely independent, and "the landlord did not invest anything."
Rent deposit system: The tenant farmer was given more control over the land by paying a deposit to buy the tenancy.
Permanent tenancy system: Hereditary management rights, a kind of possession.
Top-soil right: The tenancy became a property right and a right of possession.
Capital model: Hired labor operation. Usually a large-scale and market-oriented operation; generally referred to as "large tenant farmer" (*da diannong*), rich tenant farmer (*dian funong*).

This variety of contracts allowed the tenant farmer and the landowner to decide based on their preferences and market prices.

Finally, the optimal subsistence farmer theory is still a kind of economic mindset in a shortage economy. Under the historical conditions of economic ruin in modern China, the lack of land and widespread poverty exacerbated the situation for peasants. However, the fundamental way to lift peasants out of poverty lies in technological progress and productivity improvement, in industrialization and urbanization. The movement of peasants to the cities or factories to earn a living reduces the number of peasants on limited land, thus giving more land to those who remain in the countryside. However, if everyone is confined to their own small piece of land, how can technological development and productivity increase be generated?

Under traditional technological conditions, human beings cannot solve the problem of poverty. Therefore, there will always be poor tenants and subsistence farmers in human society. If all workers remained subsistence farmers, it would be impossible to eliminate poverty and create permanent stagnation. In contrast, under the tenancy system, there were types of tenant farmers, rich tenant farmers, and large tenant farmers. There was competition between landowners and tenant farmers and between superiority and inferiority. When the land was concentrated in the hands of capable farmers, it indicated that resources were allocated to efficient farms, which may lead to progress. Although the tenancy system could not eliminate poverty, it had the potential to bring about structural change and progress.

A Theory of Optimal Farmland Rights

In the past, it was understood that land tenancy occurred when many peasants were forced to lose their farmland under difficult circumstances and had to rent farmland from landlords. If such an understanding holds, a higher tenancy rate is likely in places where natural disasters were severe and production is backward. However, this was not the case. According to the percentage of tenant farmers and semi-tenant farmers (or semi-tenant farmers) in each province of Republican China, it can be seen that the tenancy rate in developed areas was much higher than that in backward areas. For example, North China, which was relatively backward in economic development, had the lowest tenancy rate, while the more economically developed southern region had a higher tenancy rate (Table 6.1).

In terms of individual regions, those with more developed economies also tended to have more developed tenancy systems. As shown in Table 6.1, among the four areas in Wuxing County, Zhejiang, Yuanjiahui's farming economy was the most backward, and its percentage of subsistence farmers was the highest. Among them, Nanxun Town was the most developed area. Its tenancy system was also the best developed, with only 8.72% of farmers being subsistence farmers and nearly 90% being semi-subsistence and tenant farmers based on the tenancy system.

Another example was that of the 11 rural villages in Danyang County, Jiangsu Province, Guixian Town was the richest, with the highest unit

Table 6.1 Shares of the subsistence, semi-subsistence farmers, and tenant Farmers in Wuxing County. *Sources*: Zhongguo jingji yanjiusuo (Institute of Chinese Economy), 1939, pp. 751–752

Regions	*Subsistence farmers (%)*	*Semi-subsistence farmers (%)*	*Tenant farmers (%)*
Nanxun	8.72	82.56	5.81
Linghu	33.64	58.88	2.34
Shuangxiu	55.56	40.43	0.31
Yuangjiahui	58.38	35.53	1.52

production of all kinds of agricultural products and the largest proportion of farm households with a standard of living above the well-off. Correspondingly, its tenancy ratio was also the highest in all of Danyang County, with 65% of partially self-employed farmers and tenant farmers, much higher than in other areas.[5] Further, among the five regions in Jiaxing County, Zhejiang Province, Yuxi Town had the highest agricultural productivity in the county, with the proportion of semi-subsistence farmers and tenant farmers at 94.82%, much higher than the other regions in the county.[6]

By introducing the theory of optimal ownership structure of firms, Zhao Liang and Long Denggao propose the theory of optimal land rights structure at the level of farmers' operations.[7] Zhao and Long argue that in the case of free trade, the land rights structure with the largest total institutional surplus will dominate. The transaction cost of land rights, the return function of land investment, and the labor cost of farm operations determine the total surplus of the system. Since these factors vary significantly across regions, environments, and even farm households, theoretically, the land rights structure should be diverse. Thus, the subsistence farming system, the hired labor system, the share tenancy system, and the fixed-rent tenancy system each have their own conditions of applicability. In this paper, Zhao and Long conducted two types of empirical tests, and the results were as follows:

One type was the factors that affect the return on land investment. In general, the higher the rate of return on land investment, the greater the willingness of landowners to invest in land, and thus the higher the tenancy rate. By examining the degree of commercialization of agricultural products and the relationship between transportation costs and tenancy rates, this chapter finds that the easier the agricultural products were to transport or the greater the degree of commercialization, the higher the tenancy rate. The other category was landownership and the area of land operation. The test results found that the average area of land

[5] Zhang Hanlin, *Danyang nongcun jingji diaocha* (Danyang Rural Economy Survey), Jiangsu sheng nongmin yinhang zonghang, 1930, 789–835.

[6] Feng Zigang, *Jiaxing xian nongcun diaocha* (Jiaxing County Rural Survey), Zhejiang University and Jiaxing County Government, 1936, 236.

[7] Zhao Liang and Long Denggao, "Tudi zudian yu jingji xiaolü" (Land Tenancy and Economic Efficiency), *Zhongguo jingji wenti* (China Economic Studies), no. 2 (2012): 3–15.

rights was negatively related to the tenancy rate in both the south and the north, while the area of land capable of being operated per unit of labor was positively related to the tenancy rate.

This chapter compares the economic efficiency of historical tenant farming with subsistence farming and finds that tenant farming tends to be more advantageous than subsistence farming. Based on statistics from various sources in several typical regions, the paper compares subsistence farming and tenant farming in these regions in terms of the size of the family workforce, the size of the land operation, and the profitability of operating the farm. Zhao and Long find that, in most cases, semi-subsistence farmers have larger families, larger farms, and higher profits. In addition, semi-subsistence farmers who rented a portion of their land made up a significant proportion of the rich farmers, and fewer were pure subsistence farmers.

In general, the tenancy had adaptability and advantages in three ways. First, the tenancy system separated the investment function of land from the production factors, thus lowering the threshold for farmers to acquire land to cultivate and landlords to invest in land. It promoted cooperation and allocation among those with different factor endowments. Second, the tenancy system regulated the contradiction between the areas of landownership and operation. Since there were different mechanisms for determining the titled area of land and the optimal operating area, tenancy allowed the operating area to be free from the constraints of the titled area. Third, the tenancy system achieved meritocracy for cultivators. Subsistence farmers who were good at land management could expand their business scale through other tenancy and land rights transactions, while those who were not faced elimination.

Growth of Subsistence Farmers

In traditional China, a subsistence farmer could not set up a large-scale operation. He was no longer a subsistence farmer if he acquired land or labor from the market to expand his production. When a subsistence farmer rented land from the market, he became a tenant farmer; when a subsistence farmer hired workers from the market, he became a business or even a capitalist farm. From this point of view, there was no such thing as a strict "subsistence farmer," who inevitably had to obtain or supplement some market production factor.

A tenant farmer, of course, acquired land from the market. When tenant farmers expanded their land operations, they generated economies of scale, known as large tenant farmers (*da diannong*). In Taiwan in the nineteenth century, large tenant farmers were the main driving force behind the great development of the local agricultural economy; in England in the seventeenth and eighteenth centuries, large tenant farmers drove the change of traditional business methods and led to the English agricultural and property rights revolutions. When large tenant farmers hired workers to run the business, they promoted the emergence of capitalist agricultural operations.

In traditional China, the development of large tenant farmers was often inhibited because small individual family farms were highly competitive and viable. However, the number of wealthy tenant farmers was not insignificant. In fact, tenant farmers existed in all classes. According to the agricultural demographic statistics in 1934, there were landlords and tenant farmers, subsistence farmers and tenant farmers, and semi-subsistence farmers and tenant farmers. In other words, each class could rent land from the market. Likewise, hired farmers could rent out their small plots of land, including the subsoil and top-soil rights.

In the land rights market characterized by "multi-level land rights" and "diversification of transaction types," on the one hand, there was a trend where "tenant farmers turned into middle peasants," and on the other hand, there was a trend where subsistence farmers transformed into non-subsistence farmers, such as tenant farmers and semi-tenant farmers, which can be called "tenantization of middle-income farmers." In other words, it was difficult for farmers to improve their operating capacity and living standard without using the market to rent land. These farmers did not hold full land titles, but they were distinct from the traditional tenant farmers who simply rented the use of land. They occupied different levels and sizes of land rights. They "shared" the landowner's control over the land.

As a result of the distribution of land rights, the phenomenon of "non-subsistence-farming" (*fei zigengnong hua*) occurred because a large number of land titles were divided and transferred to different farmers through various types of transactions and continued to be traded freely. In such a situation of fragmentation and trading of land rights, the number of subsistence farmers with complete land titles naturally decreased. In terms of the transaction preferences of land operators, a large number of operators were actively involved in various kinds of transactions of tenancy rights, *dian* rights, and land top-soil and subsoil rights and were not confined to the traditional form of irrevocable sales (*juemai*); there were even many cases in which subsistence farmers sold their land and switched to tenancy farming.

Since the phenomenon of "non-subsistence-farming" was inconsistent with the traditional understanding of "subsistence farming optimal," it is necessary to explore further why farmers chose to give up subsistence farming in the land rights market. By constructing a dynamic optimization model that optimizes the utility of farm households under an infinite period, Tang Yunjian analyzes the changes in the optimal land rights allocation strategies of farmers at different periods and different levels of wealth and poverty and demonstrates the self-generating mechanism of the choice of "giving up subsistence farming" from the perspective of farm households' independent operations. This chapter points out that the multi-level land rights trading system was of great significance for the independent operation of farm households, and therefore it was necessary to rethink the proposition of "optimal subsistence farming."[8]

Economic efficiency stems from the rational allocation of resources. In agricultural societies, land circulation was one of the prerequisites for the efficient combination of production factors. Resource allocation and land transfer can only be realized in transactions and markets, and smooth transactions were based on clear property rights. Since the Ming and Qing dynasties, the division of land rights and the diversification of their transaction types have enabled land circulation to break through the limits of personalized transactions and to take place over a larger area and among a broader range of people. The market for land rights also became an instrument of integration.

First, farmers could use the land rights market to combine their family assets and transfer their current and future earnings to help them overcome difficulties and hardships. Second, labor and land were combined in the land rights market. The land rights market could adapt to changes in the composition of the household labor force and promptly meet the diverse choices and preferences of farmers in terms of land cultivation, sideline business, industrial and commercial business, or geographical

[8] Tang Yunjian, "Jinshi 'fei zigengnong hua' yuanyin yanjiu—cong nonghu diquan peizhi celue jiaodu" (A Study on the Causes of "Non-Subsistence-Farming" in Modern China: A Perspective on the Land Allocation Strategy of Farming Households), Master thesis, Tsinghua University, 2016.

migration. Third, various land rights transactions could circulate land to the most efficient labor force. Farmers rich in labor or good at land cultivation could trade land rights to obtain access to land operation rights, input work costs, and increase land output. At the same time, urban and external residents could get rid of the constraints of land entities and invest in land for income through asset-based land rights. Thus, capital flows to the land in various ways.[9]

As the types of land transactions become more diverse, the more options for farmers to trade become available, and the more possibilities for combining factors of production. For example, during the Republican Era, the Chinese government banned transactions such as rent deposits and tenant transfers to protect vulnerable tenant farmers. In reality, however, this policy restricted the free choice of farmers and was therefore not accepted and practiced by the local people. Instead, traditional land trading practices continued in an orderly manner.[10]

Although the constraints differed, historical land rights transactions and resource allocation still offer practical lessons and insights. Only a dynamic combination of labor and land can optimize the allocation of resources. Thus, the "good" desire to divide the land equally and restrict its transfer, or to keep peasants fixed or even tied to the land, hindered large-scale operations and lagged behind the trend of peasants moving to the cities under rapid urbanization.[11]

[9] A number of scholars have questioned why the traditional Chinese economic system could not be transformed into a capitalist or modern economy, given its dynamism. Traditional China's land-based resource allocation and economic operation brought economic efficiency under the prevailing technological conditions, but also solidified and reinforced the original system. The truly logical and testable conclusion was that the more mature a traditional economy based on land rights is, the more difficult it was to produce the opposite factor—a modern capital-centered economy—originally and endogenously. In fact, original institutional innovations tend not to produce heterogeneous factors opposed to them in mature economies; in the midst of turbulent changes, the new or heterogeneous factors generally break through the constraints of the old system, which was not so strong in the first place.

[10] Many scholars have begun to move away from this simplistic assumption of questioning the rationality of the traditional economy based on the backwardness of the modern Chinese economy. China's modern economy collapsed for a variety of reasons.

[11] It was originally published in the third issue of *Hebei xuekan* (Hebei Academic Journal) in 2018. I thank Li Yiwei for the proofreading.

6.3 From "Equalization of Farmland Rights" to "Advocation of Farmland Circulation"

In the twentieth century, the idea of "equalizing farmland rights" (*pingjun diquan*) became a mainstream idea in China and was also put into practice. In the early 1950s, China implemented an equalization of farmland ownership; in the early 1980s, it implemented an equalization of farmland use rights. However, the initial equalization was quickly broken under the influence of variables such as women marrying off, changes in family demographic membership, and population movements; together with other variables, the dynamic combination of land and labor was difficult to sustain. With the advent of the twenty-first century, China moved to encourage land circulation, shifting from government allocation to market allocation of agricultural land.

In the middle and late twentieth centuries, the political slogan "equalization of farmland rights" gradually became the dominant ideology and was implemented throughout China. The Land Reform Movement of 1949–1952 was a mandatory change to equalize landownership, while the Collectivization Movement of the late 1950s and the Family Joint Production Contract Responsibility System of 1981 aimed to equalize land use rights. Historically, each of the above land reforms was a significant change in property rights, even a major shift that was unprecedented in human history. From an academic perspective, the way the land rights situation changed after the "equalization of land rights" was a rare economic experiment that provided valuable research material.

The book also starts at this point. Despite much writing on "equalization of farmland rights" and the previous three land reforms, a thorough, cogent, and systematic examination was still lacking. Throughout Chinese history, land reforms have profoundly affected society, the economy, and politics. Therefore, a systematic study of the historical changes in Chinese land rights can not only serve as inspiration for current land reforms and as a reference for understanding the fundamental principles of the reforms but can also be used to better understand and summarize the historical meaning of "Chinese characteristics."

Equalization of Farmland Ownership: A Mandatory End

The equalization of land rights was a mainstream idea in the twentieth century, first proposed by Sun Yat-sen. The "People's Livelihoods" (*minsheng zhuyi*) from the "Three Principles of the People" (*sanmin zhuyi*) included equalization of land rights and restraint of capital, which was a new understanding at that time. However, from the logic of economics, many interpretations of the "Three Principles of the People" were more of a sentimental appeal. For example, in reality, Sun Yat-sen's idea of "increasing prices to the public" (*zhangjia guigong*) was challenging to realize. Sun believed that the concentration of land in China at that time had led to the bankruptcy and exile of peasants and therefore saw the concentration of land rights as the root cause of China's economic decline in modern times. In some areas, land concentration was indeed severe, and this, combined with widespread peasant poverty, caused the perception of a causal link between the two. Nevertheless, recent research shows that, according to the most authoritative survey data on land reforms in 1949–1952, the top 10% of the wealthy in the southern provinces held only 25–35% of the land, far less than the 70–80% social perception or political propaganda; and the southern provinces were also generally considered to be more uneven in terms of land tenure than the north.

Despite the slogan, Sun Yat-sen and the Kuomintang failed to specify how to implement equal farmland rights. Accordingly, "equalization of land rights" was paradoxical because since private property rights in land were recognized, farmland should be freely disposed of by its owners, so it was not the place of the government to distribute it equally. At the First National Congress of the GMD in 1924, Sun Yat-sen replaced the slogan "equalization of farmland rights" with "land to the tiller." It was only in 1949, after the defeat of the GMD in Taiwan, that land reforms were implemented in Taiwan through redemption.

Equal Distribution of Farmland in the Land Reforms

In the 1920s and 1930s, the Communist Party of China (CCP) implemented the "fight against the landlords and share the land" (*da tuhao, fen tiandi*) in the base areas; during the War of Resistance, the CCP implemented the policy of "reduction of rent and interest" (*jianzu jianxi*); and in the early years of the founding of the People's Republic of China, the Land Reform Movement was launched in the liberated areas. In order to mobilize the peasants and win the War of Liberation, on May 4, 1946, the Central Committee of the Communist Party of China issued the "Instruction on Land Issues." With this, the policy of "reduction of rent and interest," implemented during the War of Resistance, was transformed into a land policy aimed at realizing "farmland to the tiller." In the early stages of land reforms, the most common methods of redistributing land were settling accounts (*qingsuan*), persuading landowners to sell their fields, and expropriating landowners' land. In 1947, the National Land Conference put forward the slogan "equal distribution of land" (*pingfen tudi*). Since then, the land reform policy confiscated land from landlords and distributed it to peasants without compensation.

In 1949–1952 there was a top-down, mandatory shift in farmland property rights that was both sweeping and revolutionary. So, how did the land property system in China change before and after that? Before that, the idea of private property rights of land was deeply rooted. The prevalence of land transaction contracts indicated that peasants could dispose of their land at their discretion within the limits of the law, including the sale, tenancy, and other forms of transactions. Land transaction deeds can also be used for land transfers and transactions, detailing the parties' economic interests.

What kind of changes occurred in the land ownership system after the land reforms? There used to be a view that the revolution was about overthrowing private ownership of land and establishing collective ownership through land reforms. In fact, after the Land Reform Movement, from 1952 to 1957, peasants obtained landownership certificates and were still free to dispose of their land, including buying and selling. In other words, the landownership system was still a system of private property rights. Moreover, the starting point of the revolution was to give peasants access to landownership through land reforms and change the inequality of land rights in the past.

The Agrarian Reform Law (*Tudi gaige fa*) enacted and implemented in 1950 further guaranteed peasant landownership at the legal level. Article 30 states, "After the completion of the land reforms, the government shall issue landownership certificates and recognize the right of all landowners to operate, buy and sell and lease their land freely." In other words, the peasants had the same right to dispose of their land freely before the land reforms.

On June 28, 1950, the Eighth Session of the Central People's Government Committee adopted the Land Reform Law of the People's Republic of China (*Zhonghua renmin gongheguo tudi gaige fa*). Article 30 states, "After the completion of land reforms, the People's Government shall issue landownership certificates." On November 10, 1950, the 18th

Council of State adopted the "Regulations on Land Reforms in Urban and Suburban Areas" (*Cheng jiaoqu tudi gaige tiaoli*). Article 17 stipulated that "after the completion of the land reforms in the urban suburbs, landownership certificates shall be issued to those with private agricultural land to guarantee their landownership." On November 25, 1950, the Ministry of the Interior's Instruction on the "Issuance of Land and Property Ownership Certificates" (*Guanyu tianfa tudi fangchang suoyouzheng de zhishi*) further clarified that after the completion of the land reforms, all peasants would be issued "Land and Property Ownership Certificates" (*tudi fangchan suoyouzheng*), regardless of their newly subdivided land and existing land and houses. The certificate was issued to households to show that the land and property were common to the household members. The land and property ownership certificate had three copies, the first for the family, the second for the county government, and the third for the village administration.

On September 20, 1954, the First Session of the First National People's Congress adopted the Constitution of the People's Republic of China. The Constitution provided that "the state shall protect the landownership rights of the peasants in accordance with the law." It was a solemn political promise and declaration by the new regime to the people of the country and to the people of the world. The "equalization of land rights," implemented in the Soviet and liberated areas and gradually covered in full after the founding of the New PRC, was the political and economic result of a long revolution.

The Land Reform itself was also achieved through violent revolution. Landowners' land and all their property were confiscated and redistributed equally; the old social land transaction deeds and land titles were burned. Further, there were also violent acts of repression during the agrarian revolution. For example, 2024 people were killed in Xing County, including landlords, many rich and middle peasants, and even poor and hired peasants. At the time, violence was a revolutionary ethic. "Everywhere it was proposed that the tendency to divide the land peacefully should be prevented and that this automatic surrender of land by landlords should be treated with a clear policy of rejection." Because "without the struggle for settling accounts, the class hatred between landlords and peasants will not be obvious, and the peasant class consciousness will not be raised."[12] It should be noted that the violence during the agrarian revolution was a product of the times. This does not need to be whitewashed, but it cannot be judged by today's market ethics.

At that time, the idea of equal land rights was already deeply rooted and became the basic consensus of the whole society. The story of a former academic who graduated from SWLU demonstrates this point. On the one hand, his family's land was equally divided in the land reforms (in those days, most professors came from wealthy families that owned quite a lot of land); on the other hand, he joined the land reform working group in another county and participated in confiscating the land of the local landlords. He admitted that he was inevitably conflicted when faced with his family's land being divided equally. However, he thought that land reforms were a good policy, so he concentrated on the work of land reform without any reluctance.

One of the few people who openly opposed land reforms at that time was Professor Dong Shijin, a doctor of agricultural economics from Cornell University. On April 12, 1948, 6 months after the release of the Outline of China's Land Law (*Zhongguo tudifa dagang*), Ta Kung Pao (Shanghai) published the proceedings of a discussion on "land issues." Dong Shijin was the first to speak, and he opposed the land reforms. Dong argued that China's land problem was not serious, the difference between the rich and the poor in China's countryside was not as big as in the cities, and the uneven distribution of land in China was not as severe as in other countries. He argued that the land in China was not unevenly distributed but that there was too much population and too little land, resulting in a large surplus of rural labor. Among the 19 participants, most advocated for the government to acquire land through bonds; three supported the CCP's land reform policy; three supported the land collectivization policy; but none supported Dong Shijin's proposal.[13] At the beginning of the founding of the PRC, Dong Shijin wrote a letter to Mao Zedong, stating that the land reforms should be halted.[14] He said:

[12] Luo Pinghan, *Tudi gaige yundongshi* (History of the Land Reforms Movement), Fuzhou: Fujian People's Press, 2005, 184.

[13] Zheng Yefu, "Tugai: Fei Xiaotong yu Dong Shijin" (Land Reforms: Fei Xiaotong and Dong Shijin), *Mingbao yuekan* (Hongkong) (Mingpao Monthly), no. 8 and no. 9, 2011.

[14] "Guanyu Dongshijin shangshu fandui tudi gaige wenti" (On the issue of Dong Shijin's Petition Against Land Reforms), *Guancha* (Observation), no. 6, December 1950.

> "The reason landlords and rich peasants became landlords and rich peasants, except for a few special cases, was that they were more capable, worked harder, and spent less. Although many of them inherited the savings from their grandfathers, many rose from poor farmers. Even if it is due to their grandfather's savings, they must be non-disabled; otherwise, they were bound to decline. Namely, most landlords and rich peasants were the best members of society, the driving force for social progress, and should be protected and rewarded by the state. However, this does not mean that the poor peasants were all inferior because most did not have the opportunity to improve their situation during the war and the lack of prosperity. However, no poor peasant does not want to become a landlord or a rich peasant. It is not credible to say that they did not become landlords or rich peasants because they had an exceptionally high moral character and did not want to exploit others."
>
> "The state should undoubtedly help these poor farmers improve their situation. However, the proper way to help them is to make efforts to develop production and construction after peace is restored and to create more employment opportunities so that everyone can work and earn much income, not to give them a few pieces of land and tie them up in small plots of land so that they can continue to live in the countryside where the farmers were already too many. They cultivate such a small piece of land, and the result of their hard work all year round is not enough to maintain the minimum living standard after the food tax and all the expenses."

However, Mao Zedong did not read his report as he was visiting the Soviet Union then. According to Dong, peasants could become rich peasants by acquiring more land to make their lives better. Only by allowing land to be allocated to capable laborers could land production be made more efficient and social and economic development possible. On the contrary, who would want to increase land inputs if farmers accumulated land and wealth only to have their wealth distributed away equally? If land output and productivity did not increase, there would be no socioeconomic development. Unfortunately, under the revolutionary fervor of the time, Dong Shijin's vision was drowned in the flood of revolution.

Collectivization Movement

Although the original intention of mutual aid groups, cooperatives, and collectivization was to improve farmers' business efficiency, it was distorted by the extreme "left" trend. Chinese farmers were usually a family of five, primarily self-employed, and their risk-bearing capacity was small due to their small scale. If mutual aid groups and cooperatives were implemented, they could realize large-scale operations and promote economic efficiency. First, membership in cooperatives was basically mandatory at that time. All peasants had to join, and the right to use the land belonged to the collective. Moreover, from elementary societies and cooperatives to senior societies and then to the People's Commune in 1958, collectivization was achieved within 1 or 2 years, called the "Great Leap Forward." As a result, the "peasant land ownership" achieved by the land reforms in the past was changed to "collective land ownership." Second, there was no exit mechanism for cooperatives, which was another kind of coercion, and the peasants had no right to choose.[15]

Through collectivization and corporatization, peasants' land use and ownership rights were taken back to the collective. On June 30, 1956, the Third Session of the First National People's Congress adopted the "Model Statute for Advanced Agricultural Production Cooperatives" (*Gaoji nongye shengchan hezuoshe shifan zhangcheng*). Article 13 stipulated those farmers who joined the cooperative had to transfer their private land to the collective ownership of the cooperative. In other words, individuals no longer had ownership of land. It was only 2 years before the 1954 Constitution. On September 27, 1962, the Tenth Meeting of the Eighth Central Committee of the Communist Party of China adopted the Draft Amendment to the "Regulations on the Work of Rural People's Communes" (*Nongcun renmin gongshe gongzuo tiaoli xiuzheng an*, referred to as "Article 60"). The Draft stipulated that all land within the production team should be owned by the production team, including the land reserved for the community members (*ziliudi*), their own hills (*ziliushan*), and houses (*zhaijidi*). They were not allowed to be rented or traded.[16] After the Third Plenary Session of the Eleventh Central Committee, the Chinese government seriously reflected on this series of extreme "leftist" ideologies and officially negated the "Great Leap Forward" and the People's Commune.

[15] Wen Guanzhong, "Tudi zhidu bixu yunxu nongmin you tuichu ziyou" (The Land System Must Allow Farmers the Freedom to Exit), *Shehui guancha* (Social Sciences Digest), no. 11 (2008): 10–12.

[16] In 1962, the "Certificate of Land Use and Property Ownership for Members of Anhua County, Hunan Province" stated that "Iiquan People's Commune, Wangcheng Team, Meibei Production Team, Liu's 3 *fen* of land reserved for the family's long-term use; and the house belongs to the family forever, "no unit or individual shall violate."

If the People's Commune of 1958 marked the realization of collective ownership, when did the Constitution recognize collective ownership? In 1975, China promulgated its second Constitution. This Constitution was deeply marked by the "Cultural Revolution" and the "leftist" ideology. By 1978 and 1982, the Constitution had undergone massive revisions. Some people argue that the collective landownership system and rural collectivization were not recognized by the Constitution for the 20 years from 1957 to 1975. However, we believe that the collective landownership system was a historical fait accompli, despite the "leftist" policy, and that the current collective ownership system should not be denied. Moreover, a careful review of the collective ownership system's history, background, and evolution can clarify many misconceptions and stereotypes.

Equalization of User Rights: Vitality of Family Farms

Under the People's Commune system, what rights did the peasants have to the land? Since land use and ownership rights were collectively owned, labor was organized collectively. Whenever the whistle blew or the gong sounded, the peasants went to the fields to do collective work. The lack of incentives for collective labor led to the phenomenon of "free-riding." At the same time, since the peasants lost their most important property, the land, they were not motivated to produce. By the end of the Cultural Revolution, China's agricultural economy was on the verge of collapse.

In 1981, the "contract to the household" (*baochan daohu*) was introduced, which meant that the right to use collective farmland was reallocated to individual peasant families. However, at that time, the "contract to the household" was a terrible ideological prohibited area. The peasants in Xiaogang Village wrote blood letters and fingerprints to distribute the farmland to each family; they promised each other that if they were taken away, other peasants should take care of their families. Du Runsheng also coined the long name "household contract responsibility system" (*jiating lianchan chengbao zeren zhi*) to replace the de facto "contract to the household," thus circumventing the ideological debate. Fortunately, this new name also allowed later reforms to bypass the legal definition of tenure.

The change in property rights policy had an immediate effect, which has rarely been seen before. The people's communes and collective labor led many peasants to flee for food because they did not have enough to eat. However, once the policy of "contract to the household" was promoted, the problem of famine was soon solved. It was called "collective labor leads to famine, but the policy of contract to the household offers a surplus of food."

It has been argued that significant changes occurred because farmers regained access to land and were thus motivated to produce. This explanation was valid but incomplete. The real explanation was that although the peasants did not gain ownership of the land, by owning the right to use the land, the peasants could establish their family farms and thus become agricultural entrepreneurs who could have both business income and entrepreneurial remuneration. In this way, the peasant received not only a wage payment for his labor (under the people's commune, members only received work credits, that is, labor income, and their role was equivalent to that of a commune hired hand); but more importantly, the farm, as a kind of enterprise, had the right to surplus control and surplus claim. The peasants also had the power to dispose of the surplus of production, which was a strong incentive to produce.

Historically, there has been a vast difference between farmers renting land, setting up family farms, and working as hired laborers to get paid for their work. One might ask if tenant farmers were considered agricultural entrepreneurs? Of course, they are, just as a firm's office was usually rented nowadays. If the business owner does not own the office or the factory but only had the right to use them, do the factory and the business belong to him? Of course, they do. Therefore, the business owner gets paid as an entrepreneur and had residual control and a residual claim beyond his salary.

Generally speaking, 50% of the land rent was based on the production of one crop season. Suppose the farmer works hard and pays the rent for the first season and usually does not need to pay for the second season; but if the farmer raises rice fish inside the farm or grows vegetables on the ridge, he does not need to give the landowner the fresh rice fish or vegetables, because they were income outside the contractual provisions, called a residual claim. The income outside the contract was the reason for the massive difference between the tenant farmer's and the hired worker's income. After the implementation of the policy of "contract to the household," farmers were motivated not only to cultivate their own farmland but also to establish their family farms to obtain entrepreneurial rewards and residual claims, as well as risky returns.[17] This was the institutional basis for the dramatic and resilient growth of agriculture in the 1980s. It seems to have been overlooked and not systematically revealed.

Unsustainability of Equalization of Farmland Rights

Equalization of farmland rights was a wonderful idea. However, can the initial equilibrium state after equalization be maintained in the long run?

Equalization of Farmland Rights: Family Property Division and Governmental Force

The equalization of farmland rights at the micro-level was practiced in China since ancient times, namely, the system of "equal division among sons." In order to divide the family's land, house, movable property, and debts equally among the male children, the peasant household usually signed a contract or drew lots to determine their ownership. However, even after equal division, the second generation with the same starting point and blood background could have completely different developmental results. For example, the difference in abilities between sons and grandsons, the difference in the size of their nuclear families and resources of their maternal families, and the difference in opportunities after the separation of families all made the differences between the second and third generations likely to grow larger. Dong Shijin's "Two Families" (*Lianghu renjia*) describes in literary form the differences in the development of the next generation after a family was divided equally into two families.

If the parents' wealth was divided equally among the sons, the second generation soon becomes unequal in wealth. Then, does the third generation of sons change the unevenness by equalizing it again among themselves? Absolutely not. If so, individuals would have no incentive to increase wealth creation and accumulation, and economic and social development would regress. Therefore, there was usually only equalization among sons; or rather, there can be only one equalization among the

[17] Long Denggao, Pengbo, "Jinshi diannong de jignying xignzhi yu shouyi bijiao" (A Comparison of the Nature of Business and Earnings of Tenant Farmers in Modern Times), *Jingji yanjiu* (Economic Research Journal), no. 1 (2010): 138–147.

second generation, but not another equalization among the third generation. The "equal division among sons" guarantees an equal starting point but not an equal outcome. In fact, there was usually a race between sons.

How can a country achieve an even distribution of wealth and maintain this equilibrium in the long run when a family's wealth was distributed in this way? Of course, it was even more impossible. Nor should the state seek permanent averages of outcomes. If a country wants to narrow the gap between rich and poor, it can do so through taxes and benefits rather than by redistributing land and property.

The first round of equalization of farmland rights was the equalization of landownership. Under private ownership, peasants could sell, rent, pawn, and mortgage their land. These land transactions quickly changed the equalization of land rights and led to the emergence of new rich peasants and rich tenant peasants.[18] When the land was concentrated back into the hands of the farmers, the original purpose of the "equalization of land rights" was shaken. What should be done then? During the land reforms, Mao Zedong said:

The egalitarianism of the peasants was revolutionary before the distribution of land, so we should not oppose it; what we should oppose is the egalitarianism after the distribution of land. It does not matter if the land is distributed evenly once, but not often. In fact, we are going to infringe on some old-style rich peasants; however, the new-style rich peasants should not be infringed.[19]

The most important goal of equalizing land rights and the agrarian revolution was to get a better combination of the two factors of production: labor and land. Since some farmers did not have or lacked land, it was thought that the equalization of land rights would give them access to land for cultivation. In fact, however, the averaging of land rights was soon followed by the concentration of land among the best cultivators, a result of the optimal allocation of land and labor through the land rights market. However, on the face of it, the initial equilibrium state was quickly altered. So, what can be done to ensure that the initial equilibrium

[18] Su Shaozhi, "Geming genjudi xin funong wenti yanjiu" (A Study on the New Rich Peasants in the Revolutionary Base Areas), *Jindaishi yanjiu* (Journal of Modern Chinese Studies), no. 1 (2014).

[19] Zhonggong Zhognyang wenxian yanjiushi (Central Documentary Research Office of the Communist Party of China), ed., *Mao Zedong nianpu (1893–1949)* (Mao Zedong Chronology), vol.2, Beijing: People's Press, 1993, 78–79.

state of averages was not changed? Only by not allowing land to be traded, that is, by land rights being taken away. Therefore, the second stage of land reforms was the equalization of land use rights. Under collective property rights, peasants could no longer buy or sell land. Nevertheless, was it possible to keep the equalization of tenure rights? As a matter of fact, it would still be difficult to maintain.

Unsustainability of the Original Equalization Status

Both equalization of farmland ownership and farmland use rights were subject to variables and shocks that change the initial averaging state.

First is the issue of women's marriage and the distribution of land rights. Should women be allocated land from their mothers' or their husbands' families? If a woman is allocated land from her mother's family, she generally cannot bring it to her husband's family after marriage. This is because the land is usually distributed on a household basis and according to the population; even the equalization of tenure in the collectivization movement was distributed within the collective; and the husband's family, often not a collective member of the village, could not use the land of the mother's family. However, if women were allocated land from within their husbands' families, unmarried women and divorced women could not be allocated land.

The prerequisite for a woman to receive a share of land when she married was that the collective land in which the husband's family was located needed to be divided equally on a regular or irregular basis. Under such a system, many young people might marry and have children earlier (or, in a few cases, later) to catch up with the equalization of land shares, or else they would be left without land for a long time. In fact, more and more regions were now implementing the system of "when the number of people in the household increases, the amount of land allocated to the household does not increase; when the number of people in the household decreases, the amount of land allocated to the household does not decrease" (*Zengren bu zengdi, jianren bu jiandi*) which means that newly married women and their newborn children will not be allocated land from their husband's collective, except for the land they inherit.

Since marriage, for example, changes the status of rural women as family members (e.g., from the mother's family to the husband's family), this change in status also leads to the "uncertainty" or even "disappearance" of their land rights. The fact that rural women's land rights and interests were already vulnerable in reality was solidified by the current land titling process in 12 provinces.[20] Since the titling of agricultural land rights, according to a sample survey conducted by the Agricultural Research Center of the Ministry of Agriculture commissioned by the All-China Women's Federation at fixed observation sites, 30.4% of women have not registered their names on the land contract management right certificate, and 80.2% of women have not registered their names on the residence base use right certificate.[21] In the traditional period, farmers married their daughters with a "dowry field" (*liantian*), which is now collectively owned and cannot be brought to the husband's family with the women. Thus, it seems logical that when a rural woman marries, the woman's family demands a high dowry gift, equivalent to compensation for the woman's family's property, such as farmland and houses.

Second is the issue of population mobility and migration. China's rural population is moving more and more frequently. In the past two decades, with the rapid urbanization and industrialization, about 15 million peasants move to the cities every year or live in the cities for a long time and become migrant workers. This is contrary to the principle of "those who cultivate farmland have their own land" and is not in line with the original intention of combining farmland and labor. In terms of the general trend, the transformation of farmers into city-dwellers and the decrease in the number of farmers is irreversible. Since everyone's preferences and choices were different, it would be a waste of time to make a uniform arrangement for farmers or to tie them to the land. However, the trend of peasant migration to the cities was poorly understood in the past. During the first constitutional debate, when freedom of movement was discussed, some people argued that farmers should just grow their land and did not need freedom of movement.

[20] "Jiusan xueshe Zhongyang jianyi: wanshan nongcun funü tudi quanyi baozhang" (Jiu San Society Central Committee Suggestions: Improve the Protection of Rural Women's Land Rights and Interests), *Zhongguo funü bao* (China Women's News), March 9, 2018.

[21] Rural women are vulnerable to losing their land rights as collective members due to marriage. Since rural women belong to at least two separate families before and after they reach adulthood (the situation was even more complicated for divorced and remarried women), the land contract rights and interests and the rights to use residential bases acquired by women according to their status as family members face special changes. If rural women cannot remarry soon enough after divorce, most of them will be trapped in a situation where they have "no house, no land, and no money." "Guanyu Shenhua nongcun gaige zhong weihu funü tudi quanyi" (Proposal on Safeguarding Women's Land Rights and Interests in Deepening Rural Reforms), *Zhongguo funübao* (Chinese Women's News), March 5, 2018.

Third, the number and composition of family members change. The marriage of women, the birth of children, and the passing away of the elderly all lead to the number of family members changing. In addition, the labor capacity of farming households also changes due to the changes in the composition of family members. When men were underage or old, their labor capacity is weaker, and they cannot cultivate much land; when men were in their prime, they may not have enough farmland to cultivate. This initial equilibrium state can be broken at any time. The author has investigated a case in the field. In 1949, during the land reforms in Hunan, a 14-year-old boy surnamed Jiang in Anhua County, whose mother was paralyzed, was given two shares of the land of about two *mu*, but the mother and son could not work their share of land; half a year later, his mother died, and the boy had two shares of land, which he still had to rent out to others because he was unable to work it (of course, the farmers would not see it as exploitation because they rented the land). In another example, a neighbor's family, an able and strong man, was given only one *mu* of land, and his labor was largely idle; a year later, the strong man married and had children, but the family of three still had only one *mu* of land. For a family of three, one *mu* of land was not enough.[22] Such situations were quite common. In addition, since there were differences in farming ability and management ability, the equal distribution of farmland may seem fair, but it is not. If the land is not concentrated in the hands of capable farmers, it is likely to lead to economic inefficiency.

How should we respond to these variables that change the initial equilibrium state? Although periodic equalization of farmland can ensure absolute parity, it can lead to fragmentation, higher farming costs, and reduced land fertility. Moreover, land redistribution usually requires a mix of fertility and proximity. After two or three redistributions, the contracted land owned by each farming family becomes scattered and fragmented. For example, the Xiang family of four people in the Anhua County of Hunan Province owned less than five *mu* of land, but it was scattered over eight places, making farming it inconvenient, costly, and inefficient. As a result, the Xiang family simply gave up farming or gave it to others for free, which is the fragmentation of farmland and its inefficiencies, among other problems.

[22] Field survey in Anhua County, Hunan Province, January 2016.

In addition, due to the expectation of future subdivision and the lack of guaranteed future returns from investing in land, most farmers were reluctant to invest their labor costs in water conservation and soil fertility, resulting in a lack of maintenance of the land's productivity. As a result, equalizing farmland rights did not achieve its original intent—both equity and efficiency cannot be achieved.

If equalization of farmland is not sustainable, is it sustainable to leave it unchanged for a long time? China's forest land property rights system has remained unchanged for 30 years, which avoids fragmentation due to multiple allocations but raises other issues. For example, in a village in Anhua County, Hunan Province, there were two families initially with two *mu* of forest land per capita. Family A originally had six people, but only three people remained after 10 years, and its per capita forest land became four mu. Family B originally had four people and had eight *mu* of land, 2 *mu* per capita at the time. After 10 years, the population of family B increased to 8, so that only one *mu* of land per capita remained. The difference between 4 *mu* per capita and one *mu* per capita is large. If the forest land is not redistributed, the difference between the rich and the poor may continue to grow.

Thus, whether the land was redistributed periodically or kept constant for 30 years, the initial state of equilibrium will be disrupted due to variables, leading to inequality and inefficiency. The so-called when the number of people in the household increases, the amount of land allocated to the household does not increase; when the number of people in the household decreases, the amount of land allocated to the household does not decrease (*Zengren bu zengdi, jianren bu jiandi*), as practiced in many places nowadays, means that newborn children do not get a share of land; women married to their husbands do not get a share of land; and after the death of an old man, the household still keeps his share of land, which was inherited by the next generation. Such a policy creates a situation of private ownership of land by families. Since the increased population was not given land, but the reduced family still holds land, was this not private ownership of land by the family? Also, private land transactions would be widespread, just not recognized by law. These potential risks were concerning. The policy of keeping land shares intact also reinforces the idea of patriarchy since women do not have land to share when they marry into their husband's families. The policy of keeping land shares intact also reinforces the idea of patriarchy since women do not have land to share when they marry into their husbands' families.

Land Market and Land Circulation

The many land reforms and "experiments" in modern China have been costly in terms of optimally combining labor and land. From the perspective of production factor allocation, the only way to reform now is to use the market mechanism to allow various factors to flow and trade. Only in this way can we find a reasonable solution to the above dilemma of equal farmland rights. There were four reasons.

First, land and labor capital were dynamic and can only be allocated dynamically by the market. In terms of the changes in family labor force composition, Jiangxi Province was typical. In the Qing dynasty, there was a household of four sons in Jiangxi. When the sons were young, they proved inefficient and incapable of farming, so the farmer leased their land. However, after 10 years, all four sons had grown up and needed more land. This was when the farmer's family had to buy, *dian* purchase, or rent land to release all four sons' labor. The case shows that only through the land rights market can land and labor be combined in an optimal way.

In addition, why do farmers participate less in agricultural land circulation than expected despite the current encouragement? The legacy and historical experience of China's traditional land system deserve attention. Until the eighteenth century, Chinese economic growth dominated the world, feeding more than a quarter of the planet's population and, at its height, nearly a third. It was a miracle in an era of shortage when the ability to feed such a large population required corresponding land production. The fundamental reason for the high output, given a certain level of technology, is that an active land rights market allows a good allocation of resources.[23] There were different levels of land rights (including ownership, possession, and use rights) available on the market as clear property rights, which created a multi-level and diversified transaction system such as tenancy, rent deposit, *dian*, revocable sale, and irrevocable sale. Farmers could select the preferred method of transaction based on their price preferences and current or long-term requirements. Additionally, redemption mechanisms can also serve as a buffer between the

[23] Long Denggao, *Diquan shichang yu ziyuan peizhi* (Land Rights Market and Resource Allocation), Fuzhou: Fujian People's Press, 2012, 197–198.

delivery of rights and the concentration of land.[24] To promote land circulation in the present, we should first clarify land ownership rights and, second, diversify how land rights were traded.

Third, demand and trends for land circulation will continue to grow over time. First is the need for large-scale operations. The land will be concentrated with capable cultivators or agricultural companies, which will benefit agricultural efficiency, and farmers will benefit more. The second factor is urbanization. Urbanization is a trend that cannot be reversed. The number of farmers will decrease, increasing the amount of land and resources per capita; at the same time, the land will be transferred to the most efficient farms or companies. There is also a new interpretation of "the one who cultivates has his own land" (*gengzhe you qitian*), namely, the right to cultivate or occupy land through the land transaction is also a form of "the one who cultivates has his land." The "ownership-only theory" and static egalitarianism should be abandoned, and land rights at different levels and at different times should be traded separately on the market to achieve the dynamic combination of labor and land. Labor and land can only combine dynamically when land rights at different levels and times were traded separately in the market.

Fourth, marketization is the only way to ensure farmers' freedom of choice. Farmers and households each have their own preferences and needs, so how can the collective or the government make decisions that satisfy all of them? Individual farmers or groups of farmers can only choose according to market signals and realize the combination of production factors through the market. The market plays a crucial role in resource allocation.

To put it briefly, from average land rights to encouraging land transfers, it is a change in the system from the government's mandated distribution to the market allocation of resources, which can also be seen as a deepening of the market economy system. From equalization of land rights to encouraging land circulation, it is a system shift from the government's mandated distribution to the market allocation of resources, otherwise

24 Long Denggao, Lin Zhan, and Peng Bo, "Dian yu Qingdai diquan jiaoyi tixi" (Dian and the Qing's Land Rights Transaction System), *China's Social Science* (Social Sciences in China), no. 5 (2013): 125–141.

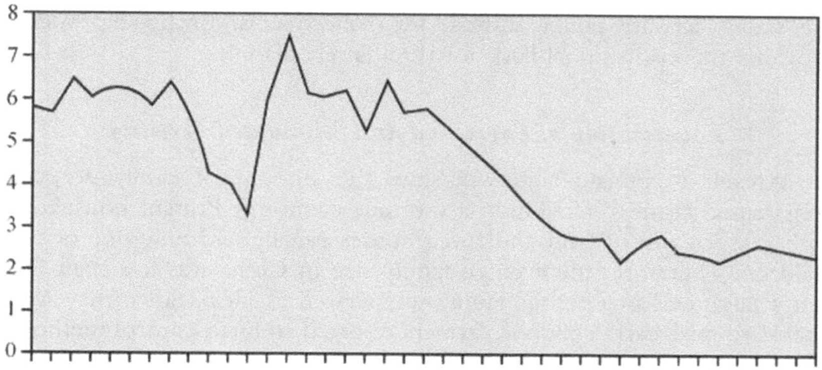

Fig. 6.1 Changes in fertility rate of Chinese women, 1950–90

known as the deepening of the market economy system in the field of production factors (Fig. 6.1).[25]

6.4 Prologues: Equalization of Farmland and Reproduction Behavior

Since the founding of the PRC, collective landownership has encouraged peasant fertility and contributed to population peaks, so the government had to switch from encouraging fertility to birth control.[26] In turn, when

[25] We are grateful to Professors Bo-Chong Li, Jingping Chen, Weimin Zhong, and Yuping Ni of Tsinghua University and Jianbo Zhou of Peking University for their discussions and guidance.

[26] Since 1978, family planning has been a basic state policy in China; in 1982, family planning was written into the Constitution of the People's Republic of China. The Constitution stipulates that every citizen has the rightsand obligation to practice family planning. During this period, a large family planning work organization was created in China. The number of institutional departments and staff engaged in family planning from the central to local levels grew to indescribable proportions, especially at the county and township levels, where the number of relevant departments and staff was particularly large. In one township, there were 84 government employees, including seven stations, eight institutes, with the family planning office occupying 21 staff members at a very high salary. See Wen Dongliang, "Yige xiangzhen ganbu jianzheng jihua shengyu sishinian shouji" (Handbook of a Township Cadre Witnessing 40 Years of Family Planning), *Xiangcun faxian* (Rural Discovery), February 12, 2018.

the state's fertility policy shifted, the collective landownership system provided the institutional basis for rural family planning.

Equalization of Farmland and Stimulated Fertility

As a result of private landownership, the amount of family property constrained farmers' fertility in a shortage economy. Peasant households with just ten *mu* of land and three houses usually had only one or two children. Therefore, the average family size in China was less than five, and a large and prosperous family was viewed as ideal. Since they were unable to raise extra children, farmers resorted to birth control methods, such as drowning infants in the Qing dynasty, as discussed by Professor Li Bozhong. The level of medical care was, of course, another natural constraint. Before the advent of penicillin in the twentieth century, premature infant death was prevalent. As medical care improved, family size increased.

As a result of the land reforms, the equalization of land per capita stimulated the fertility rate. After the completion of the land reforms in 1952, the total fertility rate increased significantly; the fertility rates in 1950 and 1951 were 5.81 and 5.70, respectively, which were already not low; in 1952, the rate was as high as 6.74 and remained high; in 1957, it reached 6.41; the fertility rate plummeted during the "Great Leap Forward" period.

In collective ownership of land, all people could share in the collective cake. During the time of the people's commune, rations were distributed on a per capita basis with the number of work points. The more children there were, the more shares were allocated. According to a survey conducted by Professor Zhou Jianbo of Peking University, a family had seven children. The male owner thought, "It is economical to have children because when the ration is divided, children were counted as half adults. Since [children] have less to eat, if we have more children, won't we become rich? At least not poor."

It can be seen that the system of per capita distribution allows for "intergenerational reallocation" (or intergenerational transfer between young and old) within a household, between older and younger children. For example, the share of infants and toddlers can be used to "supplement" older children who eat more or older parents who work, which is a rare means of family reallocation in a shortage economy. Having more children during this period would help family members survive and reduce risk. The same is true for rationed products such as cloth. The eldest son could use his younger sibling's cloth tickets, while the younger sibling could wear his older sibling's clothes. In this way, the cost of raising a second and third child also decreased.

There were, of course, constraints. The total fertility rate plummeted during the 3 years of the Great Chinese Famine, from 4.3 in 1959 to 3.29 in 1961. If even the minimum basis for survival is not available, it is difficult for newborns to survive and grow up. As a result, the more children there were, the poorer the family became. For example, some professors or senior officials in their sixties now recall that they did not wear pants for the first time until the first or second grade. The fertility incentives of the people's communes were significant, with the total fertility rate exceeding 6.0 in most years from 1962 to 1971, and with improved medical care, the number of premature deaths was greatly reduced. Thus, although China was still in a shortage economy in the mid-twentieth century, fertility rates peaked, creating a subsequent population peak. However, the government had to adopt extremely coercive family planning policies due to the rapid overpopulation. In 1972, China fully implemented a family planning policy. The total fertility rate dropped below 5.0 that year and below 3.0 after 1977.

After 1978, under the household contract responsibility system, land use rights were distributed equally, and all new people received a share of land. The new land policy also provided incentives for farmers to have children. In the trend of decreasing total fertility rate year by year, the fertility ratio increased from 2.24 in 1980 to 2.63 in 1981 and 2.86 in 1982. Meanwhile, due to the high implementation costs and obstacles in rural areas, the Chinese government stepped up its efforts to intensify family planning and make it a fundamental state policy in China.

Nowadays, many regions were implementing the policy of "when the number of people in the household increases, the amount of land allocated to the household does not increase; when the number of people in the household decreases, the amount of land allocated to the household does not decrease" (*Zengren bu zengdi, jianren bu jiandi*), and agricultural land has become de facto private land, resulting in the absence of incentives for rural fertility. Thus, the farmers' willingness to give birth is reduced. It is probably one of the realistic bases for the government's courage to liberalize the "two-children" policy (Fig. 6.1).

Reproduction Preferences and Restrictive Conditions in Different Eras

There is concern that if private ownership of land in a shortage economy is a natural constraint on fertility, then in a saturation and surplus economy, fertility will probably be unconstrained by the amount of land and property and will be able to support more children even if there is less land. At this time, private ownership of land will lead to an uncontrolled population. However, when the economy and standard of living develop to a certain level, it becomes a common choice for people to marry later and have fewer children. As in the developed countries of the West, fertility rates continue to decline despite government encouragement.

Human society undergoes natural evolutionary processes, and any institution has its own constraints or negative feedback mechanisms. In a shortage economy, people have fewer children because they were poor; in a saturation economy and a surplus economy, when the material conditions for raising children were improved, people were much less willing to have children. This natural evolutionary process also creates a corresponding order (Hayek's so-called autopoietic order). If the government interferes with one of these processes, it will inevitably cause a distortion of the other processes and the natural order. That is, forced government intervention in one phenomenon or area will lead to an unanticipated situation that will leave the government stretched to its limits. For example, when the government controls the landownership system, it is not expected that collective ownership will stimulate reproduction; this leads to the need for the government to intervene and control people's reproductive behavior. Since land control requires a large number of government officials, and family planning requires a large bureaucracy, the size of government grows, taxes and fees increase, and the burden on the public increases, along with rent-seeking and corruption.

In recent years, some scholars have also discussed the institutional context in which patriarchal attitudes were reinforced. The people's commune was one of the reasons,[27] and the household contract responsibility system also led to a preference for men over women. It was not expected by those who were committed to pursuing gender equality.

[27] Huang Yingwei, Li Jun, and Wang Xiuqing, "Jitihua moqi nonghu laodongli touru de xingbie chayi—yige cunzhuang 'beitaizi' de yanjiu" (Gender Differences in Farmers' Labor Inputs at the End of Collectivization: A Study of Beitaizi Village), *Zhongguo jingjishi yanjiu* (Researches in Chinese Economic History), no. 2 (2010): 29–39.

Many people believe it is a Confucian tradition to have many children and that cultural mores have led to a large population in China. This has been disproved by the facts and, more critically, challenged by new phenomena that have emerged as a result of changing constraints. For example, the Taiwan region and South Korea, which were also influenced by Confucian traditions, rank at the bottom of the world regarding fertility rates. Residents of Hong Kong, China, and the Chinese in Singapore and Malaysia also have very low fertility rates. Clearly, fertility rates were related to living standards, economic development, and private property rights.

Collective landownership has fundamentally undermined the Confucian tradition of filial piety. One of the economic foundations of the filial tradition is property inheritance. With the total regency of land and property rights by the parents, the property inheritance of the unfilial son may be restricted and limited. In reality, wealthy people with property or resources were treated with special filial piety or respect by their children and neighbors, while older people without property often face abandonment or abuse. In a collective landownership system, since the children's land no longer comes from the parents, the parents lose the power to pass on their property and thus bind their children and grandchildren. Since the children were no longer dependent on the parents but on the village community collectively, the traditional model of the family and the concept of filial piety were then under attack. For example, as Professor Chen Zhiwu argues, financial instruments gradually replaced the need to raise children for old age.

Collective Landownership and Institutional Effect on Family Planning

As collective members, peasants were governed and controlled by the rural collective organization and the hukou system. In all aspects of land distribution, children's education, and hukou and welfare, farmers depend on and were subject to the organization. If any farmer disobeys the instructions, he may be punished to varying degrees. Thus, an organizational system based on collective landownership is the institutional basis for the effective implementation of compulsory family planning.

In government and public institutions, where the organizational system is tighter and members were more dependent, control over family planning by government employees and public institution workers is more efficient, and penalties were easier. However, at the same time, if one has one's own independent property and does not have to rely on resources and benefits under government control, one can stray from the family planning system. For example, if the rich have more children, they can choose to attend private schools in the future. Family planning policies cannot bind the rich. Second, peasants can choose to leave their hometowns and work in cities, allowing them to break out of collective control and family planning constraints with relative ease. With the increasing mobility of peasants, the land becomes a lesser part of the peasant family property structure. By this point, the options available to peasants had become increasingly diverse, and the effectiveness of village and township collective organizations had decreased.

Without one's own property, one is dependent on and subject to other people or organizations, and there is no real sense of free choice.

CHAPTER 7

The Traditional Presentation of the Essence of Economy and Its Modern Disorientation

7.1 Tradition, Disorientation, and Contemporary Trend

Under the traditional economy, the nature of human beings and the origin of the economy were more easily presented. Therefore, from a methodological point of view, revealing the core and essence of things in a simple state first and then adding other variables to observe the changes in complex phenomena and affairs can avoid putting the cart before the horse.

Nature and Essence of Economy

The essence of the economy is a reflection of the most basic elements of human existence and nature, but it is also the most easily forgotten or denied right. The essence (or origin) of the economy includes the following levels:

The first level is the right to own property and create wealth. For Chinese peasants, the most important manifestation of wealth is their land and individual family farms. The second level is the path of realizing and increasing wealth through various transactions. These were intergenerational transactions, between power protection and personal

D. Long and X. Chi, *The Institutions of Land Property Rights in China*, Palgrave Studies in Economic History,
https://doi.org/10.1007/978-981-97-5112-9_7

attachment, or means of production and labor.[1] Market transactions were the main form of wealth creation and realization because only market-based transactions were equal, fair, mutually beneficial, universal, and expansive.

Take private land property rights and their transactional forms as an example. Land deeds in traditional China were certificates of private property rights, by which the land's physical boundaries and the landowner's rights were determined. Landowning peasants established family farms on their land. In contrast, land-deficient peasants acquired land from the land market by renting, mortgaging, *dian* purchasing, or buying, and then established their own farms, thus becoming agribusiness entrepreneurs, the "middle class" of agricultural society. This is the basis for the survival and development of peasants.

There was a gradual development in land rights transactions in traditional China. During the Warring States, Qin, and Han dynasties, only tenancy of use rights and sale of ownership rights existed; during the Wei and Jin dynasties, mortgages of security interests began to appear; during the Tang and Song dynasties, possession rights were added on to land rights transactions; and during the Ming and Qing dynasties, new types of transactions such as rent pledges and live sales emerged. The diverse types of land rights transactions met farmers' different needs and preferences, reduced systematic risks, and enhanced the ability of individual farmers to operate independently. Without land rights trading and markets, farmers would have had difficulty gaining economic independence or been forced to rely on some force, for example, the government, local powers, estates, lineages, or other organizations.

Clear land property rights guarantee farmers' survival and development, as well as acting as an incentive and constraint mechanism for wealth creation. Relying on the land rights market to realize resource allocation, individual farmers can reduce disputes and transaction costs and improve land returns and economic efficiency. At the level of transactions and markets, in addition to the land rights market, China had already formed a national market during the Ming and Qing dynasties, and the flow of commodities, information, and capital became increasingly active.

[1] For example, raising sons in case they have no one to rely on in old age. During the traditional period, when there was no socialized retirement system, the older generation raised their sons, and the sons were responsible for taking care of their parents in old age.

At that time, there were no taboos or crimes such as speculation, illegal fundraising, or employment exploitation.

The functioning of the private economy relies not on external instructions but on the coordinated and spontaneous formation of orderly transactions according to specific rules. Over a long period, the rules of the private economy naturally move from disorderly to orderly, from low to high. The rules embodied in the land transactions gradually became the agreed-upon customs and practices of the people. The buyers and sellers kept cooperating and forming rules to minimize the loss of disputes. This is what Hayek called "the spontaneous order," which is similar to the theory of the "invisible hand" proposed by Adam Smith and is also the "rule by doing nothing" (*wuwei erzhi*) promoted by the ancient Chinese, which is said to be translated by French scholars as "laissez-faire."

> The style of governance proposed by Sima Qian is still compelling: "[The most intelligent way for those in power to deal with the people] is to follow their human nature, followed by guiding them, followed by educating them, followed by binding them with rules and regulations, and the most foolish way is to compete with them for profit".

The way of the state should follow human nature. A government that goes against human nature should not exist, and coercive rule is not sustainable. The worst way to govern a state is to compete with the people for profit. For example, Sang Hongyang and Wang Anshi let officials sit in rows to engage the government directly in business for profit in order to solve the financial crisis. However, the state economy is not the mainstream of the traditional Chinese economy and is much maligned. As Lao Tzu said, "Governing a large country is like cooking a small meal." In other words, the imperial court should not bother the people.

Modern Disorientation and Contemporary Rerelease

In the nineteenth century, China's economy suffered a precipitous fall, and the impact from outside triggered an increasingly strong response. Chinese intellectuals at that time were eager to find ways to strengthen the country and enrich the people, or blamed foreign capital for China's backwardness and thus blindly excluded foreigners; blamed private ownership as the source of all evils; or blamed free-market transactions as the cause of economic chaos and turmoil; some even blamed Confucian culture. From the May Fourth Movement to the Cultural Revolution, revolutionaries have been trying to destroy traditional culture.

Amid national peril, collectivism and economic nationalism flourished. People looked to the government to control resources, allocate them, and organize the economy. At the same time, government power continued to expand and tried to take absolute control of the local communities. During the planned economy, China's national economy reached the brink of collapse. It was not until the reforms and opening-up policy that China's economy gradually got on the right track.

The causes of modern China's backwardness and defeat were complex and were discussed in detail in the third section of Chapter 8. The hardships and pain of economic transformation in modern China were so rare in the history of other countries that few comparable objects can be found. From a traditional to a modern economy, from an agricultural to an industrialized economy, modern China's economic and social transformation has been comprehensive and profound, facing insurmountable obstacles and intense social pain. However, some people still blame the traditional system for China's modern backwardness, arguing that the Chinese idealistic understanding of economic development has led to inevitable twists and turns and repeated trials and errors in realistic exploration.

It may be difficult for contemporary people or foreigners to understand revolutionary ethics. However, at that time, the idea that individuals could be sacrificed for the sake of the group and that certain groups could be sacrificed for the overall good of the country was typical. For a good ideal, everything in the old world had to be broken; sacrifices had to be made to rebuild a new world. The strugglers who came from the war had experienced the brutal struggle and had dealt a merciless blow to all counterrevolutionaries. The revolution was not a "gentle and frugal" one. For example, the Land Reform of 1949–1952 was a violent deprivation and redistribution of land. To try to conceal the violence is to fail to understand the character of the time and the nature of the Land Reform Movement.

Collectivism and strict organization have been increasingly strengthened in modern China's pursuit of national wealth and power. Chinese communists were willing to sacrifice their interests, even their lives, for the sake of the organization and the country. This understanding was maintained even long after the founding of the country. At that time, private property and personal ideas were considered "selfish thoughts" that should be overcome. During the planned economy period, the very essence of the economy was distorted. People could not own their property and factors of production, establish their farms and enterprises, or even engage in trading; the government arranged everything. The government controlled and allocated the resources, and the market almost disappeared.

After reforms and opening-up, China's planned economy began transforming into a market economy. The property rights system is the foundation of the economy, and the market is the way to achieve economic independence. After more than 30 years of exploration, in 2013, the Third Plenary Session of the 18th Central Committee established that "the market is the decisive factor in resource allocation." Since then, Premier Li Keqiang has also proposed that the main principle is always the simplest, and good governance is to respect the people and simplify administration. After three centuries of deliberations and debates, painful transformations, and trial-and-error explorations, Chinese people have gradually faced up to the origin of the economy. However, there were still obstacles to people's thinking that must be further corrected.

The fundamental institutional basis for the economic miracle of the 40 years of reforms and opening-up has been the market economy. The fundamental reason for the recovery of the rural economy in the 1980s was the ability of farmers to set up family farms with land management rights. State-owned enterprises were internationally competitive today, from having been unprofitable during the planned economy and the early years of transition. The fundamental path is also marketization, corporatization, and internationalization.[2] The basis for establishing the contemporary market economy path is that the economic fundamentals can function properly again. The foundation on which the path to a market economy in contemporary China was established is, in fact, the economic fundamentals.

[2] Long Denggao, Chang Xu, and Xiong Jinwu, "Jieshu yu" (Conclusion), *Guo zhi run, zi shujun shi: Tianjin hangdaoju 120 nian fazhan shi* (The Wetness of the Country Begins with Dredging: A History of the Development of the Tianjin Dredging Bureau in 120 Years), Beijing: Qinghua University Press, 2017.

Case Study: Evolution of Credit Patterns

The twists and turns in understanding the economic essence and the corresponding institutional arrangements at different times were highlighted in the evolution of credit patterns. Compared with the "high-trust societies" in the US, UK, and Japan, China is a low-trust society, and Fukuyama's argument is quite representative.[3] However, some scholars argue that marketization has led to the current loss of trust in society. Is this the case?

For example, in the nineteenth century, American society was plagued by credit fraud and default for a long time. Driven by strong demand, the American personal credit system formed spontaneously through market transactions. In the twentieth century, this personal credit system was gradually institutionalized as a mechanism of behavioral restraint and, to some extent, internalized into the morals and ethics of American society. In addition, the image change of "Made in Germany" and "Oriental Goods" also reflects a similar evolutionary process—from a synonym of counterfeit to a highly trusted multinational brand. On the one hand, this shows that the so-called high-trust society is not a specific cultural or national characteristic but a process of establishing and operating a credit system; on the other hand, the credit system is a product of market demand and is an endogenous product of the market economy.

Traditional Chinese markets and society have always had a simple form of credit and have generated a corresponding sense of property rights and contractual spirit. The first appearance of paper money as credit money in China and its use for hundreds of years were associated with the development of credit. In traditional China, "honesty" (*chengxin*) was commonly used as a credo in family instructions, and merchants passed it on to their children as the essence of business. If the Confucians' moral requirement of "benevolence, righteousness, deference, wisdom, and trust" (*ren yi li zhi xin*) contains didactic elements, then what is passed on to one's children is always heartfelt. In fact, the Confucian moral requirement had a long history of connection with other religions and cultures, which shows that trust and credit originate from the pursuit of the human heart.

[3] Francis Fukuyama (Fulang xisi fushan), *Xinren: Shehui meide yu chuangzao jingji fanrong* (Trust: Social Virtues and the Creation of Economic Prosperity), translated by Guo Hua, Hainan: Hainan Press, 2001.

However, under the revolutionary struggles of the twentieth century, especially since the May Fourth Movement, the old Confucian principles were denounced as premodern hypocrisy, and the traditional credit mechanism was eradicated. During all the movements, especially the Cultural Revolution, there were phenomena such as mutual denunciations and struggles between husband and wife, father and son, teacher and student, and between ordinary people. After the Cultural Revolution, people were still worried about "struggles between acquaintances" (*douzheng shuren*). In the planned economy and the subsequent period, everything depended on the "institutional credit" (*danwei xinyong*) endorsed by the government; thus, when some individual households and private enterprises lacked the backing of their public institutions or the government, they were discriminated against because they lacked long-term credit records and evaluations.

China's transition from a planned economy to a market economy has led to the socialization and marketization of more and more people away from institutional credit. However, as China's credit system is still being explored, there is no credit mechanism. Since China has long lacked an effective credit system, traditional credit mechanisms, and Confucian moral constraints have only recently begun to be re-established, and thus the phenomenon of social default is still severe, although there was an improvement during the 1960s. Obviously, marketization cannot be blamed for the loss of credit. On the contrary, the credit system will gradually expand and improve as marketization progresses. New types of credit have emerged under Internet technology, such as Sesame Credit, whose scores were trusted by the consulates of many countries to issue visas. The essence of a market economy is a cooperative and credit economy, which is why mature market economies were generally more credit-oriented.

7.2 Grassroots Autonomy and China's Grand Unification: Institutional Cornerstones and Historical Logic

It has long been a dominant view that maintaining unity requires tight regulation of the grassroots. This is still the case in some mainstream views. Compared with Western Europe, unification is a prominent tradition and characteristic of China. So, how did historical China maintain unity? Was the state's management of grassroots society tightly controlled or indirect? Was it direct management or self-governance at the grassroots? These were questions that have long been of interest to the academic community.

Traditional Chinese self-government at the grassroots level had an institutional basis and internal logic. Although centralized and authoritarian governments were known for their harsh control, the control is mainly over the bureaucracy and local governments. As for the governance of local society, China has long upheld simple liberalism in economic management and local self-governance in political management.

A simple tradition of economic liberalism can be found in the traditional Chinese economy (as discussed earlier). For example, factors of production such as land, labor, and capital were largely free to move, local society was self-governed, religious beliefs were free, and associations were basically free; the government and the law recognized private property rights and transaction practices. Further, the government's orientation is to "store wealth among the people" (*cangfu yumin*) and not to "compete with the people for profit" (*yumin zhengli*). The rise of various cities and market towns (*shizhen*) also reflects the role of the private economy and the market in promoting urbanization.

With limited state intervention in the private sector and at the local level, economic liberalism effectively promoted the rational allocation of resources. It maintained the stability of the economic and social order, allowing a unified state to continue for a long time based on low-cost governance. Meanwhile, limited technological conditions and insufficient social surplus also served as a hedge or constraint against heavy taxation, autocracy, and centralization of power in successive dynasties, and the "following their human nature" (*shanzhe yinzhi*) approach became a simple tradition.

The comparison reveals that simple economic liberalism was an important basis for China's economic ability to lead the world for a long time in history. Moreover, simple economic liberalism waxed and waned in the game against authoritarian centralism. When the constraints changed, it could not counteract the expansion of government power, especially in the modern trend that demanded strengthening government control. As a result, the simple tradition of economic liberalism declined and gradually disappeared.[4] The author will elaborate on this basis.

Private Self-Organization and Local Self-Governance

Traditional Chinese local self-governance is represented in the following five aspects: First, diversified types of private organizations, which have undertaken various public affairs and formed a self-management and self-operation system, include:

1. The clan and the ancestral temple were the core of local society, and the clan field was the corporate property owned by the clan. The proportion of clan fields was huge in Guangdong and Fujian, accounting for about 30%.
2. In terms of construction of public facilities, private organizations for public welfare built and maintained bridges, free ferry (*yidu*), teahouses, roads, water conservancy projects, and so on. These public facilities were independent corporate property and could be operated continuously in the long term.
3. In terms of charity, although the government may offer some grants, civil organizations were more sustainable as charities, and this avoided rent-seeking behavior by power-holders.
4. In terms of education, private education was mainly undertaken by private schools, free schools, and academies. The most prominent example is Wu Xun, a beggar in the late Qing dynasty who raised money through financial management to build and maintain a free school with corporate assets.[5]
5. In terms of religion, historically, China's prevalent religions were free and diverse, in contrast to the sectarian rivalries among the European religions. In traditional China, Buddhist and Taoist temples and local deities were scattered, supported by civilian donations. Since the Wei and Jin dynasties, Chinese popular religion had

[4] Long Denggao, "Lishi shang Zhongguo minjian jingji de ziyou zhuyi pusu chuantong" (The Simple Tradition of Liberalism in Chinese Private Economy in History), *Sixiang zhanxian* (Thinking), no. 3 (2012): 84–91.

[5] Long Denggao, Wang Miao, "Wu Xun de licai xingxue zhidao" (Wu Xun's Way of Managing Money and Promoting Education), *Zhongguo jingjishi yanjiu* (Researches in Chinese Economic History), no. 3 (2018): 182–189.

a tradition of lending money,[6] which is also quite different from the original Catholicism and Islam, which forbade lending money at interest.

6. Free association. From the Song dynasty, people in various professions begun associating freely, and different guilds and chambers were formed. These associations not only set the rules in different professions, dealing with the coordination of internal affairs but also dealt with various relations with the external government and society. Guilds also abounded in the fields of finance, sports, and recreation. For example, in the Song dynasty, Hangzhou private citizens organized surfing competitions. Due to the annual casualties, Su Shi had ordered its cancelation, but the order was not enforced. This was because of the great interest and strong organizational capacity of the local society for surfing. In addition, secret societies also existed in China's traditional society, such as the "Society of Brothers" (Gelaohui), "Chinese Freemasons" (Hongmen), and Chee Kung Tong (Zhigongtang).

It is evident that a general and all-encompassing system of self-organization existed in Chinese society and has a long history. Alternatively, the various levels and areas of society complemented and cooperated with each other to promote civic self-management and self-operation. Of course, in historical reality, local organizations did not fully achieve the idealized state. However, due to the limited power of the government, they also had to manage the local society indirectly.

Second, the labor force could freely choose and have an independent economic base. In traditional China, the labor force had access to basic freedom of mobility and choice. For example, the people could improve their economic status by creating and accumulating wealth.[7]

[6] Zhou Jianbo, Zhang Bo, Zhou Jiantao, "Zhonggu shiqi siyuan jignji xingshuai de jingjixue fenxi" (An Economic Analysis of the Rise and Fall of the Economy of Monasteries in the Ancient and Middle Ages), *Jingjixue jikan* (China Economic Quarterly), no. 3 (2011): 1219–1236.

[7] During the Warring States, Qin and Han dynasties, the common people (commoners) began to break through the hierarchy and freely engage in commercial activities to gain wealth. See Li Yan, "Taishigong lun shuren zhifu: du shiji huozhi liezhuan zhaji" (Taishi Gong's Discussion on the Wealth of the Common People: Notes on Reading the *Records of the Grand Historian: Biographies of Wealthy Merchants*), *Sixiang zhanxian* (Thinking), no. 1 (2002): 67–70. From the Tang and Song dynasties, Chinese society was a "society

They could also improve their political status through the imperial examination system, thus making social mobility in traditional China different from the strict hierarchy of the medieval period in Western Europe. However, it must be emphasized that the right to free choice of labor was based on private property rights of land and the right to operate independently. Individual farmers could survive independently by operating their own businesses, which was the fundamental economic basis for guaranteeing their free choice. In contrast, medieval Western European farmers were more dependent on the manor. They could not easily establish an independently run individual farm if they were separated from the manor. The number of proletarians who could not operate independently was much higher in Western Europe than in China (2–3%) under the influence of, for example, primogeniture. Pomeranz estimates that the population of premodern Western Europe was about 10% of the total population.[8]

Third, the growth of cities and market towns (*shizhen*) highlights the dynamism of a self-generating private economy. Market towns were not the same as municipal towns during the Song, Yuan, Ming, and Qing dynasties. Market towns were basically formed under the impetus of the private economy and generally did not establish formal ranking officials. However, because of the expansion of their transactions, the government would also set up tax agencies to collect money and establish security agencies to maintain order. The emergence of market towns reflects the ability of the market and the private economy to drive the process of urbanization.

The tone of the traditional Chinese state was to "leave wealth with the people" rather than to "compete with the people for profit." Although a government monopoly system existed, it was limited in the variety of goods it could sell. The state mostly shifted to market-based operations

of the rich common people" (*fumin shehui*) and began to develop into a "civil society" (*shimin shehui*) during modern times. See Lin Wenxun, "Zhongguo gudai 'fumin shehui'de xingcheng jiqi lishi diwei" (The Formation of *Fumin Shehui* and its Historical Status in Ancient China), *Zhongguo jingjishi yanjiu* (Researches in Chinese Economic History), no. 2 (2006): 30–37.

[8] Kenneth Pomeranz, "Chinese Development in Long-Run Perspective," Proceedings of the *American Philosophical Society* 152, no. 1 (2008): 83–100. As the proletarians in Western Europe were forced to become industrialists and traders, autonomous cities gradually formed outside the manor. This became an important trigger for change in Western Europe.

after the Song dynasty.[9] Before the Song dynasty, there was no general formal commercial tax in China, indicating that commerce lacked a certain degree of protection and regulation by the government. The Song state began to levy commercial taxes while reducing state-run commerce. In this way, the state shifted from making direct profits through state-run commerce to profiting from or sharing profits with merchants through the imposition of merchant taxes.

Fourthly, in the core areas, the imperial power did reach the county; the frontier areas were "ruled with a loose reign" (*jimi*). County had the lowest level of formal government institutions in traditional China. Generally, the number of county government officials was small, only the magistrate and a few officials (*li*). Since the management of the county officials was limited to the county town and its surrounding areas, the sub-county was basically run autonomously by the villagers, and the *baozhang* and the *jiazhang* were not part of the civil service. In frontier areas, the state implemented the *jimi* system and the *tusi* system. Namely, the central government tried not to interfere with the polity, religion, and taxation systems in frontier areas. Thus, within the framework of the unification, the regions maintained a high degree of autonomy, and the state maintained a unified order with low control costs.[10]

Fifth, limited government under natural constraints, with centralized power constrained by transportation and financial instruments.[11] In Chinese history, autocracy and centralization were often portrayed as omnipresent and arbitrary. In fact, in traditional Chinese society, autocracy and centralization were usually limited due to the constraints of

[9] During the Tang and Song dynasties, the monopoly system shifted from a direct monopoly system to an indirect monopoly system, with the government sharing profits with merchants. During the Ming and Qing dynasties, the monopoly system went into full decline. See Lin Wenxun, Huang Chunyan, *Zhongguo gudai zhuanmai zhidu yu shangpin jingji* (Ancient Chinese Monopoly System and Commodity Economy), Kunming: Yunnan University Press, 2003.

[10] Zhuge Liang's seven captures of Meng Huo were to achieve low-cost rule without stationing troops and officials. During the Han and Jin dynasties, the dual governance of native and circulatory officials was implemented, with both the native chiefs enthroned and the circulatory officials (*liuguan*) stationed. Since neither local taxation nor local troops were stationed, the cost of rule was high, and conflicts intensified. This probably provided a lesson for the implementation of the native official (*tuguan*) system after the Tang and Song dynasties.

[11] I thank Professor Chen Zhiwu for the inspiration.

technological conditions. First, the emperor and the central government had limited tools and abilities to collect wealth from localities due to transportation and information transmission limitations. As a result, the scope and extent of wealth concentration for the central government were not high, and the amount of local specialist products, tributes, or luxury goods for imperial consumption was always limited. The second was the limitation of financial instruments. In the traditional period, due to the lack of state-owned financial instruments, the social surplus could only flow to the government through the channel of taxation. In contemporary times, efficient financial institutions have led to the flow of people's money to financial institutions such as banks. When the government monopolizes the financial institutions, the social surplus flows to the government through these financial intermediaries.

Property Rights as the Cornerstone of Civil Self-governance

The prerequisite for civil self-governance is the independence of individuals and civil organizations. The cornerstone of individual independence is private property rights and self-management; the independence of civil organizations is the property rights of corporate bodies and their autonomous development.

The institutional basis of civil self-government is law and property rights. In terms of law, "the government has a proper code, the people comply with the private contract" (*guanyou zhengdian, mincong siqi*), and the contract has played a legal role in the handling of civil disputes. In the traditional era, when a dispute arose, it was first coordinated by the middleman, the clan chief, or the gentry; if it did not work, it went to the county court. The magistrate also made a judgment according to the provisions of the contract. Even when the emperor gave a general amnesty, if the amnesty order conflicted with the contract, then the amnesty gave way to the contract. In addition, the patriarchal law (*zongfa*) also had specific legal effects. The clan had the autonomy to enforce the law, the right to participate in the trial process, and the right to assist in the execution process.

Regarding property rights, the institutional basis of local self-government was private property rights and corporate property rights. For peasants, having independent and exclusive property rights on their farms was the basis of their livelihood; otherwise, it would be difficult for them to get rid of personal or economic dependence. For example, in the period of the Wei, Jin, and Northern and Southern dynasties and the Middle Ages of Western Europe, peasants were dependent on the manor; or, as in the case of the people's communes under the planned economy, peasants were dependent on the government and public institutions. For organizations and institutions, having exclusive corporate property rights makes it possible for them to exist independently and develop autonomously. Corporate property rights can be said to be a derivative form of private property rights, reflecting the degree of development of private property rights. Corporate property rights were also represented in nonprofit organizations such as public welfare organizations, charitable organizations, guild houses, clan lands, temple lands, and school lands. These legal entities were property rights units, which were registered in government records, as well as transaction units and sometimes tax units. For more details on the study of corporate property rights, please refer to my article "Civil Organizations and Corporate Property Rights in the Traditional Period" [*Chuantong shiqi de minjian zuzhi yu faren chanquan*]. We will not repeat it here.

The Chinese private economy can be described as a self-organizing system to a large extent. It does not operate primarily by external directives but coordinates itself to form an orderly structure according to specific rules within the system. Prime facie, this spontaneous force is soft and weak, but it is fairly resilient. From its long history, the rules of the private economy were moving from disorder to order, from low- to high-level order. The rules of the land rights market and transaction contracts have gradually become customs and practices agreed upon by the people. These customs were not able to be prescribed by the government but were formed spontaneously by the people and then approved and prescribed by the government from the state law. The evolution of the rules of *dian* transaction from Song to Qing is a typical case. The state respected folk practices and maintained harmony rather than confronting them. This shows that the state always respected private practices and maintained harmony. It was not until the modern era that the relationship between the state and society changed significantly. The traditional Chinese market was also fundamentally a self-organizing system, or what Hayek called a "spontaneous order."

This explains why traditional economies have grown under authoritarian centralization, with technological and institutional innovations.[12] It is rooted in the fact that authoritarian governments have less influence on the functioning of self-organized systems such as the local level, the private sector, and the market. The dynastic government's orientation toward economic liberalism of the people guaranteed the space for factor mobility and free choice. The people had private property rights of land and wealth; in terms of production and wealth creation, individual farmers were dynamic and competitive; in terms of morality and tradition, the government advocated to "store wealth among the people" (*cangfu yumin*); in terms of ruling techniques, the government advocated "allowing the people to rest and recuperate by lightly imposing taxes and duties" (*yumin xiuxi*) and "following their human nature" (*shanzhe yinzhi*). Thus, under the technological conditions of the time, the factors of production could flow freely, and the people were free to choose and operate independently, ultimately maximizing wealth creation. As a result, China could support a large population with limited land, and its economy led the world for a long time.

Despite the centralization of the bureaucracy, China's dynastic governments have generally followed a simple liberal economic orientation toward the private sector and local communities. It was a low-cost way of governing a large empire and a practical guarantee of the long-term survival of the dynasty and the Great Unification. It was not so much a clever ruling technique of the dynasties as it was a natural, back-to-basics approach to governance: responding to the economic and faith-based choices of the people to make a living and providing them with the appropriate infrastructure, social services, and information delivery services.[13] If the government deprives the people of their private property and independent business rights, the country's long-term interests will not be guaranteed. Under the technological conditions and shortage economy,

[12] Innovations arise from time to time. For example, the world's earliest paper money was first created by Chengdu merchants on their own initiative. It was first innovated by the private sector, then granted a government charter, then directly regulated by the government, and finally established as a formal system.

[13] The United States is a federation under which each state has its own tax rules, education system, community services, and even laws and regulations, while the federal government is responsible for foreign affairs, the military, and national security. States are free to choose their own policies, adapt to local conditions, and develop their own competitiveness.

the dynastic government could only choose to adopt economic liberalism due to the natural constraint of limited social surplus.

Role of Grassroots Autonomy in Support of the Grand Unification: Intuitive Logicism and Historical Evidence

Grassroots autonomy can be a check on bureaucracy. This point may have received less attention in previous studies. As agents of the emperor, bureaucrats were responsible for maintaining the stability of civil society. However, agents and principals may have had incompatible incentives due to their conflicting interests. Therefore, on the one hand, the government had to incentivize officials to collect taxes effectively instead of plundering the people's wealth; on the other hand, the government had to restrain them from enriching themselves. The emperor's primary concern was corruption in the bureaucracy, which is the same in both ancient and modern times. Therefore, the system of internal supervision and external checks and balances were critical.

Where do the external forces of checks and balances come from? One of the important forces comes from grassroots autonomy. If the bureaucracy fully controls the local community, the peasants may become "serfs" under the bureaucracy; however, when the local community is autonomous, they can serve to check and balance the bureaucracy. On the one hand, officials' self-governance at the grassroots level can reduce the room for rent-seeking. On the other hand, it can counteract official corruption and even echo the central government by monitoring officials from the bottom up and putting power in a cage. An extreme example of this was during the Ming dynasty when the emperor Zhu Yuanzhang allowed people to "bind what they considered to be unscrupulous officials for punishment" (*bangfu fujing zhizui*). China has achieved excellent results in fighting against corruption, mainly due to the leadership of the CPC Central Committee. In the United States, the fight against corruption is primarily done by the private sector. The media and society serve as a whole to monitor officials. Although local self-governance is better in the United States today than in the Qing dynasty, local self-governance in the Qing was also strong.

When power is restrained, the government's ability is enhanced, as demonstrated in the history of England after the Glorious Revolution. When the government was restrained and supervised by the Parliament, its behavior tended to be regulated, its politics tended to be stable, its credibility was improved, and its ability to finance itself was ultimately enhanced. That was the institutional basis for Britain's emergence as a latecomer to the hegemony of Western Europe.

The second force of checks and balances is the power, responsibility, and risk of local self-governance. Given the decentralized and diverse nature of grassroots society, the officials around the people directly influence their perception of the regime. Typically, people at the grassroots level do not oppose the central government in one voice but may oppose their respective local officials. In addition, when a local problem arises, if the local self-governance system is relatively sound, its internal self-digestion and resolution of the problem can be accomplished; even if the problem cannot be solved for a while, it will not be linked to or blamed on the central government. Therefore, when power and responsibility were devolved to the grassroots, the country's overall risk will be dispersed. When government power can reach the grassroots, the advantage is that the government has a powerful mobilization capacity; the disadvantage is that it is very costly, and the risk is reinforced by concentration. This is the case with the US system of government.

In traditional China, people were usually "against corrupt officials, not against the emperor" (*fan tanguan, bufan huangdi*). The threat to the emperor and the central government does not come from the grassroots. According to a recent study by Chen Zhiwu and Lin Zhan, the emperors in Chinese history died in three main circumstances: by ministers (38%), by clan members (26%), and by hostile states (26%); only 1.6% died because of the people (peasant uprisings). Thus, the real threat to the regime did not come from the people.[14]

During the planned economy, state power reached the grassroots to control the people and collect taxes. Since the people did not have property rights then, the government could control resources to the maximum extent. Now that the people own their property and can operate independently and choose freely, and the agricultural tax has been abolished, what is left to mobilize? Controlling the grassroots by proxy is difficult and costly to control but also leaves a negative impression of being a nuisance to the people.

[14] Chen Zhiwu, Lin Zhan, "Zhenming tyanzi yi sangming–lishi Zhongguo Huangdi ming'an de lianghua yanjiu" (Are Emperors Prone to Lose Their Lives? A Quantitative Study of Emperor Fatalities in Historical China), Hongkong University working paper, 2017.

Third, grassroots autonomy can stimulate the people's creativity and is conducive to institutional innovation. Grassroots democracy or simple democracy, as expressed in grassroots autonomy, is more open and transparent and can stimulate people's creativity. Through innovative attempts and mutual comparisons in different places, people can freely choose, transplant, and improve viable systems; otherwise, systems that were not competitive will be eliminated. For example, facilities that provide free services, such as *yidu*, bridges, and tea houses, tend to get better by comparing those in other places.

Fourth, grassroots autonomy can reduce the management costs of unification. In the traditional shortage economy, the government could not afford to support many officials due to limited tax revenue. Thus, the cost of grassroots administration under the unification was a huge burden to the government. There have been many previous studies on ancient government taxation. One of the most important reasons why "imperial power did reach the county" (*huangquan bu xiaxian*) was that the dynastic state could not afford the enormous financial burden of public construction at the grassroots level. According to Li Bozhong's empirical analysis, the proportion of government taxation to GDP in Jiangnan, represented by the Hualou region, was 4–5%[15]; Ma Debin also estimated that taxation in the Qing dynasty accounted for about 5% of GDP[16]; Shi Jinjian's study showed that the proportion of fiscal revenue to GDP in the Ming dynasty declined steadily from 9% at the beginning of the fifteenth century to about 4% at the end of the century. In horizontal and vertical comparisons to England and the Song dynasty, taxation in Ming and Qing China was relatively low.

The number of local officials from the second to the ninth rank in the Ming dynasty was 5,836, and the national public construction costs in the Qing dynasty were only 1.5 million taels per year. The state could not afford the high cost of exercising complete power over the grassroots, in

[15] Li Bozhong, *Zhongguo de zaoqi jindai jingji—1820 niandai huating-louxian diqu GDP yanjiu* (China's Early Modern Economy—A Study of GDP in the Huating-Lou County Region in the 1820s), Beijing: Zhonghua Books, 2010, 251, 515.

[16] Shi Jinjian, "Zhongguo lishi shang caizheng shouzhi he zhengquan wending guanxi de yanjiu, 1402–1644" [A Study of the Relationship between Fiscal Revenues and Expenditures and Regime Stability in Chinese History (1402–1644)], Doctoral thesis, Xiamen University, 2017.

terms of either human or financial resources. Therefore, grassroots self-government undoubtedly reduced government administration costs and maintained local society's basic stability.

The grand unification at the national level and a large economic market were very attractive to the grassroots and can bring many benefits. On the one hand, the scale effect and low transaction costs brought by the unification and the large market effectively enhance the "centripetal force"; on the other hand, the cross-regional transfer under the unification can enhance risk resistance. The so-called centrifugal force or even independence is only for freedom; when the grassroots have freedom, they will not enjoy the benefits of unification and a large market. Therefore, it is in the interests of grassroots society to support national unification and the big economic market.

From the above logic and historical evidence, we can find that in Chinese history, grassroots autonomy, and unification have been able to complement and supplement each other, forming an institutional basis to support the relative stability of local socioeconomics.

Decline in Economic Liberalism Under Increasing Government Control

In traditional China, government management of the grassroots was mainly mediated through the *baojia* system and civil organizations rather than direct control by the central government. Wang Rigen, Yang Guo'an, and Wu Xuemei argue from different perspectives about civil organizations and grassroots social order, revealing a complex relationship between civil organizations and the government that complements each other.[17] The development of the market and society in the Qing expanded the power of grassroots society, strengthened the ties of maintenance,

[17] Wang Rigen, "Lun mingqing xiangyue shuxing yu zhineng de bianqian" (On the Change of Attributes and Functions of Community Compacts in Ming and Qing dynasties), *Xiamen University xuebao (zhexue shehui kexue ban)* [Journal of Xiamen University (Arts & Social Sciences)], no. 3 (2003): 69–76; Yang Guo'an, "Kongzhi yu zizhi zhijian: guojia yu shehui hudong shiye xiade mingqing xiangcun zhixu" (Between Control and Autonomy: Rural Order in the Ming and Qing dynasties in the Perspective of the Interaction between State and Society), *Guangming ribao* (Guangming Daily), November 29, 2012; Wu Xuemei, "Duo zhongxin huqian: xiangcun shehui zhixu de you yizhong leixing" (Polycentric Embeddedness: Another Type of Rural Social Order), *Guangming ribao* (Guangming Daily), December 15, 2011.

and added market-oriented ties of connection between the government and the grassroots. Societies involved in public facilities and charities, guilds and public offices engaged in commerce and industry, academies and free schools responsible for education, families, clans with blood ties, and monasteries and temples of popular religion. These civil societies were autonomous subjects or organizational managers in different fields and served as the link between the government and the people. Through these civil organizations, traditional China achieved, at low cost, grassroots autonomy for diversity under a unified regime.

When the above intermediaries and agents were included in the bureaucratic system, they were the minions of the government or officials; when they were not in the bureaucratic system, their nature remains the same. Tax farms (*baoshuishang*) existed in large numbers in China and abroad, and the "chaoguan jingshu" in Linqing was similar to a tax farm. The so-called profit-making brokers of Duara should include both the tax farm and the *baoxie*. The *baohu xiejia*[18] was a market-oriented connection between the county government and the grassroots society in the Qing dynasty. It made a living from the market and used its information and activity to transmit information between the government and the grassroots. Meanwhile, it also accepted the government's commission to perform certain functions, such as tax collection, on behalf of the government. *Xiejia* was not a government official and did not require a government salary, thus reducing government management costs.

The simple orientation of economic liberalism waxes and wanes in playing with authoritarian centralization. As a simple pursuit of human nature, it is strong and long-standing but lacks a formal system of binding institutions. When the constraints change, the liberal economic orientation cannot counteract the expansion of government power. It becomes vulnerable in the face of strong governments. For example, this orientation was often undermined at the end of dynasties or during periods of tyranny; the dynasties then collapsed with socioeconomic decline.

In modern times, the tradition of economic liberalism has been reversed and distorted, mainly for the following reasons:

[18] Hu Tieqiu, *Mingqing xiejia yanjiu* (Study of *Xiejia* during Ming and Qing dynasties), Shanghai: Shanghai guji Press, 2015.

1. With the increased public facilities and public affairs in modern times, government functions have gradually expanded. Functions that were previously performed by the private sector were transferred to the government.
2. With the deepening of urbanization, some gentry moved into the cities after the nineteenth century; in the early twentieth century, with the abolition of the imperial examinations, a power vacuum emerged at the grassroots level, while the government increasingly strengthened its control over the grassroots.
3. As a result of colonial aggression, the ideal of "enriching the country and strengthening the army" and the demand for collectivism intensified in modern China, and the idea of strengthening government control became increasingly common.
4. After the Great Depression, all countries strengthened government control, as represented by Fascist Germany and the Soviet Union. In terms of economic thought, the Keynesian theory of government intervention and Marx's theory of a planned economy dominated intellectual circles in China.

With the increasing penetration of direct central management to the grassroots and increased public affairs, civil organizations that used to act as government intermediaries were gradually bureaucratized or replaced and eliminated. During the planned economy, clans were regarded as "feudal" and were banned; various "associations" and "societies" either ceased to exist or were transformed into quasi-governmental institutions. In order to strengthen its control over the grassroots, the government took over almost everything and became the subject of unlimited responsibility, assuming most of the public affairs and all the risks. Public infrastructure, such as education, health care, and public utilities, must and can only be provided by the government. As the government was funded by taxes, the financial system and the taxpayers were overwhelmed, and both the government and the private sector lost vitality.

The decline of the Chinese economy in the modern era and its failure to move spontaneously toward "capitalism" led to strong doubts about the vitality of the traditional Chinese economy and the belief that an authoritarian and centralized government had impeded economic development. Another view looked to strong government control to drive China's modernization, which became the dominant trend of thought in twentieth-century China. Both opposing views ignore the tradition of civil and economic liberalism. Especially amid China's national crisis, private economic liberalism and traditions of grassroots autonomy declined and were gradually forgotten or misinterpreted.

CHAPTER 8

Farmland Rights System and Economic Transformation

8.1 Traditional China Versus Premodern Western Europe: Property Rights and Management Practices

Traditional China and premodern Western Europe differed in many ways and contrasted sharply. For example, equal inheritance versus primogeniture; early marriage and early childbearing versus late marriage and birth control; labor-intensive versus labor-saving; individual family farm operation versus large-scale manorial operation; intensive farming versus a combination of agriculture and pastoral farming, and so on (Table 8.1).

Comparison of Operations

In the traditional era, Chinese agriculture emphasized intensive farming, a labor-intensive operation rather than a labor-saving one. Due to the small amount of land per household, most Chinese farmers ran family farms independently and could not operate on a large scale. Based on a developed land rights market, family farms were divisible, easy to replicate, and easy to recover. However, the king, nobles, and the church controlled most of the land, manors, and serfs in medieval Western Europe. Due to

D. Long and X. Chi, *The Institutions of Land Property Rights in China*, Palgrave Studies in Economic History,
https://doi.org/10.1007/978-981-97-5112-9_8

Table 8.1 Comparison of traditional china and premodern Western Europe

Traditional China	*Premodern Western Europe*
Individual family farms	Estate economy
Arable farms	Agro-pastoral farms
Labor-intensive (intensive farming)	Labor-saving
Early marriage and early childbearing	Late marriage and birth control
Preference for son (male farming and female weaving)	Female labor (pastoral labor)
Private land property rights	Corporate property rights under the feudal system
Free trade of land rights	Land cannot be bought or sold
Equal inheritance	First-born son inheritance system (primogeniture)
Replication and duplication of individual farming operations	Heterogeneous growth outside the system
Stability (intrinsic factors assimilate heterogeneous factors)	Change (heterogeneous factors change the essential factors)

the strong holistic nature of the manorial economy and corporate property rights, individual farmers tended to have a strong attachment to the manor.

The Western European feudal system was a top-down system of granting fiefs and manors, with the manor owners contributing their income and military service in return. The manors included:

1. *Manorial domain*: This accounted for 25–30% of the total area and was cultivated by farmers without compensation. The territory included the means of production, such as the lord's mansion, barns, stables, workshops, orchards, and household appliances such as mills, kilns, grape presses, and ovens. The lack of large or expensive equipment made the farmers dependent on the lord of the manor. Farmers paid for their use.
2. *Farmers' share of land*: This was cultivated by the farmers themselves. However, the farmers relied on the manor for their livelihood and reproduction, including dependence on large farming tools and utensils and public pastures, and the serfs were physically dependent on the lord.
3. *Commons*: These included pasture, grazing land, and woodland.

Manors were holistic in nature. To some extent, the manor was an iron-clad camp (*yingpan*) with a constant change of lords. Serfs depended on the manor for production, livelihoods, and even personally. In terms of production, since the cultivation of land in Western Europe required heavy plows and two to four cattle to cultivate the land, the ordinary farmer could not obtain these means of production. Therefore, the individual farmer had to rely on the tools of the manor. Second, stock raising requires large areas of pasture which could only be provided by the manor. In addition, because of the fallow and rotational agriculture system in Western Europe, farmers depended on the manor owners to allocate their arable land. In terms of livelihood, farmers also relied on tools such as ovens and mills provided by the manor.

These characteristics made British agriculture primarily based on the production unit of the manor, which combined agriculture and stock raising so that the production of individual British farmers was subordinated to the manorial economy. In contrast, Chinese soils were soft and plowshares were light; by using simple tools, Chinese farmers were able to develop integrated individual farm productivity and survive independently. For example, using a hoe, Chinese peasants could reclaim wastelands in migratory areas and quickly establish independent farms, which led to the development of mountainous areas during the Ming and Qing dynasties.

In Western Europe, winters are wet, summers are dry, and the crops are primarily drought-resistant cereals (wheat, barley, oats, or rye), fruits, and vegetables. With low rainfall, low temperatures, and limited sunlight in the summer, crop yields and nutrient densities are low, and the capacity of land to feed the population is limited. Under the influence of the Atlantic current, winters are wet and warm, and the cost of wintering livestock is low, so pastoral farming is more developed and meat is more abundant.

East Asia is influenced by the monsoon climate, with dry and cold winters and high costs to overwinter livestock, so animal husbandry is limited, and there is a diminished supply of beef, lamb, and dairy products. However, summers are hot and rainy, with enough rain and heat for higher crop yields. As a result, North China produces enough wheat, millet, and beans, while South China produces enough rice, to feed a large population.

Agricultural production in China and East Asia requires more labor, especially during the busy farming season, when men must brave the heat to harvest and plant. Agricultural production is heavy on physical labor, which is the source of patriarchy. In labor-intensive production, additional labor is still required, even though labor efficiency is marginally decreasing. Regardless of the input–output ratio, such labor can only be implemented in individual family production and is difficult to achieve in large-scale hired operations. Therefore, individual farmers are more competitive in their modes of management. Relatively speaking, traditional Chinese large-scale farms or hired labor operations were inhibited. Although some large farming tools were more technologically advanced, they were not further developed because they were not suitable for individual farming operations. For example, the Yuan dynasty's water spinning wheel (*dafangche*) was higher than the Jenny spinning machine in terms of power and number of spindles. However, during the Ming and Qing dynasties, the water spinning wheel gradually disappeared due to a lack of demand,[1] while in Western Europe, the Jenny spinning machine stimulated the improvement of British machines and further advanced the Industrial Revolution.

In traditional China, the emphasis on manual labor and the model of intensive farming created a preference for sons over daughters and a need for more children. Due to the natural constraints of land size per household, the average size of a Chinese farming family was usually less than five members. However, during the period of Land Reform, the period of the People's Commune, and the early years of Contracting Production to Households (*baochan daohu*), new policies encouraged fertility, and family size grew. However, the collective labor system of the People's Commune introduced different pay for men and women for the same work, reinforcing the custom of giving preference to sons over daughters.[2]

The medieval and premodern periods in Western Europe were very different. The lack of land output on combined agro-pastoral manors to support a limited population and the low nutritional density of the population inhibited labor-intensive operation modes. Second, several waves of

[1] Li Bozhong, "Chucai jinyong: Zhongguo shuizhuan dafangche yu Yingguo akelai shuili fangzhiji" (Water Spinning Wheel and British Ackley Hydrospinning Machine), *Lishi yanjiu* (Historical Research), no. 1 (2002): 62–74.

[2] Huang Yingwei, Li Jun, and Wang Xiuqing, "Jitihua moqi nonghu laodongli touru de xingbie chayi: yige cunzhuang 'beitaizi' de yanjiu" (Gender Differences in Farmers' Labor Inputs at the End of Collectivization: A Study of Beitaizi Village), *Zhongguo jingjishi yanjiu* (Researches in Chinese Economic History), no. 2 (2010): 29–39.

the Black Death swept through Europe, resulting in massive population declines, creating labor-saving operations and incentives to marry later and have fewer children. Third, the labor input of combined agro-pastoral manors was relatively low, so female labor was adaptable in pastoral operations. Fourth, the larger the size of the agro-pastoral manor, the greater the marginal decrease in labor input required and the greater the marginal increase in female labor, thus incentivizing the operation of large-scale estates.

The prevalence of late marriage and birth control in Western Europe also inhibited population growth. In the seventeenth century, the age of first marriage for women in France, England, Belgium, Germany, and Scandinavia ranged from 24.6 to 26.7 years old. In contrast, in traditional China, the age of first marriage for women was around 16 years old, which was 8–10 years lower than the age of first marriage in Western Europe. This means that in two generations of Western European women, Chinese women have already had three generations. At the same time, about 17.5% of women in Western Europe chose not to marry or have children, so population growth in Western Europe was even slower. In China, almost all women were married, except for a few nuns (Fig. 8.1).

The late marriage of women was adapted to the needs of manorial labor. Women's labor ratio in pastoral operations was high, with the number of women working per 100 acres of the estate at 26% for arable

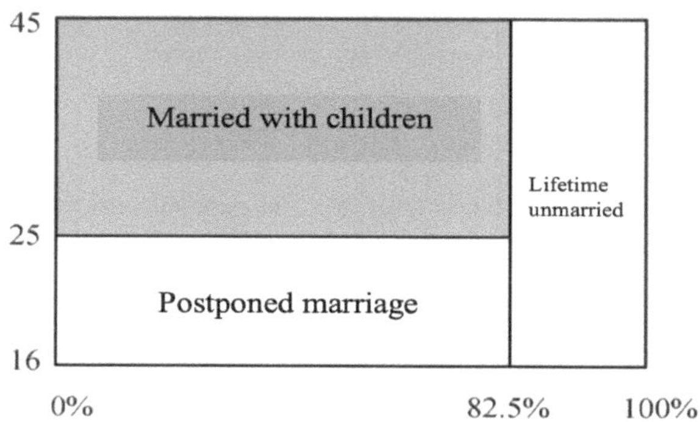

Fig. 8.1 Marriage and childbirth patterns in Europe in the seventeenth century. *Sources* Clark, G. A., *Farewell to Alms: A Brief Economic History of the World* (Princeton: Princeton University Press, 2007)

farming and 34% for pastoral farming, almost equal to male labor (36%). The ratio of female labor per 250-acre estate was only 19% for arable farming and still 31% for the pastoral type. In contrast, men's farming and women's weaving were the traditional division of labor between men and women in China, with women's labor playing a supporting role in the cultivation of the fields. However, even during the period of Collectivization, when equality between men and women was advocated, women's work points were lower than men's for the same number of work hours (Fig. 8.2).

Regarding labor costs, arable farms were higher than pastoral farms on the same scale. Generally, the average size of an arable farm was small, about 87 acres, while the average size of a pastoral farm was more than six times larger, at 546 acres. The ratio of labor costs per acre was 1.11–0.27. Therefore, the higher the proportion of pastoral farming, the more land-intensive and labor-saving the farm tends to be; the larger the farm, the more land-intensive and labor-saving it tends to be (Fig. 8.3).

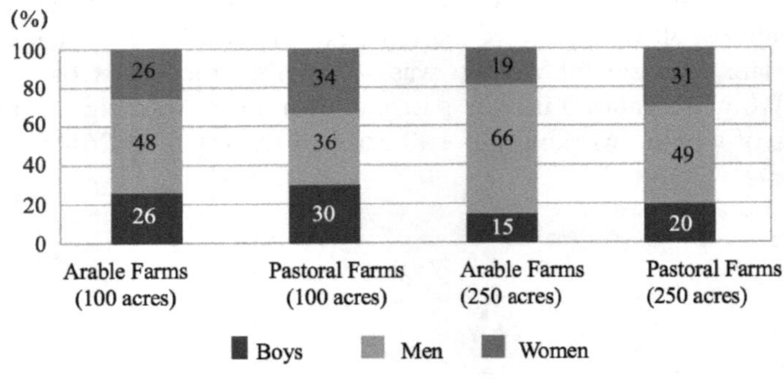

Fig. 8.2 Share of types of labor in arable and pastoral farms (high labor ratio of women in pastoral farms). *Sources* Nico Voigtländer and Hans-Joachim Voth, "How the West 'Invented' Fertility Restriction," *American Economic Review* 103, no. 6 (2013): pp. 2227–2264

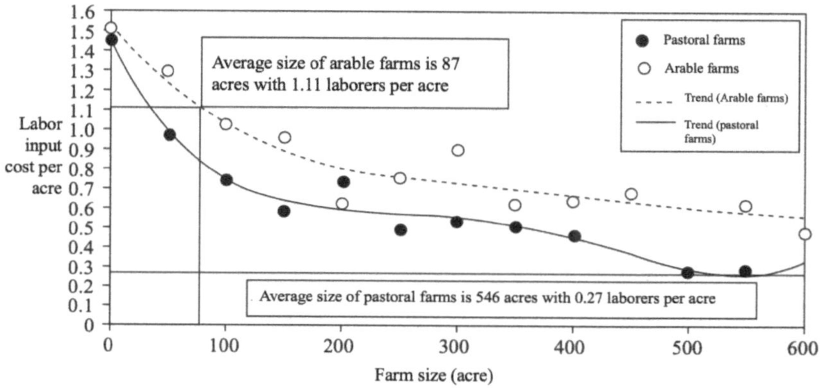

Fig. 8.3 Labor costs of arable and pastoral farms. *Sources* Nico Voigtländer and Hans-Joachim Voth, "How the West 'Invented' Fertility Restriction," *American Economic Review* 103, no. 6 (2013): pp. 2227–2264

Comparison of Property Types

The manor system was similar to corporate property rights, with its land property rights unclear and its owners absent (just like collective ownership).[3] The estate was nominally owned by the village and township collective but had to follow the orders of the higher government; land use rights were vested in individual farmers. Neither village and township collectives nor peasant families had the right to mortgage the land. The power of the Lord was limited and could change constantly. Serfs were no longer the property of their masters but appendages of the land.

Corporate property rights were holistic and inseparable, so only a single inheritance system could guarantee their integrity. If the system of equal inheritance was implemented, the property rights and the estate would be divided. The peasant's share of land could not be divided autonomously either. In an era when life expectancy was only 40 years, the system of primogeniture was the appropriate one. However, the indivisibility of land

[3] Qiu Yimeng, "16–19 shiji yingguo tudi zhidu bianqian—cong bu wanquan siyou chanquan xiang wanquan siyou chanquan de guodu" (Changes in the British Land System From the 16th to the 19th Century: Transition from Incomplete Private Property Rights to Complete Private Property Rights), Doctoral Thesis, Liaoning University, 2008.

discouraged the trading of land rights; in particular, the buying and selling of ownership rights was not allowed.

The manor's operation as a whole, once divided, would damage its efficiency. For example, pastures and rangelands that were common land would no longer be suitable for grazing if they were divided, especially as pastures that provided large-scale grazing for horses, cattle, and sheep. Large-scale means of production such as mills also could not be divided, because once the manor was divided into two, it could require two or four mills. The wholeness and indivisibility of corporate property rights and the manorial economy inhibited the division and trading of land rights, making the primogeniture system more adaptable.

Primogeniture and Equal Inheritance

Throughout history, China practiced equal inheritance, while Western Europe practiced primogeniture. Previously, it was thought that cultural differences were responsible for this. However, if Chinese traditional culture emphasizes collectivism and Western European culture emphasizes individualism, then Western European plurality and Chinese succession of the eldest son should be logical.

What is the rationale behind the Western European system of maintaining manor integrity? If you want to maintain the integrity of the manor, it is necessary to have a system of primogeniture. The same is true of corporate property rights, which may collapse if the business is divided. The same logic applies to manors in Western Europe. When the lord divided the estate among the eldest sons, most younger sons had to leave the estate to go out and earn a living, unless they stayed to manage the estate or were employed by it. Those who went out to earn a living were engaged in fields such as:

1. Industrialists and traders. They operated outside the feudal castles and converged on the emerging cities. The city was independent of the original system and did not belong to the manor or the nobility. In the cities, the merchants and industrialists were autonomous. The emergence and independent development of commercial and industrial towns also became an important force for change.
2. Pirates, seafarers, or explorers travel the lesser known geographical world. The development of overseas trade and colonization may not be unrelated to this.

3. Professional clergymen, promoting Christianity and theological development. This was an important reason for Christianity's relatively independent existence and development as a secular force.
4. Theology, in turn, drove the development of philosophy and science. Theology, philosophy, and science in Europe were relatively independent and self-contained and thus formed the modern intellectual system of the world. In contrast, the Chinese system of knowledge emphasized practicality, especially in serving the rulers; its path of independent evolution by the logic of the knowledge system itself was relatively weaker.
5. Knights or mercenaries. At that time, there was a constant war between small European countries and a great demand for soldiers.
6. If they could not gain a foothold in any of the above areas, they would fall into proletarianism. As mentioned before, then they would become a potential revolutionary force.

In all these, the younger sons made a living outside the old system, outside the original manor; they were self-sustaining, and could grow to become a force to challenge and change the old system. In this way, the heterogeneous factors kept increasing to impact the original homogeneous factors, and eventually, the heterogeneous factors replaced the original homogeneous factors; thus, qualitative change occurred. The first point concerns the development of industry, commerce, and market development. The latter five points are somewhat less developed in China. In fact, industry and commerce in traditional China were not inferior but rather were even more prominent. However, the market in traditional China also blended with and complemented the traditional institutions.

In Western Europe, the surplus population that the manor could not accommodate was redirected and became the antithesis of the manorial economy. In contrast, under the Chinese system of equal inheritance, additional populations formed new individual family farms. The population that the original land could not support established individual farms elsewhere through migration or land reclamation, but their method of agricultural operation did not essentially change. Supported by the developed land rights market, the family farm model was replicated and sustained stably and dynamically. However, as the homogeneous factors continued to intensify, qualitative change became increasingly difficult. That is the real meaning and path of involution.

The policy of "equal inheritance" was adapted to the vitality and competitiveness of individual family farming in China. The main body of traditional Chinese society was the independent agricultural family households and tenant farmers who ran family farms. They have different levels of land rights. Farmers who owned family farms were the proletarians of the time, constituting the "middle class" of the agricultural era. Family farms contributed to the stability of the social economy and became the main form and essential feature of the dominant traditional Chinese economy. Thus, land property rights and their trading system were an important institutional guarantee for the vitality of independent Chinese farming, but they also became a disincentive for modernizing large or wage farms. That was the basic characteristic of the traditional Chinese economy and its divergence from the economic development path of Western Europe. What is too stable is difficult to change qualitatively.

Traditional Stability: A Comparison with Premodern Western Europe

There is a long-standing social belief that dynastic changes occur in China every one or two centuries and that such periodic dynastic changes lead to instability in Chinese society. However, on a global scale, it is already a wonder that such a large empire lasted for more than two thousand years through dynastic changes. The source of its stability is the "middle class." However, when a society is too stable, change does not occur easily, and new factors are inhibited. Stability inhibits change, resulting in a delayed growth of budding capitalism, the failure of the Industrial Revolution to grow endogenously, and delayed and costly post-industrialization.

The proletariat is the opposite of the middle class and comparing China with Western Europe yields interesting differences. The purely hired peasants in China were the proletariat. According to Mao Zedong's survey, the hired peasants had no economic basis to marry and raise children, no ability to build their own families and farms, and no ability to reproduce population and materials independently; therefore, the hired peasants were cruelly eliminated. However, the number of such peasants was very small in China, accounting for only 2–3%. Thanks to the development of the land rights market, those who did not have land could establish farms by renting land, and only those who really lacked the basic capacity or were inherently deficient were eliminated. In fact, some hired peasants rented out small plots of land (or the field bottom rights) and worked for themselves. These people were not proletarians in the strict sense.

According to Pomeranz's estimate, the proletariat in Western Europe was roughly 10% of the total population before the Industrial Revolution.[4] Why was there a large number of proletarians in Western Europe in the Middle Ages? The root cause was the weakness of the individual farmer's ability to operate independently. The peasants were too dependent on the manor to be able to carry out agricultural operations independently. After leaving the manor, they failed to establish their own farms and eventually became proletarians.

Primogeniture was also associated with the manor's operation. Why could the manor and its property not be equally distributed among future generations? Because if the manor was repeatedly divided, its holistic operation would be destroyed, leading to a decrease in efficiency. Meanwhile, the nature of the vanity title led to the fact that the superior lord did not allow the subordinate lord to divide the manor. In an era when the average life expectancy was no more than 40 years, primogeniture became the appropriate choice. Nevertheless, sons other than the eldest had to find other ways out, and some became proletarians.

The proletariat in Western Europe was large and was constantly reproducing itself, preparing the labor force for the industrial workers needed for the Industrial Revolution. Especially after the "Enclosure Movement," the sources of purely hired labor increased. The impact of the proletariat on society was the most revolutionary and destructive, as Carl Marx and Mao Zedong have argued, so the revolution depended on the proletariat, who "lost only their chains."[5] Before and after the Industrial Revolution, the revolution in England lasted two or three hundred years. Since the Chinese proletariat was small in number, it had less power to push for social change. In modern times, the main body of industrial laborers in China consisted mainly of peasant workers who went to cities to work in industry or services. However, migrant workers were and still were inextricably tied to the land and their hometowns.

As can be seen from the comparison between the "middle class" and the proletariat, the relative stability of traditional societies is due

[4] Kenneth Pomeranz (Peng Mulan), *Da fenliu: Ouzhou, Zhongguo, ji xiandai shijie de fazhan* (The Big Divergence: China, Europe, and the Making of the Modern World Economy), translated by Shi Jianyun, Nanjing: Jiangsu People's Press, 2004.

[5] Friedrich Engels, Carl Marx, *Makesi Engesi xuanji* (Selected Works of Marx and Engels), translated by Zhongyang bianyiju (Central Compilation and Translation Bureau), Beijing: People's Press, 1995, 307.

to a large number of independently owned family farms. Such family farms were made possible because of land property rights and markets. Without fairly developed land property rights and markets, it would be difficult for individual family farms to dominate and develop a long-term continuity of life. The model of establishing and operating family farms through markets is resilient and vital and dominates the traditional Chinese economy's main form and essential features, and the two were mutually reinforcing. Land property rights and their markets, together with individual farming, were the distinctive and fundamental features of the traditional Chinese economy, with its inherent logic. Therefore, the land property rights transaction system is an important institutional guarantee for the vitality of individual Chinese farmers.

Compared with Western European manors, the operation of individual agricultural households had a lower threshold and the characteristics of divisibility—easy to replicate and easy to recover. Even if the family size of a farmer increases, it is possible to achieve independent operation by clearing wasteland. Because of the divisibility of farms, land could be distributed equally to future generations, and large families with four generations together were usually not competitive. Although the emperor honored four generations together, it was not the dominant form or norm. In addition, large-scale operations and "capitalist" farming that focused on the market were relatively rare in traditional China.

In conclusion, clear land property rights and a diversified market for land rights, together with independently operated individual family farms, constitute the distinctive features and developmental vein of China's traditional economy. The allocation of production factors such as land through the market resulted in the higher land output and efficiency of farms in the shortage economy, which also inspired reform of the agricultural land system on the road to marketization.

8.2 Economic Backwardness in Modern China: Root Causes

China's economic backwardness in modern times disappointed Chinese people. The root cause of this is still a source of confusion. As a result of violence and intrusions by imperialist powers, modern China's large, a unified market was shattered, with its economy disordered, which resulted in a market panic. The imperfection of international rules affected China's opening to the outside world and also created anxiety about opening-up and even economic nationalism. This book reflects on established theories and reveals the most important but long-overlooked cause of negative economic growth due to prolonged war, the failure of economic transformation, and the resulting turmoil and chaos.

Exploring the reasons for the economic backwardness of modern China is not only a matter of basic judgment of the traditional economic system but also a major issue of the perception of Chinese characteristics and the choice of the Chinese road. In the 100 years between 1850 and 1949, China's economic output barely grew but remained the same; per capita income fell from 43.8 yuan to 34.98 yuan (Table 8.2).[6] The share of China's industrial added value in the world total was still 7.2% in 1850 and fell to 0.3% in 1953. China's industrial output per capita, 19 US dollars in 1850, was slightly higher than India's; it was reduced to 8 US dollars a century later, only a third of India's. At the beginning of reforms and opening-up in 1980, China's per capita industrial output value was comparable to that of India, at more than 60 US dollars. However, the gap between China and developed countries was getting bigger, and the difference in 1980 was about 100 times[7] (See Tables 8.3, 8.4 for details).

China's aspirants have been seeking the path to recovery. People searched hard, either blaming China's backwardness on private ownership of land, believing that the market led to the chaos in modern China, blaming the emperor and autocracy, or blaming foreign capital, and some even believed that the root cause of China's backwardness lay in Confucian culture.[8] All of the above became objects of revolution under emotional demands and political passions. These myths are, in fact, not academically tested. Past ideologies criticized the so-called feudal system, feudal culture, feudal rule, imperialist invasion, etc. However, it is rare to find a serious academic discussion of the causes of modern economic backwardness, and few papers systematically examine them from the perspective of economic history. This book will reflect on the myths about the causes of modern China's backwardness and then explore the real

[6] Wang Yuru, "Zhongguo jindai de jingji zengzhang he zhongchang zhouqi bodong" (Economic Growth and Medium- and Long-Cycle Fluctuations in Modern China), *Jingjixue (jikan)* (China Economic Quarterly), no. 1 (2005): 461–490.

[7] It only jumped to USD 1405 in 2010, which was not only much higher than India's USD 241, but the gap with Europe and the United States was also narrowing significantly.

[8] There are so many references that it is difficult to form a brief literature review.

Table 8.2 China's national income per capita (*yuan*), 1850–1949. *Sources* Wang Yuru, "Zhongguo jindai de jingji zengzhang he zhongchang zhouqi bodong" [Economic Growth and Medium- and Long-Cycle Fluctuations in Modern China], *Jingjixue (jikan)* [China Economic Quarterly], no.1 (2005): 461–490

Years	*1850*	*1887*	*1914*	*1936*	*1949*
National income (billion *yuan*)	181.64	143.43	187.64	257.98	189.48
Population (*qianren*)	414,699	377,636 400,000*	455,243	510,789	541,670
Per capita income (*yuan*)	43.8	38.0 35.9*	41.22	50.51	34.98

Years	*1850–1887*	*1887–1914*	*1914–1936*	*1936–1949*
Average annual growth	– 0.38	0.30	0.92	– 2.87
National income (billion yuan)	– 0.54*	0.51*		

Notes The figures marked * above for 1887 wereper capita income and average annual growth rates derived by the original authors from more desirable population figures

Table 8.3 Estimated shares in world total industrial output of three countries (%), 1850–2012. *Sources* Xu Yi, Basi Fanluwen (Bas van Leeuwen), "Zhongguo gongye de changqi biaoxian jiqi quanqiu bijiao, 1850–2012 nian: yi zengjiazhi hesuan wei zhongxin" [Long-Term Performance of Chinese Industry and Its Global Comparison, 1850–2012: Focusing on Value Added Accounting], *Zhongguo jingjishi yanjiu* [Researches in Chinese Economic History], no.1 (2016): 39–50

Years	*China*	*United State*	*Britain*
1850	7.2	11.1	18.7
1913	1.1	32.8	12.5
1953	0.3	39.3	9.4
1980	1.1	23.6	4.7
2012	15.1	20.3	3.5

Table 8.4 Estimated industrial output per capita by country (USD). *Sources* Xu Yi, Basi Fanluwen (Bas van Leeuwen), "Zhongguo gongye de changqi biaoxian jiqi quanqiu bijiao, 1850–2012 nian: yi zengjiazhi hesuan wei zhongxin" [Long-Term Performance of Chinese Industry and Its Global Comparison, 1850–2012: Focusing on Value Added Accounting], *Zhongguo jingjishi yanjiu* [Researches in Chinese Economic History], no.1 (2016): 39–50

Years	*Britain*	*Germany*	*United States*	*India*	*China*	*Peru*
1850	539	336	397	15	19	102
1880	1085	843	929	16	20	48
1890	1159	710	1175	16	15	51
1900	1359	918	1515	18	14	86
1910	1430	1216	2042	22	16	148
1920	3183	988	1765	16	16	138
1930	2162	1112	2244	15	16	221
1940	2743					
1950	3371	1625	4512	25	8	350
1960	4268	3997	5205	35	25	491
1970	5561	6533	7267	49	33	635
1980	5859	7721	6957	60	68	740
1990	7202	8446	7654	90	165	548
2000	8262	8511	9147	132	496	701
2010	8643	9418	8807	142	1405	1182

roots of modern backwardness and its revelations from the perspective of economic history.

Rethinking the Backwardness of China: Misconceptions and Trial and Error Exploration

Due to the backwardness of modern China, the mainstream thinking and views in the twentieth century rejected the traditional Chinese system and culture in almost all aspects and regarded them as the root cause of backwardness.

First, the prevailing view in the past was that private property rights of land and free trade led to China's economic backwardness. Under private ownership of land, peasants may be forced to sell their land while landlords and gentry purchase it extensively, resulting in land annexation and concentration. Landless peasants were exploited by landlords and were bankrupted and exiled, eventually leading to social unrest and peasant revolts.

However, this argument is problematic. First, land concentration was grossly exaggerated. The proportion of land held by landowners and rich peasants was expressed in political slogans as 70–80%, while the concentration of land in the southern provinces was only about 30%, according to provincial survey data on Land Reform. If there was disorder in the land rights market in some areas in modern times, it was due to the intrusion of power and violence. In the traditional period, the land rights market was mainly well-ordered. For example, the system regulated potential disruptions of land rights transactions—officials were prohibited from buying land in their jurisdictions. However, the disrupted land rights market in the modern era has shaped people's perception of China's land property system, even being regarded as the root of all evil. Second, land rights transactions promoted the combination of production factors and resource allocation, improved economic efficiency and land output, and became the institutional basis for China's traditional economy to lead the world.[9] How did the land rights market become the source of economic collapse in modern times? Furthermore, after several explorations of equalization of land rights in the twentieth century, China in the new century has turned to land titling and encouraging land transfer—that is, advocating the market allocation of production factors. It can be seen that the claim that land property rights led to backwardness does not stand up to the test.

Second, another mainstream view influencing present-day policies is that the emperor and the premodern dynasty were the root cause of backwardness. Scholars bemoaned the misfortune of Chinese history, where dynastic changes had a cycle of roughly 200 years and where China was unable to achieve long-lasting peace and stability during dynastic cycles, with revolutions being accomplished in the form of peasant uprisings or wars of destruction. Regime change was often accomplished in the form of peasant revolts or wars. However, if we look at the history of the world, a cycle of about 200 years is already quite long, even a miracle, in both the

[9] Long Denggao, "Diquan jiaoyi yu shengchan yaosu zuhe, 1650–1950" (Land Rights Transactions and Production Factor Combinations, 1650–1950), *Jingji yanjiu* (Economic Research Journal), no. 2 (2009): 146–156; Long Denggao, Lin Zhan, Peng Bo, "Dian yu Qingdai diquan jiaoyi tixi" (Dian and the Qing dynasty Land Rights Transaction System), *China's Social Science* (Social Sciences in China), no. 5 (2013): 125–141.

ruling and economic cycles. Imagine if a dynasty remained unchanged for hundreds or even thousands of years—that is, the realization of the ideal of the first Qin emperor to rule the dynasty ruled by his descendants for ten thousand generations, which would be incredible in the history of humankind. In the Western world, only the modern United States has achieved stability for more than 150 years since the Civil War; Western Europe has gained stability for more than 60 years after the World War II. Previously, Europe was involved in far more internal and external wars than China, including the Dutch War of Independence, the English Glorious Revolution, the Anglo-Spanish War, the Anglo-French War, the Hundred Years' War, and the Napoleonic Wars, not to mention the two world wars. It can also be seen that the expectation that China would achieve centuries of unchanged political and economic stability actually reflected that people's insistence on national revitalization at that time had reached an unrealistic level. It is not surprising that various acts of correction and utopian ideals have been perpetrated against traditional China in recent times.

Third, it was once widely believed that if the private economy was allowed to develop freely or if the market was allowed to develop, the economic order could fall into chaos. The economic crisis in modern China could hardly be avoided. Today, we finally realize that cyclical fluctuations were an inevitable part of economic development. However, there was a time when people naively hoped that the economic system would run smoothly forever and that the government would have complete control over resources and allocate them to achieve stable economic development. In the 1950s, China established a planned economy of state-run enterprises and government control. Even small restaurants and barbershops were brought under state control, and private vendors and peddlers were banned. Until the early 1990s, private individuals transporting and selling goods across regions were still severely punished for speculation. After nearly 30 years of trial and error, it became clear that a planned economy with the government in complete control and allocation of resources was a dead end and a market economy was an irreversible path. China returned to its traditional economic path of private control and market allocation of resources.[10] Government-run

[10] Long Denggao, *Zhongguo chuantong shichang fazhanshi* (History of the Development of Traditional Markets in China), Beijing: People's Press, 1997.

enterprises were "competing with the people for profit," which our ancestors avoided. After the twists and turns and the pain, China accepted that it is the basic nature of human beings to pursue their own wealth creation, just as everyone pursues their own knowledge accumulation, and any other reason should be subordinated to and serve this nature. The transition from a planned economy to a market economy through reforms and opening-up has led to the outstanding achievements of today. The restructuring of state-owned enterprises through marketization, corporatization, and internationalization has led to international competitiveness.[11]

Fourth, blaming the backwardness of modern China's economy on the plunder and exploitation of foreign capital gave rise to Boxer-style xenophobia, leading to economic nationalism.

Fifth, it is even widely believed that traditional culture hindered the development and transformation of modern China. As a result, there were movements to clean up or even end traditional culture in China, and it was hoped that by introducing certain Western ideas, traditional Chinese culture could be fully replaced to promote modernization. The revolution in the field of culture, from Confucian morality and ethics to popular customs and practices, from religious beliefs to political and economic systems, was extensive and profound. In this vein, the "Cultural Revolution" reached an unprecedented level, and the so-called revolution was carried out in the name of "opposing feudalism, capitalism, and revisionism." Buddha statues were torn down, Confucius statues were trampled on, ethics were torn apart, and families, their ancestral halls and genealogies, were destroyed and abandoned. In the name of revolution, the cultural movement exposed the primitive ugliness of human beings. The subversion and revolution of traditional Chinese culture were the main lines of Chinese cultural thought in the twentieth century, and the "Cultural Revolution" was not an accidental event but a comprehensive presentation of a historical vein. Essentially, it was not something one person or a group could promote or stop. Learning from the pain, China gradually realized that traditional culture was not a sin and that

[11] Long Denggao, Chang Xu, and Xiong Jinwu, "Jieshu yu" (Conclusion), *Guo zhi run, zi Booksn shi: Tianjin hangdaoju 120 nian fazhan shi* (The Wetness of the Country Begins with Dredging: A History of the Development of the Tianjin Dredging Bureau in 120 Years), Beijing: Qinghua University Press, 2017.

the country's backwardness in modern times was not caused by traditional culture or the so-called inferiority of Chinese people. Destroying tradition does not build a new society; it is better to build a harmonious society rather than engage in struggle and revolution. In recent years, there has been a strong call for the revival of tradition,[12] and people even look to Neo-Confucianism to promote the ideal of world harmony, so much so that some scholars have forgotten that traditional culture also has its constraints. Traditional cultures and institutions that were trampled on in the twentieth century were being reawakened and even cherished today. China is returning to tradition to some extent, both culturally and economically.

Root Cause of China's Economic Backwardness

What is the cause of modern China's economic backwardness, since it is not due to the traditional culture and economic system?[13]

First, the great destruction of the long war was the chief cause of the economic decline and poverty of the people in modern times.

Modern China has had frequent domestic wars and aggressions by external colonial powers, including the Anglo-French alliance, the Taiping Rebellion, the Sino-Japanese War, the Eight-Power Allied Forces, the Warlords' Conflict, the War of Resistance against Japan, and the Communist Civil War. In terms of the extent, scope, and continuation of the economic damage caused by the wars, the War of Resistance against Japan and the Taiping Rebellion were massive disasters that led to severe long-term negative economic growth. As shown in Table 8.1 above, China's growth averaged about − 0.54% per year for 27 years between 1850 and 1887; it reached a staggering − 2.87% per year between 1931 and 1945. China's economy and society were devastated by 14 consecutive years of total war.

[12] Since the 18th Party Congress, General Secretary Xi Jinping has discussed the inheritance and promotion of China's traditional culture, which has also become an important source of his governance. Xi Jinping has repeatedly emphasized the historical influence and importance of Chinese traditional culture and given it a new contemporary relevance.

[13] Some of the following points have been overlooked and forgotten, some have not been deeply investigated, some lack historical perspective, some are too emotional and have ignored basic logic, and some are derived from stereotyped thinking and lack of reflection.

The second was the Chinese civil war and the warlord chaos. The invasion of China by the Eight-Power Allied Forces and the Sino-Japanese War itself did not involve a large area, but the war reparations caused a heavy burden on the Chinese people. Many years of positive exponential growth were needed to recover from the long war's negative economic growth of more than 40 years. The People's Republic of China started its recovery and development on a foundation of 100 years of failure.

In stages, the Chinese people have struggled during this century of catastrophe. During short periods of peace, the Chinese people created economic growth. The 1920s and 1930s, following the reunification of China by the Nationalist government, were a rare golden period of economic development for modern China. From 1914 to 1936, China achieved an average annual growth rate of nearly 1%. During the New Deal period of the late Qing dynasty, China's economy grew despite the presence of the Great Powers, and the total economy also achieved a slow growth of about 0. 3% from 1887 to 1911. There is no doubt that prolonged warfare was the main reason for China's economic backwardness and defeat in the modern era. The majority well understand it, but people always turn a blind eye to it and look for other reasons. Under war and turmoil, it is impossible for a country to have a well-functioning system and to experience peacetime economic growth.

The second was fracture and pain of transition from a traditional economy to a modern one.

The traditional economy fell behind relatively sharply under external stimuli. Before the Industrial Revolution, economic development was slow in both the East and the West. China was still on the economic and cultural high ground compared to its neighboring countries. Nevertheless, with the invasion of the Western powers, China's economic structure gradually changed, and the modern economy entered a period of profound transformation that had never been seen before. Any transformation is accompanied by change and pain, and even more so in modern China's economic transformation, which included an all-round transformation from agriculture to industrialization, from closed to the outside world to open to the outside world, and from a traditional to a modern economy. In fact, this transformation had its first results. For example, the New Deal at the end of the Qing and the Golden Decade of the Nationalist Government were not sustained because they were interrupted.

It was difficult to avoid turbulence and the ensuing poverty and backwardness during the long transition period. On the one hand, the old economic structure was broken, and the old economic order was in disarray; on the other hand, the new economic structure and order were slow to be established and stabilized, so the economy withered, and people suffered hardship. By contrast, the Western economy, which had already completed its modern transformation, was growing fast, and Western goods and capital were entering the Chinese market. In contrast, the stagnation and backwardness of China stood out. The pain and chaos of the modern transition period were typical worldwide, but it is particularly prominent in modern China.

The change in industrial structure and economic transformation in modern China was essentially a squeeze and elimination of labor-intensive products and industries, thus increasing the number of unemployed and semi-unemployed people. By the middle of the Qing dynasty, the Chinese economy had reached the limits of its technological conditions. After the development of mountainous areas, the population increased. Economic growth slowed due to decreased land and resources per capita. More importantly, the structure of the Chinese economy changed with the importation of Western commodities beginning in the mid-to-late nineteenth century. In the traditional period, the textiles and handicraft products produced by peasant households were sold in the domestic market, and such income became an indispensable part of the household income. However, with the growing impact of cheap Western industrial products, peasant household handicrafts gradually became unable to compete, their products lost their markets, and peasant families lost an important source of income. This was a structural change brought about by technological progress. As a result, artisans or semi-craftsmen lost their jobs, affecting other industries. From the late nineteenth century, large numbers of cotton artisans began to lose their jobs, followed by other craftsmen. As their food and other consumption had to be reduced, other industries were depressed. Due to the slow progress of urbanization and industrialization, rural society could not absorb the new labor force, and the people were increasingly impoverished. By the end of the nineteenth century, the international market, where Chinese goods such as tea and silk used to have a monopoly, was also successively seized by goods from Britain, India, and Japan. With a new wave of traditional industries under attack, the Chinese economy was in a long and painful transition.

Transition is inevitably accompanied by pain, both in China and abroad. Britain and France also underwent such a transition in the modern era, with the burning of churches between different religious denominations, constant struggles between interest groups, and revolutions. The United States was no exception, and in the late nineteenth century, Mark Twain called it the "Gilded Age," a period of superficial glamor and internal ugliness.

Third, the benefits of China's opening were limited, and the risks were high because international rules were not yet established.

China was beaten in foreign invasions because of the imperfection of international rules, and the rule of force played a dominant role. That is also why China's reforms and opening-up was unsuccessful during the late Qing dynasty and the Republican Period.[14] The benefits of opening-up to the outside world in modern China were limited, and the negative impact on the economy and people's lives was much greater than the benefits. As a result, xenophobia became more widespread and intense, reaching its peak during the Boxer Rebellion and the Cultural Revolution.[15] Under the WTO rules of equal trading in today's world, China's reforms and opening-up have gained a favorable external environment. In contrast, other backward and small countries have not suffered the fate of being beaten.

Fourth, another prominent cause of economic turmoil and decline was the destruction and fragmentation of the sizeable unified market that supported the development of the traditional economy.

A unified market was once a major advantage of China's traditional economy over that of Western Europe, but in modern times the chaotic political situation, especially local warlordism, has fragmented the market. From the mid to the late nineteenth century, the Taiping Rebellion swept through the whole of South China, and since then, there have been internal and external troubles and little peace in the country. The

[14] Chen Zhiwu, *Jinrong de luoji* (The Logic of Finance), Beijing: Guoji wenhua chuban gongsi, 2009.

[15] Similarly, the current export of Chinese manufacturing to Europe and the United States has impacted local industries, causing workers to lose their jobs and causing a backlash among local people, such as the anti-Chinese riots in Spain, Italy, and Russia in recent years, as well as the anti-globalization demonstrations of the working class in Europe and the United States. The burning of Chinese goods in Spain, Italy, Russia, and other places in recent years was in fact a popular catharsis of fear and anxiety. This xenophobia was the same as that of modern China.

advantages of a unified market were gradually lost and turned into disadvantages and obstacles due to various factors, such as massive reparations, and separatism by the powers and warlords.[16]

In modern times, warlordism has been abusive, and violence and power have invaded the market, destroyed the market's original rules and triggering economic chaos. However, this chaos is not inevitably accompanied by the market economy itself, much less insurmountable. On the contrary, it is the result of the destruction of the market. However, the chaos caused by the disrupted modern market went so far as to create a kind of fear for the market. For a time, most Chinese people saw economic chaos as an inevitable flaw inherent in the market and believed that only government control and resource allocation could overcome it. Be that as it may, this trend of thinking was understandable given the historical context of the time.

Fifth, Japan's aggression interrupted and reversed China's modernization process.

The Japanese war of aggression against China not only caused untold economic losses and catastrophe, but war, poverty, and disorder also reversed the trajectory of China's development. Before 1937, China's economy gradually got on the right track and embarked on an exploratory trajectory of market economic development. During the war, the government's control over the economy was unprecedentedly strengthened under the wartime economic system. After the victory of the war against Japan, the Chinese state confiscated enemy assets, and the state-owned economy became dominant. After the War of Liberation, when the state again confiscated enemy property and foreign investment, the state-owned economy became dominant. In the middle of the twentieth century, the mainstream thinking of economics, reinforced government control, and the Soviet model of a planned economy came into favor in China.

These factors, reinforced by each other, led to chaos in government administration and social disorder; in a disordered social economy, the destructive effects of natural disasters were also more likely to intensify.

[16] In the mid-twentieth century, national unification was completed. But immediately afterward, under the planned economy, a unified market was divided into segments, market rules were trampled on and disappeared as never before, and the market was rejected by the government. Even today, 40 years after the reforms and opening-up, the market rules are still distorted from time to time by the government's squeeze.

Thus, a peaceful and unified open environment is the most fundamental guarantee for economic development.

Comparison and Inspirations

The traditional economic system and culture and the system of private property rights on farmland were not the root causes of modern China's economic backwardness. However, there were still many questions about this.

> First, China's traditional economic system is mature and stable, yet difficult to transform.

There is a view that the failure of China's traditional economy to produce an indigenous Industrial Revolution and be the first to enter modern society indicates the lack of dynamism of the traditional economy. In fact, when Britain completed the Industrial Revolution, the rest of the world was far behind Britain, and China was not the only one lagging. A better way to think about this question should be why the traditional Chinese economy did not transform and could not generate an Industrial Revolution like the one that occurred in Britain. This question has been asked not only by Chinese scholars but also by scholars from France and Spain, India, Islamic countries, and Africa. For example, the traditional view is that the Great Voyages opened up the maritime trade and colonial economies of Western Europe and that the accumulation of capital contributed to the Industrial Revolution. However, Spain was the first to benefit from the opening of new routes and colonies in America, but the Industrial Revolution did not occur in Spain but in Britain, which was a latecomer.[17]

The fact that the Industrial Revolution took place in Britain is considered by some scholars to be accidental.[18] Therefore, the occurrence of the Industrial Revolution cannot be used as a criterion to measure the

[17] Acemoglu D., Johnson, S., & Robinson, J. "The Rise of Europe: Atlantic Trade, Institutional Change, and Economic Growth," *The American Economic Review* 95, 3 (2005): 546–579.

[18] Kenneth Pomeranz (Peng Mulan), *Da fenliu: Ouzhou, Zhongguo, ji xiandai shijie de fazhan* (The Big Divergence: China, Europe, and the Making of the Modern World Economy), translated by Shi Jianyun, Nanjing: Jiangsu People's Press, 2004.

dynamism of the economic system and the economic development of any region in history. In fact, the economy of the Jiangnan region in China during the Ming and Qing dynasties was as developed as that of the Netherlands or Scotland in Europe, each in its own way.[19] Moreover, in the traditional era, change often occurred under crisis and in an immature pattern; in a generally mature economy, the stimulus and impetus for change did not exist. In other words, the traditional Chinese economy probably did not change because it was mature and stable, not because it was in crisis, which took place in modern times.

Although no countries and regions except Britain could produce Industrial Revolution, the process of advancing their industrialization through learning and imitation may be more common. After Britain, Western Europe, and the United States completed their Industrial Revolutions, Japan and other countries followed, and in the 1970s, countries and regions such as the Four Little Dragons of Asia and Israel completed their industrialization. In the 1990s, China and Russia began to establish market economic system. Under this perspective, the real issue is to explore why China in the nineteenth to twentieth centuries was so slow to learn and emulate the progress of industrialization or the modern market economic system.

It is true that in the late nineteenth century, China was able to begin the industrialization process as Japan did. However, the initial results of the late Qing reforms were disrupted by the warlord chaos. The period of the Nanjing Nationalist Government was a golden decade in which China's modern economic development was beginning to bear fruit. However, unfortunately, it was interrupted by the Japanese invasion, and the trajectory of China's market economy was thus reversed. Thus, the process of industrialization in China in the twentieth century was a troubled road, and establishing a market economic system was obstructed. The main reason for this was that the war interrupted and distorted the original path of China's economic development, not because it was influenced by the world trend to embark on a planned economy.

Third, the Industrial Revolution in Britain was only completed after the dramatic and tumultuous changes of the seventeenth to nineteenth centuries. During its nearly two centuries of existence, it was constantly accompanied by turbulence and risk. Even long after the completion of

[19] Li Bozhong, *Jiangnan de zaoqi gongyehua (1550–1850)* (Early Industrialization in Jiangnan), Beijing: Zhongguo renmin University Press, 2010.

the Industrial Revolution, the social and economic turmoil in Britain were still abhorrent to Marx and Engels, who wanted to eliminate them. Third, the Industrial Revolution in Britain also underwent dramatic and tumultuous changes from the seventeenth to nineteenth centuries before it was completed. In other words, even by the middle of the nineteenth century, the system initiated in Britain was not regarded as a good system. It underwent turbulence and change for more than 100 years before stabilizing after World War II.

> Second, there were lessons and inspirations we should learn from the modern era.

China's traditional economy had its own characteristics, but it can hardly be said to be uniquely superior, but nor is it an inferior culture or system; Confucianism was not incompatible with capitalism, as Weber argued, nor was Chinese inferiority irredeemable, as some have claimed, and nor can so-called Neo-Confucianism save China.

War and turmoil were the main reasons for China's backwardness in the modern era, and the present situation is hard-won and should be cherished by all the people of China. In cases of civil unrest or war, it will be a national disaster, and no one will be spared. Moreover, the failure of China's economic transformation in modern times led to chaos. Today we are in the process of a new transition, which will be accompanied by different degrees of turmoil and change. We must objectively look at the problems that arise in the transition process and not deny them or hinder them because of various problems. Finally, difficult exploration and continuous trial and error have determined China's market economic path. The country should never again make a destabilizing mistake or a directional error.

> Third, moral judgments may constrain economic development and may also fall into misconceptions and even traps.

The traditional Chinese economy is neither superior nor inferior in terms of culture and institutions. It cannot change the world with neo-Confucianism, as some scholars claim; nor is it incompatible with capitalism, as Weber argues; nor is it irredeemably inferior, as some claim. The Chinese tradition does have its uniqueness, which is worth exploring.

It would be biased to look at any economic form, phenomenon, or system from a purely moral perspective. For example, the tenancy system is considered exploitative and therefore denounced or prohibited. However, the prohibition of tenancy de facto eliminates the peasants' right to choose and means peasants may be tied to the land forever. Conversely, if morality is used as a criterion, an ethical economic system may not necessarily have room for development; in the long run, it may lose its vitality. For example, in the Qing dynasty, the free provision of public facilities by private organizations for the public good was touching and worthy of eulogy. However, the lack of profit accumulation to promote reproduction in the long run generally limits its development space. The original intention of a planned economy was to try to eliminate chaos in economic activity, especially economic crises, with total government control. However, when such good intentions replace the choices of market actors, it leads to the opposite of its original purpose.

Fourth, respect history instead of blindly following the sages.

In the twentieth century, against the historical background of saving the country and the people, it was challenging for the nation to recognize the characteristics of the traditional economy with today's market economic logic or to explore the reasons for modern economic backwardness. The dominant thinking in twentieth-century China, as well as in many other countries, was a non-market or anti-market economy. We can understand the choices made during the historical period. However, China cannot limit its perception of today's market economy by the thoughts and choices made by predecessors under specific historical conditions or even deny the market economy of some chaotic phenomena that emerged in the process of market economic transformation. In that case, China will neither be able to correctly grasp and understand the fundamental causes of its economic backwardness in modern times nor will it be able to understand the path to building a market economy today. Today, in the twenty-first century, only by reflecting on the historical perspective of the market economy can China grasp the historical origin of the flow and general trends.[20]

[20] The choices of the twentieth century have left a profound impact in a way that has become the premise of today's Chinese market economy and constitutes a concrete

8.3 Institutional Legacy and Its Impact

The historical practice of allocating factors of production and resources such as land, labor, and capital through the market, as well as the historical experience and institutional legacy, are worthy of the market-based land reforms currently underway.[21]

Risk Buffer Mechanism for Farmland Transfer

Currently, the phenomenon of illegal sale and purchase of agricultural land around the country is full of hidden dangers. Promoting farmland transfer while effectively resolving risks is a complex problem that needs to be solved in the current reforms of the agricultural land system. Farmers have both the desire to leave the land for development and the need to rely on the land for security and safety. Therefore, it is necessary to establish a risk buffer, security, and transition mechanism, so that farmers and collectives can eliminate their worries and resolve the contradiction between development and security in a virtuous cycle of promoting agricultural land transfer. The institutional legacy and experience of diverse land rights transactions in China's history can provide feasible inspirations and lessons.

First, diversified transaction types can promote agricultural land transfer, curb illegal land sales, and reduce systemic risks.

According to our research in Zhejiang, Jiangsu, Hunan, Hubei, Jiangxi, Fujian, and Yunnan Provinces, it is not uncommon for farmers to sell their land. Farmers sell their land illegally because there were too few types of transactions, and farmers have no choice. Therefore, it is urgent to innovate the form of land transfer and provide farmers with guidance rather than obstruction.

1. Diversified types of land rights transactions in traditional societies
   In traditional societies, farmers would not sell their land unless they had no choice but to do so because they had no other options.

element of Chinese characteristics. Therefore, it cannot simply be abolished on the basis of its non-market economy but can only be adapted and reformed on a historical basis.

[21] I thank Dr. Zhang Hudong for his cooperation in this section.

In traditional China, there were both multi-level land rights[22] and diverse types of transactions, including tenancy and rent-deposit for use rights, pawn and *dian* transaction for other rights, mortgage for security rights, and revocable and irrevocable sale of ownership rights. The essence of this system was that land rights were divided into different levels and periods of rights that could be traded independently in their corresponding markets. The system included use, possession, and ownership rights (or usufruct, security, other rights, and proprietary rights), as well as the transfer of current and future interests across time.

This land rights system effectively lowered the transaction threshold, facilitated land transfer and resource allocation, and met farmers' diverse needs and choices. The security of farmers' land property was effectively guaranteed in diversified transactions, thus reducing systemic risks.

2. *Carrying out land titling and allowing farmland as collateral can broaden the way farmland is traded*
   Although the existing legal types of agricultural land transfer were known by various names, such as subcontracting (*zhuanbao*), leasing (*chuzu*), borrowing (*jieyong*), and swapping (*huhuan*), they were all within the framework of the right-to-use transaction. Therefore, the fewer choices farmers have, the more difficult it is to meet their needs. As farmers' rights and interests were not easily protected, the risks were greater.[23] With the implementation of land titling, the form of property rights of contractual management rights and homesteads is becoming more and more perfect, and these transaction types will definitely break through the framework of user

[22] This includes clearing fields (*qingyetian*), subsoil rights, top-soil rights, and public fields (i.e., clan fields and school fields). For more details on the top-soil rights, please refer to Long Denggao's 2013 report, "Jiejian Mingiqng tianmianquan zhidu, chuangxin gudi chanquan gaige moshi" (Learning from the "Top-soil Right" System in the Ming and Qing dynasties and Innovating Land Property Reforms Model). The basic results of this report were published in authoritative journals such as *China's Social Science* (Social Sciences in China), *Jingji yanjiu* (Economic Research Journal), and others.

[23] For example, the Republican government ordered those transactions such as rent deposit (*yazu*) and subtenancy (*zhuandian*) to be prohibited. However, *yazu* was a system whereby the tenant farmer secured his rightsto lease the land and the landowner secured the future rent; *zhuandian* was a form of transaction whereby the tenant farmer was free from the bondage of the land. Ultimately, these prohibitions became a dead letter due to resistance from the people.

rights transactions. Since land contractual management rights in the form of property rights were now allowed to be used as mortgages, the historical transactions of pawn and *dian*, revocable sales, and rent deposits will also be justified and feasible. In terms of jurisprudential logic, since collective land in the form of self-interest can be separated into other property rights—that is, land contractual management rights—then collective land transactions can have multiple transaction types that were not limited to the right to use.

Allowing a variety of transaction types for farmers to choose from, which means that farmers can realize future gains from their land without selling it, will minimize the space for illegal selling of contractual management rights. In terms of the legal provisions, the form of contractual land management property rights should be clarified further, and the right to contractual land management should be more than a right to use.

3. *Diversified transactions can expand rural financial inclusion and reduce systemic risk*
   The more diversified land rights transactions are, the more room there is for farmers to choose, the better their needs can be met, and the risks reduced. Active and diversified land rights transactions were the fundamental system to guarantee farmers' property security and value-added income and an effective means to break the bottleneck of rural finance.

Rural finance is the weakest link in the overall financial system, and it is difficult for existing financial instruments to work in rural areas. In the future, the diversification of types of agricultural land transaction is expected to expand to rural finance.

Farmers can dispose of their land freely, smoothly, and conveniently and were able to realize future earnings through land transfers. With these funds, farmers were better able to move to the city to work or do business. In this way, the more channels there are for transferring future and current gains, the more likely it was that farmers' needs will be realized.

Diversification of types of transaction allows for a smoother flow of capital into farmland and agriculture. Currently, the state does not allow urban residents to buy farmland and residential land, but it can open up various types of investment in lands, such as leasing (including rent deposits), pawning, and revocable sales. The more types of land transactions, the more it will reduce systemic financial risks.

Second, the redemption mechanism possesses the function of risk buffer and security.

1. The unique "redemption" system in traditional societies
   Traditional land rights transactions, such as *dian*, revocable sales (*huomai*), and rent deposits (*yazu*), all have a redemption mechanism. Using land as security was an institutional legacy that was popular in China for over a thousand years.[24] The landowner cedes the right to the land for an agreed period to obtain a loan and pays interest on the capital with the right to operate the land with all the proceeds; the landowner (*dian* seller) retains ultimate ownership of the land and redeems the land by repaying the loan at maturity. During the term of the transaction, the *dian* buyer owns almost the entire interest in the land; not only can he lease the land, but he can also mortgage the land to obtain a loan or convert it to cash. A "revocable sale" was when the seller retains the right of first refusal. In a rent deposit, the tenant pays a variable amount in advance to gain control of the land over the ordinary tenant, while the owner receives a stable rent. At the end of the transaction, the landowner pays the deposit and redeems the right to the land. If the tenant owes rent, the landowner deducts the corresponding deposit.

   The redemption mechanism makes it possible for farmers to regain their original land, revive, and operate their businesses after receiving cash through land rights transactions to survive hard times. It was an effective transition mechanism with a risk-cushioning function and some degree of security. This institutional barrier that avoids the eventual transfer of property rights reduces the space for land annexation that may be caused by irrevocable sales (*juemai*)

[24] A conditional sale (*dian*) was different from a mortgage. The existing Western jurisprudence-based concept of *dian* was subject to reinterpretation and there are different views in the academic community. The rightsof *dian* has been valid in China for thousands of years and was still a legal transaction in Taiwan. Since the reforms and opening-up, China has restored many types of transactions from the historical period. For example, pawnshops, private banks, and the securities market have been borrowed, as well as European and American financial instruments such as venture funds and private equity funds. *Dian* trading should also be, and can be, restored.

or usurious mortgages and effectively maintains farmers' willingness to secure and restore their land rights.[25]

The redemption system enriched the diversified types of land rights transactions, making the transactions between land and capital more flexible and meeting the needs of farmers for capital financing and land transactions at different times. The problems associated with changes in land prices are dealt with by such methods as "supplementary payment" (*zhaojia*).[26]

2. *Redemption mechanisms are still viable for the current time.* Redemption mechanisms can give urban farmers a cushion or a mechanism for security. Some farmers, especially those who have encountered setbacks in the urbanization process, can return to farming through pawn, revocable sale, or rent-deposit transactions that allow them to redeem their farmland as needed. In this way, farmers will have fewer worries about land transfer and will not be afraid to trade or not to trade, thus further reducing the risk of farmers in the urbanization process.

   We can learn from the traditional land rights transaction mechanism to systematically design land transactions in conjunction with modern transaction and financial systems and set up flexible transaction and redemption procedures according to the actual situation and policy objectives: for example, rural cooperatives, government-authorized private financial institutions, various trading platforms, and qualified intermediary companies or enterprises; we can also learn from the land banks in some countries. These can all play an intermediary role in selling and redeeming agricultural land.[27]

[25] This was one of the institutional safeguards for the long-standing dominance of the individual peasant economy in traditional China and a hedging factor for land annexation. Recent scholarship suggests that historical land concentration and annexation have been grossly exaggerated, and that negative feedback mechanisms in the market (including the "equal inheritance" (*zhuzi junfen zhi*) and other mechanisms have actually mitigated the concentration of land rights).

[26] There are two types of "supplementary payment" (*zhaojia*), one was the buyer and seller agreeing to realize and compensate for future gains on their investment as the buyer increases investment in the land over a longer transaction period, and the other was the compensation for gains as both parties extend the time frame of the transaction.

[27] The compensation mechanisms such as "supplementary payment" (*zhaojia*), interest income, and investment income are designed to respond to and deal with the problems caused by changes in land prices.

Third, the exit and transition mechanisms are paired with the risk buffer mechanisms to meet farmers' needs.

While there are risks associated with the marketization of land rights transactions, hedging factors also create a negative feedback mechanism. If institutional design and innovation can be strengthened in this area, it can facilitate agricultural land reforms and ensure farmers' welfare. For example, agricultural land could be better utilized and developed by transferring it to skilled growers or family farms. Or, if a farmer, who "fails in migrating to the city," wants to return to his hometown, or wants to return to his land for other reasons, he can do so through a process such as redemption. The redemption would be compatible with "land rights" that guaranteed his rights to work in agriculture. A redemption period of 10–20 years can be considered essentially a transitional period given to farmers in the process of urbanizing.

The redemption system can not only broaden the exit mechanism for farmers in the land rights market and form a transition mechanism but also maximize the social security function of land and build a risk buffer and safety valve in the process of agricultural land transfer so that farmers can choose flexibly according to market prices and risk preferences to meet their different needs. In this way, land contractual management rights and homesteads can smoothly enter or exit the market, reducing the fettering of land to farmers or the phenomenon of agricultural land abandonment; at the same time, the level of agricultural land utilization was improved and better adapted to agricultural scale operation, which helps promote the development of family farms in the process of urbanization and meets the diversified choices of farmers.

With full consideration of relevant supporting mechanisms, the abovementioned ideas will have important practical significance. On the one hand, a new "channel" (*zhuashou*) can be found for promoting agricultural land transfer and family farm construction; on the other hand, a new path to buffer and prevent the risk of agricultural land transfer can be explored.[28]

[28] The core content of this section, as the result of a major project of the National Social Science Foundation, received a special letter of recognition from the National Office of Philosophy and Social Science to Tsinghua University in 2013.

Empowerment of the Peasantry: Learning from the Top-Soil Right System

Promoting the titling of rural land, strengthening the protection of real rights of various types of land contractual management rights, and effectively safeguarding farmers' property rights were the core contents of 2013 Central Document No. 1 and the institutional cornerstone of rural economic and farmers' development. However, under the framework of the existing land contract management rights as the right to use, land titling was restricted by the existing collective ownership system.

How should the relationship between farmers' contractual land management rights and collective ownership rights be dealt with, to minimize the implementation costs of institutional changes, and truly apply the real property rights of contractual land management rights? In this regard, China's rich institutional heritage, especially the top-soil right system, was expected to provide inspiration and lessons.

The purpose of land registration and titling was to allow farmers to obtain "property certificates"[29] like urban citizens so that the land becomes their property. If the contractual right of land management was limited to the right of use only, then this land tenure does not have the real right form of property attributes, and the right certificate does not have substantial meaning. If farmers only have the user rights, they will not be able to secure the value-added income from their land; if the agricultural land cannot be mortgaged then the future income of the land cannot be realized. Security rights are an indispensable attribute of land titling and an important condition for enhancing and activating land transfer. Under a mere right of use, not only are mortgages and other types of transactions illegal, but other types of land transfer such as tenancy or exchange are also significantly constrained.[30] With the trend of urbanization and population mobility accelerating and farmers moving to cities, the need for rural land transfer becomes more obvious.

[29] The huge increase in wealth of urban residents is mainly due to the issuance of real estate licenses. If only the use rights are available, even if every family has a house to live in, it is still difficult for urban residents to become property owners.

[30] The central government encourages land transfers. However, the institutional obstacles to the extremely limited willingness and performance of agricultural land transfer are: first, the lack of clear land property rights; and second, the extremely limited means of transaction and transfer.

Granting real property rights to contractual land management rights will greatly promote land transfer. It was also the most important way to increase farmers' property and wealth. When we strive to improve and protect farmers' rights and interests on the one hand but deny them access to their most valuable properties due to a variety of reasons, on the other, the impact of the policy on farmers will be severely reduced. In fact, the real attributes of contractual land management rights have already been realized to various degrees in rural practices throughout the country. Only when legal recognition becomes an essential link can future land disputes and problems of all kinds be reduced and various obstacles to smooth agricultural land transfers removed.

Why do we not advance the property rights reformation by granting real contractual land management rights to allow farmers to make use of their most important property? The obstacle lies in the existing land property rights system. How can that be remedied without changing the nature of collective land ownership? China's legacy of field bottom and top-soil right can be helpful.

First was the institutional heritage of top-soil right and inspiration.

It was a unique Chinese institutional legacy that a piece of land was divided into subsoil and top-soil rights. The owner of the subsoil rights owns the land, harvests the rent, and can use the field bottom right to make various transactions freely; while the owner of the top-soil rights had the right to manage the land independently, as well as the right to dispose of the income and transactions other than the rent. Moreover, the top-soil right owner can not only rent, transfer, and exchange the top-soil right, but also mortgage, guarantee, and sell them. By renting out the top-soil right, the top-soil right owner can obtain another share of the land rent (called *dinggeng* or *dianzu*); by mortgaging the top-soil right, he can obtain a loan. The rent from the subsoil rights remains the same during the transaction or after the transfer.

The subsoil and top-soil rights are interrelated and mutually binding. The top-soil and subsoil rights owners negotiate and enter into contracts to clarify their respective rights and interests. In the centuries of history from the Ming and Qing dynasties to the modern era, China developed unique rules and orders for land rights transactions that facilitated resource allocation and land output. Its success was evident: it supported 200–300 million more people without significantly increasing land area.

This system worked well for five or six hundred years and had its own logic and rationality.

First, from the perspective of real rights, landownership was exclusive, while real rights can be divided into self-interest and other-interest (or fixed-limit real rights).[31] Under this framework, the subsoil rights are self-interested rights, and the top-soil rights are other property rights. As a result, the top-soil rights have the usufruct and security rights of other property rights, and can freely engage in various transactions, including mortgages, and thus acquire property attributes. As rights in rem, subsoil rights also have the same properties of usufruct and security rights. The two are not incompatible.

Second, analyzed from the perspective of land rights stratification, since land rights can be divided, the investment and management of the same piece of land can be undertaken by different subjects. In this way, land harvest, value-added rights, and management risks can be distributed or apportioned among different land rights subjects. In other words, each level of land rights can form income rights of varying degrees, and each independently enters the market in the form of a transaction corresponding to it.

The fact that top-soil rights were freely tradable was a product of the increasing intensification of tenancy rights. Usually, the tenant farmer increases the output of the land through investments (that is, inputs of labor, manure, and grass, or improvements to farming and water facilities), thereby gaining direct control over the incremental amount of land and thus strengthening his right to operate the land independently. Tenant farmers may also purchase such rights. For example, a tenant farmer may contract with the landowner for the right to freely dispose of the land for a certain number of years through a rent charge and mortgage; that is, the landowner may sell independent other property rights.

The top-soil right system was prevalent from the Ming and Qing dynasties to the modern era, along with other land types such as rent-deposit, permanent tenancy, and *dian* rights. Overall, this type of land

[31] It is also known as limited real rights. For the sake of analysis, we can treat self-interest and ownership and other-interest and possession as roughly equal; usufruct and rights to use are also treated similarly, although usufruct is usually higher than rights to use.

rights had a high proportion in the economically developed eastern regions and around the cities.

The top-soil right system had many positive implications.

First, it expands farmers' freedom of choice and lowers the threshold for land transactions and transfers. Peasant families who lack labor, or operators who leave the land, can choose to hold the subsoil rights. In this scenario, farmers can still retain their landownership and enjoy land rent when they leave the land to engage in industry and commerce. A peasant family rich in labor can choose to hold the top-soil rights and cultivate the land independently. For example, capable farmers can expand their land operations at a low cost by transferring field rights, increasing total land output, and reaping the benefits of scale. Thus, almost all means of land rights trading were suitable for top-soil rights trading, such as tenancy, rent deposits, *dian* (conditional sales), mortgages, revocable sales, and irrevocable sales.

Second, it expands investment in land, especially by providing incentives for tenant farmers to invest in land. With the long-term property rights incentive, tenant farmers spared no effort to invest in water facilities and soil improvement to improve land output and gain value-added interests.

Third, the top-soil rights owner owns the right of land as property in rem, thus alleviating the uneven distribution of land rights. Although top-soil rights owners do not have ownership of the land, they have property rights by owning top-soil rights with real property attributes. This has been completely ignored in previous statistics. If factors such as top-soil rights are added, the Gini coefficient of land occupation in modern times will be greatly reduced.[32]

Second, the realization of real rights attributes of contractual land management rights under collective ownership: a feasible solution.

Contractual land management rights can take the form of real rights similar to top-soil rights. In other words, as the landowner, the village and township collective can retain the self-interest rights and then grant the

32 Zhao Gang, *Zhongguo chuantong nongcun de diquan fenpei* (Distribution of Land Rights in Traditional Rural China), Beijing: Xinxing Press, 2006; Ding Qian, "Minguo shiqi Zhongguo diquan fenpei de yanjiu" (A Study of the Distribution of Land Rights in China during the Republican Era), Master thesis, Tsinghua University, 2008.

contractual land management rights the attributes of real rights, adding the function of security interest to its original use right. In this way, management rights and collective ownership rights are complementary, interrelated, and binding and can jointly promote the rights and interests of farmers and collectives. As long as national laws and government policies regulate this and properly negotiate between farmers and village and township collectives, institutional innovation can be promoted in an orderly way with low implementation costs. For example, we can consider granting long-term and stable titles to agricultural land based on the 70-year property rights in cities. The well-performing combination of state-owned urban land and private property has not only activated the real estate market but also made it a pillar for China's economic growth in the last decade. Therefore, the realizing real rights attributes of agricultural land was also bound to become a new round of economic growth.

First, under the current collective ownership, agricultural land does not have the function of a security interest. Neither the collective nor the farmer can mortgage farmland. As a result, farmland has almost no property function, which hinders the capitalization of land, prevents the realization of future gains, and inhibits land appreciation and wealth creation. It was a severe loss to the farmers, the collective, and the state.

Suppose farmers can be issued land certificates that give them real property rights[33] over their land use rights. Then, farmers can mortgage their land, borrow against their land,[34] or transfer their land rights in rem in exchange for a certain amount of money to move to the city. It will not only revitalize 1.8 billion *mu* of land in rural areas and create tens of trillions of *yuan* of capital credit flowing to the "three rural" (*sannong*) areas and cities but also enable most farmers to exchange for citizenship through the market and buy more urban products and services.[35] For

[33] The management rights are supposed to have the attributes of real rights. Land contract management rights are broader in connotation and extension than use rights.

[34] When a farmer mortgages his land, if he cannot repay it, he loses only his other property rights and does not affect his self-property rights (that is, collective ownership). In traditional transactions such as *dian* transactions and revocable sales, farmers can also redeem the land in the future.

[35] Liu Hengzhong has made a specific estimate of this. See Liu Hengzhong, *Lun Zhongguo da fazhan: bayi nongmin bian shimin* (On China's Great Development: 800 million Peasants Become Citizens), Beijing: Zhongguo jingji Press, 2008.

example, 260 million rural migrant workers have now moved to cities. If they could trade their contractual rural land management rights for 1–20 years and realize future earnings through liquidation, their ability to purchase or rent housing in the cities would be enhanced,[36] and their ability to survive in the cities would be accordingly improved, thus reducing social unrest in the urbanization process.

Land titling can attract socialized capital to invest in land, thus protecting farmers' rights and interests, especially value-added rights and interests and transaction realization proceeds. At the same time, farmers with land property rights will gradually increase their awareness of their rights and interests and have a stronger voice to resist the powerful. It will effectively reduce rent-seeking and corporate corruption by grassroots officials and promote a more harmonious rural society.

Some people may worry that farmers will sell their land. In fact, with land certificates, many farmers will value their land as much as they value and care for their ancestral homes and graves. They will carefully consider before selling or transferring their landownership at will.

Third, along with the land titling, there was bound to be a richness and diversity of means of trading land rights. Land transactions such as subleases, transfers, and shares will be developed and perfected, and mortgages and sales will be legal. As a result, farmers will have more diverse choices and opportunities to realize and expand their benefits and welfare. If there was only one transaction option, the benefits will likely be minimized; "no other way" (*biewu tatu*) was often a painful choice. In other words, real property rights of land and its transfer will create the necessary conditions for the intensive operation and scale economy of agriculture, which was the basis of family farms and agricultural modernization.

The reform in realizing real rights attributes of contractual management rights was less costly to implement. In contrast, although private property rights to agricultural land are in the interest of farmers, there was more resistance under the current system, and the specific implementation costs and risks may also be higher. To promote the reform of contracted land management rights, pilot reforms can be allowed and encouraged in some regions, especially in areas that retain the heritage of

[36] According to Lai Ming, a member of the National Committee of the Chinese People's Political Consultative Conference, due to the lack of market-based exit mechanisms for contracted land, homesteads, and houses, farmers in the cities are unable to obtain the capital to settle in the cities through the proceeds of land transfer.

these land systems.[37] In this way, the reforms can be carried out steadily under the existing land system without making significant changes, which was conducive to promoting social stability and harmony in rural areas.

In conclusion, the realization of real rights attributes of contractual land management rights had both institutional heritage and historical foundations, and theoretical logic and rationale; there was a strong practical need and a feasible solution. As long as misunderstandings can be prevented, institutional innovation with low implementation costs can be promoted; there can be fundamental changes for farmers and the rural economy in the urbanization process, forming a strong domestic demand and a new growth point for economic development after the real estate industry.

[37] At present, actual transactions in rural areas have long exceeded the use rights. On the one hand, there is a need for legal recognition of this private demand; on the other hand, if not recognized, these "illegal transactions" will result in endless problems.

CHAPTER 9

Conclusion and Interpretation Framework

Based on the achievements of the previous research and by exploring the original materials, such as the deeds in the Tsinghua University Library Collection, we examine the historical transformation and characteristics of China's land tenure system in the past millennium, study its role in the traditional Chinese economy and its impact on economic changes in modern China, and seek academic originality and realistic theories revolving around China's land tenure system. As a result of the completion of major projects of the National Social Science Fund, this book follows my previous study, *Diquan shichang yu ziyuan peizhi* (Land Rights Market and Resource Allocation). It provides an in-depth study of the topic and strengthens the systematic discussion to form an interpretative framework.

The book explores the land property types and land transaction system under the historical transmutation of China's land system, discusses the role and influence of the land market, and examines the impact on the vitality of individual family farms (including tenant farms) at the micro-level and on traditional economic efficiency and social mobility at the macro-level, including the impact on China's economic development and its characteristics. Finally, it analyzes the exploration of modern land reforms, especially through historical references and insights from the

D. Long and X. Chi, *The Institutions of Land Property Rights in China*, Palgrave Studies in Economic History,
https://doi.org/10.1007/978-981-97-5112-9_9

current agricultural land reforms. The following summary can be said to be an extended introduction to the book.

9.1 Types of Land Property Rights

Private property rights in land, corporate property rights, and state-owned property rights coexist in traditional China, and this book focuses on the form of private property rights in land and, for the first time, on corporate property rights. Both private land and corporate land are titled and traded under deeds. The simple awareness and system of property rights are rooted in the civil customs and rules of the village and are recognized and protected by state laws.

Legal property rights are a derivative extension of private property rights, reflecting the degree of development of the private property rights system. If private landownership rights are the cornerstone of peasants' independent management, legal property rights are the basis for the independent development of civil organizations, such as clans, religious temples, colleges, private schools, nonprofit organizations, charitable organizations, and various associations (*hui*) and societies (*she*) in the industrial, commercial, financial, cultural, sports, and entertainment industries, that can all form a property unit, a transaction unit, and a taxing unit, with features such as integrity, indivisibility, and exclusivity, developing an efficient management model based on independence. Through the governance model centered on the council (*lishihui*), nonprofit public interest corporations manage their own properties and engage in public services. The comprehensive and multi-level civil self-organization play a unique and vital role in rural society.

Property rights are obtained through investment in capital (except for inheritance and other means); non-landowners can also control the appreciation of land proceeds through investment and thus acquire the corresponding rights of land disposition, sharing land rights with the owners. The typical form was the top-soil right of land (*tianmianquan*), which coexists with the subsoil right of land (*tiandiquan*) as a property right and was qualitatively different from ordinary tenancy rights. Similarly, rights to conditional sale (*dianquan*) and rights of the top-soil have become distinctive types of landownership.

Land property rights have multiple levels of rights and functions that are interrelated and mutually reinforcing. First and foremost are rights to cultivate (*gengzuoquan*), which are to realize the dynamic combination of land and labor in circulations and transactions. The tenancy system was one of the systems of agricultural land tenancy discounted by future labor income or land gains. The second was land appreciation rights and interests (*tudi zengyi quanyi*). Future earnings are secured and incentivized by property and can be realized through transactions, thus facilitating people's investment in land. Finally, land-mediated types of diversification have a financial function of intertemporal adjustment (*kuaqi tiaoji*), which meets the peasants' needs for financing.

9.2 Land Transaction System and Its Evolution

China's land rights transaction system took shape with a land market over thousands of years, from the Warring States, Qin, and Han to the Ming and Qing dynasties. The system of *taijie* (loans through the land as collateral), *zudian* (tenancy), *yazu* (rent deposits), *dian* (conditional sales), *diya* (mortgages), *huomai* (unfinalized or revocable sales), and *juemai* (finalized or irrevocable sales) was a hierarchical system with an internal logic. They are interconnected but also confusing. For example, people might miss the slight distinctions between the right of *di* (using some portion of land rights as repayment of debt), *huomai* (unfinalized or revocable sales), and *dian* (conditional sales), or between the right of *yazu* (rent deposits), *yongdian* (permanent tenancy), and *dian* (conditional sales), and so on. This book provides clear distinction and analysis of them. Moreover, the redemption mechanism of China's land rights transaction system, which includes the right of *dian*, *huomai*, and *yazu*, adequately safeguards the willingness of peasants to secure and restore their land rights and compresses the space for the complete transfer of land rights caused by *juemai* (finalized sales) and *diya* (mortgages) of a usurious nature. A multi-level land rights transaction system thus enables peasants to make choices according to market prices and risk preferences to meet their own needs. It helps to achieve intertemporal adjustment between current and long-term gains, thereby promoting the combination of land transfer and production factors to improve economic efficiency.

This book particularly focuses on *dianquan* (rights to the conditional sale), a practice with Chinese characteristics. *Dian* was a transaction between the land tenure and all proceeds thereof and the interest on land during an agreed period, rather than the superficial understanding that "rent offsets interest." The right to a conditional sale was not a right to use or an ownership right. It was a property right that was limited in the form of real right and clearly distinct from a mortgage. Chapters 4 and 5 clarify the misconceptions about rights to the conditional sale in the fields of Legal History and Economic History and reveal the nature and role of *dian* rights. According to their own preferences and needs, the *dian* receiver (*chengdianren*) can choose the operating income, investment income, or realization of future income from the land, which highlights the shared land rights structure built by the three parties—the landowner, the *dian* receiver, and the tenant peasant—through market transactions.

Regarding the historical evolution of the land rights system, since the Warring States Period and the Qin and Han dynasties, China increased land rights transactions with in the variety of land rights. The Song Dynasty witnessed the emergence of *yondianquan* (permanent tenancy rights) and *dian* rights, and the Ming and Qing dynasties saw the emergence of *tianmianquan* (rights of the top-soil), *yazu* (loan through land as guarantee), and *huomai* (unfinalized sales). Among them, the evolution and differences of *dian* rights from the Song Dynasty to the Qing Dynasty highlight how land rights transaction rules evolved from spontaneous generation to gradual improvement and standardization.

The Song Dynasty's provision that "the *dian* has to be separated from the original property" indicates the very nature of the *dian* (conditional sales). However, its derived rights and its diverse manifestations give rise to ambiguity. For example, the practice of the *dian* receiver renting land to the owner was not recognized in the Song Dynasty, while in the Qing Dynasty, this form was widely popular. The time difference of *dian* rights was also reflected in the government provisions. For instance, in the Song Dynasty, both parties to a transaction of *dian* needed to visit the local government to make a contract deed, divide the land tax, and pay transaction tax. In contrast, in the middle and late Qing Dynasty, transaction tax was exempted, land tax division was no longer required, and a single form of contract was adopted, making the *dian* transfers and the relevant subsequent transactions more convenient. All these differences and characteristics reveal that in the course of the development of *dian* rights, the transaction rules and social understanding also underwent a tortuous transformation. Long-term comparisons help us to grasp the origin and diversity of *dian* rights, and to form a more comprehensive understanding of traditional Chinese land property and transaction patterns.

In modern times, the system and order of China's land rights were undermined by power and violence, and this deterioration led to the socioeconomic upheaval and decline in the late Qing Dynasty and the early Republican Era. The decline of the modern economy has often been blamed on the private property system itself, and there have even been calls to eradicate it to revive the rural economy.

9.3 Land Rights and Economic Efficiency

The development of land rights patterns and the diversification of their transactional types have led to an active land circulation, facilitating a combination of production factors and resource allocation. Through the land rights market, peasants can adjust their current income and future returns and freely choose and diversify their arrangements between various elements and their returns to meet their financing needs. As a result, the various production factors are in a dynamic combination, with capital flowing from the social strata to the land. Land was allocated to the productive labor force through various transactions, promoting agricultural economic efficiency.

The redemption mechanism also contributes to economic efficiency. Practices such as *yazu* (loan through land as guarantee), *huomai* (unfinalized sale), and *dian* (pawnage) can all be redeemed, which scholars believe affects efficiency, and this book responds to related queries. In the redemption of *dian* rights, at least five ways for both parties to negotiate the contract can solve many problems such as investment return or loss of interest. The redemption mechanism not only ensures the rights and investment incentives of the *dian* receiver but also gives the *dian* owner flexibility to respond to different demand levels. Such a mechanism has clear property rights, which allow investment in agricultural production to be maintained effectively and resource allocation to be optimized.

Regarding the economic efficiency of the land tenancy system, the tenancy and land rights transactions enabled effective cooperation between factor owners, which not only increased the mobility and efficiency of the use of factors of production but also brought about changes in class and management, reflecting the social mobility of the time.

Previous studies have generally considered tenant peasants to provide the landowners' labor, similar to hired labor, and remunerated on a par with hired labor. This stereotype leads to mistaken economic interpretation and historical understanding. In fact, tenant peasants combine various factors and resources of production of their own, their landlords', markets', families', and society's through various means of personification and marketization to create wealth through independent farm management and therefore dominate surplus claims. Moreover, they take risks and reap the benefits of the risks, operate for the market and reap profits, and reap future benefits through investment in the land. Therefore, tenant peasants are paid for their talents in a way that was fundamentally different from the wages for their labor. In the case of tenant farming, when the best tenant was selected for good land, land and other factors of production are allocated to the more efficient tenant peasants and the wealthier farmers in the transaction. Consequently, the transfer of factors of production and the allocation of resources under land rights transactions and tenancy systems have contributed to economic efficiency and increased land output.

The prevailing argument that the owner-peasant farming system was fair and efficient and that the tenant peasants are exploited by landlords and are less efficient under the tenancy system has been challenged in recent years by historical facts and theories. In a free market context, the structure of land tenure depends on transaction costs and the level of the total surplus of the system. By analyzing the total institutional surplus of owner-peasants, tenants, and hired labor, based on the theory of optimal ownership structure, this book finds that the optimal scale of land operation, technical level, land endowment, market conditions, and other factors affect the choice of land rights structure, and farming land as an owner-peasant was not necessarily the optimal choice. This book uses statistical methods to examine the effects of the degree of marketization of agricultural products, transportation costs, the scale of land operation, and the degree of dispersion of land rights on the tenancy rate. After comparing the production scale and profits of modern owner-peasants and tenants, it is found that the tenancy economy exhibits advantages in many aspects. The reason for this was that the tenancy system separates the asset function of land from the factor function of production, separates the use of land from the ownership of land, and thus achieves the selection of the best cultivators.

9.4 Role of the Land Rights

Compared to Western European societies, China's traditional economy had two fundamental features, namely land rights transactions and independent operations by individual peasant households, which are related and form the unique development path of China's traditional agricultural economy.

Multi-level land property rights and diversified types of transactions enable landless peasants or those with few plots of land to establish family farms and operate independently through various types of land transfer. Previous claims of "optimality of owner-peasant farming" and average land rights failed to take into account the market's dynamic nature and ignored peasants' autonomy to choose between risk preferences and prices at different levels in diversified land rights transactions. Peasants can rent land, obtain land user rights, and gained greater control over land through *yazu*. Moreover, they can also obtain "other rights in rem" (*tawuquan*), such as rights to the conditional sale (*dianquan*) and top-soil rights. Rights to dispose of land, rights to proceeds, and rights to transactions can be freely exercised without conflict with ownership. It can be seen that the diversification and differentiation of transactions can meet the needs of different orientations, reduce transaction costs and systemic risks, and stimulate and realize land circulation and resource allocation.

The previous view was that land transactions were prone to trigger land annexations. However, this book finds that the traditional view exaggerates the concentration of land rights while ignoring the negative feedback mechanisms of the land rights market, including at least five aspects, such as the equal inheritance system (equal distribution of family property among the sons). Moreover, the redemption mechanism can actually protect vulnerable groups' rights and interests, delay the transfer of land rights, provide the possibility for peasants to overcome difficulties, restore and rebuild their farms to operate independently, and form a hedging factor for the concentration of land rights. These institutional arrangements have allowed peasants' independent farming to gain ongoing competitiveness and become a fundamental feature of China's traditional economy.

Individual family farms had a significant impact on Chinese society. Owner-peasants, semi-owner-peasants, and tenant peasants can establish their own farms through transactions such as tenancy, *yazu* (rent deposits), *diandang* (conditional sales and pawning), and top-soil rights and can obtain operating income, investment income, and venture returns, with the attributes or potential of agricultural entrepreneurs. This makes the peasant middle class in traditional Chinese society both landowners who receive property-based income and farm owners (peasant entrepreneurs) who receive business-based income, and purely hired peasants—the proletariat only account for 2–3% of the agricultural population. The multi-layered nature of landownership and the diversity of land transactions have contributed to long-term stability in Chinese society, demonstrating the resilience of family operations.

The separability, low threshold, easy replication, easy recovery, and other characteristics of individual peasant households that rely on the land rights market, as well as the corresponding system of equal inheritance, have led to the continuous replication and strengthening of family farms, to some extent inhibiting the emergence of large, modernized farms or farms that hire laborers, resulting in the differences between the development paths of China and Western Europe. The medieval manorial system in Western Europe and its first-born inheritance system were in stark contrast. In Europe, younger sons or new populations cannot be absorbed by the estate nor can it be challenging to establish a self-employed family to operate independently. They often survive outside the old system, for example, by becoming proletarians or working in industry and commerce in the cities, whose gradual growth, in turn, pushes the old system to change.

Independent farms with autonomous property or the market's help allow peasant households to be autonomous and self-reliant. Peasants are free to choose, including free association and local self-governance. These have contributed to the social mobility and economic vitality of traditional China.

9.5 Centennial Quest and Its Reflection

There were two explorations of equalizing land rights in the mid-to-late twentieth century, one around 1950 and the other in 1981. However, unexpectedly, the initial equilibrium state was difficult to sustain because of population size and migration, household composition, farming capacity, and others. As a result, not only was the top-soil equity being destroyed, but efficiency losses are becoming severe. Under the average ownership, as peasants could trade land freely, new rich peasants and tenants soon reemerged. Under the average land user right, the regular distribution of land resulted in fragmentation and discouraged investment in the land, such as the construction of water conservancy facilities, and restricted land circulation. The combination of factors of production, such as land and labor, was inefficient under government resource allocation and it was difficult to ensure equity. After rounds of land reforms, trial and error, and exploration, China finally embarked on the path of market allocation of production factors and resources.

There is a view that in the twentieth century, average land rights became the dominant trend because of the concentration of land and peasant bankruptcies caused by private ownership of land. Therefore, private property has been a source of economic backwardness in recent times. However, several important factors are overlooked here, one of which was the fact that the disorder in the modern land rights system and market order was due precisely to the destruction of that system and order by power and violence and not to the system itself. Second, ideology overemphasizes phenomena such as exploitation caused by tenancy while ignoring the rationality of the market allocation of land. Third, the concentration of land-holding has been seriously exaggerated, and the cutting-edge achievements of academia have not been transmitted to society or textbooks. Fourth, it ignores the existence of a negative feedback mechanism in land concentration.

This negative feedback mechanism was reflected in the following aspects: (1) diversified transaction types, including the redemption mechanism that postpones the final transfer of land tenure; (2) the emperor's and the central government's restrictions on bureaucratic power to intervene in the market; (3) occupation of private land by legal persons' property rights, such as clan land, temple land, school land, and society property (*huichan*); (4) the system of equal distribution of land among all sons; (5) the competitiveness and vitality of individual peasant households' operations are fundamental. In addition, the frequent wars and natural and man-made disasters of recent times have also led to the fragmentation of land rights in some areas.

The reason why the exaggeration of land concentration and average landownership became the dominant trend in modern times was the decline of the Chinese economy in the modern era. The root cause of China's economic backwardness in the late nineteenth century lies not in the system itself but in the following reasons: first, successive years of war and turmoil have caused China's economy to grow negatively for a long time; second, the fractures and pain that inevitably accompany the transformation of the traditional economy into a modern one; and third, international rules have not yet been established and the opening-up of China in the late Qing Dynasty failed by imperial violence. Thus, the disorder in the land rights system and the market order was due to the destruction of this system and order by power and violence. The land system that once propelled China's economy ahead of the rest of the world was not the root cause of China's modern economic backwardness. However, its stability and vitality have also somewhat inhibited China's shift from a traditional economy to a more modern one.

In the end, the book comes up with the following lessons and takeaways:

Equalization of Landownership and Fertility Incentives

Under the privatization of land, the size of the family property became a natural constraint on the fertility of peasant households in a shortage economy, so the average family size in China declined to less than five people. The equal distribution of land according to headcount stimulates fertility rates. During the People's Commune Period, rations were distributed according to headcount and work point, and the greater the number of children, the greater the share of the distribution, which facilitated intertemporal adjustment within the household. Thus, choosing to have more children was conducive to family survival and reduced risk. The equal distribution of land use rights under the Household Contractual Responsibility System, where new populations are given a share of land, also stimulates the reproductive behavior of peasant households. Fertility rates declined after the land was no longer divided equally. It was not until recent years that harsh family planning policies were liberalized and even shifted to encouraging births.

Promoting the Household Contract Responsibility System by Drawing on the Top-Soil Right System

There are two kinds of property rights on the same piece of land: the top-soil and subsoil rights; the village collective owns the subsoil right, while the individual peasant household had the top-soil right, both of which have the nature of property rights. Peasants with top-soil rights can carry out various transactions, including mortgages, pawns, and guarantees, not to mention renting out to tenants as well as buying and selling. The historical operation of top-soil rights was stable and provided a blueprint for the current peasant household contract management rights to become property rights. The owner of the top-soil had rights in the property, such as use, proceeds, mortgage, and transfer, and was in exclusive possession, free from interference by the owner of the rights to the subsoil. The top-soil right and the subsoil right are interrelated and mutually binding, and the two parties enter into a contract through negotiation to specify their respective interests. In sum, the two kinds of rights trade and circulate relatively independently, forming their own corresponding market prices.

Peasants should have full property rights, or at least real rights to their land. General Secretary Xi Jinping once pointed out: "Conditions should be created to give farmers more property rights." Most peasants' proprietary rights, of course, are still land.

Redemption Mechanisms and Buffer Mechanisms

Currently, local governments in many parts of China are turning a blind eye to their regularities in selling agricultural land, which has led to numerous problems. Promoting the transfer of agricultural land while effectively resolving the risks was an intricate problem that needs to be solved in the current reforms of the agricultural land system. Peasants have both a desire to leave their land for other development and a need to rely on it for security and safety. Therefore, a risk buffer, safeguard, and transition mechanism must be put in place to allow peasants and peasant collectives to resolve the contradictions between development and security in a virtuous circle that promotes the transfer of agricultural land.

Diversified types of transactions include a redemption system, which will not only expand a peasant's trading options but also form an exit and transition mechanism, maximizing the use of the social security function of land and creating a risk buffer mechanism and safety valve in the process of agricultural land circulation so that peasants can make flexible choices according to market prices and risk preferences to meet their different needs. Second, the redemption system allows for smooth and convenient access to or exit from the market for contracted land management rights and residential land, reduces land constraints on peasants or agricultural land abandonment, and increases agricultural land use. Third, the system will also be adapted to farm-scale operations, advancing the diversification of peasants' choices in popularizing family farms and urbanization.

Appendix 1: Beggar Wu Xun's Methods of Managing Money and Promoting Education

Wu Xun was a highly acclaimed historical figure with significant achievements and special status.[1] He was included in official history by establishing free schools through financial management instead of begging. Wu Xun entered the financial market by selling his ancestral property. He efficiently controlled risks in commercial, agent, and small and macro lending and successfully gained financial returns. He invested in land and raised funds with the legal entity "Loyalty, Learning, and Righteousness" (Yi Xue Zheng), whose income from the land supported the long-term development of free school operations. Wu Xun shifted between capital and land income and organically combined long-term and short-term gains, all of which were made possible by making full use of private financial instruments, a developed land rights market, and a mature corporate property rights system to integrate market and social resources under the goal of establishing a free school.

Wu Xun (1838–1896), a beggar in the northwest region of Shandong Province, established three free schools using all his financial resources. He was therefore included in the "Biography of Filial Piety" (*xiaoyizhuan*) volume of the "Draft History of Qing" (*Qingshi gao*) as "a

[1] The paper was written with Doctor Wang Miao and was originally published in the third issue of *Researches in Chinese Economic History* in 2018.

D. Long and X. Chi, *The Institutions of Land Property Rights in China*, Palgrave Studies in Economic History,
https://doi.org/10.1007/978-981-97-5112-9

righteous beggar in a thousand years" (*qiangu qigai*).[2] As a legendary figure, who came from a lowly background and a humble profession but did extraordinary deeds in establishing free schools, Wu Xun was honored by the Qing government, celebrated by the Republican government, and praised by all the educators of modern times.[3] In 1950, a biographical film, "The Life of Wu Xun" (*Wu Xun Zhuan*), was released; in 1951, the film wrongly criticized,[4] but in 1986, China's State Council decided to restore Wu Xun's honor.

[2] Zhao Erxun et al., "Xiaoyi san Wu Xun zhuan" (Filial Piety and Righteousness Three: Biography of Wu Xun), *Qingshi gao* (Draft History of Qing), vol. 499, Beijing: Zhonghua Books, 1977.

[3] After Wu Xun's death, the Guoshiguan (Academia Historica) of the Qing dynasty produced a biography of him and built a shrine and a monument for him. See *Qingshi gao* (Draft History of Qing), vol. 499. The original materials about Wu Xun, as well as the award application form, detailed documents, letters, the memorials, epitaphs, monuments, portraits, chronicles, songs of promotion of education, and others, are collected in the book *Wu Xun ziliao daquan* (Wu Xun's Complete Collection) (Zhang Ming ed., Wu Xun ziliao daquan (Wu Xun's Complete Collection), Jinan: Shandong University Press, 1991, hereinafter referred to as "Daquan"). This book is informative and has more than 800,000 words. Xing Peihua and Zhang Qingnian has provided brief introduction to Wu Xun's historical documents. See Xing Peihua, Zhang Qingnian, "Wu Xun Dang'an wenxian shiliao shulue" (A Brief Description of Wu Xun's Archival Documents and Historical Materials), *Dang'anxue yanjiu* (Archives Science Study), no. 3 (1993): 46–48. Previous studies on Wu Xun have mainly focused on the historical evaluation of Wu Xun himself, including two historical periods, the late Qing and Republican Periods and the 1950s. The introduction and evaluation of Wu Xun in the late Qing and Republican Periods are recorded in the collection of *Daquan*; evaluation of Wu Xun in the 1950s was carried out in the political movement, and the important material of *Wu Xun lishi diaocha ji* (Wu Xun History Survey Record) was published later. In July 1951, in order to clarify thoughts on the issue of Wu Xun, the *People's Daily* and the Ministry of Culture initiated a Wu Xun History Survey Mission, which carried out research work for 20 days in Tanyi, Linqing, and Guantao counties. After visiting local people from all walks of life and collecting written materials about Wu Xun in the late Qing and Republican Periods, the final publication was *Wu Xun lishi diaocha ji* (Wu Xun History Survey Record) (People's Press, 1951, hereinafter referred to "Survey Record"). This survey also found some transcripts of the deeds of land purchased by Wu Xun. In 1975, the People's Publishing House published a photocopy of *Wu Xun dimu zhang* (Wu Xun's Account Book of Land) (hereinafter referred to as "Account Book of Land").

[4] On May 20, 1951, *People's Daily* published an editorial entitled "The Discussion on the Film Wu Xun Zhuan (The Life of Wu Xun) Should Be Taken Seriously," which was revised and approved by Mao Zedong himself. The article pointed out that "the discussion on the film Wu Xun Zhuan and other writings and essays on Wu Xun should be launched, to thoroughly clarify the confusing ideas on this issue." Thus, the nationwide criticism of Wu Xun began.

Previous studies of how Wu Xun, a beggar, accumulated sufficient financial resources to build a school have mainly emphasized his reliance on begging and hard work. However, building a school was not easy even for local governments and wealthy merchants in the late Qing Dynasty, and constructing a school building, hiring teachers, and operating it for a long time were all costly and complicated. Moreover, the fact that it was a free school meant there were no tuition fees to support the school's operation and continued development. Although Wu Xun was a beggar, the money he used to start the school was not accumulated by begging. He was actually a skilled financial manager, which has not been recognized.[5] Ignoring this will create misunderstanding and may result in misinterpretation of traditional society.[6]

This section does not focus on his status as a beggar and the establishment of the school but on the means by which he gathered wealth and how he managed money and business. Wu Xun's assets for the school were spread over three counties, and among them were land, houses, stores, and interest-bearing capital, including 230 *mu* of land for the Liulin school in Tangyi County; one house for the school, with 20 rooms; 7 *mu* of land and three stores for the school in Yushi Lane, Linqing Prefecture; 1300 *qianwen* of interest-bearing capital for the stores; and 300 *qianwen* of capital for the Yang Erzhuang school in Guantao County.[7] The total amount of assets was about 10,625.8 *guan*.[8]

[5] *Survey Record* (Diaocha ji) criticizes Wu Xun for "high-interest loans, exploitation of land rent, house rent, and forced donations." Yang Yinqiu's article "Xingqi xingxue yishi Wu Xun xiansheng shilue" (A Brief History of Wu Xun, the Righteous Man who Begged to Support Education) has characterized Wu Xun's deeds as "fundraising" (*choukuan*), "generating interest" (*shengxi*), and "renewing principal" (*xuben*). See *Daquan*, 106–107. Guo Yukuan has provided an evaluation of Wu Xun's investment talent and righteous deeds in promoting education. Guo Yukuan, "Zuowei touzijia de Wu Xun" (Wu Xun as an investor), *Tongzhou gongjin* (A Shared Journal Forward), no. 5 (2013): 79–81.

[6] Pure begging could not accumulate the huge amount needed for running free schools. When begging for the purpose of promoting education, it is transformed into fundraising, the scale and nature of which are very different from ordinary begging.

[7] "Linqing zhou zhizhou Zhuang Honglie, Tangyi zhixian Wang Fuzeng, Guantao xian zhixian Xiang Zhihui qingzou zili an bing" (The Governor of Linqing Prefecture, Zhuang Honglie, the Magistrate of Tangyi County, Wang Fuzeng, and the Magistrate of Guantao County Reporting and Requesting the Case to be Filed), *Daquan*, 21.

[8] This figure was an account of Wu Xun's personal investment when he ran the school. The total capital cost of the school should include the 1578 *guan* raised during the construction of *Liulin Yixue* (Free School of Liulin), making a total of 12,203.8 *guan*.

Capitalizing on Land and Lending It to Generate Interest

Selling ancestral property was always considered a disgraceful act, if not desperate. Therefore, it was rare at the time to turn land into capital. It took courage and boldness to sell land and turn it into much-needed commercial capital, which was only occasionally seen among the merchant class.[9] However, in 1862, Wu Xun sold four *mu* of his ancestral land for 120 *qianwen*; together with the money he had accumulated over the years, the total amount was more than 210 *qianwen*. Wu Xun took the 210 *qianwen* as the principal and asked someone to lend it to him to earn interest.[10] With 210 *guan* of principal and 3% interest, the total interest for one year was 210*3% *12 = 75.6 *guan* of money, which was a considerable amount of interest. The risk of transforming land into interest-bearing capital was very high, so the case of Wu Xun was unusual. However, Wu Xun had the courage to take the risk and set up the free school. By the winter of 1886, "according to the money generated from interest, in addition to the cost of buying 230 *mu* of land, there was still a balance of 2800 *guan* of capital and profit."[11] Within 24 years, Wu Xun had expanded his original capital of 210 *guan* to more than 7000 *guan*.[12]

[9] Zhang Haipeng, Wang Tingyuan eds., "Wang Yanshou maitian chiqi" (The Red Contract of Land Sales of Wang Yanshou), "Huishang ziben de laiyuan he jilei" (The Source and Accumulation of Capital of Huizhou Merchants), *Mingqing huishang ziliao xuanbian* (Selected Materials of Huizhou Merchants in Ming and Qing Dynasties), Hefei: Huangshan shushe, 1985, 58.

[10] The 90 *qianwen* or so here may include the money obtained from the sale of Wu Xun's belongings, because at that time Wu Xun had been begging for only a few years. About the lender, "Jubing Tangyi xianshu qingjiang biaowen" (Reporting to the County Office of Tangyi and Requesting for the Award) wrote Lou Junling and Lou Songling, and "Ji Wu Xun xingxue shimo" (Record of Wu Xun's Promotion of Education) recorded Yang Shufang as the lender on behalf of Wu Xun, see *Daquan*, 3, 151. *Wu Xun xiansheng xingqi xingxue ge* (A Song for Mr. Wu Xun's Begging and Promoting Education) recorded that "Save the capital, generate interest, and seek Scholar Lou from Tangyi County for help." See *Daquan*, 82.

[11] "Jubing Tangyi xianshu qingjiang biaowen" (Reporting to the County Office of Tangyi and Requesting for the Award); "Tangyi zhixian Guo Chunxu zaosong yixue fangwu dimu xiangwen" (The County Magistrate of Tangyi, Guo Chunxu, sending a Detailed Document on the Land and House for the Free School), *Daquan*, 3, 5.

[12] The total cost of land purchase of around 230 *mu* was 4263 *guan*. See "Shandong xunfu Zhangyao zouqing jianfang pian" (Shandong Governor Zhang Yao Requesting the Construction of a Workshop), *Daquan*, 10.

Therefore, capital lending was an important way for him to accumulate wealth.

Due to the scarcity of financial instruments and insufficient supply of capital, the interest rate for lending in the traditional era was rather high. Wu Xun had both large commercial lending and microlending, "he got Lou Junling and Yang Shufang and others to operate large loans for him, and he ran small ones himself."[13] He focused on the liquidity of the funds and did not let them settle down, "he refused even to have five hundred *yuan* with him, believing that the interest rate would rise every other day." Wu Xun had his vision and brilliant means of granting loans, and his business practice of lending to generate interest was reflected in the following five aspects.

First was the emphasis on commercial lending. Previous studies on commercial loans in history are relatively scarce, but commercial loans may be the main way of lending in traditional China. Wu Xun "often lent money to rich store owners at a 3% interest rate and settled accounts monthly,"[14] and "whether he lent money in Tangyi, in Guantao, or Linqing, the interest rate was the highest standard at the time, with a monthly interest rate of 3%," and "one *diao* of coins cost thirty *zhiqian* of interest per month." Wu Xun's commercial lending was mainly to the local store owners. Linqing in Shandong, where he was located, was the commercial center of north China during the Ming and Qing dynasties when the canal flourished.[15] Although in the late Qing Dynasty, with the blockage of the canal, the docking and diversion of the Yellow River, canal transportation was declining, and Linqing was no longer in its prime. However, the commercial development of Linqing continued, and it was a place for the exchange of goods between the north and the south; the

[13] *Survey Record* (Diaocha ji), 25.

[14] In the nineteenth century, the private interest rate was usually 20%, as a rural example. See Peng Kaixiang, Chen Zhiwu, Yuan Weipeng, "Jindai Zhongguo nongcun jiedai shichang de jizhi—jiyu minjian wenshu de yanjiu" (The Mechanism of Rural Lending Market in Modern China: A Study Based on Private Instruments), *Jingji yanjiu* (Economic Research Journal), no. 5 (2008): 147–159.

[15] Xu Tan, "Mingqing shiqi de qinqing shangye" (Linqing Commerce in the Ming and Qing Dynasties), *Zhongguo shehui jingjishi* (Researches in Chinese Economic History), no. 2 (1986): 135–157. For more details on the development of the canal economy in Shandong during the Qing Dynasty, see Wang Yun, *Mingqing Shandong yunhe quyu shehui bianqian* (Social Changes in the Canal Region of Shandong in the Ming and Qing Dynasties), Beijing: People's Press, 2006, 106–224.

local grain ships were inundated, and the market was active. According to the "Survey Record" (*Diaocha ji*), there were 70–80 shops (*yinhao*) for the exchange of ingots, silver, and bank notes alone (including small money stores). The largest three were "Jiyuan" at the Horse Market Street (Mashijie), "Juxing" at the Pot Market Street (Guoshijie), and "Yonghengzeng" at the Green Bowl Market Entrance (Qingwanshi kou).

Commercial loans usually have a specific scale effect. Wu Xun chose the well-known money exchange shops with relatively low lending risk. "He lent tens of *diao* of money to those money exchange shops, stores, and landowners in Linqing." Wu Xun had transactions with several big money exchange shops. He lent the money to these shops or the branch firms (*zihao*) they opened; each time, he deposited 20–30 or 50–60 *diao* of money. Wu Xun frequented the Xu family compound (Dafu di). "Xu was a big landlord, a big gentry, and was the boss of the big money exchange shops 'Jiyuan.' Wu Xun often went to deposit at 'Jiyuan,' in and out of Dafu di."

In Linqing, Wu Xun worked with a big merchant Shi Shanzheng to manage his money. Shi was one of the wealthiest and most influential people in the area and also one of the tax farmers (*baoshuishang*) of Linqing chaoguan (an institution directly under the central government to oversee tax collection in grain) along the canal.[16] Linqing chaoguan was created in the early Ming Dynasty. In the middle of the Qianlong period, the central government appointed Linqing Prefecture Governor to administer the taxation. At that time, the tax collection was as much as 60,000 to 70,000 taels, or as little as 20,000 to 30,000 taels. The rest of the floating revenue went to some people to enrich themselves.[17]

In Linqing, Wu Xun gave a substantial portion of his money to people like Shi Shanzheng, who was responsible for collecting chaoguan taxes to lend. According to the statistics after Wu Xun's death: "the tax farmer of Linjing chaoguan lent six hundred taels of *kupingyin* with an interest of 2.2%; [the depositor] may take the interest with the passbook and everything was all well-documented. Feng Changtai was in charge of

[16] Jing Yang, "Mingqing linqing yunhe chaoguan yanjiu" (Study on Ming-Qing Linqing Canal Chaoguan), Master thesis, Shandong University, 2018.

[17] Zhang Ziqing et al., *Minguo linqing Xianzhi* (Linqing County Records in the Republican Era), Nanjing: Fenghuang Press, 2004, 122.

lending"[18] [临关经书等使, 库平银六百两, 二分二厘行息, 凭折取利, 有卷可查, 系冯长泰承管].

It was said that when Wu Xun walked in the street, he was "always with his head down and not looking at people." However, he never missed the door of a "good store" (*haohu*) and big store. "He either went to raise money or money lending and debt collection." Whenever he saved up one *diao* of money, he took it to the landlords, rich buyers, and sellers to earn interest. On the one hand, the Survey Record said that Wu Xun only befriended rich people, but on the other hand, it criticized him for exploiting peasants, which was obviously contradictory.[19]

A beggar could do business with wealthy merchants and as a money lender, which was very rare. At this point, WuXun was no longer a beggar but a private financier. However, in the beginning, the wealthy merchants ignored him. Wu Xun had kneeled for several days in Yang Shufang's home, "having saved ten *guan* of silver, he kneeled to beg the local elites to deposit the money for him to generate interest."[20] Eventually, Wu Xun moved the local elite with his sincerity. So that he was able to "get Lou Junling and Yang Shufang and others to operate large loans for him, and he ran small ones himself."[21]

Running a commercial loan was a smart strategy. First, commercial lending is, after all, less risky than microlending to the poor. Poor people borrow money to make ends meet, such as when they are ill and need medical treatment or are unproductive. In such cases, the poor are likely to have trouble repaying the loan.[22] Second, loans to large merchants can reduce the risk of repayment, as their ability to repay loans was more

[18] "Linqing zhou shishen Zhang Zhuang qingzhuan xiangcun an bing" (Linqing Prefecture gentry Zhang Zhuang Reporting and requesting to Transfer the Details of the Case), *Daquan*, 18.

[19] The theory of exploitation mainly refers to the exploitation of workers' labor, not to the exploitation of others' money. In fact, Wu Xun's lending was mostly oriented to merchants, fundraising was mostly from large families, and most of the funds for establishing schools did not come from the poor; however, free schools may allow the poor to have more access to schooling.

[20] Sha Mingyuan, "Ji Wu Xun xingxue shimo" (Record of Wu Xun's Promotion of Education), *Daquan*, 151.

[21] *Survey Record*, 25.

[22] Usury was always attacked morally. In fact, it was not "usury" that caused the borrower to be unable to repay the loan and end up with no way out. Without usury, the tragedy of the poor would have happened much sooner.

secure. Third, the capital needs of store merchants are large and stable. The information search cost of lending to stores was low, and the unit cost was also low. As Wu Xun cooperated with several of the largest local money exchange shops and asked Shi Shanzheng, Yang Shufang, and other big merchants to lend money on his behalf, he made substantial and reliable profits.

Besides large loans, Wu Xun also paid attention to "small lending." He seized every opportunity to grant small loans. After the death of Wu Xun, in his Linqing heritage, small household loans reached more than 1000 *diao* of coins.[23] "Wu Xun was begging for money in his village. When he encountered people who would not give it to him and said they had no money, Wu Xun immediately pulled out the money and said, 'I have money. I will give you a loan.'" He improvised on his dual identity as a beggar on one side and a financier on the other. Such microloans are so important in addressing the root causes of poverty among the poor that Yunus was awarded the Nobel Peace Prize for microlending.[24]

Wu Xun asking the money exchange shops and wealthy merchants to lend money can be seen as his choice of wealthy merchants and money exchange shops as his agents for capital lending or as lending money to those store owners and money exchange shops; if so, they had to pay him the interest rate every month. Small lenders usually need to choose an agent. First, as the customers of small and micro lenders are scattered, agents can grasp the credit and information of the lenders more efficiently, which can solve the dilemma of information asymmetry. Second, since it was not easy for the poor to repay the loan, a variety of means of frequent collection and sometimes even resorting to violence can be required. In Linqing town, Wu Xun's cooperative agents included Li Huilan, a large landowner in Jiaochang village, Li Tingyang, a landowner in Hexi, and Shi Shanzheng, the abovementioned Linqing chaoguan tax farmer. Wu Xun also cooperated with a "rascal" called Lüla Yue'er, often lending through him to the small traders who sold buns, had small businesses, or sold paper *yuanbao* on the street. In Yaowangmiao Street, Wu Xun often went to lend and collect debts in small amounts. Moreover, Wu Xun's ability to choose his agents was also a reflection of his managerial

[23] *Survey Record* (Diaocha ji), 53.

[24] Yunus (You Nusi), **Qiongren de yinhang jia—Nuobei'er heping jiang dezhu You Nusi zhuanji** (Bankers of the Poor: A Biography of Nobel Peace Prize Winner Yunus), translated by Shihong, Beijing: shenghuo dushu xinzhi sanlian shudian, 2006.Wu

skills. When he was known to have set up a free school under "Yi Xue Zheng," his agents became partners in raising funds for the school.

Wu Xun traveled around begging all year round. In the process, he learned about the credit situation of his customers, so he was better able to control the risk when lending and choose the appropriate business strategy. For example, the wife of a chicken intestine peddler was a gambler and often gambled with Wu Xun's money. Wu Xun provided her with a loan of no more than two *diao* at a time, with an interest rate of 3%. Worrying that she could not pay off the loan, Wu Xun required that the loan term be one month, and the principal and interest must be repaid at the end of the term. This was to use short-term lending to hedge the risk.

Wuxing valued credit and often lent through institutions and individuals with high credit, such as landlords, gentry, and money exchange shops. For these relatively low-risk institutions, Wu Xun chose to lend large amounts of money to them on a long-term basis. When he lent money himself, he usually chose "good customers" (equivalent to customers with "high credit score" as he assessed it) who could pay back the capital and interest. Wu Xun's lending had an incidental principle that the applicant had to be from a family of "three generations," so that when the debtor passed away, his descendants could still be called upon to settle the debt. Alternatively, this was a way for Wu Xun to examine credit.

Wu Xun did not lend easily to the poor or those with low credit. If a poor person wanted to borrow money, he had to have collateral, and he usually "lent money by requiring the land as a deposit" (*zhidi fangdai*). According to "Survey Record," Wang Xinyuan of Guantao County borrowed money from Wu Xun for many years. As Wang Xinyuan could not repay, he had to give "forty *mu* of land and nine houses to Wu Xun." Another case was that Zhang Yu Chi's great-grandfather borrowed money from Wu Xun, and when he couldn't repay it, he pawned the land to Wu Xun. Wu Xun's principle of lending was to follow the market rules, regardless of favoritism: "money matters instead of kinship" (*renqian bu renren*). Wu Xun was Tang Qinxi's uncle, and Tang Qinxi's father begged Wu Xun to lend him ten *diao* of money. Despite being his relative, Wu Xun insisted that he needed collateral, and said to Tang Qinxi's father, "Okay, which piece of land do you give to me as collateral."

Finally, investing in houses while capital lending. Wu Xun had a discerning eye for opportunities and focused on the future. He once lent a sum of money (about ten *diao*) to two gatekeepers who managed the canal gates, using their riverbank hut as collateral. The riverbank hut was a temporary building far from downtown, but Wu Xun found its value and potential appreciation. After borrowing the money, the gatekeepers could no longer afford to pay the loan. Wu Xun executed the claim, collected the hut, and rented it to a barber household surnamed Wang. As there were often boatmen visiting this area to transit and rest, the barber opened a barber store at the mouth of the canal. Wu Xun collected the hut rent at 800 *wen* per month. He also pawned another nearby storehouse at the price of 100 *diao* and rented it at the price of two *diao* and 400 *wen*.[25]

In the past, the academic community formed some stereotypes about capital lending or usury. In fact, usury always had its space and inner logic. It satisfies a certain demand, it was a high-risk form of private lending in a diversified system of financial instruments, and it was difficult for other financial instruments to completely replace usury; second, usury reduces the systemic risk in a diversified system with its market positioning and industry segmentation.[26] Therefore, Muhammad Yunus's microlending was awarded the Nobel Peace Prize instead of being denounced as exploitation. Although Wu Xun's lending was criticized in the record, his ability in financial management was still worthy of attention.

Corporate Property Rights: Future Land Revenue Ensures the Free School's Operation

In addition to capital lending, Wuxing also valued the return on land. While capital lending had a short return period and high risk, the return of land was more stable, low risk, and more secure in the long run. According to the Survey Record, Wu Xun had more than 300 *mu* of land in Tangyi, Linqing, and Guantao counties, among which Tangyi County had the most land. Most of the documents of Wu Xun's land transactions were kept in a brief copy of the account book, called "Account Book of Land" (*Dimu zhang*). The "Account Book of Land" records that Wu Xun bought and *dian* purchased more than 280 *mu* of land from 1868

[25] "Linqing zhou shishen Zhang Zhuang qingzhuan xiangcun an'bing" (Linqing Prefecture gentry Zhang Zhuang Reporting and requesting to Transfer the Details of the Case), *Daquan*, 18.

[26] Long Denggao, Pan Qingzhong, and Lin Zhan, "Gaolidai de qianshi jinsheng" (The past and present life of the Usury), *Sixiang zhanxian* (Thinking), no. 4 (2014): 13–19.

to 1893. The three-volume "Account Book of Land" transcribes 74 land documents, 38 of which are below three *mu* and 5 of which are above ten *mu*. In the nearly 280 *mu* of land transactions recorded by 74 documents, there was one exchange of land, the area of which was two *mu* two *fen*; eight land pawns and transfers totaled 28. 6 *mu*, and the rest were land purchases. Wu Xun's land rights were traded in various ways, from revocable and irrevocable sales to mortgages and *dian* purchases (Table A.1). The active market for land rights provided the conditions for Wu Xun to seek future income from land rent.

From the above statistics, we can see that before 1878, Wu Xun only "pawned land" three times; after 1879, he began to buy land for the first time. In the following two years, Wu Xun bought a large amount of land, reaching 63.29 *mu* and 104.45 *mu*, respectively, and after 1882, Wu Xun continued to purchase land. The land purchase was not under the natural name of Wu Xun but under the legal name of "Yi Xue Zheng." In March 1880, the name of "Yi Xue Zheng" began to appear in the land purchase deed, "sold under the name of "Yi Xue Zheng;" after that, the land was

Table A.1 Wu Xun's land acquisitions (1868–1893). *Sources*: "Account Book of Land" (*Dimu zhang*) in *Survey Record* (Diaocha ji), pp. 65–71. The total of 279.38 *mu* is calculated by the author and differs from the total of the *Survey Record* by about five *mu*

Years	*Purchase methods*	*Area (mu)*
1868	1 land pawn	1.50
1878	2 land pawns	12.00
1879	1 land purchase	0.55
1880	20 land purchases, 1 land transfer, and 3 land pawns	63.29
1881	21 land purchases	104.45
1882	6 land purchases	12.74
1883	4 land purchases	17.78
1884	1 land purchase	0.53
1885	2 land purchases	15.67
1891	1 land purchase	1.46
1892	6 land purchases, 1 land transfer and pawn	35.57
1893	4 land purchase	13.84
Total	279.38	

purchased under this name.[27] In other words, at the latest from 1880, the government should have been recognized Wu Xun's act of setting up a free school; that is, the legal entity of "Yi Xue Zheng" was confirmed and became a legally valid subject.[28] In traditional China, legal persons can also become landowners in addition to natural persons. For example, "Yongxi Bridge Pier" (*yongxi qiaozhu*), the hall (*tang*) of the clan, the temple, the "association," and the "society."[29] In addition, in order to prevent the descendants from competing for these lands, Wu Xun set up more than 190 *mu* of land as "permanent free school land" (*yongwei yixue zhidi*), with "Yi Xue Zheng" as the main body of property rights, thus eliminating the possibility of encroachment by other natural persons. It was worth emphasizing that, due to the lack of school funding, the annual tax on the free school's land was exempted from the government's taxation by about 70 *guan* and was classified as a "government donation" (*guanjuan*).[30] This shows that the Qing government set up a special tax-free "government donation." However, this point has not been revealed because there are few records of the exemption from land tax of the fields of *yidu*, bridges, and other public welfare corporations.

Generally speaking, a land sale deed must go through the formalities of title delivery and payment of land transaction tax at the government office before it becomes a legally valid title certificate. However, the *dian* purchase and sale of land did not require the delivery of property rights, so there was no need to go through the governmental procedures. Before establishing the legal entity of "Yi Xue Zheng" in 1880, Wu Xun rarely used the land rights market to seek added value, and there were only three land transactions of *dian*. Once the "Yi Xue Zheng" legal entity was

[27] "Account Book of Land" (*Dimu zhang*), 15, 23.

[28] On April 13, 1879, "Wu Xue Zheng" first appeared in land purchase deed. The name "Wu Xue Zheng" is only found in this deed. See "Account Book of Land" (*Dimu zhang*), 7.

[29] Long Denggao, "Langqiao yimeng: Qingdai gonggong sheshi de jingying moshi yu chanquan xingtai" (The Legacy of Corridor Bridge: Operation Mode and Property Rights Form of Public Facilities in Qing Dynasty), Keynote Speech, Zhongguo jingji shixuehui nianhui, July 2016.

[30] "Tangyi xian zhixian Guo Chunxu chuci qingjiang xiangwen" (A Detailed Document of Guo Chunxu, Magistrate of Tangyi County, First Requesting for Award); "Tangyi zhixian Guo Chunxu zaosong yixue fangwu dimu xiangwen" (The County Magistrate of Tangyi, Guo Chunxu, sending A Detailed Document on the Land and House for the Free School), *Daquan*, 6–7.

formally established, Wu Xun used the funds he had accumulated in the financial market to purchase a large amount of land to obtain corporate property rights and secure future income. Since part of the land was used as a home base for building school buildings, there were also land transfer transactions.

Wu Xun was unusual in several ways. First, Wu Xun purchased land without signing a deed in his natural name. It shows that he was clear from the beginning that his purpose was to promote education rather than for personal gain.

Second, Wu Xun had a good understanding of legal regulations. The purchase of land with the legal entity "Yi Xue Zheng" could transcend a natural person's life span and limitations and be protected by the law. The land of the legal entity no longer belonged to Wu Xun personally, and the school management was not under Wu Xun's personal responsibility or control. After the establishment of the free school, the school council presided over the specific management affairs.

Third, the accumulation of land wealth in the name of "Yi Xue Zheng" could guarantee the source of income of the free school and ensure its perpetual development. This example of developing a business with a corporate property rights institution was also applied to the *shuyuan*, *yidu*, temples, and *shantang* (benevolent society). This system provided the basis for Wu Xun's establishment of the free school. Therefore, it was not valid for the Survey Record to conclude that Wu Xun was a big landlord.

Fourth, Wu Xun's establishment of a free school had both long-term planning and strong action. From the large-scale land purchases in 1880 and 1881, it can be seen that Wu Xun had been planning to buy land for a long time and probably had already reached a preliminary agreement with the seller and made cash preparations. After 1882 Wu Xun's land-buying behavior and quantity gradually normalized. Among the land sellers, there were many supporters of the free school. They were also a kind of support by selling land to the free school. By the winter of 1886, Wu Xun had pawned and purchased a total of 230 *mu* of land at the cost of 4263.874 *qianwen* of Beijing local currency (*jingqian*).[31]

The land purchased by the "Yi Xue Zheng" was usually rented out for future rental income. The land under the name of "Yi Xue Zheng"

[31] "Tangyi xian zhixian Guo Chunxu chuci qingjiang xiangwen" (A Detailed Document of Guo Chunxu, Magistrate of Tangyi County, First Requesting for Award), *Daquan*, 5.

received an annual rent of 380 *guan* to support the daily expenses of the school.[32] Many of the original landowners rented the land they sold. Specifically, the original landowner transferred the right to the land but retained the right to use the land for a certain period, which was called "selling the horse without leaving the trough" (*mai ma bu li cao*). However, if the tenant could not pay the rent when it was due, "Yi Xue Zheng" would take back the right to use the land.

On the 6th day of March 1882, Chi Wande sold the house base with an area of one *mu*, six *fen*, eight *li*, five *hao*, and three *si* to Wu Xun. On the contract, it was written:

> "The price is 2670 *wen*, due on August 15. If not paid after the deadline I will take back the house base."[33]

On December 14, 1882 (New Year's Eve), Zhang Hengsong sold his land with an area of three *mu*, one *fen*, four *li*, and five *hao* to Wu Xun. The deed reads:

> "On the same day, Zhang Hengsong rented the land back. The total price of the land is 4730 *wen*, due on August 15. If not paid on time, the penalty is 300 *wen*, guaranteed by Zhang Yansong."[34]

As a result of giving the seller the offer to lease back the same day, Wu Xun was granted permission to defer payment (or to pay in installments; perhaps Wu Xun was cash-strapped at the time; perhaps he used the eight months to lend money to generate interest). In short, the buyer acquired ownership of the land while leasing the use of the land to the original landowner for the benefit of both parties. The development of a mature land rights market and diverse trading methods facilitated the continued operation of free schools.

[32] "Jubing Tangyi xianshu qingjiang biaowen" (Reporting to the County Office of Tangyi and Requesting for the Award); "Tangyi zhixian Guo Chunxu zaosong yixue fangwu dimu xiangwen" (The County Magistrate of Tangyi, Guo Chunxu, sending A Detailed Document on the Land and House for the Free School), *Daquan* 3, 5.

[33] "Account Book of Land" (*Dimu zhang*), 157.

[34] "Account Book of Land" (*Dimu zhang*), 158–159.

Fundraising

When the initial conditions were in place for establishing a free school, and the local gentry supported, and the government approved it, Wu Xun was able to raise funds for the free school in name only. Wu Xun obtained the "donation book" (*yuanbu*) approved by the local government and could legally mobilize others to raise funds.[35] When Wu Xun begged to raise money for the school, begging was transformed into raising money. Wu Xun raised 1578 *guan* in cash, accounting for 18.3% of the total 8641 *guan* raised for Chongxian free school in 1887 (Table A.2). In addition, the land for the construction of the school was partly donated by others (for example, Guo Fen donated 1.87 *mu* of land).

Begging income was for beggars' personal alms, and donations are the sponsorship of the free school; the nature of the two are different, and the amounts are also very different. If you distinguish the income of Wu Xun as begging, it will lead to misunderstanding. Wu Xun often "took the donation book around to solicit donations and promoted 'good books' (*shanshu*) such as '*Taishang ganying pian*' '*Yinzhi wen*' '*Zaowang jing*' and '*Quanshi wen*.'" The names of the donors in the donation books were

Table A.2 Construction cost and property of Chongxian Yishu in Liulin Town (1886). *Sources* "Jubing Tangyi xianshu qingjiang biaowen" [Reporting to the County Office of Tangyi and Requesting for the Award]; "Tangyi zhixian Guo Chunxu zaosong yixue fangwu dimu xiangwen" [The County Magistrate of Tangyi, Guo Chunxu, sending a Detailed Document on the Land and House for the Free School]; "Shandong xunfu Zhangyao zouqing jianfang pian" [Shandong Governor Zhang Yao Requesting the Construction of a Workshop], See Daquan, 3–10

	Cost (guan)	*Sources of funding*
Total	8641	
Material and labor costs of school building	2800	Wu Xun's financial management
	1578	Donations by the gentry
School property of more than 230 *mu*	4263	The legal entity of "Yi Xue Zheng" established by Wu Xun

35 *Daquan*, 5, 227.

usually inscribed on monuments or included in memorial books, and Wu Xun also marketed spiritual products as an incentive.

Wu Xun, who traveled around begging, also had information about many parties, which was helpful for fundraising. In fact, his begging was quite similar to monks traveling around to raise funds. Monks have a natural advantage in collecting donations. First, they are trusted by the people; second, they travel around the four quarters of the world, are familiar with the people's ability to donate, and therefore often become an important force for fundraising. For example, in Fujian in the Song Dynasty, monks were important participants in constructing local bridges. The situation of Wu Xun was similar. When he set up a free school and got the support of the gentry and the government, he also gained the people's trust.

There are certain correlations and similarities between begging (*qitao*), donation collecting (*huayuan*), and fundraising (*mujuan*), and sometimes it was difficult to distinguish them clearly. The monk's donation collecting was not very different from begging, "*huayuan*" was basically a term for monk's begging. Fundraising, too, was a kind of donation collecting, also known as "*muhua*" and "*muyuan*"; if a monk collects donations for the development of the temple, then fundraising was usually for public causes. Therefore, fundraising requires a legal "donation book," approved by the government with a seal. We say that Wu Xun was begging at the beginning, but when the government recognized him for setting up a free school, his begging became fundraising; to be precise, he changed from personal begging to fundraising for public causes, which greatly enhanced his ability to raise funds.

Historically, there was a similarity in terms of "donation collection" (*mujuan*) and "tax collection" (*nashui*). For example, "donations and taxes" (*juanshui*) are used together, and "taxes" are sometimes called "donations." Strictly speaking, donations are voluntary, and taxes are mandatory. However, sometimes the collection of donations amounts to collecting mandatory taxes in the name of "voluntary donations."[36]

[36] Tianjin Customs levied a surcharge for the construction of the Wuanguo Bridge, known as the "bridge donation" (*qiaojuan*). See Long Denggao, Gong Ning, Meng Dewang, "Jindai gonggong shiye de zhidu chuangxin: liyi xiangguan fang hezuo de gongyi faren moshi–jiyu haihe gongchengju zhong waiwen dang'an de yanjiu" (Institutional Innovation of Modern Public Utilities: A Public Benefit Corporation Model of Stakeholder Cooperation–A Study Based on the Chinese and Foreign Language Archives

For example, in the tax donations contained in the "*Yongxi qiaozhi*," more than 100 people donated 1000 *wen*. Here the "donation" was no different from the "tax." Wu Xun would sometimes persuade people to donate money to the free school in a compulsory way. In any case, Wu Xun spared no effort to raise funds for the free school; he was good at performing, even sacrificing his dignity in exchange for alms and donations.

The Origin of Wu Xun's Way of Managing Money and Business

Wu Xun lost his father when he was young and begged with his mother, so he was not familiar with farming, whose knowledge was passed on to children by male parents. Wu Xun was the seventh in line, with two older brothers and four older sisters. Although the "Survey Record" describes Wu Xun in a very derogatory way, the content was generally factual. Wu Xun "acquired the habit of being a vagrant who did not care about crop work and did not like to work." At the age of 16 or 17, his mother managed to send him to his distant relative Zhang Bianzheng's house in Xuedian, Guantao County, to "carry out work" (*kanghuo*, a dialect of Shandong). Due to the lack of basic knowledge of crop work, he was assigned to take care of the orchard or to do some light work of feeding pigs and livestock.[37] As a result, Wu Xun received the lowest wages at the standard of "three whips" (*sanbian*)—4 *diao* of money.[38] It was said that "Wu Qi left after a big fuss and did not work again."[39] Since the income

of the Haihe Engineering Bureau), *Qinghua University xuebao* (Journal of Tsinghua University (Philosophy and Social Sciences)), no. 6 (2017): 170–182.

[37] It is said that "Doumo [Wu Xun's nickname] did not know how to do crop work and could not even distinguish beans from cotton. Once people asked him to go to the field to pick the cotton tip, he pinched off the bean tip." "He couldn't do any farm work; he couldn't carry night soil or hoe. He couldn't hold the cart and swayed; he carried water without using his hands and swayed around." Zhang Bianzheng was Zhang Laobian, a distant relation of Wu Xun, and a tribute student. His family had four or five *mu* of land and hired several people to cultivate it. See *Survey Record* (Diaocha ji), 21–22.

[38] At that time, the strongest laborers were called "first whip" (*toubian*), and their annual wages were eight or nine *diao*; the wages of "second whip" (*erbian*) were five or six *diao*. See *Survey Record* (Diaocha ji), 21.

[39] On the question of whether to do farm work or ask for food, Wu Xun clashed with his mother and brother. Wu Xun believed that "it is better to beg for food as I like,"

from farm work was low and the work was undignified, it was no different from begging.

Wu Xun was not a qualified farmer but had outstanding potential for financial management, and he befriended different people from all walks of life.[40] His uncle Cui Laohua had been the "Chief of the Land Tax" (*fufang laozong*) in the government office, and Wu Xun and he "got along best." This experience opened the door to financial management for Wu Xun. Although he did not go to school, he had a fantastic memory, sensitivity, and talent for numbers.[41] Wu Xun tied many knots on his belt to mark the loans he gave to others and never made a mistake.

From one to a thousand *min*, the interest accumulation was different and complicated, and the daily interest, monthly interest, and annual interest are rich and complicated, changing from time to time. Wu Xun could not read and write and could not understand mathematics, so he did not know the books of accounts and contracts. He mastered the size of the various debt and payments only by memorization. Therefore, as a creditor for decades, he never had a debt dispute.[42]

At the peak, Wu Xun collected rent from more than 200 *mu* of land scattered in several counties, as well as dozens of loans. Wu Xun's financial management skills were thus evident.

For those who are interested, a begging career can exercise marketing skills. Wu Xun traveled around to beg, so he was well-informed and could better grasp the market and customer information than ordinary people.

"I'll become a monk, and you don't have to bother me!" See *Survey Record* (Diaocha ji), 22.

[40] According to *Survey Record,* "From then on, he befriended all the rascals, bachelors, landlords, bullies, rich monks and big and small bureaucrats. The local people said that when he was young, he liked to go to Cuizhuang to visit his uncle Cui Laohua, who was a famous bachelor, and 'specialized in earning other people's money.' Wang Tangchuan said that Cui Laohua had been the '*fufang laozong*' in the government office, and Wu Xun and he got along best. It is conceivable that Wu Xun learned a lot from Cui Laohua, who specialized in making money. Later, Wu Xun begged in many counties, befriended the rogues of each county, and became a powerful rogue leader." See *Survey Record* (Diaocha ji), 22.

[41] There are many entrepreneurs who have a talent for numbers, such as Sudono Salim (Lin Shaoliang), Eka Tjipta Widjaja (Huang Yicong), Lucio Tan (Chen Yongzai), and other famous Nanyang Chinese businessmen. Although they did not receive much formal education, their numerical ability was extraordinary.

[42] Sha Mingyuan, "Ji Wu Xun xingxue shimo" (Record of Wu Xun's Promotion of Education), *Daquan*, 151.

He was good at identifying opportunities and finding the right people to lend to. Also, he recognized people's preferences and found ways to meet their needs. For example, he could get handouts from others by pretending to be crazy and making them happy. He was humble, a good communicator and coordinator, and articulate.[43] After the official preparation and inauguration of the free school, Wu Xun moved people with his affection and righteousness, integrating individuals and resources from all sides to promote the school's operations. He mobilized the gentry and celebrities to form a council of 41 chiefs to manage the school affairs and hired scholars as schoolteachers. The council model of governance had a long tradition and was a mature institutional arrangement in Chinese civil society, providing the institutional foundation for Wu Xun's success.[44]

Wu Xun had the extreme frugality of a miser, which was the pattern of wealth accumulation in the era of a shortage economy. Even when he acquired wealth later, he still begged for a living and lived a frugal life: "In winter, he was dressed in a shabby robe, and in summer, he had a short and a long shirt; he refused to throw away his food, even if it stank. In the year of his death, he suffered from abdominal disease for several months and had diarrhea, probably because he was usually overly frugal."[45] Wu Xun was also very distant to his family, a practice that was one of the means of accumulating wealth.[46]

[43] Wu Xun called people "old grandfather" (*lao yeye*), "old grandmother" (*lao nainai*), or "grandfather" (*yeye*), and "grandmother" (*nainai*). The children of the landlords were all called "little uncle" (*xiao shushu*) and "little aunt" (*xiao gugu*). The landlords of Tangyi and Guantao said that Wu Xun was "sweet-talking" "He was good-tempered and didn't get annoyed even if he was fooled." See *Survey Record* (Diaocha ji), 24.

[44] Long Denggao, "Langqiao yimeng: Qingdai gonggong sheshi de jingying moshi yu chanquan xingtai" (The Legacy of Corridor Bridge: Operation Mode and Property Rights Form of Public Facilities in Qing Dynasty), Keynote Speech, Zhongguo jingjishi xuehui nianhui (Annual Conference of Chinese Economic History Society), July 2016.

[45] "Linqing zhou zhizhou Li Weicheng chengsong Zeng Sheng Jin Eqiu suozao Wu Xun shishi" (Submittsion by Li Weicheng, Magistrate of Linqing Prefecture, Facts of Wu Xun made by Zeng Sheng and Jin E'qiu), *Daquan*, 24. Another example is that on the day when Chongxian Yixue, the free school he ran, was opened, he refused to be seated at the dinner table. Later he was given a *jin* of bun and a bowl of vegetables. But in a short time, he had already run to the kiln and returned with a few bricks. See "Wu Xun xiansheng de yishi: jinian Wu Xun xiansheng de yishi: jinian Wuxun 109 zhounian danchen" (Anecdotes of Mr. Wu Xun: Commemorating the 109th Birth Anniversary of Mr. Wu Xun), *Daquan*, 252.

[46] "His mother his brother did not enjoy the wealth of Wu Xun, and his mother died not like a dog" "Wu Xun would rather sell the food he asked for to others to feed their

The reason for Wu Xun's success, in addition to his extraordinary personal qualities, the environment and the system he was in at that time were also indispensable conditions. First, the developed commodity and financial markets around Linqing enabled him to lend money to generate interest with the help of stores and money exchange shops. Second, the active market of land rights and tenancy relations enabled him to invest in land and stores and obtain stable rental income.[47] Moreover, the system of corporate property rights allowed him to purchase land and accumulate wealth in the name of "Yi Xue Zheng" and receive legal protection. Finally, the civil organization and mobilization ability of traditional China empowered Wu Xun, who was a beggar, to initiate and organize a free school and to manage it in the long run through the school council.

Wu Xun sold his ancestral property to realize funds, and then lent the funds to generate interest; he used the principal and interest to buy land to obtain land rent, and then sold part of the land to raise funds for the free school; he used the proceeds of the land with corporate property rights as a source of funding to ensure the long-term stable operation of the free school. All this came from a beggar, which is impressive. Behind Wu Xun's success was the support of the market environment and institutions, including Linqing's financial market, land rights market, corporate property rights, and civil organizations. Wu Xun used the "free school" as a pretext to gain the support of the gentry, the assistance of prominent merchants, as well as the permission of the government. Shedding the appearance of a beggar, Wu Xun was a Master of Financial Management in the traditional era.

animals but would not give his mother and brother a bite to eat. He was such a heartless and unrighteous man." See *Survey Record* (Diaocha Ji), 27–28. Later, among the land donated by Wu Xun to the school, forty mu were allocated to him "as a capital for Wu Xun to marry and have children." However, he did not marry, but used the land as a sacrificial field and asked his nephews to pay ten *guan*, for the use of the free school, and the remaining funds were used for the daily needs of his second brother and nephews, in addition to the needs of worshiping his ancestors. See "Linqing zhou zhizhou Li Weicheng chengsong Zeng Sheng Jin Eqiu suozao Wu Xun shishi" (Submittsion by Li Weicheng, Magistrate of Linqing Prefecture, Facts of Wu Xun Made by Zeng Sheng and Jin E'qiu), *Daquan*, 24.

[47] Long Denggao, "Diquan jiaoyi yu shengchan yaosu zuhe, 1650–1950" (Land Rights Transactions and Production Factor Combinations, 1650–1950), *Jingji yanjiu* (Economic Research Journal), no. 2 (2009): 146–156; Long Denggao, Lin Zhan, Peng Bo, "Dian yu Qingdai diquan jiaoyi tixi" (Dian and the Qing Dynasty Land Rights Transaction System), *China's Social Science* (Social Sciences in China), no. 5 (2013): 125–141.

Appendix 2: Land Deeds of Tsinghua Collection

Sale Deed, the 11th year of Wanli's reign (1583), Ming Dynasty.

Li-Guangming collections of folk documents, Tsinghua Center for Chinese Economic History

D. Long and X. Chi, *The Institutions of Land Property Rights in China*, Palgrave Studies in Economic History,
https://doi.org/10.1007/978-981-97-5112-9

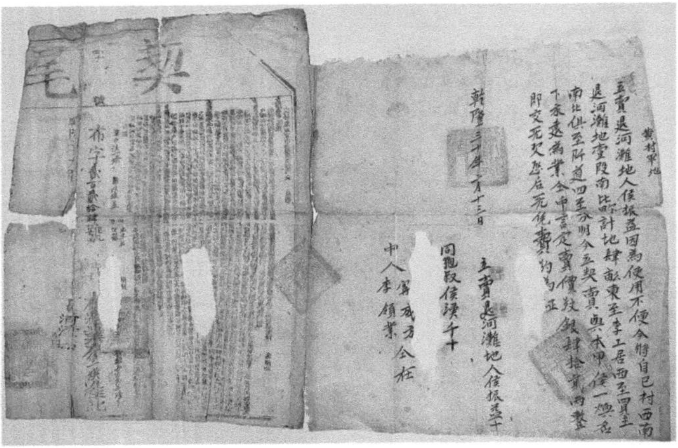

Sale Deed of Mudflats, Hejin County. Deed Tail: "No. Cloth 224," the 30th year of Qianlong's reign (1765), Qing Dynasty.

Zhang-Wenda collections of folk documents, Tsinghua Center for Chinese Economic History

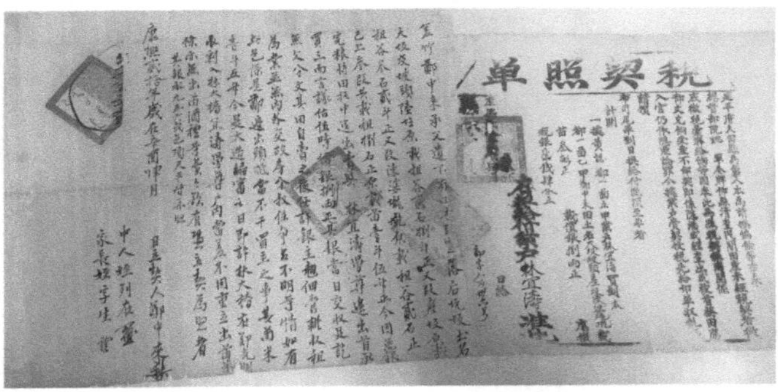

Tax certificate, the 20th year of Kangxi's reign (1681), Qing Dynasty.

Li-Guangming collections of folk documents, Center for Chinese Economic History, Tsinghua University.

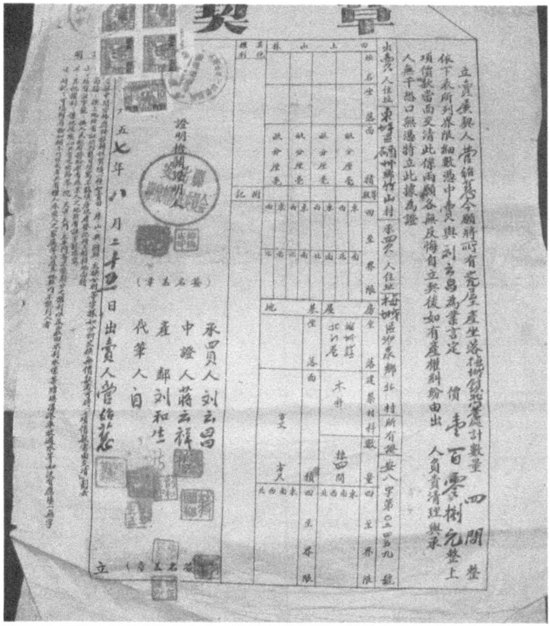

契 草

立賣屋契人曾紹蕖今願將所有瓦屋產坐落梅城鎮□□□計數量四間整
依下表所列界限細數憑中賣與刘云昌為業言定 價壹百零捌元整上
項價款當面交清此係兩願各無反悔自立契後如有產權糾紛由出 人負責清理與承
人無干恐口無憑特立此據為證

出賣人住址 東坪區硒州鄉竹山村 承買人住址 梅城區邓家鄉北 村 所有證 安八字第0二四五九號

承買人 刘云昌
中證人 蔣云祥
產 鄰 刘和生
代筆人 自

五七年八月二十五日出賣人曾紹蕖

Sale Deed of House, Anhua County, 1957
Provided by Xiang Xinzhuang, Anhua County, Hunan Province.

References

Folk Documents

Li-Guangming collections of folk documents, Center for Chinese Economic History, Tsinghua University.

Zhang-Wenda collections of folk documents, Center for Chinese Economic History, Tsinghua University.

"Tsinghua Collection of Deeds" 清华藏契约

Archival Sources

Chen Yanen 陈延恩 et al. *Jiangyin xianzhi* 江阴县志 [Gazetteer for Jiangyin County], Nanjing: Fenghuang chubanshe, 2011.

Daming lü 大明律 [Ming Law Code]

Daqing lüli 大清律例 [Qing Law Code]

Daqing huidian shili 大清会典事例 [The Collected Institutes and Precedents of the Great Qing]. *juan* 247

Wenxian tongkao 文献通考 [Comprehensive Examination of Literature]. *juan* 19

Dayuan shengzheng guochao dianzhang hubu 大元圣政国朝典章 [Statutes of the Yuan dynasty, Ministry of Revenue]. *juan* 5. Beijing: Zhongguo guangbo dianshi chubanshe, 1998.

Dayuan tongzhi tiaoge 大元通制条格 [Comprehensive Regulations of the Great Yuan Dynasty]. *juan* 16. Collated by Guo Chengwei 郭成伟. Beijing: falü chubanshe, 2000.

Songxingtong 宋刑统 [Song Criminal Code]. *juan* 4. Collated by Xue Meiqing 薛梅卿. Beijing: falü chubanshe, 1999.

D. Long and X. Chi, *The Institutions of Land Property Rights in China*, Palgrave Studies in Economic History,
https://doi.org/10.1007/978-981-97-5112-9

Feng Zigang 冯紫岗. *Jiaxing xian nongcun diaocha* 嘉兴县农村调查 [Jiaxing County Rural Survey]. Zhejiang University and Jiaxing County Government, 1936.

Kong Zhaoming 孔昭明. ed. *Fujian shengli·tianzhai li·dianye mianshui* 福建省例·田宅例·典业免税 [Fujian Province Example, Examples of Lands and Houses, The Tax Exemption for *Dian* Properties]. Taipei: datong shuju, 1987.

Fujian shifan daxue lishixi 福建师范大学历史系 [Fujian Normal University History Department]. ed. *Mingqing Fujian jingji qiyue wenshu xuanji* 明清福建经济契约文书选辑 [Selected Economic Contracts of Fujian in the Ming and Qing Dynasties]. Beijing: renmin chubanshe, 1997.

Guomin zhengfu zhujichu tongjiju 国民政府主计处统计局 [The Bureau of Statistics, Office of the Comptroller of the National Government]. ed. *Zhongguo zudian zhidu zhi tongji fenxi* 中国租佃制度之统计分析 [Statistical Analysis of the Tenancy System in China]. 1942.

Qian Nanjing guomin zhengfu sifa xingzheng bu 前南京国民政府司法行政部 [The Former Ministry of Justice and Administration of the GMD Government of Nanjing]. ed. *Minshi xiguan diaocha baogao lu* 民事习惯调查报告录 [Record of Survey Reports on Civil Customs]. Beijing: Zhongguo zhengfa daxue chubanshe, 2000.

Hong Mai 洪迈. *Yi Jian Zhi* 夷坚志 [Records of Yi Jian]. Collated by He Zhuo 何卓. Beijing: Zhonghua shuju, 1981.

Huadong junzheng weiyuanhui tudi gaige weiyuanhui 华东军政委员会土地改革委员会 [Land Reforms Committee of the East China Military Commission]. *Zhejiang sheng nongcun diaozha* 浙江省农村调查 [Survey of Rural Areas in Zhejiang Province]. December 1952.

"Huadong tudi gaige shishi banfa de guiding" 华东土地改革实施办法的规定 [Provisions of the East China Land Reforms Implementation Measures], 1950-aa-26. Jiangsu Provincial Archives: 3006-Chang-22.

Jingui chenshi wenshu 金匮陈氏文书 [Chen's Documents in a Golden Box]. Institute for Advanced Studies on Asia.

Lin Xinchuan 李心传. *Jianyan yilai xinian yaolu* 建炎以来系年要录 [Summary of the Years Since Jianyan]. Shanghai: Shanghai guji chubanshe, 1992.

Lin Zhen 林真. ed. *Taiwan sifa wuquan bian* 台湾私法物权编 [A Compilation of Taiwan Private Law Property Rights]. Taipei: datong shuju, 1987.

Liu Zhiwei 刘志伟. ed. *Zhang Shenghe jiazu wenshu* 张声和家族文书 [Zhang Shenghe Family Papers]. Hongkong: Huanan chubanshe, 1999.

Nanchuan Xianzhi 南川县志 [Gazetteer for Nanchuan County], eds. Liu Langsheng 柳琅声 et al. Taipei: Chengwen chubanshe youxian gongsi, 1976.

Ma Jianshi 马建石. Yang Yuchang 杨有裳. eds. *Daqing luli tongkao jiaozhu* 清律例通考校注 [A General Examination of Statutes and Substatutes of the Great Qing]. *juan* 9. Beijing: Zhongguo zhengfa daxue chubanshe, 1992.

Minggong shupan qingmingji 名公书判清明集 [Collections of Well-Crafted and Just Verdicts of Scholar-Bureaucrats in the Song Dynasty]. Beijing: Zhonghua shuju, 1987.

Nongye tuiguangbu 农业推广部 [Ministry of Agricultural Extension], "Nanchang quanxian nongcun diaocha baogao 南昌全县农村调查报告" [Report on the Rural Survey of Nanchang County], *Jiangxi sheng Nongyeyuan zhuankan* 江西省农业院专刊 [Special Issue of Jiangxi Province Agricultural Institute], 1935.

Xingzheng sifabu 司法行政部 [Ministry of Justice and Administration], *Min shangshi xiguan diaocha baogaolu* 民商事习惯调查报告录 [Report of the Survey of Civil and Commercial Customs]. 1930.

Tudi weiyuanhui 土地委员会 [Land Commission]. ed. *Quanguo tudi diaocha baogao gangyao* 全国土地调查报告纲要 [Outline of the National Land Survey Report]. 1937.

Wang Anshi 王安石. *Wang Anshi ji* 王安石集 [Works of Wang Anshi]. Nanjing: Fenghuang chubanshe, 2006.

Wang Shiqing 王世庆. ed. *Taiwan gongsi cang guwenshu huibian* 台湾公私藏古文书汇编 [Collection of Antique Documents from the Public and Private Collections of Taiwan]. FSN01-10-479. Fu Ssu-nien (Fu Sinian) Library, Academia Sinica, Taipei.

Wu Xun lishi diaocha tuan 武训历史调查团 [Wu Xun History Survey Group]. *Wu Xun lishi diaocha ji* 武训历史调查记 [Wu Xun History Survey Record]. Beijing: Renmin chubanshe, 1951.

Wu Xun lishi diaocha tuan 武训历史调查团 [Wu Xun History Survey Group]. *Wu Xun dimu zhang* 武训地亩账 [Wu Xun's Account Book of Land]. Beijing: Renmin chubanshe, 1975.

Xie Shenfu 谢深甫. *Qingyuan tiaofa shilei* 庆元条法事类 [The Law Code of the Qingyuan Reign]. Harbin: Heilongjiang renmin chubanshe, 2002.

Xinhua shudian Huadong zongfen dian 新华书店华东总分店 [Xinhua Bookstore East China Main Branch]. *Tudi gaige shouce* 土地改革手册 [Handbook of Land Reforms]. Beijing: Xinhua shudian huadong zong fendian, 1950.

Xinbian shiwenlei juyao qizha qingqian waiji 新编事文类要启札青钱 [The New Series of Writings of Official Documents]. *juan* 11. Reprinted copies in1324. China's National Library.

Xingke tiben 刑科题本 [Board of Punishments Routine Memorials]. 6120. September 12, 1823.

Song huiyao jigao 宋会要辑稿 [Song Government Manuscript Compendium]. Beijing: Zhonghua shuju, 1957.

Taiwan yinhang jingji yanjiushi 台湾银行经济研究室 [Bank of Taiwan Economic Research Office], *Taiwan sifa wuquan bian* 台湾私法物权编 [Private Law Property Rights in Taiwan]. Taipei: Taiwansheng wenxian weiyuanhui, 1999.

Taiwan yinhang jingji yanjiushi 台湾银行经济研究室 [Bank of Taiwan Economic Research Office]. *Qingdai Taiwan dazu diaochashu* 清代台湾大租调查书 [Survey on the Great Lease of Taiwan in the Qing Dynasty]. Taipei: Taiwansheng wenxian wekyuanhui, 1999.

Ying Liangeng 应廉耕. *Sichuan sheng zudian zhidu* 四川省租佃制度 [The Tenancy System in Sichuan Province]. Zhongnong yinshua suo, December 1941.

Yu Xiufeng 余修风, *Dingyuan tingzhi* 定远厅志 [Gazetteer for Dingyuan Prefecture], 1879. Taipei: Chengwen chubanshe youxiangongsi, 1969.

Qingshi gao 清史稿 [Draft History of Qing], ed. Zhao Erxun 赵尔巽 et al. Vol. 499. Beijing: Zhonghua shuju, 1977.

Zhengzhi guanbao 政治官报 [Political Official Newspaper], no. 620, "Dian guanxi" 典惯习 [Customs of Dian].

Zhonggong sunanqu dangwei nongwei hui 中共苏南区党委农委会 [the Agricultural Committee of the Party Committee of the Communist Party of China, Sunan District]. *Sunan nongcun tudi zhidu chubu diaocha* 苏南农村土地制度初步调查 [Preliminary Survey of the Rural Land System in Sunan]. 1 May 1950. JF328.8-2431.

Zhongguo nongmin yinhang weituo Jinling daxue nong xueyuan nongye jingji xi 中国农民银行委托金陵大学农学院农业经济系 [Department of Agricultural Economics, College of Agriculture, Jinling University, commissioned by Chinese Peasant Bank]. *Yu'e wangan sisheng zhi zudian zhidu* 豫鄂皖赣四省之租佃制度 [The Tenancy System in the Four Provinces of Henan, Hubei, Anhui and Jiangxi]. Nanjing: Jinling University, 1936.

Zhongguo diyi lishi dang'anguan 中国第一历史档案馆 [China's No. 1 Archives]. Zhongguo shehui kexueyuan lishi yanjiusuo [Institute of History, CASS]. eds. *Qianlong xingke tiben zudian guanxi shiliao zhiyi: Qingdai dizu boxue xingtai* 乾隆刑科题本租佃关系史料之一：清代地租剥削形态 [The Documents of Tenancy Relationships in Grand Secretariat Memorials on Criminal Matters in Qianlong's Reign, and Forms of Exploitation of Land Rents]. Beijing: Zhonghua shuju, 1988.

Zhongguo diyi lishi dang'anguan 中国第一历史档案馆 [China's No. 1 Archives]. Zhongguo shehui kexueyuan lishi yanjiusuo 中国社会科学院历史研究所 [Institute of History, CASS]. eds. *Qianlong xingke tiben zudian guanxi shiliao zhier: Qingdai tudi zhanyou guanxi yu diannong kangzu douzheng* 乾隆刑科题本租佃关系史料之二：清代土地占有关系与佃农抗租斗争 [Land Tenure Relations and Tenant Struggle Against Rent in the Qing Dynasty in Grand Secretariat Memorials on Criminal Matters in Qianlong's Reign, and Types of Exploitation of Land Rents]. Beijing: Zhonghua shuju, 1988.

"Zhuojia shiban shuiqi zhangcheng 酌加试办税契章程" [Regulations on Additions of Deed Taxes]. *Jilin guanbao* 吉林官报 [Jilin Official Journal]. Vol. 26. 1909

Japanese References

Kusano, Yasushi 草野靖. *Chugoku no jinushi keizai: Bun tane-sei* 中國の地主經濟: 分種制 [Landlords' Economy in China: Tenancy Segregation System]. Tokyo: Kyuko shoin, 1985.

Kusano, Yasushi 草野靖. *Chugoku kinsei no kiseijinushisei: Tadzura kanko* 中国近世の寄生地主制—田面慣行 [Parasitic Land System in the Early Modern China: Land Top-soil Customs]. Tokyo: Kyuko shoin, 1989.

Minami Manshū Tetsudō Kabushiki Kaisha 南满洲铁道株式会社 [South Manchurian Railway Company]. *Manshū Kyukan Chōsa Hōkoku-sho* 满洲旧惯调查报告书 [Report on the survey of Old Customs in Manchuria]. Minami Manshū Tetsudō Kabushiki Kaisha. 1915.

Tamashita, Takeshi 滨下武志. et al. eds. *Dongyang wenhua yanjiusuo cang Zhongguo tudi wenshu mulu jieshuo* 东洋文化研究所藏中国土地文书目录解说 [Explanation of the Catalogue of Chinese Land Documents in the Collection of the Institute of Advanced Studies on Asia]. Institute of Advanced Studies on Asia, Tyoko University. 1983.

Kawakatsu, Mamoru 川勝守. *Meisei Kōnan nōgyō keizai-shi kenkyū* 明清江南農業経済史研究 [A Study on the Agricultural Economy History in Jiangnan in the Ming and Qing Dynasties]. Tokyo: Tokyo University Press, 1992.

English References

Acemoglu D., Johnson, S., & Robinson, J. "The Rise of Europe: Atlantic Trade, Institutional Change, and Economic Growth," *The American Economic Review* 95. 3(2005): 546–579.

Cheung, S. N. S. *The Theory of Share Tenancy*. Chicago, IL: University of Chicago Press, 1969.

Kenneth Pomeranz, "Chinese Development in Long-Run Perspective," *Proceedings of the American Philosophical Society 152, no. 1 (2008): 83–100.*

Kenneth Pomerantz, "Land Markets in Late Imperial and Republican China," *Continuity and Change*. 23.1 (2008): 101–150.

Buoye, Thomas M. *Manslaughter, Markets, and Moral Economy, Violent Disputes Over Property Rights in Eighteenth-century China*. Cambridge: Cambridge University Press, 2000.

Chinese References

Bian Li 卞利. "Mingqing diandnag he jiedai falü guifan de tiaozheng yu xiangcun shehui de wendin 明清典当和借贷法律规范的调整与乡村社会的稳定" [The Adjustment of Pawning and Lending Laws and the Stability of Rural Society in the Ming and Qing Dynasties]. *Zhongguo lishi* 中国农史 [Agricultural History of China], no. 4 (2005): 66–75.

Bucking, John [Bu Kai 卜凯]. ed. *Zhongguo tudi liyong* 中国土地利用 [China's Land Use]. Nanjing: Jinling daxue nongxueyuan jingjixi. 1941.

Cai Jiming 蔡继明 and Cheng Shiyong 程世勇. "Zhongguo de chengshihua: cong kongjian dao renkou" 中国的城市化: 从空间到人口 [Urbanization in China: From Space to Population]. *Zhongguo xiangcun faxian* 中国乡村发现. Vol. 14. Changsha: Hunan renmin chubanshe, 2010.

Cao Shuji 曹树基. "Su'nan diqu 'tianmian quan'de xingzhi 苏南地区"田面田"的性质" [The Nature of Top-soil Land Rights in Southern Jiangsu Province], *Qinghua daxue xuebao (zhexue shehui kexue ban)* 清华大学学报 (哲学社会科学版) [Journal of Tsinghua University (Philosophy and Social Sciences], no. 6 (2007): 59–71.

Cao Shuji 曹树基. "Liangzhong 'tianmian quan'yu Zhejiang de 'er'wu jianzu' 两种'田面田'与浙江的'二五减租'" [Two Kinds of Permanent Tenancy and Rent Reduction in Zhejiang Province]. *Lishi Yanjiu* 历史研究 [Journal of Historical Research], no. 2 (2007): 108–121.

Cao Shuji 曹树基. "Chuantong Zhongguo xiangcun diquan biandong de yiban lilun 传统中国乡村地权变动的一般理论" [The General Theory of Land Rights Changes in Traditional Chinese Villages], *Xueshu yuekan* 学术月刊 [Academic Monthly], no. 12 (2012): 117–125.

Cao Shuji. and Li Feiqi 李霏霁. "Qing zhonghou qi zhenan shanqu de tudi diandang—jiyu songyang xian shicang cunde 'dangtian qi'de kaocha 清中后期浙南山区的土地典当—基于松阳县石仓村'当田契'的考察" [Land Mortgage in Mountainous Regions of Southern Zhejiang during the Mid- and Late Qing: A Study Based on 'Land Mortgage Contracts' from Shicang Village, Songyang County]. *Lishi Yanjiu* 历史研究 [Journal of Historical Research], no. 4 (2008): 40–54.

Cao Xingsui 曹幸穗. *Jiu Zhongguo sunan nongjia jingji* 旧中国苏南农家经济研究 [A Study of the Farming Economy in Old China's Southern Jiangsu Province]. Beijng Zhongyang bianyi chubanshe, 1996.

Cui Yangyang 崔杨杨. *Tianmianquan jiqi lishi qishi* 田面权及其历史启示 [Top-soil Rights of land and Their Historical Inspirations]. Master thesis, Tsinghua Unversity, 2010.

Chai Rong 柴荣. *Zhongguo gudai wuquanfa yanjiu—yi tudi guanxi wei yanjiu shijiao* 中国古代物权法研究—以土地关系为研究视角 [Research into Property Rights Law in Ancient China: Land Relations as a Research Perspective]. Beijing: Zhongguo jiancha chubanshe, 2007.

Chen Jiru 陈继儒. "Chidu shuangyu 尺牍双鱼" [Paired Carp (Personal Correspondence)]. In *Zhongguo lisdai qiyue huibian kaoshi* 中国历代契约会编考释 [Examinations of the Compilation of Chinese Deeds of Each Dynasty], ed. Zhang Chuanxi 张传玺. Vol. 2. Beijing: Beijing daxue chubanshe, 1995, 1029–1030.

Chen Mingguang 陈明光. "Lun Tang wudai taotian chanquan zhidu bianqian 论唐五代逃田产权制度变迁" [On the Change of the Property Rights System of Fugitive Fields in the Tang and Five Dynasties]. *Xiamen daxue xuebao* 厦门大学学报 [Journal of Xiamen University], no. 4 (2004): 59–67.

Chen Qiukun, *Qingdai Taiwan tuzhu diquan*–guanliao, handian, *yu anli sheren de tudi bianqian, 1700–1895* 清代台湾土著地权—官僚、汉佃与岸里社人的土地变迁, 1700–1895 [Indigenous Land Rights in Taiwan during the Qing Dynasty: Bureaucrats, Han Tenants, and the Land Changes of the Lahodobool Community]. Taipei: Institute of Modern History, Academic Sinica, 2009.

Chen Yixin 陈意新. "Meiguo xuezhe dui Zhongguo jindai nongye jingji de yanjiu 美国学者对中国近代农业经济的研究" [American Scholars' Studies of China's Modern Agricultural Economy]. Zhongguo jingjishi yanjiu 中国经济史研究 [Researches in Chinese Economic History], no. 1 (2001): 118–137.

Chen Zhiwu 陈志武. *Jinrong de luoji* 金融的逻辑 [The Logic of Finance], Beijing: Guoji wenhua chuban gongsi, 2009.

Chen Zhiwu 陈志武. and Lin Zhan 林展. "Zhenming tyanzi yi sangming--lishi Zhongguo Huangdi ming'an de lianghua yanjiu 真命天子易丧命?—中国历代皇帝非正常死亡的量化研究" [Are Emperors Prone to Lose Their Lives? A Quantitative Study of Emperor Fatalities in Historical China]. Hongkong University working paper, 2017.

Chen Zhiying 陈志英. *Songdai wuquan guanxi yanjiu* 宋代物权关系研究 [A Study of Property Rights Relations in the Song Dynasty]. Beijing: Zhongguo shehui kexue chubanshe, 2006.

Crook, Isabel. and Crook, David (Ke Luke 柯鲁克). *Shilidian: yige zhongguo cunzhuang de qunzhong yundong* 十里店: 一个中国村庄的群众运动 [Ten Mile Inn: Massive Movement in a Chinese Village]. Beijing: Beijing chubanshe, 1982.

Dai Jianguo 戴建国. "Songdai de mintian dianmai yu 'yitian liangzhu zhi' 宋代的民田典卖与'一田两主制'" [The Dian Transactions of Civil Lands and the System of "One Piece of Land with Two Owners" in the Song Dynasty]. *Lishi yanjiu* 历史研究 [Historical Research], no. 6 (2011): 99–117.

Ding Qian 丁骞. "Minguo shiqi Zhongguo diquan fenpei de yanjiu 民国时期中国地权分配的研究" [A Study of the Distribution of Land Rights in China during the Republican Era]. Master thesis, Tsinghua University, 2008.

Duan Yinshou 段荫寿. *Pinghu nongcun jingji zhi yanjiu* 平湖农村经济之研究 [A Study of Pinghu's Rural Economy]. Taipei: Chengwen chubanshe youxian gongsi, 1977.

Engels, Friedrich [Engesi 恩格斯]. Marx, Carl [Makesi 马克思]. *Makesi Engesi xuanji* 马克思恩格斯选集 [Selected Works of Marx and Engels]. Translated by Zhongyang bianyiju 中央编译局 [Central Compilation and Translation Bureau]. Beijing: Renmin chubanshe, 1995.

Fang Shaowei 方绍伟. Chixu zhizheng de luoji: cong zhidu wenhua faxian zhongguo lishi 持续执政的逻辑: 从制度文化发现中国历史 [The Logic of Sustainable Governance: Discovering Chinese History through Institutional Culture]. Beijing: Zhongguo fazhan chubanshe, 2016.

Fang Xing 方行. "Zhongguo fengjian shehui nongmin de jingying dulixing 中国封建社会农民的经营独立性" [Operation Independence of Peasants in Chinese Feudal Society]. *Zhongguo jingjishi yanjiu* 中国经济史研究 [Researches in Chinese Economic History], no. 1 (1995): 10–23

Fang Xing 方行. "Zhongguo fengjian shehui de tudi shichang 中国封建社会的土地市场" [The Land Market of China's Feudal Society]. *Zhongguo Jingjishi Yanjiu* 中国经济史研究 [Researches in Chinese Economic History], no. 2 (2001): 8–22.

Fang Xing 方行. "Qingdai diannong de zhongnong hua 清代佃农的中农化" [The Middle Peasantization of Tenant Farmers in the Qing Dynasty]. *Zhongguo xueshu* 中国学术 [China Scholarship]. Vol. 2. Beijing: Shangwu yinshuguan, 2000.

Fei Xiaotong 费孝通. Xiangtu Zhongguo 乡土中国 [Rural China]. Beijing: Beijing daxue chubanshe, 1998.

Francis Fukuyama (Fulang xisi fushan 弗朗西斯•福山), Xinren: Shehui meide yu chuangzao jingji fanrong 信任: 社会美德与创造经济繁荣 [Trust: Social Virtues and the Creation of Economic Prosperity]. Translated by Guo Hua 郭华. Hainan: Hainan chubanshe, 2001.

Gao Nan 高楠. *Songdai minjian caichan jiufen yu susong wenti yanjiu* 宋代民间财产纠纷与诉讼问题研究 [Study on Civil Property Disputes and Litigation in Song Dynasty]. Kunming: Yunnan daxue chubanshe, 2009.

Gong Jun 龚君. and Wei Zhiwen 魏志文. "Guazhen yiduju shimo 瓜镇义渡局始末" [The Beginning and End of the GuaZhen's Free Ferry Bureau]. *Dang'an yu jianshe* 档案与建设 [Archives and Construction], no. 5 (2016): 58–59.

"Guanyu Dongshijin shangshu fandui tudi gaige wenti 关于董时进上书反对土地改革问题" [On the issue of Dong Shijin's Petition Against Land Reforms]. *Guancha* 观察 [Observation], no. 6 (1950).

Guo Yukuan 郭宇宽. "Zuowei touzijia de Wu Xun 作为投资家的武训" [Wu Xun as an investor]. *Tongzhou gongjin* 同舟共进 [Together in the Boat], no. 5 (2013): 79–81

Han Dezhang 韩德章. "Zhexi nongcun zhi jiedai zhidu 浙西农村之借贷制度" [The System of Loan in the Villages of the Western Zhejiang Province]. *Shehui kexue zazhi* 社会科学杂志 [Journal of Social Sciences], no. 2 (1932).

Han Xiao 韩啸. "Tangmo wudai dianquan falü zhidu zhi tantao 唐末五代典权法律制度之探讨" [A Discussion of the Legal System of *Dian* Rights in the Late Tang and Five Dynasties], *Henan caijing zhengfa daxue xuebao* 河南财

经政法大学学报 [Journal of Henan University of Economics and Law], no. 1 (2013): 159–167.

He Guoqing 何国卿. "Chuantong nongdi yazuzhi duochong gongneng de zhidu jignjixue yanjiu 传统农地押租制多重功能的制度经济学研究" [An Institutional Economics Study of the Multiple Functions of the Traditional Farmland Tenancy System]. Master thesis, Tsinghua University, 2012.

He Menglei 何梦雷. "Suzhou Wuxi Changshu sanxian zudian zhidu diaocha 苏州无锡常熟三县租佃制度调查" [Investigation of the Tenancy System in Wuxi, Suzhou and Changshu Counties]. In *Minguo ershi niandai Zhongguo dalu tudi wenti ziliao* 民国二十年代中国大陆土地问题资料 [Information on Land Issues in Mainland China in the 1920s], ed. Xiao Zheng 萧铮. Vol. 63. Taipei: Chengwen chubanshe youxian gongsi, 1977.

Huang Yingwei 黄英伟. Li Jun 李军. and Wang Xiuqing 王秀清. "Jitihua moqi nonghu laodongli touru de xingbie chayi: yige cunzhuang 'beitaizi' de yanjiu 集体化末期农户劳动力投入的性别差异: 一个村庄 (北台子) 的研究" [Gender Differences in Farmers' Labor Inputs at the End of Collectivization: A Study of Beitaizi Village]. *Zhongguo jingjishi yanjiu* 中国经济史研究 [Researches in Chinese Economic History], no. 2 (2010): 29–39.

Jin Liang 金亮. Yang Dachun 杨大春. "Zhongguo gudai qishui zhidu tanxi 中国古代契税制度探析" [An Analysis of the Ancient Legal System of Deed Tax in China]. *Jiangxi shehui kexue* 江西社会科学 [Jiangxi Social Sciences], no. 11 (2004): 99–102.

Jing Yang 井扬. "Mingqing linqing yunhe chaoguan yanjiu 明清临清运河钞关研究" [Study on Ming-Qing Linqing Canal Chaoguan]. Master thesis, Shandong University. 2018.

"Jiusan xueshe Zhongyang jianyi: wanshan nongcun funü tudi quanyi baozhang 九三学社中央建议: 规范确权工作完善农村妇女土地权益保障" [Jiu San Society Central Committee Suggestions: Improve the Protection of Rural Women's Land Rights and Interests]. *Zhongguo funü bao* 中国妇女报 [China Women's News], March 9, 2018.

Kong Qingming 孔庆明. Hu Liuyuan 胡留元. and Sun Jiping 孙季平. *Zhongguo minfa shi* 中国民法史 [The History of Chinese Civil Law]. Changchun: Jilin renmin chubanshe, 1996.

Li Bozhong 李伯重. *Zhongguo de zaoqi jindai jingji—1820 niandai huating-louxian diqu GDP yanjiu* 中国的早期近代经济—1820 年代华亭-娄县地区GDP 研究 [China's Early Modern Economy—A Study of GDP in the Huating-Lou County Region in the 1820s]. Beijing: Zhonghua shuju, 2010.

Li Bozhong 李伯重. "Chucai jinyong: Zhongguo shuizhuan dafangche yu Yingguo akelai shuili fangzhiji 楚材晋用: 中国水转大纺车与英国阿克莱水力纺纱机" [Water Spinning Wheel and British Ackley Hydrospinning Machine], *Lishi yanjiu* 历史研究 [Historical Research], no. 1 (2002): 62–74.

Li Bozhong 李伯重. *Jiangnan de zaoqi gongyehua (1550–1850)* 江南的早期工业化 (1550–1850) [Early Industrialization in Jiangnan]. Beijing: Zhongguo renmin daxue chubanshe, 2010.

Li Bozhong 李伯重. *Jiangnan nongye de fazhan, 1620–1850* 江南农业的发展 (1620–1850) [Development of Agriculture in Jiangnan, 1620–1850]. Shanghai: Shanghai guji chubanshe, 2006.

Li Li 李力. "Qingdai minjian tudi qiyue duiyu dian de biaoda jiqi yiyi 清代民间土地契约对于典的表达及其意义" [The Expression and Significance of Qing Dynasty Civil Land Deeds to the Dian]. *Jinling falü pinglun* 金陵法律评论 [Jinling Law Review], no. 1 (2006): 111–118.

Li Rujun 李如钧. "Cong 'minggong shupan qingmingji' kan songdai tianzahi maimai zhongde 'dian' 从⟨名公书判清明集⟩看宋代田宅典卖中的'典' " [The Song Dynasty's 'dian' in the Sale of Lands and Houses from "Minggong shupan Qingmingji"]. In *Songdai shehui yu falü* 宋代社会与法律 [Society and Law in the Song Dynasty], ed. Songdai guanzhen yanduhui [Song Dynasty's Official Regulations Study Semianr]. Taipei: dongda tushu gongsi, 2001.

Lin Wenxun 林文勋. "Zhongguo gudai 'fumin shehui de xingcheng jiqi lishi diwei 中国古代'富民社会'的形成及其历史地位" [The Formation of *Fumin Shehui* and its Historical Status in Ancient China]. *Zhongguo jingjishi yanjiu* 中国经济史研究 [Researches in Chinese Economic History], no. 2 (2006): 30–37.

Lin Wenxun 林文勋. and Huang Chunyan 黄纯艳. Zhongguo gudai zhuanmai zhidu yu shangpin jingji 中国古代专卖制度与商品经济 [Ancient Chinese Monopoly System and Commodity Economy]. Kunming: Yunnan daxue chubanshe, 2003.

Lin Yifu 林毅夫. *Zhidu, jishu, yu Zhongguo nongye fazhan* 制度、技术与中国农业发展 [Institutions, Technology and Agricultural Development in China]. Shanghai: Shanghai sanlian shudian, 1992.

Liu Hengzhong 刘恒中. *Lun Zhongguo da fazhan: bayi nongmin bian shimin* 论中国大发展, 八亿农民变市民 [On China's Great Development: 800 Million Peasants Become Citizens]. Beijing: Zhongguo jingji chubanshe, 2008.

Liu Zemin 刘泽民. ed. *Pingpu baishe guwenshu* 平埔百社古文书 [Pingpu Baishe Ancient Documents]. Taipei: "Guoshiguan" Taiwan wenxian guan, 2002.

Long Denggao 龙登高. "Qingdai diquan jiaoyi de duoyanghua fazhan 清代地权交易形式的多样化发展" [The Diversification of Land Transactions in the Qing Dynasty]. *Qingshi yanjiu* 清史研究 [Research into Qing History], no. 3 (2008): 44–58.

Long Denggao 龙登高. "Lishi shang Zhongguo minjian jingji de ziyou zhuyi pusu chuantong 历史上中国民间经济的自由主义朴素传统" [The Simple Tradition of Liberalism in Chinese Private Economy in History]. *Sixiang zhanxian* 思想战线 [Thinking], no. 3 (2012): 84–91.

Long Denggao 龙登高. *Diquan shichang yu ziyuan peizhi* 地权市场与资源配置 [Land Rights Market and Resource Allocation]. Fuzhou: Fujian renmin chubanshe, 2012.

Long Denggao 龙登高. "Diquan jiaoyi yu shengchan yaosu zuhe, 1650–1950 地权交易与生产要素组合: 1650–1950" [Land Rights Transactions and Production Factor Combinations, 1650–1950]. *Jingji yanjiu* 经济研究 [Economic Research Journal], no. 2 (2009): 146–156.

Long Denggao 龙登高. "Cong pingjun diquan dao guli liuzhuan 从平均地权到土地流转" [From the Equalization of Land Rights to Encouragement of Circulation]. *Hebei Xuekan* 河北学刊 [Hebei Academic Journal], no. 3 (2018): 142–147.

Long Denggao 龙登高. *Zhongguo chuantong shichang fazhanshi* 中国传统市场发展史 [History of the Development of Traditional Markets in China], Beijing: Renmin chubanshe, 1997.

Long Denggao 龙登高. "Jiejian Mingiqng 'tianmianquan' zhidu, chuangxin tudi chanquan gage moshi 借鉴明清'田面权'制度, 创新土地产权改革模式" [Innovate Land Property Rights Reforms Model by Learning From the Ming and Qing Dynasties' Top-soil Rights System]. Chengguo yaobao 成果要报. 2013.

Long Denggao 龙登高. "Diquan shichang yu ziyuan peizhi: jiyu Qingdai diquan jiaoyi anli de jieshi 地权市场与资源配置: 基于清代地权交易案例的解释" [Land Rights Market and Resource Allocation: An Explanation Based on the Case of Qing Dynasty Land Rights Transactions]. *Jidiao yu bianzou* 基调与变奏 [Keynote and Variation]. Vol. 2 Taipei: National Chengchi University and Academic Sinica, 2008.

Long Denggao 龙登高. and Wen Fangfang 温方方. "Lun zhongguo chuantong dianquan jiaoyi de huishu jizhis—jiyu qinghua guancang shanxi qiyue de yanjiu 论中国传统典权交易的回赎机制—基于清华馆藏山西契约的研究" [On the Redemption Mechanism of Traditional Chinese *Dian* Transactions: A Study Based on the Shanxi Deeds in the Tsinghua Collection]. *Jingji kexue* 经济科学 [Economic Science], no. 5 (2014): 172–182.

Long Denggao 龙登高. Wen Fangfang 温方方. and Qiu Yongzhi 邱永志. "Diantian de xingzhi yu quanyi—songdai yu qingdai de bijiao yanjiu 典田的性质与权益—基于清代与宋代的比较研究" [The Nature and Rights of Dian Land—A Comparative Study of the Song and Qing Dynasties]. *Lishi yanjiu* 历史研究 [Historical Research], no. 5 (2016): 54–70.

Long Denggao 龙登高, and Pengbo 彭波. "Jinshi diannong de jignying xignzhi yu shouyi bijiao 近世佃农的经营性质与收益比较" [A Comparison of the Nature of Business and Earnings of Tenant Farmers in Modern Times]. *Jingji yanjiu* 经济研究 [Economic Research Journal], no. 1 (2010): 138–147.

Long Denggao 龙登高. Lin Zhan 林展. and Peng Bo 彭波. "*Dian yu Qingdai diquan jiaoyi tixi*" 典与清代地权交易体系 [Dian and the Qing Dynasty Land

Rights Transaction System], *Zhongguo shehui kexue* 中国社会科学 [Social Sciences in China], no. 5 (2013): 125–141.

Long Denggao 龙登高. Chang Xu 常旭. and Xiong Jinwu 熊金武. "Jieshu yu" [Conclusion], *Guo zhi run, zi shujun shi: Tianjin hangdaoju 120 nian fazhan shi* 国之润, 自疏浚始: 天津航道局120年发展史 [The Wetness of the Country Begins with Dredging: A History of the Development of the Tianjin Dredging Bureau in 120 Years]. Beijing: Qinghua daxue chubanshe, 2017.

Long Denggao 龙登高. and Wang Miao 王苗. "Wu Xun de licai xingxue zhidao 武训的理财兴学之道" [Wu Xun's Way of Managing Money and Promoting Education]. *Zhongguo jingjishi yanjiu* 中国经济史研究 [Researches in Chinese Economic History], no. 3 (2018): 182–189.

Long Denggao 龙登高. Pan Qingzhong 潘庆中. and Lin Zhan 林展. "Gaolidai de qianshi jinsheng 高利贷的前世今生" [The Past and Present Life of the Usury]. *Sixiang zhanxian* 思想战线 [Thinking], no. 4 (2014): 13–19.

Long Denggao 龙登高. Gong Ning 龚宁. and Meng Dewang 孟德望. "Jindai gonggong shiye de zhidu chuangxin: liyi xiangguan fang hezuo de gongyi faren moshi--jiyu haihe gongchengju zhong waiwen dang'an de yanjiu 近代公共事业的制度创新: 利益相关方合作的公益法人模式—基于海河工程局中外文档案的研究" [Institutional Innovation of Modern Public Utilities: A Public Benefit Corporation Model of Stakeholder Cooperation--A Study Based on the Chinese and Foreign Language Archives of the Haihe Engineering Bureau]. *Qinghua daxue xuebao* 清华大学学报 (哲学社会科学版) [Journal of Tsinghua University (Philosophy and Social Sciences)], no. 6 (2017): 170–182.

Long Denggao 龙登高. He Guoqing 何国卿. "Dizhu funong zhanyou duoshao tudi: jiyu tudi pucha de diquan fenpei jianyan 地主富农占有多少土地—基于土改普查的地权分配检验" [How Much Land Do the Landlords and Rich Peasants Own? A Test and Explanation of Land Rights Distribution on the Eve of Land Reforms]. *Dongnan xueshu* 东南学术 [Southeast Academic Research], no. 3 (2018).

Long Denggao 龙登高. Deng Yongbing 邓勇兵. and Yin Wei 伊巍. "Tudi jiti suoyouzhi yu nongmin shengyu lü 土地集体所有制与农民生育率" [Collective Land Ownership and Peasant Fertility]. *Jinrong bolan* 金融博览 [Financial View], no. 2 (2016): 20–21.

Luo Pinghan 罗平汉. *Tudi gaige yundongshi* 土地改革运动史 [History of the Land Reforms Movement]. Fuzhou: Fujian renmin chubanshe, 2005.

Mo Hongwei莫宏伟. and Zhang Chengjie 张成洁. *Xinqu nongcun de tudi gaige* 新区农村的土地改革 [The Land Reforms in the Rural New Areas]. Nanjing: Jiangsu University Press, 2009.

Niu Jie 牛杰. "Lun songdai qiyue guanxi yu qiyuefa 论宋代契约关系和契约法" [On Contractual Relations and Contract Law in the Song Dynasty].

Zhongzhou xuekan 中州学刊 [Academic Journal of Zhongzhou], no. 2 (2006).

Peng Kaixiang 彭凯翔. Chen Zhiwu 陈志武. and Yuan Weipeng 袁为鹏. "Jindai Zhongguo nongcun jiedai shichang de jizhi—jiyu minjian wenshu de yanjiu 近代中国农村借贷市场的机制—基于民间文书的研究" [The Mechanism of Rural Lending Market in Modern China: A Study Based on Private Instruments]. *Jingji yanjiu* 经济研究 [Economic Research Journal], no. 5 (2008): 147–159.

Perkins, Dwight H. [Bo Jinsi 铂金斯]. *Zhongguo nongye de fazhan 1368–1968* 中国农业的发展, 1368–1968 [Agricultural Development in China, 1368–1968]. Translated by Song Haiwen 宋海文. Shanghai: Shanghai yiwen chubanshe, 1984.

Pomeranz, Kenneth (Peng Mulan彭慕兰). *Da fenliu: Ouzhou, Zhongguo, ji xiandai shijie de fazhan* 大分流: 欧洲, 中国及现代世界的发展 [The Big Divergence: China, Europe, and the Making of the Modern World Economy]. Translated by Shi Jianyun 史建云. Nanjing: Jiangsu renmin chubanshe, 2004.

"Guanyu Shenhua nongcun gaige zhong weihu funü tudi quanyi 在深化农村改革中维护妇女土地权益" [Proposal on Safeguarding Women's Land Rights and Interests in Deepening Rural Reforms], *Zhongguo funübao* 中国妇女报 [Chinese Women's News], March 5, 2018.

Ren Zhiqiang 任志强. *Nongdi chanquan jiqi zibenhua* 农地产权及其资本化 [Property Rights in Agricultural Land and Their Capitalization]. Postdoctoral Report, Tsinghua University, 2011.

Shi Jinjian 石锦建. "Zhongguo lishi shang caizheng shouzhi he zhengquan wending guanxi de yanjiu, 1402–1644 中国历史上财政收支和政权稳定关系的研究 (1402–1644)" [A Study of the Relationship between Fiscal Revenues and Expenditures and Regime Stability in Chinese History (1402–1644)]. Doctoral thesis, Xiamen University. 2017.

Shi Zhihong 史志宏. "20 shiji sansi shi niandai Huabei pingyuan nongcun de zudian guanxi he guyong guanxi—yi Hebei sheng qingyuan xian sic un weili 20世纪三四十年代华北平原农村的租佃关系和雇佣关系—以河北省清苑县4村为例" [Tenancy and Employment Relations in Rural Areas of the North China in the 1930s and 1940s: The Case Study of Four Villages in Qingyuan County, Hebei Province]. *Zhongguo jingjishi yanjiu* 中国经济史研究 [Researches in Chinese Economic History], no. 1 (2003).

Su Shaozhi 苏少之. "Geming genjudi xin funong wenti yanjiu 革命根据地新富农问题研究" [A Study on the New Rich Peasants in the Revolutionary Base Areas]. *Jindaishi yanjiu* 近代史研究 [Journal of Modern Chinese Studies], no. 1 (2014).

Sui Hongming 眭鸿明. *Qingmo minchu shangshi xiguan diaocha zhi yanjiu* 清末民初民商事习惯调查之研究 [A Study of Civil and Commercial Customs in the Late Qing Dynasty and Early Republican Period]. Beijing: falü chubanshe, 2005.

Tang Yunjian 唐云建. "Jinshi 'fei zigengnong hua' yuanyin yanjiu—cong nonghu diquan peizhi celue jiaodu 近世"非自耕农化"原因研究—从农户地权配置策略的角度" [A study on the Causes of "Non-Subsistence-Farming" in Modern China: A Perspective on the Land Allocation Strategy of Farming Households]. Master thesis, Tsinghua University. 2016.

Wang Rigen 王日根. "Lun mingqing xiangyue shuxing yu zhineng de bianqian 论明清乡约属性与职能的变迁" [On the Change of Attributes and Functions of Community Compacts in Ming and Qing Dynasties]。*Xiamen daxue xuebao (zhexue shehui kexue ban)* 厦门大学学报 (哲学社会科学版) [Journal of Xiamen University (Arts & Social Sciences)], no. 3 (2003): 69–76.

Wang Yuru 王玉茹. "Zhongguo jindai de jingji zengzhang he zhongchang zhouqi bodong 中国近代的经济增长和中长周期波动" [Economic Growth and Medium- and Long-Cycle Fluctuations in Modern China], *Jingjixue (jikan)* 经济学 (季刊) [China Economic Quarterly], no. 1 (2005): 461–490.

Wang Yun 王云. *Mingqing Shandong yunhe quyu shehui bianqian* 明清山东运河区域社会变 [Social Changes in the Canal Region of Shandong in the Ming and Qing Dynasties], Beijing: Renmin chubanshe, 2006, 106–224.

Wang Zhenghua 王正华. "Wanqing minguo huabei xiangcun tianzhai jiaoyi zhongde guanzhong xianxiang 晚清民国华北乡村田宅交易中的官中现象" [Phenomenon of *Guanzhong* in the Dealings of Land and House in Rural North China in the Late Qing and Republican Period]. *Zhongguo jingjishi yanjiu* 中国经济史研究 [Researches in Chinese Economic History], no. 6 (2017): 104–119.

Wei Tian'an 魏天安. "Songdai de qiyue 宋代的契税" [Deed Tax in the Song Dynasty], *Zhongzhou xuekan* 中州学刊 [Academic Journal of Zhongzhou], no. 3 (2009): 19–201.

Wen Dongliang 文栋梁. "Yige xiangzhen ganbu jianzheng jihua shengyu sishinian shouji 一个乡镇干部见证计划生育四十年手记" [Handbook of a Township Cadre Witnessing 40 years of Family Planning]. *Xiangcun faxian* 乡村发现 [Rural Discovery]. February 12, 2018.

Wen Guanzhong 文贯中. "Tudi zhidu bixu yunxu nongmin you tuichu ziyou 土地制度必须允许农民有退出自由" [The land system must allow peasants to exit freely]. *Shehui guancha* 社会观察 [Social Observation], no. 11 (2008).

Wu Xianghong 吴向红. *Dianzhi fengsu yu dianzhi falü* 典之风俗与典之法律 [Customs and Laws of Dian]. Beijing: falü chubanshe, 2009.

Wu Xuemei 吴雪梅. "Duo zhongxin huqian: xiangcun shehui zhixu de you yizhong leixing 多中心互嵌: 乡村社会秩序的又一种类型" [Polycentric Embeddedness: Another Type of Rural Social Order]. *Guangming ribao* 光明日报 [Guangming Daily]. December 15, 2011.

Xiao Ben 肖奔. *Cong Qingchao minguo duzhi kan hunan yidu* 从清朝民国渡志看湖南义渡 [Free Ferry of Hunan from the Perspective of *Duzhi* (Records of Ferries) in the Qing and Republican Era]. Master thesis, Hunan Normal University. 2014.

Xing Peihua 邢培华, and Zhang Qingnian 张庆年. "Wu Xun Dang'an wenxian shiliao shulue 武训档案文献史料述略" [A Brief Description of Wu Xun's Archival Documents and Historical Materials]. *Dang'anxue yanjiu* 档案学研究 [Archives Science Study], no. 3 (1993): 46–48

Xiong Boheng 熊伯蘅, and Wan Jianzhong 万建中. eds. *Shaanxi nongye jingji diaocha* 陕西农业经济调查研究 [Shaanxi Agricultural Economy Survey Research]. Xi'an: Guoli Xibei nongxueyuan, 1942.

Xu Tan 许檀. "Mingqing shiqi de qinqing shangye 明清时期的临清商业" [Linqing Commerce in the Ming and Qing Dynasties]. *Zhongguo shehui jingjish*i 中国社会经济史 [Researches in Chinese Economic History], no. 2 (1986): 135–157.

Xu Qing 许庆. "Canyu shichang yu nongcun pinkun: yige weiguan fenxi de shijiao 参与市场与农村贫困: 一个微观分析的视角" [Market Participation and Rural Poverty: a Microanalytical Approach]. *Zhongguo jingjixue* 中国经济学 [China Economics], no. 9 (2009).

Yang Guo'an 杨国安. "Kongzhi yu zizhi zhijian: guojia yu shehui hudong shiye xiade mingqing xiangcun zhixu 控制与自治之间: 国家与社会互动视野下的明清乡村秩序" [Between Control and Autonomy: Rural Order in the Ming and Qing Dynasties in the Perspective of the Interaction between the State and Society]. *Guangming ribao* 光明日报 [Guangming Daily]. November 29, 2012.

Yang Guozhen 杨国桢. "Lun Zhongguo Yongdianquan de jiben tezheng 论中国永佃权的基本特征" [On China's Permanent Tenancy Rights: Basic Characteristics]. *Zhongguo shehui jingjishi yanjiu* 中国社会经济史研究 [Journal of Chinese Social and Economic History], no. 2 (1988).

Yang Jiping 杨际平. *Beichao Suitang "juntian zhi" xintan* 北朝隋唐"均田制"新探 [An Inquiry into the "Equal Field System" of the Northern Sui and Tang Dynasties]. Changhsa: Yuelu shushe, 2003.

Yang Wenxin 杨文新. "Songdai sengtu dui Fujian qiaoliang jianzao de gongxian 宋代僧徒对福建桥梁建造的贡献" [Song Dynasty Monks' Contributions to Fujian's Bridge Construction]. *Fujian jiaoyu xueyuan xuebao* 福建教育学院学报 [Journal of Fujian Institute of Education], no. 5 (2004): 23–27.

Ye Mingyong 叶明勇. "Xin zhongguo chengli houde tudi gaige yundong pingshu 新中国成立后土地改革运动研究述评" [A Review of the Land Reforms Movement After the Founding of PRC]. *Beijing dangshi* 北京党史 [Beijing Party History], no. 5 (2008).

Yunus, Muhammad [You Nusi尤努斯], Qiongren de yinhang jia—Nuobei'er heping jiang dezhu You Nusi zhuanji 穷人的银行家—诺贝尔和平奖得主尤

努斯传记 [Bankers of the Poor: A Biography of Nobel Peace Prize Winner Yunus]. Translated by Wu Shihong 吴士宏. Beijing: shenghuo dushu xinzhi sanlian shudian, 2006.

Yu Jiang 俞江. "'Qiyue' yu 'hetong' zhibian—yi Qingdai qiyue wenshu wei chufadian '契约'与'合同'之辨—以清代契约文书为出发点" [The Identification of "Contracts" and "Contracts"—The Qing Dynasty Contract Documents as a Starting Point]. *Zhongguo shehui kexue* 中国社会科学 [Social Sciences in China], no. 6 (2003): 134–149.

Qu Mingzhou 瞿明宙. "Zhongguo nongtian yazu di jinzhan 中国农田押租底进展" [Progress of Farmland Rent Deposits in China]. *Zhongguo nongcun* 中国农村 [China's Agricultural Villages], no. 4 (1935).

Zhang Ming 张明. ed. *Wu Xun ziliao daquan* 武训研究资料大全 [Wu Xun's Complete Collection]. Jinan: Shandong daxue chubanshe, 1991.

Zhang Weiying 张维迎. "Renlei hezuo de zhidu jichu 人类合作的制度基础" [The Institutional Basis for Human Cooperation]. *Dushu* 读书 [Reading], no. 1 (2014).

Zhang Xinbao 张新宝. "Dianquan feichu lun 典权废除论" [abrogation of *dian* rights]. *Faxue zazhi* 法学杂志 [Law Science Magazine], no. 5 (2005): 6–10.

Zhang Yan 张研. "Guanyu Qingdai zutian fenbu de chubu kaocha 关于清代族田分布的初步考察" [A Preliminary Examination on the Distribution of Clan Fields in the Qing Dynasty]. *Zhongguo jingjishi yanjiu* 中国经济史研究 [Researches in Chinese Economic History], no. 1 (1991).

Zhang Ziqing 张自清. et al. eds. *Minguo linqing Xianzhi* 民国临清县志 [Gazetter for Linqing County in the Republican Era]. Nanjing: Fenghuang chubanshe, 2004.

Zelin, Madeleine., Jonathan K. Ocko, and Robert Gardella. eds. *Contract and Property in Early Modern China*. Stanford: Stanford University Press, 2004.

Zhao Liang 赵亮 and Long Denggao 龙登高. "Tudi zudian yu jingji xiaolü 土地租佃与经济效率" [Land Tenancy and Economic Efficiency]. *Zhongguo jingji wenti* 中国经济问题 [China Economic Studies], no. 2 (2012): 3–15.

Zheng Ding 郑定 and Chai Rong 柴荣. "Liangsong tudi jiaoyi zhong de ruogan falü wenti 两宋土地交易中的若干法律问题" [Some Legal Issues in the Land Transactions of the Two Song Dynasties]. *Jianghai xuekan* 江海学刊 [Jianghai Academic Journal], no. 6 (2002): 114–121.

Zheng Yefu 郑也夫. "Tugai: Fei Xiaotong yu Dong Shijin 土改: 费孝通与董时进" [Land Reforms: Fei Xiaotong and Dong Shijin], *Mingbao yuekan* (Hongkong) 明报月刊 (香港) [Mingpao Monthly], no. 8 and no. 9, 2011.

Zheng Yougui 郑有贵 and Dong Yanbin 董彦彬, and Jiao Hongpo 焦红坡, "Tudi gaige yanjiu zongshu 土地改革研究综述" [A Review of Land Reform Studies], *Zhonggong dangshi yanjiu* 中共党史研究 [CPC History Studies], no. 6 (2000): 93–97.

Zhonggong Zhognyang wenxian yanjiushi 中共中央文献研究室 [Central Documentary Research Office of the Communist Party of China] ed., *Mao Zedong nianpu (1893–1949)* 毛泽东年谱 (1893—1949) [Mao Zedong Chronology], vol. 2, Beijing: Renmin chubanshe, 1993, 78–79.

Zhou Jianbo 周建波 and Zhang Bo 张博. and Zhou Jiantao 周建涛. "Zhonggu shiqi siyuan jignji xingshuai de jingjixue fenxi 中古时期寺院经济兴衰的经济学分析" [An Economic Analysis of the Rise and Fall of the Economy of Monasteries in the Ancient and Middle Ages], *Jingjixue jikan* 经济学季刊 [China Economic Quarterly], no. 3 (2011): 1219–1236.

Zhou Linbin 周林彬 and Li Shenglan 李胜兰. "Wuquan xinlun: yizhong fa yu jingjixue fenxi de silu 物权新论: 种法与经济学分析的思路" [A New Theory of Property Rights: A Method of Law and Economic Analysis], *Xiangtan daxue xuebao* 湘潭大学学报 [Journal of Xiangtan University], no. 6 (2000): 26–33.

Zhang, Taisu. *The Laws and Economics of Confucianism: Kinship and Property in Preindustrial China and England*. Cambridge University Press, 2017.

FSC
www.fsc.org
MIX
Papier | Fördert
gute Waldnutzung
FSC® C083411

Kolibri 360 GmbH
Ferdinand-Jühlke-Straße 7
99095 Erfurt, Deutschland
produktsicherheit@kolibri360.de